SIMD Programming Manual
for Linux and Windows

Springer
London
Berlin
Heidelberg
New York
Hong Kong
Milan
Paris
Tokyo

Paul Cockshott and Kenneth Renfrew

SIMD Programming Manual for Linux and Windows

 Springer

CENTRAL MISSOURI
STATE UNIVERSITY
Warrensburg
Missouri

Paul Cockshott, BaEcon, DipEd, MSc, PhD
Department of Computing Science
University of Glasgow
17 Lilybank Gardens
Glasgow G12 8RZ
UK

Kenneth Renfrew, BSc(Hons)
Crookhill Farm
Gateside
By Beith
Ayrshire KA15 1HQ
UK

British Library Cataloguing in Publication Data
Cockshott, W. Paul
  SIMD programming manual for Linux and Windows. - (Springer professional computing)
  1. Parallel computing (Computer science)
  I. Title II. Renfrew, Kenneth
  005.2'75

  ISBN 185233794X

Library of Congress Cataloging-in-Publication Data
Cockshott, W. Paul, 1952–
  SIMD programming manual for Linux and Windows/Paul Cockshott and Kenneth Renfrew.
    p. cm. – (Springer professional computing)
  Includes index.
  ISBN 1-85233-794-X (alk. paper)
  1. Parallel programming (Computer science) 2. Linux. 3. Microsoft Windows
  (Computer file) I. Renfrew, Kenneth, 1962– II. Title. III. Series.
QA76.642C63 2004
005.2'75–dc22   2003067311

Apart from any fair dealing for the purposes of research or private study, or criticism or review, as permitted under the Copyright, Designs and Patents Act 1988, this publication may only be reproduced, stored or transmitted, in any form or by any means, with the prior permission in writing of the publishers, or in the case of reprographic reproduction in accordance with the terms of licences issued by the Copyright Licensing Agency. Enquiries concerning reproduction outside those terms should be sent to the publishers.

ISBN 1-85233-794-X Springer-Verlag London Berlin Heidelberg
Springer-Verlag is a part of *Springer Science+Business Media*
springeronline.com

© Springer-Verlag London Limited 2004
Printed in the United States of America

The use of registered names, trademarks etc. in this publication does not imply, even in the absence of a specific statement, that such names are exempt from the relevant laws and regulations and therefore free for general use.

The publisher makes no representation, express or implied, with regard to the accuracy of the information contained in this book and cannot accept any legal responsibility or liability for any errors or omissions that may be made.

Typeset by Gray Publishing, Tunbridge Wells, UK
34/3830-54321 Printed on acid-free paper SPIN 10962251

Contents

List of Tables xvii

List of Figures xix

List of Algorithms xxiii

Introduction xxv

I SIMD Programming   1
Paul Cockshott

1 Computer Speed, Program Speed   **3**
  1.1 Clocks 3
  1.2 Width 4
  1.3 Instruction Speed 5
  1.4 Overhead Instructions 6
  1.5 Algorithm Complexity 8

2 SIMD Instruction-sets   **11**
  2.1 The SIMD Model 11
  2.2 The MMX Register Architecture 12
  2.3 MMX Data-types 13
  2.4 3DNow! 15
       2.4.1 Cache Handling 17
       2.4.2 Cache Line Length and Prefetching 18
  2.5 Streaming SIMD 19
       2.5.1 Cache Optimisation 21
  2.6 The Motorola Altivec Architecture 22

3 SIMD Programming in Assembler and C   **23**
  3.1 Vectorising C Compilers 23
       3.1.1 Dead for Loop Elimination 24
       3.1.2 Loop Unrolling 25
  3.2 Direct Use of Assembler Code 25
       3.2.1 The Example Program 26
  3.3 Use of Assembler Intrinsics 27

	3.4	Use of C++ Classes	27
	3.5	Use of the Nasm Assembler	28
		3.5.1 General Instruction Syntax	29
		3.5.2 Operand Forms	29
		3.5.3 Directives	32
		3.5.4 Linking and Object File Formats	34
		3.5.5 Summing a Vector	35
	3.6	Coordinate Transformations Using 3DNow!	38
	3.7	Coordinate Transformations Using SSE Instructions	44
4	**Intel SIMD Instructions**		**47**
	4.1	Types	47
	4.2	shrl	51
	4.3	saturate	51
	4.4	Instructions	51
		4.4.1 ADDPS	52
		4.4.2 ADDSS	52
		4.4.3 ANDNPS	52
		4.4.4 ANDPS	52
		4.4.5 CMPPS	53
		4.4.6 CMPSS	54
		4.4.7 COMISS	54
		4.4.8 CVTPI2PS	55
		4.4.9 CVTPS2PI	55
		4.4.10 CVTTPS2PI	55
		4.4.11 CVTSI2SS	56
		4.4.12 CVTSS2SI	56
		4.4.13 CVTTSS2SI	56
		4.4.14 DIVPD	56
		4.4.15 DIVPS	57
		4.4.16 DIVSD	57
		4.4.17 DIVSS	57
		4.4.18 EMMS	57
		4.4.19 FXRSTOR	58
		4.4.20 FXSAVE	58
		4.4.21 MASKMOVQ	59
		4.4.22 MAXPD	59
		4.4.23 MAXPS	60
		4.4.24 MAXSD	60
		4.4.25 MAXSS	60
		4.4.26 MINPD	61
		4.4.27 MINPS	61
		4.4.28 MINSD	61
		4.4.29 MINSS	61
		4.4.30 MOVAPS_load	62
		4.4.31 MOVAPS_store	62
		4.4.32 MOVD_load	62

4.4.33	MOVD_store		63
4.4.34	MOVD_load_sse		63
4.4.35	MOVD_store_sse		63
4.4.36	MOVHLPS		63
4.4.37	MOVHPS_load		64
4.4.38	MOVHPS_store		64
4.4.39	MOVLHPS		64
4.4.40	MOVLPS_load		64
4.4.41	MOVLPS_store		64
4.4.42	MOVMSKPS		65
4.4.43	MOVNTPS		65
4.4.44	MOVNTQ		65
4.4.45	MOVQ_load		66
4.4.46	MOVQ_store		66
4.4.47	MOVSS_load		66
4.4.48	MOVSS_store		66
4.4.49	MOVUPS_load		67
4.4.50	MOVUPS_store		67
4.4.51	MULPD		67
4.4.52	MULPS		67
4.4.53	MULSD		68
4.4.54	MULSS		68
4.4.55	ORPS		68
4.4.56	PACKSSDW		69
4.4.57	PACKSSWB		69
4.4.58	PACKUSWB		69
4.4.59	PADDB		70
4.4.60	PADDB_sse		70
4.4.61	PADDW		70
4.4.62	PADDW_sse		71
4.4.63	PADDD		71
4.4.64	PADDD_sse		71
4.4.65	PADDQ		72
4.4.66	PADDQ_sse		72
4.4.67	PADDSB		72
4.4.68	PADDSB_sse		73
4.4.69	PADDUSB		73
4.4.70	PADDUSB_sse		74
4.4.71	PAND		74
4.4.72	PAND_sse		74
4.4.73	PANDN		75
4.4.74	PANDN_sse		75
4.4.75	PAVGB		75
4.4.76	PAVGB_sse		76
4.4.77	PAVGW		76
4.4.78	PAVGW_sse		76
4.4.79	PCMPEQB		77
4.4.80	PCMPEQB_sse		77

4.4.81	PCMPEQW	77
4.4.82	PCMPEQW_sse	78
4.4.83	PCMPEQD	78
4.4.84	PCMPEQD_sse	79
4.4.85	PCMPGTB	79
4.4.86	PCMPGTB_sse	79
4.4.87	PCMPGTW	80
4.4.88	PCMPGTW_sse	80
4.4.89	PCMPGTD	80
4.4.90	PCMPGTD_sse	81
4.4.91	PEXTRW	81
4.4.92	PEXTRW_sse	81
4.4.93	PINSRW	82
4.4.94	PMADDWD	82
4.4.95	PMAXSW	82
4.4.96	PMAXUB	83
4.4.97	PMINSW	83
4.4.98	PMINUB	84
4.4.99	PMOVMSKB	84
4.4.100	PMULHUW	84
4.4.101	PMULHW	85
4.4.102	PMULLW	85
4.4.103	POR	86
4.4.104	PREFETCHNTA	86
4.4.105	PREFETCHT1	86
4.4.106	PREFETCHT0	86
4.4.107	PSADBW	87
4.4.108	PSHUFD	87
4.4.109	PSHUFW	87
4.4.110	PSxxf	88
4.4.111	PSUBx	89
4.4.112	PSUBSx	89
4.4.113	PSUBUSx	90
4.4.114	PSWAPD	90
4.4.115	PUNPCKHBW	90
4.4.116	PUNPCKLBW	91
4.4.117	PUNPCKHWD	91
4.4.118	PUNPCKLWD	91
4.4.119	PUNPCKHDQ	92
4.4.120	PUNPCKLDQ	92
4.4.121	PXOR	92
4.4.122	RCPPS	93
4.4.123	RCPSS	93
4.4.124	RSQRTPS	93
4.4.125	RSQRTSS	94
4.4.126	SFENCE	94
4.4.127	SQRTPS	95
4.4.128	SQRTSS	95

	4.4.129	SUBPS	95
	4.4.130	SUBSS	96
	4.4.131	UNPCKHPS	96
	4.4.132	UNPCLPS	96
	4.4.133	XORPS	97

5 3DNOW Instructions   99

	5.0.1	FEMMS	99
	5.0.2	PF2ID	99
	5.0.3	PFACC	99
	5.0.4	PFADD	100
	5.0.5	PFCMPEQ	100
	5.0.6	PFCMPGT	100
	5.0.7	PFCMPGE	101
	5.0.8	PFMAX	101
	5.0.9	PFMIN	101
	5.0.10	PFMUL	102
	5.0.11	PFNACC	102
	5.0.12	PFPNACC	102
	5.0.13	PFRCP	103
	5.0.14	PFRCPIT	103
	5.0.15	PFSUB	104
	5.0.16	PFSUBR	104
	5.0.17	PI2FD	105
	5.0.18	PI2FW	105
	5.0.19	PREFETCH	105

II SIMD Programming Languages   107
Paul Cockshott

6 Another Approach: Data Parallel Languages   109

6.1	Operations on Whole Arrays		109
	6.1.1	Array Slicing	111
	6.1.2	Conditional Operations	113
	6.1.3	Reduction Operations	114
	6.1.4	Data Reorganisation	114
6.2	Design Goals		116
	6.2.1	Target Machines	118
	6.2.2	Backward Compatibility	119
	6.2.3	Expressive Power	119
	6.2.4	Run-time Efficiency	120

7 Basics of Vector Pascal   121

7.1	Formating Rules		121
	7.1.1	Alphabet	121

| | | 7.1.2 | Reserved Words and Identifiers | 122 |
| | 7.2 | Base Types | | 125 |

- 7.1.2 Reserved Words and Identifiers 122
- 7.1.3 Character Case 124
- 7.1.4 Spaces and Comments 124
- 7.1.5 Semicolons 124
- 7.2 Base Types 125
  - 7.2.1 Booleans 125
  - 7.2.2 Integer Numbers 125
  - 7.2.3 Real Numbers 125
  - 7.2.4 Characters and Strings 126
- 7.3 Variables and Constants 127
  - 7.3.1 Declaration Order 127
  - 7.3.2 Constant Declarations 128
  - 7.3.3 Variable Declarations 129
  - 7.3.4 Assignment 129
  - 7.3.5 Predefined Types 129
- 7.4 Expressions and Operators 130
  - 7.4.1 Arithmetic 130
  - 7.4.2 Operations on Boolean Values 132
  - 7.4.3 Equality Operators 133
  - 7.4.4 Ordered Comparison 133
- 7.5 Matrix and Vector Operations 135
  - 7.5.1 Array Declarations 135
  - 7.5.2 Matrix and Vector Arithmetic 136
  - 7.5.3 Array Input/Output 139
  - 7.5.4 Array Slices 140
- 7.6 Vector and Matrix Products 142
  - 7.6.1 Inner Product of Vectors 142
  - 7.6.2 Dot Product of Non-real Typed Vectors 144
  - 7.6.3 Matrix to Vector Product 145
  - 7.6.4 Data-flow Hazards 146
  - 7.6.5 Matrix to Matrix Multiplication 148
- 7.7 Typography of Vector Pascal Programs 149

8 Algorithmic Features of Vector Pascal   151

- 8.1 Conditional Evaluation 151
- 8.2 Functions 152
  - 8.2.1 User-defined Functions 152
  - 8.2.2 Procedures 155
  - 8.2.3 Procedure ReadAndValidate 156
  - 8.2.4 Function H 157
  - 8.2.5 Function Log2 157
- 8.3 Branching 157
  - 8.3.1 Two-way Branches 157
  - 8.3.2 Multi-way Branches 158
- 8.4 Unbounded Iteration 159
  - 8.4.1 While 159
  - 8.4.2 Repeat 160

Contents

	8.5	Bounded Iteration	161
		8.5.1 For to	161
		8.5.2 For Downto	162
	8.6	Goto	163

9 User-defined Types   **165**
- 9.1 Scalar Types . . . 165
  - 9.1.1 `SUCC` and `PRED` . . . 166
  - 9.1.2 `ORD` . . . 168
  - 9.1.3 Input/Output of Scalars . . . 168
  - 9.1.4 Representation . . . 168
- 9.2 Sub-range Types . . . 169
  - 9.2.1 Representation . . . 170
- 9.3 Dimensioned Numbers . . . 170
  - 9.3.1 Arithmetic on Dimensioned Numbers . . . 173
  - 9.3.2 Handling Different Units of Measurement . . . 174
- 9.4 Records . . . 175
- 9.5 Pointers . . . 177
  - 9.5.1 Pointer Idioms . . . 179
  - 9.5.2 Freeing Storage . . . 181
- 9.6 Set Types . . . 182
  - 9.6.1 Set Literals . . . 182
  - 9.6.2 Operations on Sets . . . 183
- 9.7 String Types . . . 183

10 Input and Output   **187**
- 10.1 File Types . . . 187
  - 10.1.1 Binary Files . . . 187
  - 10.1.2 Text Files . . . 188
  - 10.1.3 Operating System Files . . . 188
- 10.2 Output . . . 190
  - 10.2.1 Binary File Output . . . 190
  - 10.2.2 Text File Output . . . 190
  - 10.2.3 Generic Array Output . . . 193
- 10.3 Input . . . 193
  - 10.3.1 Generic Array Input . . . 193
  - 10.3.2 Binary File Input . . . 194
  - 10.3.3 Text File Input . . . 194
- 10.4 File Predicates . . . 195
- 10.5 Random Access to Files . . . 195
  - 10.5.1 Seek . . . 195
  - 10.5.2 filepos . . . 195
  - 10.5.3 Untyped i/o . . . 196
- 10.6 Error Conditions . . . 196

11 Permutations and Polymorphism   **197**
- 11.1 Array Reorganisation . . . 198
  - 11.1.1 An Example . . . 200

		11.1.2	Array Shifts	200
		11.1.3	Element Permutation	200
		11.1.4	Efficiency Considerations	202
	11.2	Dynamic Arrays		202
		11.2.1	Schematic Arrays	203
	11.3	Polymorphic Functions		204
		11.3.1	Multiple Uses of Parametric Units	205
		11.3.2	Function dategt	206

III Programming Examples   209
Paul Cockshott

12 Advanced Set Programming   211

	12.1	Use of Sets to Find Prime Numbers		211
		12.1.1	Set Implementation	212
	12.2	Ordered Sets		213
		12.2.1	openfiles	215
		12.2.2	loadset	216
	12.3	Sets of Records		218
		12.3.1	Retrieval Operations	219
	12.4	Use of Sets in Text Indexing		219
	12.5	Constructing an Indexing Program		222
		12.5.1	dirlist: A Program for Traversing a Directory Tree	222
		12.5.2	intodir	223
	12.6	bloomfilter		224
		12.6.1	hashword	225
		12.6.2	setfilter	225
		12.6.3	testfilter	226
	12.7	The Main Program to Index Files		226
		12.7.1	processfile	227
		12.7.2	A Retrieval Program	227

13 Parallel Image Processing   229

	13.1	Declaring an Image Data Type		229
	13.2	Brightness and Contrast Adjustment		229
		13.2.1	Efficiency in Image Code	230
	13.3	Image Filtering		231
		13.3.1	Blurring	233
		13.3.2	Sharpening	233
		13.3.3	Comparing Implementations	235
	13.4	genconv		238
		13.4.1	dup	240
		13.4.2	prev	241
		13.4.3	pm	241
		13.4.4	doedges	242
		13.4.5	freestore	242

Contents   xiii

	13.5	Digital Half-toning. 242
		13.5.1 Parallel Half-tone. 244
		13.5.2 errordifuse. 245
	13.6	Image Resizing. 247
	13.7	Horizontal Resize. 249
	13.8	Horizontal Interpolation. 251
	13.9	Interpolate Vertically 251
	13.10	Displaying Images 251
		13.10.1 demoimg – An Example Image Display Program . . 251
	13.11	The Unit BMP. 257
		13.11.1 Procedure initbmpheader 260
		13.11.2 Procedure storebmpfile. 261
		13.11.3 Function loadbmpfile 261
		13.11.4 Procedure adjustcontrast. 262
		13.11.5 Procedure pconv 263
		13.11.6 Procedure convp 264

14 Pattern Recognition and Image Compression   265
14.1 Principles of Image Compression. 265
    14.1.1 Data Compression in General 265
    14.1.2 Image Compression 266
    14.1.3 Vector Quantisation of Images 266
    14.1.4 Data Structures 268
    14.1.5 encode 269
14.2 The K Means Algorithm. 271
    14.2.1 Vector Quantisation of Colour Images. 277

15 3D Graphics   279
15.1 Mesh Representation 280
15.2 linedemo: An Illustration of 3D Projection. 282
15.3 demo3d: Main Procedure of linedemo 283
    15.3.1 Viewing Matrices 283
    15.3.2 SDL Initialisation. 285
15.4 Create a Rotation Matrix 287
    15.4.1 Calculate x mod 3 288
15.5 2D Projection 288
    15.5.1 Entry Point to Line Drawing. 289
15.6 Bresenham Line Drawing Procedure. 290
15.7 Performance 292

IV VIPER   293
Ken Renfrew

16 Introduction to VIPER   295
16.1 Rationale. 295
    16.1.1 The Literate Programming Tool 295
    16.1.2 The Mathematical Syntax Converter 296

16.2	A System Overview.	296
16.3	Which VIPER to Download?	297
16.4	System Dependencies	297
16.5	Installing Files	298
16.6	Setting Up the Compiler.	298
16.7	Setting Up the System	298
	16.7.1 Setting System Dependencies.	299
	16.7.2 Personal Set-up	300
	16.7.3 Dynamic Compiler Options	301
	16.7.4 VIPER Option Buttons.	303
16.8	Moving VIPER	303
16.9	Programming with VIPER	303
	16.9.1 Single Files	303
	16.9.2 Projects.	304
	16.9.3 Embedding LaTeX in Vector Pascal	306
16.10	Compiling Files in VIPER.	306
	16.10.1 Compiling Single Files	306
	16.10.2 Compiling Projects.	306
16.11	Running Programs in VIPER	307
16.12	Making VPTEX.	307
	16.12.1 VPTEX Options.	307
	16.12.2 VPMath.	308
16.13	LaTeX in VIPER	308
16.14	HTML in VIPER	309
16.15	Writing Code to Generate Good VPTEX.	309
	16.15.1 Use of Special Comments	309
	16.15.2 Use of Margin Comments.	310
	16.15.3 Use of Ordinary Pascal Comments.	311
	16.15.4 Levels of Detail Within Documentation	311
	16.15.5 Mathematical Translation: Motivation and Guidelines.	312
	16.15.6 LaTeX Packages	313

Appendix A Compiler Porting Tools   315

A.1	Dependencies.	315
A.2	Compiler Structure.	316
	A.2.1 Vectorisation	317
	A.2.2 Porting Strategy	320
A.3	ILCG	321
A.4	Supported Types	321
	A.4.1 Data Formats	321
	A.4.2 Typed Formats	322
	A.4.3 ref Types	322
A.5	Supported Operations.	322
	A.5.1 Type Casts	322
	A.5.2 Arithmetic	322
	A.5.3 Memory.	322

Contents

	A.5.4	Assignment	323
	A.5.5	Dereferencing	323
A.6	Machine Description		323
	A.6.1	Registers	323
	A.6.2	Register Sets	324
	A.6.3	Register Arrays	324
	A.6.4	Register Stacks	324
	A.6.5	Instruction Formats	325
A.7	Grammar of ILCG		325
A.8	ILCG Grammar		326
	A.8.1	Helpers	326
	A.8.2	Tokens	327
	A.8.3	Non-terminal Symbols	329

Appendix B   Software Download   335

Appendix C   Using the Command Line Compiler   337

C.1	Invoking the Compiler		337
	C.1.1	Environment Variable	337
	C.1.2	Compiler Options	337
	C.1.3	Dependencies	338
C.2	Calling Conventions		338
C.3	Array Representation		341
	C.3.1	Range Checking	341

References   343

Index   345

List of Tables

1.1	Intel processors	5
1.2	Performance on vector kernels	9
2.1	MMX data types	13
2.2	The XMM registers support both scalar and vector arithmetic	21
3.1	Nasm constant operators	31
3.2	Register encodings	31
3.3	Object file formats and compilers that use them	34
3.4	Comparative performance of the 3DNow and SSE versions of coordinate transformation	45
6.1	Speeds of different implementations	118
7.1	Vector Pascal reserved words	122
9.1	Effect of the compiler directives $m and $r	168
9.2	The set operators	183
12.1	Comparative performances of different Pascal implementations on the Sieve program as a function of set size	213
13.1	Comparative performance on convolution	238
15.1	Relative performance	292
C.1	Code generators supported	338
C.2	Structure of an array	341

List of Figures

1.1	The use of clocked pipelines	4
2.1	The Intel IA32 with MMX register architecture	12
2.2	The MMX data formats	13
2.3	The AMD 3DNOW! extensions add 32-bit floating point data to the types that can be handled in MMX registers	17
2.4	The cache structure	18
2.5	With four banks of cache it is possible for a loop using two source and one destination array to stream data in distinct banks whilst reserving one bank for local variables	19
2.6	The Streaming SIMD extensions add additional 128-bit vector registers, with multiple formats	20
3.1	Stackframe on entry to pmyfunc	37
3.2	Mapping a one-dimensional array to a two-dimensional array suitable for vectorisation	37
3.3	Translation. The triangle a,b,c with coordinates $[1,1],[1,2],[2,2]$ is translated to the triangle d,e,f with coordinates $[3,0.5],[3,1.5],[4,1.5]$ by adding $[2,-0.5]$ to each vertex.	39
3.4	Scaling. Triangle d,e,f is obtained by multiplying the vertices of a,b,c by 2	40
3.5	Illustration of the effect of rotations by $\frac{\pi}{4}$ on the unit vectors $x=[1,0]$, $y=[0,1]$. The result is that $x \to [a,b]=[\frac{1}{\sqrt{2}},\frac{1}{\sqrt{2}}]$ and $y \to [-a,b]=[-\frac{1}{\sqrt{2}},\frac{1}{\sqrt{2}}]$	40
3.6	Contrast between the linear layout of the matrix and vectors in memory and the layout once loaded into 3DNow registers.	41
6.1	Different ways of slicing the same array	112
6.2	Reorganising by transposition	115
7.1	Projection of one vector on to another. In the example, $v2=(1,2)$, $v1=(1,1)$	143
7.2	Illustration of VPTEX formating applied to the program shown in Alg. 28 to find the mean of the first 4 primes	149
7.3	The mapping from ASCII to TEX format	150
8.1	An example of conditional evaluation	151
8.2	Three functions	152
8.3	Use of local identifiers within a function	153
8.4	Two uses of var parameters	154
8.5	Mutual recursion requires forward declaration	155
8.6	Use of unbounded iteration to sum the integers in a file up to the first 0 value	161

8.7	Use of a while loop to achieve the same result as in Figure 8.6	161
8.8	The use of a for loop to perform operations on an array contrasted with the use of explicit array arithmetic	162
8.9	The use of GOTO to escape from an error condition.	163
9.1	A program illustrating both the comparability of user-defined scalar types and their cyclical nature.	166
9.2	Illustrating how the ORD function can be used to allow arithmetic on a scalar type, in this case char	168
9.3	The use of sub-range types	169
9.4	Function oilInEuros	172
9.5	A simple program which uses dimensioned types in the context of a commodity trading problem	173
9.6	Procedure euroquote.	173
9.7	The preferred approach to using dimensioned numbers to handle different units of measure.	176
9.8	An approach to sorting a file using a fixed-size buffer. It should be noted that the inefficient bubble sort procedure is presented just for simplicity	178
9.9	A more efficient sorting program than in Figure 9.8, one which, moreover, makes use of dynamic storage allocation from the heap	180
9.10	A program which illustrates the effect of the set operators	184
10.1	The formating rules for output of multi-dimensional arrays	194
10.2	The use of ioresult to check the validity of file open calls	196
11.1	Demonstration of the use of transpose to produce tables: VPTEXed program. For the original Pascal source, see Figure 11.2	201
11.2	Demonstration of the use of transpose to produce tables: the original Pascal source	202
11.3	Use of getmem to allocate dynamically a two-dimensional array for image data	203
11.4	A polymorphic sorting unit	205
11.5	Procedure sort	205
11.6	A program that uses the integer sorting unit.	206
11.7	A unit to export dates and their order	206
11.8	The use of two instantiations of the same parametric unit within one program	207
12.1	Use of a hash function to store words in an ordinal set	221
12.2	The upper line shows the probability of false positives with a set in the range 0...1023 as the number of unique words stored in it rises. The lower trace shows the probability of false positives if unanimous results must be obtained from eight independently hashed sets	221
13.1	Test images used to illustrate brightness, contrast adjustment and filtering. The images (a)–(e) were produced by the program graphio.	232
13.2	The effect of a blurring filter on a finite impulse	233

List of Figures

13.3	The image at the top is the original. The bottom left image has been subjected to a blurring filter (0.25,0.5,0.25) and that on the right to a sharpening filter.	234
13.4	Effect of a sharpening filter on a finite impulse	234
13.5	Effect of applying a diagonal edge detection filter to Mandrill.	244
13.6	Mandrill rendered with a 4×8 mask	245
13.7	Mandrill rendered using error diffusion	246
13.8	Naive resampling used to scale pictures introduces artifacts	247
13.9	Anti-aliased rescaling using blurring and interpolation reduces artifacts	248
13.10	Horizontal interpolation of a new pixel position r between existing pixel positions p and q.	249
13.11	Effect of applying resize to Barbara.bmp	255
14.1	Outline of the vector quantisation process. Patches from the image are unwound into vectors and these are then looked up in a codebook of vectors to find the best match. Then the index of the best match is output as a surrogate for the patch	267
14.2	The process of decoding a VQ image is inherently faster than encoding since the codebook searching used during encoding is replaced by a fetch from a calculated offset into the codebook. The vector found is formed into a patch and placed in the image.	268
14.3	Effect of increasing number of iterations of the K means on image quality. All images have been compressed to 16K from an 192K original, using the program vqencode, and then decoded using vqdecode. Compare these with the images in Figure 13.3.	275
14.4	This shows how detail becomes apparent within the image blocks as iterations of the K means algorithm progress	276
15.1	The graphics pipeline used in this chapter.	279
15.2	A sequence of four frames drawn by LineDemo.	284
15.3	The pinhole camera model	285
15.4	The projection triangles. p is a vector in object space and q is its image under pinhole projection. We can treat p as either the x or y component of a point in camera coordinates. a is the focal length of the virtual camera and b is the distance from the pinhole to the base of the vector. $\frac{q}{a} = \frac{p}{b}$ by similarity of triangles, thus $q = p\frac{a}{b}$ and where $a = 1$, then $q = \frac{p}{b}$.	289
16.1	File format entries in Compiler Options	299
16.2	Dependencies window.	300
16.3	The Viper Option windows	301
16.4	Dynamic Option window	302
16.5	The right click menu.	304
16.6	The Project Properties window.	305
16.7	The Run Options panel.	307

16.8	The VPTEX Options panel.	308
A.1	Vector Pascal toolset	316
A.2	The translation of Vector Pascal to assembler	317
A.3	Sequential form of array assignment	318
A.4	Parallelised loop.	318
A.5	After applying `simplify` to the tree	319
A.6	The result of matching the parallelised loop against the Pentium instruction-set	319
A.7	The method `getParallelism` for a P4 processor	320

List of Algorithms

1	Forming a total with a for loop	7
2	Forming a total with an unrolled loop	7
3	C code to add two images and corresponding assembler for the inner loop. Code compiled on the Intel C compiler version 4.0	16
4	MMX version of Alg. 3	16
5	A simple example of prefetching	19
6	An example that makes more effective use of prefetching than Alg. 5	20
7	Assembler version of the test program	26
8	C version of the test program	27
9	C++ version of the test program	28
10	Examples of the use of section and data reservation directives	33
11	Use of MMX instructions to sum a vector of integers	36
12	Illustration of calling pmyfunc from C	38
13	3DNow routine to multiply a vector by a matrix	43
14	Matrix–vector multiplication using SSE code	44
15	C variant of the matrix to vector multiply	45
16	Inner product in assembler	82
17	Use of RCPPS	93
18	Use of RSQRTSS to normalise a vector	94
19	Use of PFRCP	104
20	Example program in Vector Pascal	117
21	Illustrating the embedding of a newline in a string	127
22	Program to compute the velocity of a falling body	128
23	Effect of string length and character values on string order	133
24	truthtab, a program to print the truth tables for all of the dyadic Boolean operators	134
25	Simple example of array operations	135
26	Element by element multiplication of each row of a matrix by a vector	137
27	Flood filling an array with a scalar	138
28	An example of operator reduction	138
29	Reduction using MAX	139
30	Illustration of how a multi-dimensional array is printed	140
31	The use of array slices	141
32	The dot product of two vectors. See Figure 7.1 for explanation	144
33	The danger of overflow when computing dot products using limited precision	145

34	Use of the dot product operator to output the number 263 as the roman number CCLXIII.	146
35	Using a spiral rotation matrix to operate on the unit x vector.	147
36	Matrix by matrix multiplication	149
37	The use of formatted output and also the use of Chinese characters in reserved words. The equivalent Standard Pascal program commands are shown as comments	192
38	The sieve of Eratosthenes, coded using sets	211
39	Main program for unique words.	214
40	Body of the function intodir.	223
41	Simple manipulations of image contrasts and brightnesses. The type pimage used is a pointer to an image	230
42	A more efficient way of adjusting contrast. Note that in this example the type line refers to a vector of pixels	231
43	The sharpening method	235
44	Standard Pascal implementation of the convolution	236
45	The program dconv, a test harness for image convolution written to work under several Pascal compilers	237
46	The procedure showtime	237
47	Vector Pascal implementation of the convolution.	238
48	Main body of the generalised convolution	239
49	The function which checks for duplicate kernel elements	240
50	Function to find a previous instance of a kernel element	241
51	The premultiplication function.	241
52	The edge processing algorithm	243
53	The release of temporary store	244
54	Parallel half-toning using a fixed mask	245
55	Classical error diffusion, non-parallel code.	246
56	Resize an image.	249
57	Horizontal resize an image.	250
58	Vertical resize routine	252
59	Horizontal interpolation routine.	253
60	Vertical interpolation of image lines	254
61	The vector quantisation routine proper. This takes a vector and searches the codebook for the vector with the closest Euclidean distance to the source vector and returns the index of the closest matching vector	270
62	The program vqdecode. This takes two parameters, a filename without extension for the encoded file and a filename with extension as the destination file. Input is assumed to be in the format generated by the vqencode program and output is a Windows BMP file	271
63	Basic training step of the vector K means algorithm	274
64	The main image encode program	274
65	Encodes an image given the codebook.	275
66	The generator function for triangle meshes	281
67	Bresenham's algorithm in Pascal.	291

Introduction

A number of widely used contemporary processors have instruction-set extensions for improved performance in multi-media applications. The aim is to allow operations to proceed on multiple pixels each clock cycle. Such instruction-sets have been incorporated both in specialist DSPchips such as the Texas C62xx (Texas Instruments, 1998) and in general purpose CPU chips like the Intel IA32 (Intel, 2000) or the AMD K6 (Advanced Micro Devices, 1999).

These instruction-set extensions are typically based on the Single Instruction-stream Multiple Data-stream (SIMD) model in which a single instruction causes the same mathematical operation to be carried out on several operands, or pairs of operands, at the same time. The level or parallelism supported ranges from two floating point operations, at a time on the AMD K6 architecture to 16 byte operations at a time on the Intel P4 architecture. Whereas processor architectures are moving towards greater levels of parallelism, the most widely used programming languages such as C, Java and Delphi are structured around a model of computation in which operations take place on a single value at a time. This was appropriate when processors worked this way, but has become an impediment to programmers seeking to make use of the performance offered by multi-media instruction-sets. The introduction of SIMD instruction sets (Peleg et al., 1997; Intel, 1999) to personal computers potentially provides substantial performance increases, but the ability of most programmers to harness this performance is held back by two factors:

1. The first is the limited availability of compilers that make effective use of these instruction-sets in a machine-independent manner. This remains the case despite the research efforts to develop compilers for multi-media instruction-sets (Cheong and Lam, 1997; Leupers, 1999; Krall and Lelait, 2000; Srereman and Govindarajan, 2000).
2. The second is the fact that most popular programming languages were designed on the word at a time model of the classic von Neumann computer.

Vector Pascal aims to provide an efficient and concise notation for programmers using multi-media enhanced CPUs. In doing so it borrows concepts for expressing data parallelism that have a long history, dating back to Iverson's work on APL in the early 1960s (Iverson, 1962).

Define a vector of type T as having type $T[\ ]$. Then if we have a binary operator $\omega : (T \otimes T) \rightarrow T$, in languages derived from APL we automatically have an operator $\omega : (T[\ ] \otimes T[\ ]) \to T[\ ]$. Thus, if x,y are arrays of integers $k = x + y$ is the array of integers where $k_i = x_i + y_i$.

The basic concept is simple; there are complications to do with the semantics of operations between arrays of different lengths and different dimensions, but Iverson provides a consistent treatment of these. The most recent languages to be built round this model are J, an interpretive language (Iverson, 1991, 2000; Burke, 1995), and F (Metcalf and Reid, 1996) a modernised Fortran. In principle, though, any language with array types can be extended in a similar way. Iverson's approach to data parallelism is machine independent. It can be implemented using scalar instructions or using the SIMD model. The only difference is speed.

Vector Pascal incorporates Iverson's approach to data parallelism. Its aim is to provide a notation that allows the natural and elegant expression of data parallel algorithms within a base language that is already familiar to a considerable body of programmers and combine this with modern compilation techniques.

By an elegant algorithm is meant one which is expressed as concisely as possible. Elegance is a goal that one approaches asymptotically, approaching but never attaining (Chaitin, 1997). APL and J allow the construction of very elegant programs, but at a cost. An inevitable consequence of elegance is the loss of redundancy. APL programs are as concise as or even more concise than conventional mathematical notation (Iverson, 1980) and use a special character set. This makes them hard for the uninitiated to understand. J attempts to remedy this by restricting itself to the ASCII character set, but still looks dauntingly unfamiliar to programmers brought up on more conventional languages. Both APL and J are interpretive, which makes them ill suited to many of the applications for which SIMD speed is required. The aim of Vector Pascal is to provide the conceptual gains of Iverson's notation within a framework familiar to imperative programmers.

Pascal (Jensen and Wirth, 1978) was chosen as a base language over the alternatives of C and Java. C was rejected because notations such as x+y for x and y declared as int x[4], y[4], already have the meaning of adding the addresses of the arrays together. Java was rejected because of the difficulty of efficiently transmitting data parallel operations via its intermediate code to a just in time code generator.

Part I
SIMD Programming
Paul Cockshott

Computer Speed, Program Speed

1.1 Clocks

Since their invention in the 1940s, the speed of electronic computers has increased exponentially. Their raw speed is usually measured in MHz or millions of cycles per second. In the last few years, MHz have been replaced by GHz, or thousands of millions of cycles per second. These figures describe what is called the clock speed of the computer.

Since the invention of escapement mechanisms in the Middle Ages, all clocks have had at their heart a device that oscillates, the regularity of whose cycles determines the clock's accuracy. In mechanical clocks the oscillator was typically a pendulum or a balance wheel bound by a spring, which might oscillate once per second. The clockwork mechanism then used toothed wheels to count these cycles and show the result in terms of seconds, minutes and hours. Such clocks were, in a sense, the first computers.

Nowadays, clocks use quartz crystals which vibrate rapidly when a voltage is placed across them. The crystals used in modern watches typically vibrate some 30 000 times per second. The vibrations produce as a side effect electronic pulses; digital circuits or *registers* count these vibrations and show or register the time on the face of the watch.

When we talk about the clock speed of a computer, we are referring to the rate of a similar sort of crystal-controlled oscillator. The pulses produced by it are used to synchronise all of the internal operations of the processor chip. Like a clock, the chip contains registers which hold the numbers on which calculations are performed. The registers are designed so that they can change their values only when a pulse arrives from the oscillator.

In between the registers are arithmetic circuits which perform the actual calculations, as shown in Figure 1.1. Register A feeds information into a calculation circuit and the result is registered in B. It takes a small but definite time for these calculation circuits to operate, and chip designers have to ensure that the results will arrive at B before the next clock pulse. As the components making up the arithmetic circuits are made smaller and smaller, the time taken for electrical pulses to propagate through them declines, allowing designers to shorten the intervals between successive clock pulses. In a modern computer the parts are so small that delays between pipeline stages are less than a nanosecond, a billionth of a second.

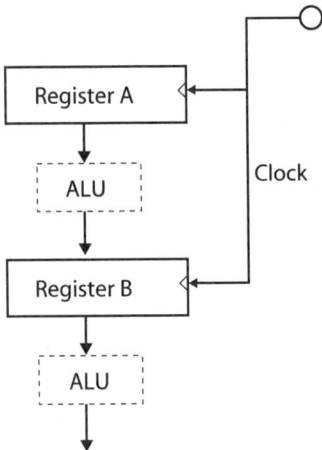

Figure 1.1. The use of clocked pipelines.

The first computer to operate with a 1 MHz clock was built in the mid-1950s. By 2000, clocks were 1000 times faster. The driving force in all of this has been the ability of the semiconductor industry to make transistors smaller and smaller, reducing the time it takes for electrons to pass through them. This reduction in size has also made computers far cheaper. Twenty years ago Cray mainframe computers had clock speeds of over 100 MHz, but they were so expensive that only major national laboratories could afford them. Two decades later we have computers with 2 GHz clocks so cheap that they are used to amuse children.

1.2 Width

Clock speeds sell computers and, historically, improvements in clock speeds have been by far the most important factor in increasing the power of computers. Clock speeds have gone up 1000-fold since the mid-1950s but individual computers are probably some 100 000 times faster than they were then. The remaining factor of 100 stems from improvements in the internal design or architecture.

Consider the problem of adding together two four-digit numbers, $1204 + 1801$. If you were to do this by hand you would proceed as follows: $1 + 4 = 5$ and carry 0, $0 + 0 = 0$ and carry 0, $2 + 8 = 0$ and carry 1, $1 + 1 + 1 = 3$, so the answer is 3005. We have done this working on at most three digits at a time. At primary school we memorised the addition tables of all the pairs of digits, knowing these we can perform the calculation in four steps.

We do pencil and paper arithmetic a single digit at a time, but using the methods of long addition, long multiplication, etc., people can perform sums on numbers of arbitrary length. A single decimal digit can be stored in a 4-bit binary number, so a computer capable of adding together two numbers each 4 bits long would be a emulate our paper and pencil methods. In one cycle it could add a single pair of digits, in the next another pair, etc., taking four cycles to do 1204 + 1801. Indeed, this is exactly how most cheap pocket calculators work, they add pairs of digits at a time. When you press the square root key of a pocket calculator a software subroutine is invoked that calculates the square root by a laborious process involving repeated single digit arithmetic, but, since the cycle time is very short compared with humans, it appears to perform the operation instantaneously.

However, if you compare a 4-bit computer with a 16-bit computer then the addition 1204 + 1801 can now be performed in a single operation. Thus, aside from clock frequency, the 16-bit machine will be four times faster than the 4-bit machine. However, this only holds so long as the calculations are four digits long. Leaving aside considerations of clock speed, a 4-bit machine will be just as efficient as a 16-bit machine on single digit arithmetic.

Taking into account both clock speed and data width, we get a measure of CPU speed s as

$$s = \frac{cb}{w}$$

where c is the clock speed, b the bit width of the machine's arithmetic and w the bit width of the operands on which the program is working.

1.3 Instruction Speed

A further complication is that the number of clock cycles required to perform an instruction varies.

Different designs of CPUs take varying numbers of clock cycles to perform an instruction. If you look at Table 1.1, you can see that the number of clocks per instruction has gone down over the years with successive models of Intel CPUs. The factors entering into this are the speed of memory relative to the clock and the depth of the data processing pipeline. Early processors took several clock cycles to access memory. On newer processors, this has been cut thanks to the ability of the CPU to fetch several instructions in one memory

Table 1.1. Intel processors

CPU	Year	Register width	Clock MHz	Clocks per instruction	Throughput MIPS
4004	1971	4	0.1	8	0.0125
8080	1974	8	2	8	0.25
8086	1978	16	5	8	0.33
386	1985	32	16	3	5.0
Pentium with MMX	1997	64	200	0.5	400
P4	2001	128	1600	0.5	3200

The first Intel microprocessor, the 4004, was targeted at pocket calculators. It had a 4-bit accumulator, just enough to hold a decimal digit. Subsequent processors have seen the widths of their registers increase by successive factors of two.

access and to the use of caches, small auxiliary high-speed memories, to reduce the mean time to read a memory location. The most recent processors are super-scalar, meaning that they can execute more than one instruction each clock cycle. A Pentium class processor can issue two instructions per clock.

This modifies our speed equation to

$$s = \frac{cb}{wi}$$

where i is the number clocks per instruction. On a given processor, the most important factor determining the number of clocks per instruction is memory access. Since memory speeds have consistently lagged behind processor speeds, an algorithm with many load and store instructions will be slower than one with fewer. Since the main technique used by CPU designers to reduce i has been the use of caches, another crucial determinant of speed is the extent to which the data used by an algorithm will fit into the cache. If the dataset is small enough, memory fetches will execute in one or two instructions. If not, they can take 10 times as long.

1.4 Overhead Instructions

When we consider an algorithm in the abstract, we can determine the minimum number of basic arithmetic operations required to perform a task. If we want to form the total of an array of four numbers, then we know that we need at least three additions. On most designs of CPU, however, it would be hard to code this with so few instructions.

If the addition is performed using a `for` loop (see Alg. 1), then there will be additional instructions to increment the iteration variable, to test it against limits and to perform jumps. Even the basic addition step `t:=t+a[i]` can involve several instructions. In Alg. 1, a total of 36 instructions are required to perform the three basic additions.

If we unroll the loop and express it in a single statement as shown in Alg. 2, then the compiler is able to make a better job of translating the code, so we end up with only five instructions to perform the three adds that are required.

The number of overhead instructions needed depends on:

- the sophistication of the compiler used
- the coding style used by the programmer
- the expressive power of the CPU's instruction-set.

We can summarise the effects of these factors in a number u, which is defined as

$$u = \frac{\text{useful instructions}}{\text{total instructions}}$$

In the program fragment in Figure 1.1 we get $u = \frac{1}{12}$ and for the unrolled code we obtain $u = \frac{3}{5}$.

Chapter 1 • Computer Speed, Program Speed

```
High Level Code             Resulting machine code
---------------             ----------------------
t:=0;
                            XOR     AX,AX
                            MOV     T,AX
for i:=1 to 4 do t:=t+a[i];
                            MOV     I,0001
                            JMP     0020
                            INC     I
                            MOV     AX,T        -+
                            MOV     DI,I         |
                            SHL     DI,1         | t:=t+a[i]
                            ADD     AX,[DI+A]    |
                            MOV     T,AX        -+
                            CMP     I,4
                            JNZ     001C
                            ============
Instructions executed       36
```

Note that the high-level code generates many more lines of assembler. Even the basic stage of computing each step of the total t:=t+a[i] requires five instructions.

Algorithm 1. Forming a total with a for loop.

```
t:=a[1]+a[2]+a[3]+a[4];
                            MOV     AX,[A]
                            ADD     AX,[A+2]
                            ADD     AX,[A+4]
                            ADD     AX,[A+6]
                            MOV     T,AX
                            ==========
Instructions executed       5
```

Note that in this case the compiler is able to optimise access to the array elements and to dispense with the loop code, giving a much better efficiency.

Algorithm 2. Forming a total with an unrolled loop.

Taking overhead instructions into account, we obtain a new equation for program speed:

$$s = \frac{ucb}{wi}$$

Another factor that one has to consider is Amdahl's law, which states that the effective speedup of a program due to parallelisation will be constrained by the fraction of the program that cannot be executed in parallel:

$$A = \frac{\psi + p}{\psi + \frac{p}{n}}$$

where A is the acceleration achievable, ψ is the number of inherently serial instructions in the program, p is the potentially parallel instructions and n is the number of processing units available to perform the operations. This means that for real programs the effective speedup tends to be less than that which might appear to be possible simply by looking at the parallelism of the instruction-set. For instance, assume we have a computer capable of performing four operations in parallel, and a program in which 8 million of the dynamically executed operations are potentially parallelisable, with a residuum of 2 million that are inherently serial:

	Serial instructions	Parallel instructions	Parallelism	Total
Problem	2 000 000	8 000 000		
Machine 1	2 000 000	8 000 000	1	10 000 000
Machine 2	2 000 000	2 000 000	4	4 000 000
Speedup				150%

1.5 Algorithm Complexity

The factors described so far relate to the speed and architecture of the CPU and to the compiler's effectiveness in using it. However, for large programs these factors are dominated by the algorithmic complexity of the program. This describes how the number of basic arithmetic operations required by the program grows as a function of the size of the problem. Thus a naive searching algorithm would require of the order of n basic operations to search a table of n elements, but a better algorithm can achieve the same function with of the order of $\log n$ basic operations. We use the notation $C(n)$ to denote the complexity of the algorithm. $C(n)$ gives the minimum number of basic arithmetic operations that are required by the algorithm assuming that $u = 1$, i.e. that we have a perfectly efficient compiler. We call this minimum number of operations the *base* operations. Thus our final model for determining the speed of a program is given by

$$s = C(n)\frac{ucb}{wi}$$

where $wi < b$, and a modified versions of Amdahl's equation in other cases:

$$s = C(n)uc\left(\frac{\psi + p}{\psi + \frac{pb}{wi}}\right)$$

Table 1.2. Performance on vector kernels

w	b					test
	16 (BP)	32 (DevP)	32 (TMT)	32 (DP)	32 (VP 486)	64 (VP K6)	
8	46	71	80	166	333	2329	unsigned byte +
8	38	55	57	110	225	2329	saturated unsigned byte +
8	23	49	46	98	188	2330	pixel +
8	39	67	14	99	158	998	pixel $\times$
16	39	66	74	124	367	1165	short integer +
32	47	85	59	285	349	635	long integer +
32	33	47	10	250	367	582	real +
32	32	47	10	161	164	665	real dot prod
32	33	79	58	440	517	465	integer dot prod

In these tests the clock speed $c = 1$ GHz is held constant, and the number of base operations is known for each row of the table. All figures are in terms of millions of base operations per second measured on a 1 GHz Athlon. Different rows of the table have different effective data type widths w. Variations in speed going down a column show the effects of w, and also measure the relative efficiency, u, of the compilers for different data types.

The rows measuring dot product also potentially show variations in i because there are opportunities in the dot product operation for caching operands in registers. Where these are taken, the effect is to reduce the mean number of clocks to access an operand, thus giving higher performances.

The bit width of the registers available varies between the columns since one compiler was targeted on the 286 instruction-set giving $b = 16$, another was targeted on the K6 instruction-set with $b = 64$ and the others on the 486 instruction-set with $b = 32$. The resulting variations in performance along the rows measure the effect of b and u varying between the compilers.

It can be seen that the combined effects of variations in bu can amount to a performance variation of 100 to 1 along the rows.

The following compilers were used: BP = Borland Pascal compiler with 287 instructions enabled range checks off, $b = 16$, release of 1992; DevP = Dev Pascal version 1.9, $b = 32$; TMT = TMT Pascal version 3, $b = 32$, release of 2000; DP = Delphi version 4, $b = 32$, release of 1998; VP 486 = Vector Pascal targeted at a 486, $b = 32$, release of 2002; VP K6 = Vector Pascal targeted at an AMD K6, $b = 64$, release of 2002.

Clearly the most important factor here is $C(n)$, since, despite gains in clock speed, etc., for sufficiently large n an $\mathbf{O}n$ algorithm will run faster on an old 8086 than an $\mathbf{O}n^2$ algorithm on a P4.

However, if we assume that the complexity of the algorithm $C(n)$ is unchanged and that we have a particular processor to work with, thus fixing c, then changes to the remaining factors can still produce dramatic changes in program speed.

If we select our numeric precision w to be no greater than required, use large register widths b and produce few overhead instructions, some programs can be speeded up by more than an order of magnitude (see Tables 1.2 and 13.1). Vector Pascal improves program performance by concentrating on these factors. To understand how this is possible we have to look at how Intel and AMD have widened the registers on their latest processors, and introduced new data-types targeted at image processing problems. This is the subject matter of the next chapter.

SIMD Instruction-sets

In the performance model presented in Chapter 1, we identified two crucial factors to be b the bit width of the machine's registers and w the width in bits of the numbers being used in the program. We examined the situation where $w > b$, taking the example of a 4-bit machine doing 16-bit arithmetic. In this case we saw that performance would vary as b/w.

In this chapter, we look at how processor manufacturers have attempted to deal with the opposite case, $b > w$, where the register widths are substantially wider than the data types being operated on. This occurs frequently when dealing with images and sound, which are typically represented by 8- or 16-bit discrete samples. Modern processors tend to have at least some 64-bit registers, since these are required for floating point operations. The challenge has been to keep performance increasing as a function of b/w whilst $b > w$.

2.1 The SIMD Model

A number of widely used contemporary processors have instruction-set extensions for improved performance in multi-media applications. The aim is to allow operations to proceed on multiple pixels each clock cycle. Such instruction-sets have been incorporated both in specialist DSP chips such as the Texas C62xx (Texas Instruments, 1998) and in general-purpose CPU chips such as the Intel IA32 (Intel, 1999, 2000) or the AMD K6 (Advanced Micro Devices, 1999).

These instruction-set extensions are typically based on the Single Instruction-stream Multiple Data-stream (SIMD) model in which a single instruction causes the same mathematical operation to be carried out on many operands, or pairs of operands, at the same time. The SIMD model was originally developed in the context of large-scale parallel machines such as the ICL Distributed Array Processor or the Connection Machine. In these systems, a single control processor broadcast an instruction to thousands of single-bit wide data processors causing each to perform the same action in lockstep. These early SIMD processors exhibited massive data parallelism but, with each data processor having its own private memory and data-bus, they were bulky machines involving multiple boards each carrying multiple memory chip, data-processor chip pairs. Whilst they used single bit processors, the SIMD model is not dependent on this. It can also be implemented with multiple 8-, 16- or 32-bit data processors.

The incorporation of SIMD technology in modern general-purpose microprocessors is on a more modest scale than were the pioneering efforts. For reasons of economy the SIMD engine has to be included on the same die as the rest of the CPU. This immediately constrains the degree of parallelism that can be obtained. The constraint does not arise from the difficulties of incorporating large numbers of simple processing units. With contemporary feature sizes, one could fit more than 1000 1-bit processors on a die. Instead, the degree of parallelism is constrained by the width of the CPU to memory data path.

The SIMD model provides for all data processors to transfer simultaneously words of data between internal registers and corresponding locations in their memory banks. Thus with n data processors each using w-bit words one needs a path to memory of nw bits. If a CPU chip has a 64-bit memory bus then it could support 64 1-bit SIMD data processors, or eight 8-bit data processors, two 32-bit processors, etc.

For bulk data operations, such as those involved in image processing, the relevant memory bus is the off-chip bus. For algorithms that can exploit some degree of data locality, the relevant bus would be that linking the CPU to the on-chip cache, and the degree of parallelism possible would be constrained by the width of the cache lines used.

Whilst memory access paths constrain the degree of parallelism possible, the large numbers of logic gates available on modern dies allow the complexity of the individual data processors to be raised. Instead of performing simple 1-bit arithmetic, they do parallel arithmetic on multi-bit integers and floating point numbers.

As a combined result of these altered constraints we find that SIMD instructions for multi-media applications have parallelism levels of between 32 bits (Texas C62xx) and 128 bits (Intel P4), and the supported data types range from 8-bit integers to 64-bit floating point numbers.

2.2 The MMX Register Architecture

The MMX architectural extensions were introduced in late models of the Pentium and subsequent processors from Intel and exist in compatible chips

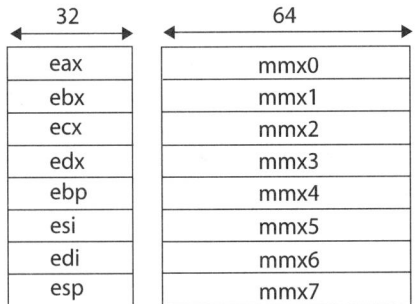

Figure 2.1. The Intel IA32 with MMX register architecture.

produced by AMD, Cyrix and others. They can now be considered part of the baseline architecture of any contemporary PC.

The data registers available for computational purposes on processors incorporating the MMX architecture are shown in Figure 2.1. The original IA32 architecture had eight general-purpose registers and an eight-deep stack of floating point registers. When designing the multi-media extensions to the instruction-set, Intel wanted to ensure that no new state bits were added to the process model. Adding new state bits would have made CPUs with the extensions incompatible with existing operating systems, as these would not have saved the additional state on a task switch. Instead, Intel added eight new virtual 64-bit registers which are aliased on to the existing floating point stack. These new multimedia registers, mm0...mm7, use state bits already allocated to the Floating Point Unit (FPU), and are thus saved when an operating system saves the state of the FPU.

The MMX instructions share addressing mode formats with the instructions used for the general-purpose registers. The 3-bit register identification fields inherited from the previous instructions are now used to index the eight multimedia rather than the eight general-purpose registers. The existing addressing modes for memory operands are also carried over, allowing the full gamut of base and index address modes to be applied to the loading and storing of MMX operands.

2.3 MMX Data-types

The MMX registers support four data formats as shown in Figure 2.2. A register can hold a single 64-bit QWORD, a pair of 32-bit DWORDS, four 16-bit WORDS or eight BYTES. Within these formats the data types shown in Table 2.1 are supported.

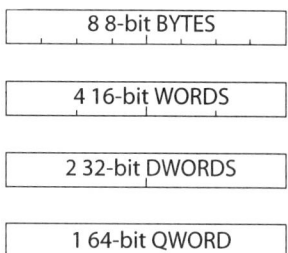

Figure 2.2. The MMX data formats.

Table 2.1. MMX data types

Format	Signed	Unsigned	Signed saturated	Unsigned saturated
BYTE	Yes	Yes	Yes	Yes
WORD	Yes	Yes	Yes	Yes
DWORD	Yes	Yes	No	No

The saturated data types require special comment. They are designed to handle a circumstance that arises frequently in image processing when using pixels represented as integers: that of constraining the result of some arithmetic operation to be within the meaningful bounds of the integer representation.

Suppose we are adding two images represented as arrays of bytes in the range 0..255 with 0 representing black and 255 white. It is possible that the results may be greater than 255. For example, $200 + 175 = 375$ but in 8-bit binary

$$\begin{array}{r} 11001000 \\ + 10101111 \\ \hline = 101110111 \end{array}$$

Dropping the leading 1, we get $01110111 = 119$, which is dimmer than either of the original pixels. The only sensible answer in this case would have been 255, representing white.

Consider the problem of applying the following vertical edge sharpening convolution kernel to an image represented as signed bytes:

−0.25	0.75	−0.25
−0.5	1.5	−0.5
−0.25	0.75	−0.25

Since the kernel is unitary, that is, its elements sum to 1, it produces no overall change in the contrast of the image. The image, being represented in signed bytes, will have pixels in the range $-128\ldots 127$, with -128 representing black and 127 representing white. The effect of the convolution should be to enhance the contrast on any vertical lines or vertical edges.

Now consider the effect of applying the kernel to the 3×4 pixel pattern

0	−70	−70	0
0	−70	−70	0
0	−70	−70	0

which represents a 2 pixel wide dark-grey vertical line on a mid-grey background. The intended effect should be to enhance the contrast between the line and the background.

If we perform the calculations for the convolution using real arithmetic,[1] the pixels p representing the dark-grey line (the −70s) are mapped to $p' = 3 \times -70 + (-1 \times -70) = -140$. The snag is that −140 is less than the smallest signed 8-bit integer. The only 'sensible' value that can be assigned to p' would be $-128 =$ black. If we simply converted −140 to an 8-bit signed value by

---

[1]For speed we might use 16-bit integers representing the convolution as

−1	3	−1
−2	6	−2
−1	3	−1

followed by a shift right two places to normalise the result, but the argument above would still hold.

truncation, we would obtain 01110011 binary or 115 decimal. The dark line, would have been mapped to a light line, contrary to intention.

To avoid such errors, image processing code using 8-bit values has to put in tests to check if values are going out of range, and force all out-of-range values to the appropriate extremes of the ranges. This inevitably slows the computation of inner loops. In addition to introducing additional instructions, the tests involve conditional branches and pipeline stalls.

The MMX seeks to obviate this by providing packed saturated data types with appropriate arithmetic operations over them. These use hardware to ensure that the numbers remain in range.

The combined effect of the use of packed data and saturated types can be to produce a significant increase in code density and performance.

Consider the C code in Alg. 3 to add two images pointed to by v1 and v2, storing the result in the image pointed to by v3. The code includes a check to prevent overflow. Compiled into assembler code by the Visual C++ compiler the resulting assembler code has 18 instructions in the inner loop. The potential acceleration due to the MMX can be seen by comparing it with the hand-coded assembler inner loop in Alg. 4.

The example assumes that v1, v2, v3 are indexed by esi for the duration of the loop. Only five instructions are used in the whole loop, compared with 18 for the compiled C code. Furthermore, the MMX code processes eight times as much data per iteration, thus requiring only 0.625 instructions per byte processed. The compiled code thus executes 29 times as many instructions to perform the same task. Although some of this can be put down to the superiority of hand-assembled versus automatically compiled code, the combination of the SIMD model and the saturated arithmetic is obviously a major factor.

2.4 3DNow!

The original MMX instructions introduced by Intel were targeted at increasing the performance of 2D image processing, giving their biggest performance boost for images of byte-pixels. The typical operations in 3D graphics, perspective transformations, ray tracing, rendering, etc., tend to rely upon floating point data representation. Certain high 2D image processing operations requiring high accuracy such as high-precision stereo matching can also be implemented using floating point data. Both Intel and AMD have seen the need to provide for these data representations. AMD responded first with the 3DNow! instructions, then Intel introduced the Streaming SIMD instructions which we discuss in the next section.

The basic IA32 architecture already provides support for 32- and 64-bit IEEE floating point instructions using the FPU stack. However, 64-bit floating point numbers are poor candidates for parallelism in view of the data-path limitations described in Section 2.1.

AMD provided a straightforward extension of the MMX whereby an additional data type, the pair of 32-bit floats shown in Figure 2.3, could be operated

```
main()
{
 unsigned char v1[LEN],v2[LEN],v3[LEN];
 int i,j,t;
 for(j=0;j<LEN;j++){
  t=v2[j]+v1[j];
  v3[j]=(unsigned char)(t>255?255:t);
 }
}
ASSEMBLER
        xor     edx, edx                            ; 9.8
                                                    ;
$B1$3:                          ; Preds $B1$5 $B1$2
        mov     eax, edx                            ; 10.9
        lea     ecx, DWORD PTR [esp]                ; 10.6
        movzx   ecx, BYTE PTR [eax+ecx]             ; 10.6
        mov     DWORD PTR [esp+19200], edi          ;
        lea     edi, DWORD PTR [esp+6400]           ; 10.12
        movzx   edi, BYTE PTR [eax+edi]             ; 10.12
        add     ecx, edi                            ; 10.12
        cmp     ecx, 255                            ; 11.26
        mov     edi, DWORD PTR [esp+19200]          ;
        jle     $B1$5           ; Prob 16%          ; 11.26
$B1$4:                          ; Preds $B1$3
        mov     ecx, 255                            ; 11.26
$B1$5:                          ; Preds $B1$3 $B1$4
        inc     edx                                 ; 9.18
        cmp     edx, 6400                           ; 9.3
        mov     DWORD PTR [esp+19200], edi          ;
        lea     edi, DWORD PTR [esp+12800]          ; 11.4
        mov     BYTE PTR [eax+edi], cl              ; 11.4
        mov     edi, DWORD PTR [esp+19200]          ;
        jl      $B1$3           ; Prob 80%          ; 9.3
\end{verbatim}
```

Algorithm 3. C code to add two images and corresponding assembler for the inner loop. Code compiled on the Intel C compiler version 4.0.

```
11: movq mm0,[esi+ebp-LEN]       ; load 8 bytes
    paddusb mm0,[esi+ebp-2*LEN]  ; packed unsigned add bytes
    movq [esi+ebp-3*LEN],mm0     ; store 8 byte result
    add esi,8                    ; inc dest pntr
    loop 11                      ; repeat for the rest
```

Algorithm 4. MMX version of Alg. 3.

Chapter 2 • SIMD Instruction-sets

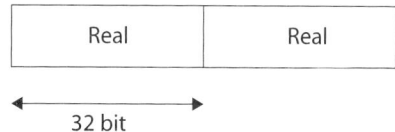

Figure 2.3. The AMD 3DNOW! extensions add 32-bit floating point data to the types that can be handled in MMX registers.

on. Type conversion operations are provided to convert between pairs of 32-bit integers and 32-bit floats.

The range of operators supported includes instructions for the rapid computation of reciprocals and square roots – relevant to the computation of Euclidean norms in 3D space.

2.4.1 Cache Handling

A significant extension with 3DNow, copied in the Streaming SIMD extensions, is the ability to prefetch data into the cache prior to its use. This is potentially useful in any loop operating on an array of data. For instance the loop in the previous section could be accelerated by inserting the marked prefetch instructions.

The instruction count rises; despite this, performance goes up since loads into the cache are initiated prior to the data being needed. This allows the loading of the cache to be overlapped with useful instructions rather than forcing calculations to stall whilst the load takes place.

To understand why this is useful, it is worth taking a closer look at how the cache on a modern processor works. We will describe the P4 cache as an example; the Athlon cache differs only in details. The account we give is simplified but sufficient to understand how the prefetch instructions work.

The P4 has an 8 kb level 1 cache with 64-byte cache lines and four-way set associativity (see Figure 2.4).

This means that it has four banks of memory each of which contains 32 lines. When a memory fetch occurs, the CPU generates a 32-bit store address. The address is split into three fields as shown. The bottom 6 bits select a byte offset within a cache line. The next 5 bits are used to select one of 32 lines in each bank. The remaining 21 bits constitute the tag field of the address. This is compared in parallel to the tag fields of each four selected cache lines. In addition to checking the tag fields for identity, validity flags associated with the lines are validated. If the tag field of one of the lines is found to match with the tag field of the address, then a cache hit occurs, otherwise a cache miss occurs.

In the event of a hit, the word in the line indicated by the byte select bits is returned as the operand of the instruction. In the event of a cache miss then a cache load is initiated to the next level of the store hierarchy – the level 2 cache. Here a similar process is repeated except that here the cache is larger and the access time longer. A miss on the level 2 cache causes a line of the level 2 cache to be loaded from main memory.

When a fetch percolates down to the main store, the processor will fetch a whole cache line as a single transaction, spread over several clock cycles. There

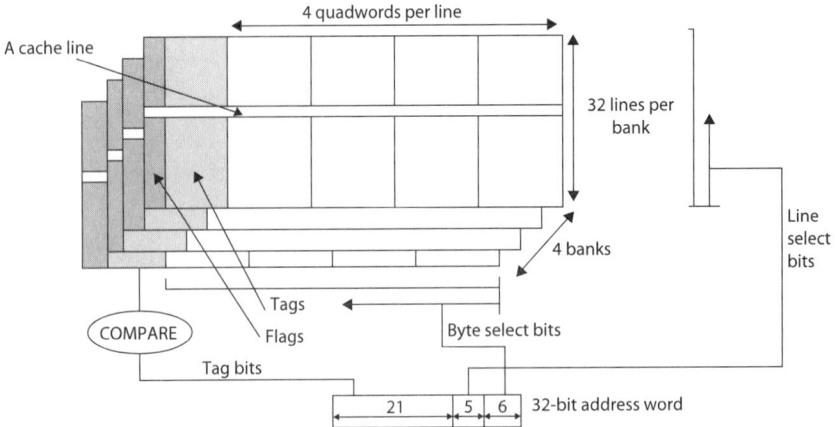

Figure 2.4. The cache structure.

is an initial memory setup time during which the address is transfered to the dynamic ram chips and an appropriate page within the dynamic ram chips is selected. Following this, eight memory cycles each transfering 8 bytes are used to fill the cache line. The reason for having relatively long cache lines is that it enables the cost of address setup to be amortised over multiple fetched memory words. This runs the risk that some of the data fetched into the cache will not be used, and will therefore show its greatest advantage either when an algorithm moves sequentially through adjacent memory locations or when a small group of frequently accessed variables can be loaded into a single cache line.

In parallel with the fetching of a new line's worth of data from memory, the CPU selects one of the four cache banks to receive the data. The mechanism used to choose which bank will get the data varies. Some caches use a pseudo random number generator to select a bank, others select the bank containing the oldest cache line to be replaced (Hennessy and Patterson, 2003). The block being replaced has its tag field replaced with the tag field of the requested word and the line is marked as invalid. Once the data has been loaded into the cache, the flags are set to indicate that it is now valid.

A moment's consideration will show that with a four-bank cache it is possible to store data from four distinct areas of memory which share the same low order address bits. As soon as a fifth block is accessed sharing these addresses, then one of the previous blocks must be discarded. However, as Figure 2.5 shows, it is still possible to perform many useful loops without such clashes occurring.

2.4.2 Cache Line Length and Prefetching

Since entire cache lines are fetched at a time, we can see that if the processor has 64-byte cache lines, Alg. 5 will issue unnecessary prefetch instructions. We only need to issue a single prefetch instruction for each use of a new cache line, that is, once every 64 bytes processed. Alg. 6 illustrates this, having two nested loops. Immediately prior to entering the inner loop, it prefetches the data that

Chapter 2 • SIMD Instruction-sets

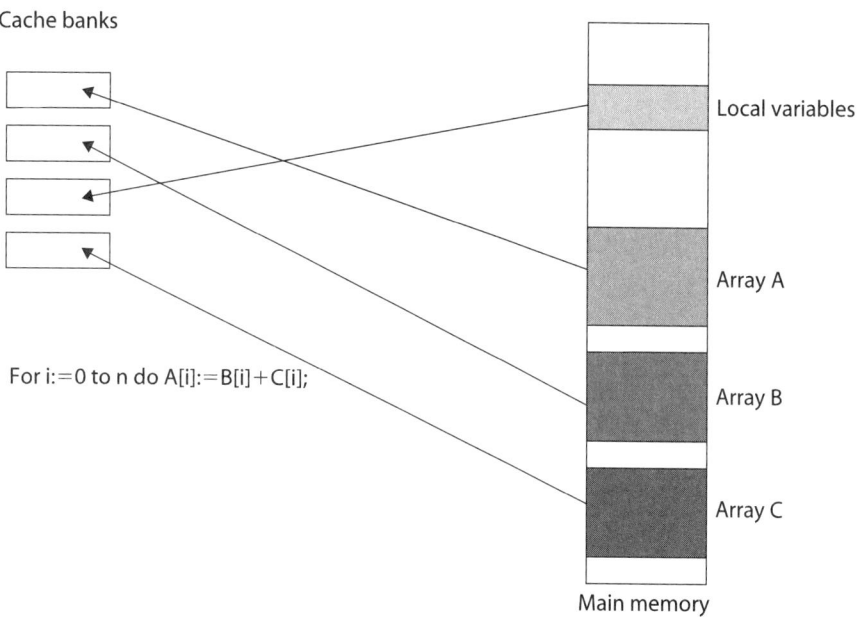

Figure 2.5. With four banks of cache it is possible for a loop using two source and one destination array to stream data in distinct banks whilst reserving one bank for local variables.

```
        mov ecx, LEN                     ; ecx gets
        shr ecx, 3                       ; number of times
                                         ; round loop
    l1: movq mm0,[esi+ebp-LEN]           ; load 8 bytes
        prefetch [esi+ebp-LEN+8]         ; get next 8 into cache
        paddusb mm0,[esi+ebp-2*LEN]      ; packed unsigned add bytes
        prefetch [esi+ebp-2*LEN+8]
        movq [esi+ebp-3*LEN],mm0         ; store 8 byte result
        prefetchw [esi+ebp-3*LEN+8]      ; set up cache to write
                                         ; 8 bytes of data
        add esi,8                        ; inc dest pntr
        loop l1                          ; repeat for the rest
```

Algorithm 5. A simple example of prefetching.

will be need for the following iteration of the *outer* loop. It does this by prefetching data that is 64 bytes on from the data to be accessed on the following iteration of the *inner* loop.

2.5 Streaming SIMD

Intel produced their own functional equivalent to AMD's 3DNOW! instruction-set with the Pentium III processor. They called the new instructions Streaming

```
        mov eax,LEN              ; eax gets
        shr eax,6                ; number of times
                                 ; round outer loop
        prefetch [esi+ebp-LEN+64]    ; get next line to cache
        prefetch [esi+ebp-2*LEN+64]  ; ditto
        prefetchw [esi+ebp-3*LEN+64] ; set up cache to write

10:     mov ecx,8                ; times round inner loop
11:     movq mm0,[esi+ebp-LEN]   ; load 8 bytes
        paddusb mm0,[esi+ebp-2*LEN]  ; packed unsigned + bytes
        movq [esi+ebp-3*LEN],mm0 ; store 8 byte result
        add esi,8                ; inc dest pntr
        loop 11                  ; repeat for the rest
        dec eax                  ; decrement outer loop count
        jnz 10
```

Algorithm 6. An example that makes more effective use of prefetching than Alg. 5.

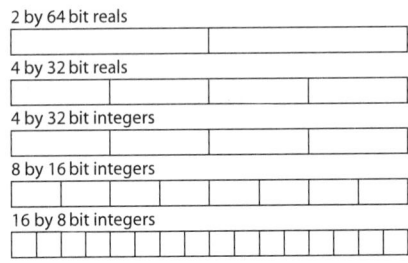

Figure 2.6. The Streaming SIMD extensions add additional 128-bit vector registers, with multiple formats.

SIMD. As with 3DNOW!, the Streaming SIMD instructions combine cache prefetching techniques with parallel operations on short vectors of 32-bit floating point operands. With the P4 these were extended to allow operations on other data types as shown in Figure 2.6.

The most significant difference is in the model of machine state. Whilst the original MMX instructions and 3DNOW! add no new state to the machine architecture, Streaming SIMD introduces additional registers. Eight new 128-bit registers (XMM0...7) are introduced. The addition of new state means that operating systems have to be modified to ensure that XMM registers are saved during context switches. Intel provided a driver to do this for Microsoft Windows NT 4.0; Windows 98 and subsequent Windows releases have this support built in.

The default format for the XMM registers is a 4-tuple of 32-bit floating point numbers. Instructions are provided to perform parallel addition, multiplication, subtraction and division on these 4-tuples. Other formats are:

1. A set of Boolean operations are provided that treat the registers as 128-bit words, useful for operations on bitmaps.

Table 2.2. The XMM registers support both scalar and vector arithmetic

Vector addition
ADDPS xmm0,xmm1

xmm0	1.2	1.3	1.4	1.5
xmm1	2.0	4.0	6.0	8.0 +
xmm0	3.2	5.3	7.4	9.5

Scalar addition
ADDSS xmm0,xmm1

xmm0	1.2	1.3	1.4	1.5
xmm1	2.0	4.0	6.0	8.0 +
xmm0	1.2	1.3	1.4	9.5

2. Scalar floating operations are provided that operate on the lower 32 bits of the register. This allows the XMM registers to be used for conventional single-precision floating point arithmetic. Whereas the pre-existing Intel FPU instructions support single-precision arithmetic, the original FPU is based on a reverse Polish stack architecture. This scheme does not fit well with the register allocation schemes used in some compilers. The existence of what are effectively eight scalar floating point registers can lead to more efficient floating point code.

The scalar and vector uses of the XMM registers are contrasted in Table 2.2. A special move instruction (MOVSS) is provided to load or store the least significant 32 bits of an XMM register.

From the introduction of the P4 processor the following data types became available:

1. The registers can hold two double-precision floating point numbers.
2. The low 64 bits of the registers can be treated as scalar double-precision floating point numbers.
3. The registers can be treated as holding four integers of length 32 bits.
4. They can hold eight integers of length 16 bits.
5. They can hold 16 integers of length 8 bits.

2.5.1 Cache Optimisation

The Streaming side of the Streaming SIMD extensions is concerned with optimising the use of the cache. The extensions will typically be used with large collections of data, too large to fit into the cache. If an application were adding two vectors of a million floating point registers using standard instructions, the 4 MB of results would pollute the cache. This cache pollution can be avoided using the *non-temporal* store instructions, MOVNTPS and MOVNTQ, operating on the XMM and MM registers, respectively.

A family of prefetch instructions is provided to pre-load data into the cache. This is more sophisticated than the equivalent 3DNOW! instruction described above. The AMD instruction applies to all cache levels. The Intel variant allows the programmer to specify which levels of cache are to be preloaded.

Whereas all previous IA32 load and store instructions had operated equally well on aligned and unaligned data, the Streaming SIMD extensions introduces special load and store instructions to operate on aligned 128-bit words. General-purpose load and store instructions capable of handling unaligned data are retained. However, these are much slower than the aligned loads and stores. For algorithms which cannot guarantee that operands will be 16-byte aligned, this can lead to significant performance penalties. For unaligned accesses to integer types it is generally more efficient to process data 64 bits at a time using the MMX registers than to process it 128 bits at a time using XMM registers.

2.6 The Motorola Altivec Architecture

Motorola have a vector extension, called AltiVec, on their G4 processor that is functionally similar to the SIMD instructions of the P4. The AltiVec unit contains 32 128-bit vector registers identified as v0 through v31. Data is represented in vector registers as either integer (byte, half, word size) or single-sized (32-bit) floating point data. The operations supported on these registers are broadly similar to those provided by Intel in the P4 with the following significant restrictions and extensions.

Restrictions

1. As a RISC processor the G4 requires all operands of arithmetic or logical instructions to be in registers. There are no memory to register instructions.
2. The alignment rules are even stricter than the P4 alignment rules. There is no unaligned load or store instruction. If an unaligned address is supplied to a load or store, the bottom 4 bits of the address are ignored.
3. Double-precision floating point numbers are not supported.
4. When using altivec instructions, a special register, the VRSAVE register, is used to indicate to the operating system which vector registers are in use. A bit set in the register indicates that your program is using the corresponding V register. The application is responsible for setting these bits and, if they are not set, the registers will not be saved during a context switch.

Extensions

1. Multiply accumulate instructions are provided.
2. Instructions are provided to produce scalar sums over vector registers.

Motorola also claim to obtain better floating point performance on their parallel single-precision instructions than Intel do. This claim, which the author has been unable to validate, must be set against the markedly slower clock speed of Motorola CPUs.

SIMD Programming in Assembler and C

There is little exploitation of the SIMD instructions described in the previous chapter because of relatively poor compiler support. When the MMX and SSE instructions became available, Intel supplied a C compiler that had low-level extensions allowing the extended instructions to be used. Intel terms these extensions 'assembler intrinsics'. Syntactically these look like C functions but they are translated one for one into equivalent assembler instructions. The use of assembler intrinsics simplifies the process of developing MMX code, in that programmers use a single tool – the C compiler, and do not need to concern themselves with low-level linkage issues. However, the other disadvantages of assembler coding remain. The Intel C compiler comes with a set of C++ classes that correspond to the fundamental types supported by the MMX and SIMD instruction sets. The SIMD classes do a good job of presenting the underlying capabilities of the architecture within the context of the C language. The code produced is also efficient. However, although the C++ code has a higher level of expression than assembler intrinsics, it is not portable to other processors. The same approach of essentially allowing assembler inserts into a high-level language was adopted by other compilers: TMT-Pascal, Free-Pascal and a release of gcc for the G4 processor used in the iMac.

3.1 Vectorising C Compilers

There has been recent interest in the application of vectorisation techniques to instruction level parallelism. Thus, Cheong and Lam (1997) discuss the use of the Stanford University SUIF parallelising compiler to exploit the SUN VIS extensions for the UltraSparc from C programs. They report speedups of around 4 on byte integer parallel addition. Krall and Lelait's compiler (Krall and Lelait, 2000) also exploits the VIS extensions on the Sun Ultra-SPARC processor from C using the CoSy compiler framework. They compare classic vectorisation techniques with unrolling, concluding that both are equally effective, and report speedups of 2.7 to 4.7. Sreraman and Govindarajan (2000) exploit Intel MMX parallelism from C with SUIF, using a variety of vectorisation techniques to generate in-line assembly language, achieving speedups from 2 to 6.5. All of these groups target specific architectures. Finally, Leupers (1999) has reported a C compiler that uses vectorising optimisation techniques for compiling code for the multimedia instruction sets of some signal processors, but this is not generalised to the types of processors used in desktop computers.

Tools of this sort have recently become commercially available with the launch of version 6 of the Intel C compiler and also the VectorC compiler from Codeplay. These allow unmodified C source programs to be compiled to the MMX and SSE instructions. The compilers are able to spot vectorisable for-loops and compile them into sequences of vector instructions.

The code generator analyses inner loops and those which have the general form

```
for(i=low;i<=high;i++)
  a[i]=b[i]Ω₁c[i]Ω₂d[i]....
```

are vectorised if vector instructions to perform operations Ω_1, Ω_2, etc. exist.

The resulting code takes the form of two loops, the quotient loop and the remainder loop. The quotient loop is executed in parallel up to the parallelism factor defined by the machine vector registers, the remainder loop is then serialised.

Suppose low = 0 and high = 10 and the type of a[i], b[i], etc., is 32-bit float and that the machine is P4, then the quotient loop translates to

```
for(i=0;i<=7;i+=4)
  a[i..i+3]=b[i..i+3]Ω₁c[i..i+3]Ω₂d[i..i+3]....
```

the remainder loop translates to

```
for(i=8;i<=10;i++)
  a[i]=b[i]Ω₁c[i]Ω₂d[i]....
```

The absence of scalar to vector arithmetic instructions on the Intel and AMD processors means that the gains from vectorisation are more limited if any of the operands in the assignment statement are scalars rather than vectors. The code generator will attempt to vectorise these, but in doing so it is forced to make multiple copies of scalars prior to loading them into vector registers, which is relatively costly.

3.1.1 Dead for Loop Elimination

The above transformations give rise to many null loops or loops with a single iteration, so the vectorisation is combined with algorithms to eliminate null loops. Given

```
for(i=e1;i<=e2;i++) c1
```

then if we know at compile time that e1 will always be greater than e2, we can remove the entire for statement.

In the loop

```
for(i=e1;i<=e2;i++) c1
```

If we know that e1=e2, then we can substitute it with

```
i:=e1;c1;
```

3.1.2 Loop Unrolling

It is advantageous to unroll loops to some degree. Unrolling loops has the advantages that:

1. Since the size of basic block is increased, the chances of pipeline stalls are reduced. This may be less significant with the very latest processors.
2. The total number of instructions executed can be reduced since in simple an inner loop the comparison and branch instructions can make up around 30% of the instructions executed. If we perform 5-fold unrolling we reduce this overhead, allowing the loop to execute about 25% faster.

A for loop of the form

```
for(i=1;i<=10;i++)   x[i]=j[i]+1;
```

can be expanded to

```
for(i=1;i<=10;i++){
  x[i]=j[i]+1;
  i=i+1;
  x[i]=j[i]+1;
  i=i+1;
  x[i]=j[i]+1;
  i=i+1;
  x[i]=j[i]+1;
  i=i+1;
  x[i]=j[i]+1;
}
```

resulting in a loop that is only gone round twice.

Since vectorisation and loop unrolling are performed prior to dead loop removal and unitary loop handling, the net effect is that:

1. Many loops are replaced with vectorised straight line code.
2. In the case of loops whose length modulo the vector register length is zero, the remainder loop is elided, giving a fully vectorised loop.

Although the VectorC and Intel C compilers do provide a means by which unmodified C code can take advantage of SIMD instructions, the compilers are expensive: several thousand dollars for VectorC, somewhat less for the Intel one.

3.2 Direct Use of Assembler Code

With instruction-sets as complex as those incorporated into the latest Intel and AMD processors, careful hand-written assembler language routines produce the highest quality machine code.

Microsoft's MASM assembler supports the extended instruction-set, as does the free assembler Nasm. The latter has the advantage of running on both

```
section .text;
global _main
LEN equ 6400
_main: enter LEN*3,0
    mov ebx,100000  ; perform test 100000 times
l0:
    mov esi,0       ; set esi registers to
                    ; index the elements
    mov ecx,LEN/8   ; set up the count byte
l1: movq mm0,[esi+ebp-LEN]     ; load 8 bytes
    paddb mm0,[esi+ebp-2*LEN]  ; packed unsigned add
    movq [esi+ebp-3*LEN],mm0   ; store 8 byte result
    add esi,8       ; inc dest pntr
    loop l1         ; repeat for the rest
    dec ebx
    jnz l0
    mov eax,0
    leave
    ret
```

Algorithm 7. Assembler version of the test program.

Linux and Windows, and provides support for MMX, 3DNOW! and SIMD instructions.

If one either cannot obtain or cannot afford better tools, then it can be worth directly coding inner loops as assembler routines. The disadvantages of using assembler are well known:

1. It is not portable between processors. A program written in assembler to use the AMD extensions will not run on an Intel processor nor, a fortiori, on a G4.
2. It requires the programmer to have an in-depth knowledge of the underlying machine architecture, which only a small proportion of programmers now have.
3. Productivity in terms of programmer time spent to implement a given algorithm is lower than in high-level languages.
4. The programmer must further master the low-level linkage and procedure call conventions of the high-level language used for the rest of the application.
5. Programmers have to master additional program development tools.

All of these militate against widespread use.

3.2.1 The Example Program

The assembler version of the example program is shown in Alg. 7. It runs in 4.01 s on the test machine, a 233 MHz Pentium II, a throughput of 160 million byte arithmetic operations per second.

```
#define LEN 6400
#define CNT 100000
main()
{
  unsigned char v1[LEN],v2[LEN],v3[LEN];
  int i,j,t;
  for(i=0;i<CNT;i++)
     for(j=0;j<LEN;j++) v3[j]=v2[j]+v1[j];
}
```

Algorithm 8. C version of the test program.

The C version is shown in Alg. 8. When compiled with the Intel C compiler (Version 4.0) it runs in 72 s on the test machine, a performance of around 8.9 million arithmetic operations per second. Thus the assembler version using MMX is about 20 times faster than the C version.

3.3 Use of Assembler Intrinsics

Intel supply a C compiler that has low-level extensions allowing the extended instructions to be used. Intel terms these extensions 'assembler intrinsics'. For example, the ADDPS instruction which adds four packed single-precision floating point numbers is mirrored by the Intel C/C++ Compiler Intrinsic Equivalent

__m128 _mm_add_ps(__m128 a, __m128 b)

which adds the four single-precision floating point values of a and b.

Syntactically these look like C functions but they are translated one for one into equivalent assembler instructions. The use of assembler intrinsics simplifies the process of developing MMX code, in that programmers use a single tool, the C compiler, and do not need to concern themselves with low-level linkage issues. However, the other disadvantages of assembler coding remain:

1. It is still not portable between processors.
2. It still requires the programmer to have an in-depth knowledge of the underlying machine architecture.
3. Productivity is unlikely to be higher than with assembler.

3.4 Use of C++ Classes

The Intel C compiler comes with a set of C++ classes that correspond to the fundamental types supported by the MMX and SIMD instruction-sets. For instance, type Iu8vec8 is a vector of eight unsigned 8-bit integers, Is32vec2 a vector of two signed 32-bit integers, etc. The basic arithmetic operators for addition, subtraction, multiplication and division are then overloaded to support these vector types.

```
#define LEN 800
#define CNT 100000
#include "ivec.h"
main()
{
Iu8vec8 v1[LEN],v2[LEN],v3[LEN];
int i,j,t;
for(i=0;i<CNT;i++)
  for(j=0;j<LEN;j++)
    v3[j]=v2[j]+v1[j];
}
```

Algorithm 9. C++ version of the test program.

Alg. 9 shows the example program implemented in C++ using the Intel SIMD class Iu8vec8. The SIMD classes do a good job of presenting the underlying capabilities of the architecture within the context of the C language. The code produced is also efficient; the example program in C++ runs in 4.56 s on the test machine, a performance of 140 million byte operations per second. However, it has to be borne in mind that the C++ code is not portable to other processors. The compiler always generates MMX or SIMD instructions for the classes. If run on a 486 processor, these would be illegal. The C++ code built around these classes, although it has a higher level of expression than assembler intrinsics, is no more portable.

There are many disadvantages to these approaches. First, programmers must have deep knowledge both of low-level architectural behaviour and of architecture-specific compiler behaviour to integrate assembly language with high-level code. Second, effective use of libraries depends on there being a close correspondence between the intended semantics of the application program and the semantics of the library routines. Finally, use of architecture-specific libraries inhibits program portability across operating systems and CPU platforms.

3.5 Use of the Nasm Assembler

The Nasm assembler is an open source project to develop a Net-wide Assembler. The assembler is included as standard in most Linux distributions and is available for download to run under Windows. It provides support for the full Intel and AMD SIMD instruction-sets and also recognises some extra MMX instructions that run on Cyrix CPUs. Nasm provides support for multiple object module formats from the old MS-DOS com files to the obj and elf formats used under Windows and Linux. If one is programming in assembler, Nasm provides a more complete range of instructions, in association with better portability between operating systems than competing assemblers. Microsoft's MASM assembler is restricted to Windows. The GNU assembler, as, runs under both Linux and Windows, but uses non-standard syntax which makes it awkward to use in conjunction with Intel documentation.

It is beyond the scope of this book to provide a complete guide to assembler programming for the Intel processor family. Instead, we will concentrate on those features of the assembly language that are needed to write SIMD subroutines that can be called from high-level languages. We document the Intel SIMD instructions in Chapter 4 and the 3DNow instructions in Chapter 5. Readers wanting a general background in assembler programming should consult appropriate text books in conjunction with the processor reference manuals published by Intel (1999, 2000) and AMD (Advanced Micro Devices, 1999).

3.5.1 General Instruction Syntax

Assembler programs take the form of a sequence of lines with one machine instruction per line. The instructions themselves take the form of an optional label, an operation code name conditionally followed by up to three comma separated operands. For example:

```
l1: SFENCE                     ; 0 operand instruction
    PREFETCH [100]             ; 1 operand instruction
    MOVQ MM0,MM1               ; 2 operand instruction
    PSHUFD XMM1,XMM3,00101011b ; 3 operand instruction
```

As shown above, a comment can be placed on an assembler line, with the comment distinguished from the instruction by a leading semi-colon. The label, if present, is separated from the operation code name by a colon.

Case is not significant either in operation code names or in the names of registers. Thus `prefetch` is equivalent to `PREFETCH` and `mm4` is equivalent to `MM4`.

In the Nasm assembler, as in the original Intel assembler, the direction of assignment in an instruction follows high-level language conventions. It is always from right to left,[1] so that

```
MOVQ MM0,MM4
```

is equivalent to

```
MM0:=MM4
```

and

```
ADDSS XMM0,XMM3
```

is equivalent to

```
XMM0:=XMM0+XMM3
```

3.5.2 Operand Forms

Operands to instructions can be constants, register names or memory locations.

---

[1] If you chose to use the GNU assembler instead of Nasm you should be aware that this follows the opposite convention of left to right assignment. This is a result of as having originated as a Motorola assembler that was converted to recognise Intel opcodes. Motorola follow a left to right assignment convention.

Constants

Constants are values known at assembly time, and take the form of numbers, labels, characters or arithmetic expressions whose components are themselves constants.

The most important constant values are numbers. Integer numbers can be written in base 16, 10, 8 or 2.

```
mov al,0a2h      ; base 16 leading zero required
mov bh,$0a2      ; base 16 alternate notation
mov cx,0xa2      ; base 16 C style
add ax,101       ; base 10
mov bl,76q       ; base 8
xor ax,11010011b ; base 2
```

Floating point constants are also supported as operands to store allocation directives (see Section 3.5.3):

```
dd 3.14156
dq 9.2e3
```

It is important to realise that due to limitations of the AMD and Intel instruction-sets, floating point constants can not be directly used as operands to instructions. Any floating point constants used in an algorithm have to be assembled into a distinct area of memory and loaded into registers from there.

Constants can also take the form of labels. As the assembler program is processed, Nasm allocates an integer value to each label. The value is either the address of the operation-code prefixed by the instruction or may have been explicitly set by an EQU directive:

```
Fseek equ 23
Fread equ 24
```

We can load a register with the address referred to by a label by including the label as a constant operand:

```
mov esi, sourcebuf
```

Using the same syntax, we can load a register with an equated constant:

```
mov cl, fread
```

Constant Expressions

Suppose there exists a data-structure for which one has a base address label, it is often convenient to be able to refer to fields within this structure in terms of their offset from the start of the structure. Consider the example of a vector of four single-precision floating point values at a location with label myvec. The actual address at which myvec will be placed is determined by Nasm, we do not know it. We may know that we want the address of the third element of the vector:

```
mov esi, myvec+3*4
```

to place the address of this word into the `esi` register. Nasm allows one to place arithmetic expressions whose sub-expressions are constants wherever a constant can occur. The arithmetic operators are written C style as shown in Table 3.1.

Registers

Operands can be register names. The available register names are shown in Table 3.2. In the binary operation codes interpreted by the CPU, registers are identified using 3-bit integers. Depending on the operation code, these 3-bit fields are interpreted as the different categories of register shown in Table 3.2.

One should be aware that in the Intel architecture a number of registers are aliased to the same state vectors, for example, the `eax`, `ax`, `al`, `ah` registers all share bits. More insidiously, the floating point registers ST0...ST7 not only share state with the MMX registers, but also their mapping to these registers is dynamic and variable.

Memory Locations

Memory locations are syntactically represented by the use of square brackets around an address expression, thus `[100]`, `[myvec]`, `[esi]` all represent

Table 3.1. Nasm constant operators

Operator	Means	Operator	Means
|	or	+	add
^	xor	−	subtract
&	and	*	multiply
<<	shift left	/	signed division
>>	shift right	//	unsigned division
%	modulus	%%	unsigned modulus

Table 3.2. Register encodings

Number	Aliased		dword reg	Aliased		sse reg
	byte reg	word reg		float reg	nnx reg	
0	al	ax	eax	st0	mm0	xmm0
1	cl	bx	ecx	st1	mm1	xmm1
2	dl	cx	edx	st2	mm2	xmm2
3	bl	bx	ebx	st3	mm3	xmm3
4	ah	sp	esp	st4	mm4	xmm4
5	ch	bp	ebp	st5	mm5	xmm5
6	dh	si	esi	st6	mm6	xmm6
7	bh	di	edi	st7	mm7	xmm7

memory locations. The address expressions, unlike constant expressions, can contain components whose values are not known until program execution. The final example above refers to the memory location addressed by the value in the `esi` register and, as such, depends on the history of prior computations affecting that register. Address expressions have to be encoded into machine instructions, and since machine instructions, although of variable length on a CISC are nonetheless finite, so too must the address expressions be. On Intel and AMD machines this constrains the complexity of address expressions to the following grammar:

memloc ::= *address* | *format address*
format ::= `byte` | `word` | `dword` | `qword`
address ::= [*const*] | [*aexp*] | [*aexp* + *const*]
aexp ::= *reg* | *reg* + *iexp*
iexp ::= *reg* | *reg* * *scale*
scale ::= 2 | 4 | 8
reg ::= `eax` | `ecx` | `ebx` | `edx` | `esp` | `ebp` | `esi` | `edi`
const ::= *integer* | *label*

The format qualifiers are used to disambiguate the size of an operand in memory where the combination of the operation code name and the other non-memory operands are insufficient so to do.

3.5.3 Directives

Directives look like operation code names, but instead of being translated into operation codes, they are used by the assembler itself to define the way in which data that follows it is to be interpreted.

Sectioning

Programs running under Linux have their memory divided into four sections:

`text` is the section of memory containing operation codes to be executed. It is typically mapped as read only by the paging system.
`data` is the section of memory containing initialised global variables, which can be altered following the start of the program.
`bas` is the section containing uninitialsed global variables.
`stack` is the section in which dynamically allocated local variables of subroutines are located.

The section directive is used by assembler programmers to specify into which section of memory they want subsequent lines of code to be assembled. For example, in the listing shown in Alg. 10 we divide the program into three sections: a `text` section containing `myfunc`, a bss section containing 64 undefined bytes and a data section containing a vector of four integers.

The label `myfuncbase` can be used with *negative* offsets to access locations within the `bss`, whereas the label `myfuncglobal` can be used with *positive* offsets to access elements of the vector in the data section.

```
section .text
     global myfunc
myfunc:enter 128,0
; body of function goes here
     leave
     ret 0
section .bss
     alignb 16
     resb 64   ; reserve 64 bytes
myfuncBase:
section .data
myfuncglobal:    ; reserve 4 by 32-bit integers
     dd 1
     dd 2
     dd 3
     dd 5
```

Algorithm 10. Examples of the use of section and data reservation directives.

Data Reservation

Data must be reserved in distinct ways in the different sections. In the `data` section, the data definition directives `db`, `dw`, `dd` and `dq` are used to define bytes, words, doublewords and quadwords. The directive must be followed by a constant expression. When defining bytes or words the constant must be an integer. Doublewords and quadwords may be defined with floating point or integer constants as shown previously.

In the bss section the directive `resb` is used to reserve a specified number of bytes, but no value is associated with these bytes.

Data can be allocated in the stack section by use of the `enter` operation code name. This takes the form

   `enter space, level`

It should be used as the first operation code name of a function. The level parameter is only of relevance in block structured languages and should be set to 0 for assembler programming. The space parameter specifies the number of bytes to be reserved for the private use of the function. Once the `enter` instruction has executed, the data can be accessed at *negative* offsets from the `ebp` register.

The last two instructions in a function should, as shown in Alg. 11, be

   `leave`
   `ret 0`

The combined effect of these is to free the space reserved on the stack by enter, and pop the return address from the stack. The parameter to the operation code name `ret` is used to specify how many bytes of function parameters should be discarded from the stack. If one is interfacing to C this should always be set to 0.

Label Qualification

The default scope of a label is the assembler source file containing the line it prefixes. However, labels can be used to mark the start of functions that are to be called from C or other high-level languages. To indicate that they have scope beyond the current assembler file, the `global` directive should be used as shown in Alg. 10.

The converse case, where an assembler file calls a function exported by a C program, is handled by the `etern` directive:

```
extern printreal
call printreal
```

In the above example we assume that `printreal` is a C function called from assembler.

3.5.4 Linking and Object File Formats

There are four object file formats that are commonly used on Linux and Windows systems, as shown in Table 3.3. This lists the name of the format, its file extension – which is often ambiguous and the combination of operating system and compiler that makes use of it. A flag provided to Nasm specifies which format it should use. We will only go into the use of the gcc compiler, since this is portable between Windows and Linux.

Assume we have a C program called `c2asm.c` and an assembler file `asmfromc.asm`. Suppose we wish to combine these into a single executable module `c2asm`. We issue the following commands at the console:

```
nasm -felf -o asmfromc.o asmfromc.asm
gcc -oc2asm c2asm.c asmfromc.o
```

This assumes that we are working either under Linux or under Cygwin. If we are using djgpp, we type

```
nasm -fcoff -o asmfromc.o asmfromc.asm
gcc -oc2asm c2asm.c asmfromc.o
```

Leading Underbars

If working with djgpp, then all external labels in your program, whether imported with `extern` or imported using `global`, must have a leading underbar character. Thus to call the C procedure `printreal`, one would write

Table 3.3. Object file formats and compilers that use them

Format	Extension	Operating system	C++ compiler
win32	.obj	Windows	Microsoft C++
obj	.obj	Windows	Borland C++
coff	.o	Windows	Djgpp gcc
.elf	.o	Windows	Cygwin gcc
.elf	.o	Linux	gcc

```
extern _printreal
call _printreal
```

whereas to export myfunc one would write

```
global _myfunc
_myfunc:enter 128,0
```

3.5.5 Summing a Vector

We will now put all this together with a simple example of calling a SIMD assembler routine from C. As an example, we take the problem of summing the elements of an integer array. If we use 32-bit integers, an MMX routine is in principle capable of doing this two words at a time, and so should outperform C code for the same purpose. Timing indicates that this is the case. Algorithm 11 runs between three and four times faster than an equivalent C function.[2]

The example illustrates a problem which has to be addressed in many vectorised algorithms. We have to add up vectors of arbitrary length, but if we are to vectorise this we need to use vector registers of fixed size. If we divide through the vector length by the size of the vector registers, 2 in this case, we may be left with a remainder that cannot be vectorised. This imposes a standard structure on vectorised MMX algorithms:

1. A parallel section that operates on the start of the array using the MMX registers.
2. A conditionally executed section that, in the presence of an odd number of elements in the array, does the rest.

The C function prototype to our array totalising routine is

```
int pmyfunc(int *v, int len);
```

The C prototype is important because it defines the configuration of parameters on the stack. Given this prototype, the C compiler will push two 32-bit words on to the stack when `pmyfunc` is called. The C convention is to push parameters on to the stack from right to left. As a result, after executing the `enter` instruction at the start of the function the local stack environment is as represented in Figure 3.1.

The `epb` register can be used to access the parameters to the function. Positive offsets from the register address parameters whereas negative offsets address local variables.

We are going to remap the one-dimensional array of integers as a two-dimensional array, whose second dimension has the range $0 \ldots 1$. Each row of the vector will fit into an MMX register. This is illustrated by Figure 3.2. The algorithm starts by using the `len` parameter to calculate the upper bound of

---

[2]On arrays of length 100, it takes 35% and 25% of the time taken for C code on Crusoe and Athlon processors, respectively. The Crusoe implements the MMX architecture only by emulation and so does not show the full gains.

```
        section .text
        global pmyfunc
pmyfunc: enter 8,0
tvec    equ  -8                  ; a temporary location
                                 ; on stack to hold a 2
                                 ; element vector
        mov edi,DWORD[ebp+12]    ; edi=len
        shr edi,1
        lea ecx,[edi-1]          ; ecx=(len/2-1)
                                 ; ecx holds number of vector
                                 ; adds to perform
        movq MM4,[dnull]         ; clear MM4
        xor edi,edi              ; clear edi as induction variable
        mov esi,DWORD[ebp+8]     ; set esi -> the array
looptop: cmp edi,ecx
        jg near loopstop
        paddd MM4,[esi+edi*8]    ; add two elements at a time
        lea edi,[edi+1]
        jmp looptop
loopstop: movq [ebp+tvec],MM4    ; save the result
        mov ebx,DWORD[ebp+12]    ; ebx=len
        mov edi,DWORD[ebp+tvec+4]
        mov eax,DWORD[ebp+8]
        mov esi,ebx
        and DWORD esi,1          ; esi=1 if len odd
        imul esi,[eax+ebx*4-4]   ; esi holds last element
                                 ; if len odd
        lea edx,[edi+esi]        ; add to tvec[1]
        mov edi,DWORD[ebp+tvec]  ; get 0th of tvec
        lea eax,[edi+edx]        ; form total
        leave
        emms
        ret 0
        section .data
dnull:   dd 0                    ; vector of two zeros
         dd 0
```

Algorithm 11. Use of MMX instructions to sum a vector of integers.

this two-dimensional array:

```
mov edi,DWORD[ebp+12]; edi=len
shr edi,1
lea ecx,[edi-1]
```

The result is stored in the ecx register. Suppose that the vector length was 7; if we shift this right, we lose the least significant bit, giving 3 in edi. Since the vector is assumed to be zero-based, we want to iterate from 0...2 so we subtract 1 to get 2 in the ecx register. The subtraction is done by using the

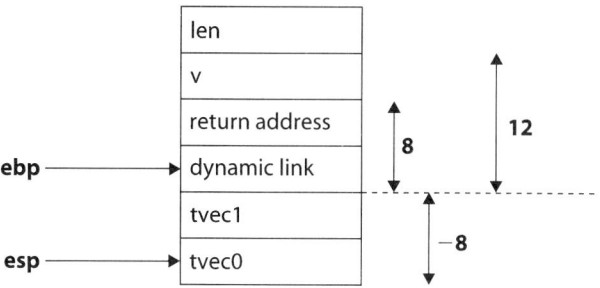

Figure 3.1. Stackframe on entry to pmyfunc.

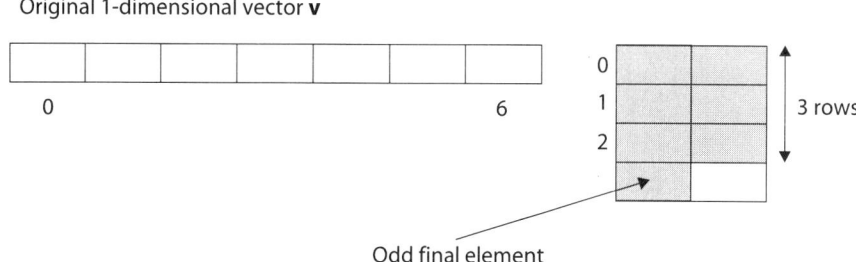

Figure 3.2. Mapping a one-dimensional array to a two-dimensional array suitable for vectorisation.

`lea` instruction. This stands for Load Effective Address; it loads the address of memory location `[edi-1]` into `ecx`, which in practice means `ecx=edi-1`. Intel recomend using lea rather than increment and decrement operations on the P3 and P4 processors, since `lea` is executed in fewer micro-ops. Next, we set up the other registers that will be used to go through the loop. We clear MM4 by loading it with the null vector:

movq MM4,[dnull]

This could have been done by xoring MM4 with itself using the PXOR instruction, but we have chosen to load a constant vector to illustrate how this is done. The constant vector itself is allocated store and initial values in the data segment. We then clear the `edi` register which will be used as the induction variable for our loop. In this case we do use an `xor` instruction to clear it:

xor edi,edi

Finally, we set the `esi` register to point to the base address of the array, by fetching the address parameter from the stack:

mov esi,DWORD [ebp+8]

The algorithm then loops round adding two elements at a time to the pairs of totals in the MM4 register. It uses base plus scaled index addressing to do this,

```
#include <stdio.h>
int pmyfunc(int *v,int len);
main(int argc, char **argv)
{ int a[10];
  int i;
  for(i=0;i<10;i++) a[i]=i;
  for(i=1;i<10;i++) printf("%d %d\n",i,pmyfunc(a,i));
}
```

Algorithm 12. Illustration of calling pmyfunc from C.

multiplying the loop induction register `edi` by eight to get the relative starting position of each row of our mapped two-dimensional array:

```
looptop:cmp edi,ecx
    jg near loopstop
    paddd MM4,[esi+edi*8] ; add two elements at a time
    lea edi,[edi+1]
    jmp looptop
loopstop:movq [ebp+tvec],MM4 ; save the result
```

At the end of the loop we have the total of the even words in `MM4[0]` and the total of the odd words in `MM4[1]`. We want to add these together along with any possible remainder word. This will be handled by scalar arithmetic, so we save the two totals in the two-element vector `tvec`. If the original array was of odd length, we want to form the sum `tvec[0]+tvec[1]+v[len-1]`, otherwise we want simply to add the two elements of `tvec` together. This could be done by testing len and branching, but it is more efficient to multiply the last element of the array by the least significant bit of the length. If the length is even, the least significant bit will be zero so that the last element is not included in the total.

```
mov ebx,DWORD [ebp+12]    ; ebx=len
mov edi,DWORD [ebp+tvec+4]; edi=tvec[1]
mov eax,DWORD [ebp+8]     ; eax=array base
MOV esi,ebx
and DWORD esi,1
imul esi,[eax+ebx*4-4]
lea edx,[edi+esi]         ; add to tvec[1]
mov edi,DWORD[ebp+tvec]   ; get 0th of tvec
lea eax,[edi+edx]         ; form total
```

The total is returned in the eax register, since this is the C convention for integer-returning functions.

3.6 Coordinate Transformations Using 3DNow!

For a second example we will look at some basic 3D graphics operations. As its name implies, one of the main aims of the AMD SIMD extensions is to accelerate 3D graphics operations. To understand the rationale for these instructions, a little background information about 3D graphics operations is necessary.

Chapter 3 • SIMD Programming in Assembler and C

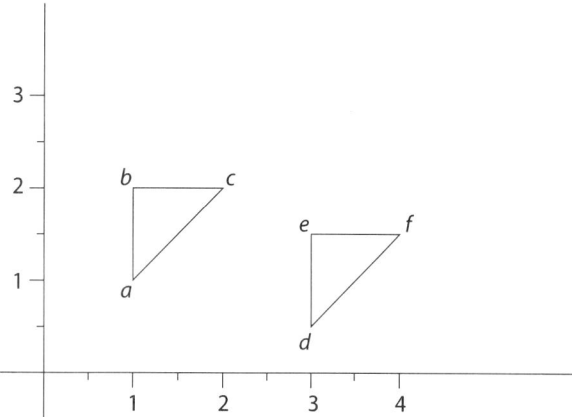

Figure 3.3. Translation. The triangle *a,b,c* with coordinates [1,1],[1,2],[2,2] is translated to the triangle *d,e,f* with coordinates [3,0.5],[3,1.5],[4,1.5] by adding [2,−0.5] to each vertex.

Points in three-dimensional space can be represented as triples of real numbers $[x,y,z]$ encoding position with respect to three orthogonal axes. Surfaces in three-space are typically represented as a set triangles, each of whose vertices is such a triple $[x,y,z]$. Manipulations of simulated solid objects break down into the primitive operations:

Translate   move all of the points in an object some common distance in three-space.
Scale   make the object larger or smaller.
Rotate   around one or other of the axes, an arbitrary rotation being decomposable into rotations about the axes.

Let us consider each of these in turn as abstract operations before going to look at how they can be implemented in the 3DNow instructions.

Translate

We can see in Figure 3.3 how we can translate a triangle by adding a constant vector to each vertex. For ease of illustration we use 2D drawings, but the principle extends to higher dimensions. The basic data-type used by 3DNow is a two-element vector of reals. Translation in two dimensions would obviously be very efficient; three-dimensional operations would at first sight seem less efficient, given that only the first two elements can use vector arithmetic, with the last requiring scalar instructions. However, when we look at the other object manipulation primitives, we shall see that this is not the case.

Scale

As Figure 3.4 shows, an object can be scaled by simply multiplying each vertex by a scalar. Thus $a = [1,1] \rightarrow d = [2,2]$ and $b = [1,2] \rightarrow e = [2,4]$, etc. Again for two dimensions, this is relatively easy to achieve, one duplicates the scalar to a two-element vector and performs parallel element by element multiplication.

Rotate

Figure 3.5 illustrates the effect of rotating unit vectors aligned with the *x*- and *y*-axes by 45°. Any point in the plane $P = [x,y]$ can be treated as the sum of two vectors, $[x,0]+[0,y]$ with one aligned with the *x*-axis and the other with the *y*-axis. These in turn are scalar multiples of the unit vectors $[1,0]$, $[0,1]$ aligned the axes. These unit vectors provide the basis of the 2D vector space. We can thus decompose P into $x[1,0] + y[0,1]$. The numbers x,y specify the amplitude of the point P with respect to these basis vectors.

We know what the effect of the rotation of these unit vectors by 45° will be, namely $[1,0] \to R = [\frac{1}{\sqrt{2}}, \frac{1}{\sqrt{2}}]$ whereas $[0,1] \to S = [\frac{-1}{\sqrt{2}}, \frac{1}{\sqrt{2}}]$. We can therefore achieve the effect of rotating P by first rotating the unit vectors, multiplying them by their original amplitudes in P and summing the result: $P \to xR + yS$. So it follows that a rotation by 45° will map a point $P = [x,y] \to Q = [\frac{x}{\sqrt{2}} + \frac{-y}{\sqrt{2}}, \frac{x}{\sqrt{2}} + \frac{y}{\sqrt{2}}]$.

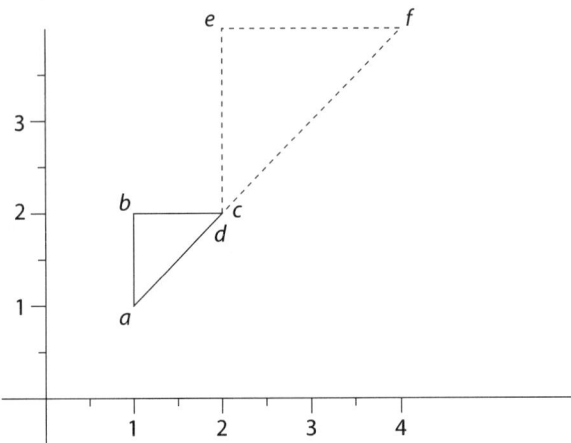

Figure 3.4. Scaling. Triangle *d,e,f* is obtained by multiplying the vertices of *a,b,c* by 2.

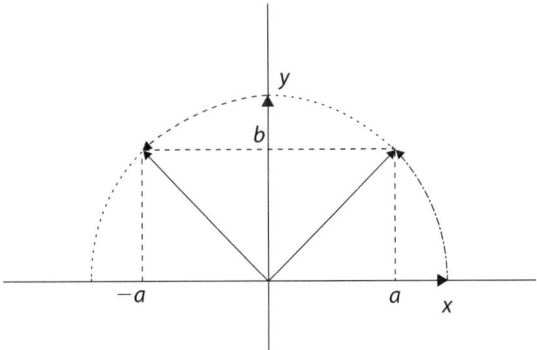

Figure 3.5. Illustration of the effect of rotations by $\frac{\pi}{4}$ on the unit vectors $x = [1,0]$, $y = [0,1]$. The result is that $x \to [a,b] = [\frac{1}{\sqrt{2}}, \frac{1}{\sqrt{2}}]$ and $y \to [-a,b] = [\frac{-1}{\sqrt{2}}, \frac{1}{\sqrt{2}}]$.

Chapter 3 • SIMD Programming in Assembler and C

We can express this as a matrix calculation $\mathbf{T}P = Q$ with

$$\mathbf{T} = \begin{bmatrix} \frac{1}{\sqrt{2}} & \frac{-1}{\sqrt{2}} \\ \frac{1}{\sqrt{2}} & \frac{1}{\sqrt{2}} \end{bmatrix} \qquad P = \begin{bmatrix} x \\ y \end{bmatrix} \qquad Q = \begin{bmatrix} \frac{x}{\sqrt{2}} + \frac{-y}{\sqrt{2}} \\ \frac{x}{\sqrt{2}} + \frac{y}{\sqrt{2}} \end{bmatrix} \qquad (3.1)$$

More generally, we can express any 2D rotation of a point P in terms of operating on P with an appropriate transformation matrix $\mathbf{T}$. This generalises to 3D points and higher.

Note that the above describes the matrix multiplication using the conventions of paper mathematics which distinguishes between row and column vectors. Computer memory is basically a one-dimensional array of words. Groups of words can be viewed as two-dimensional arrays, but the distinction between a row vector and a column vector does not make sense. Figure 3.6 shows how $\mathbf{T}$, P and Q would be represented in memory. Once loaded into 3DNow registers, their rows of individual row vectors of $\mathbf{T}$ have the same representation as the column vector P. This means that the matrix multiplication can be performed by doing parallel vector multiplications between the rows of $\mathbf{T}$ and the register form of P, followed by a summation along the rows.

Generalised Transformations

We have used two-dimensional pictures in our examples, and in consequence our rotation matrix $\mathbf{T}$ has been 2×2. Rotations in three dimensions would require a 3×3 matrix.

Suppose we want both to rotate and to scale a series of points in three-dimensional space, for example the vertices of a set of triangles. One approach is to mutliply each vertex by a rotation matrix and then multiply each vertex by a scalar. This would require 12 multiplications per vertex. If instead we premultiplied our rotation matrix by the scalar and then simply performed the matrix to vector multiplications, we would achieve the same result at a cost of nine multiplications per vertex.

T[0,0]
T[0,1]
T[1,0]
T[1,1]
P[0] or P[0,0]
P[1] or P[1,0]
Q[0] or Q[0,0]
Q[1] or Q[1,0]

Memory layout

T[0,0]	T[0,1]
T[1,0]	T[1,1]

P[0]	P[1]

Q[0]	Q[1]

Register layout

Figure 3.6. Contrast between the linear layout of the matrix and vectors in memory and the layout once loaded into 3DNow registers.

Can this technique be extended to handle translations also?

Yes, it can, but for it to do so we have to move to vectors of length 4. Consider a four-dimensional point P of the form $[x,y,z,1]$. Multiply this by a matrix T of the form

$$T = \begin{bmatrix} 1 & 0 & 0 & a \\ 0 & 1 & 0 & b \\ 0 & 0 & 1 & c \\ 0 & 0 & 0 & 1 \end{bmatrix} \qquad (3.2)$$

The result is a vector $[x+a, y+b, z+c, 1]$. The effect has been to translate P by the vector $[a,b,c,0]$. More generally, given a 3×3 rotation and scale matrix $\begin{bmatrix} d & e & f \\ g & h & i \\ j & k & l \end{bmatrix}$ and a translation vector $[a, b, c]$, then we can form a combined rotation, scaling and translation matrix **M** of the form

$$\mathbf{M} = \begin{bmatrix} d & e & f & a \\ g & h & i & b \\ j & k & j & c \\ 0 & 0 & 0 & 1 \end{bmatrix} \qquad (3.3)$$

All of our 3D graphics transforms can be expressed in terms of the same basic operation, multiplication of a four-element vector by a 4×4 matrix. In this light, the purpose of the 3DNow instructions becomes clear. They allow pairs of reals to be multiplied or added with a single instruction. A row of the transformation matrix **M** can be multiplied by a vector of four reals in just two steps. Alg. 13 gives an AMD assembler routine to perform multiplication of a four-element vector by a 4×4 matrix.

The C template of the function is

```
void mvmul(float *m, float *v)
```

where m is the start address of a 4×4 matrix of floats and v is the start address of a four-element vector of floats. This implies that the matrix address will be found at an offset of 8 from the ebp register and the vector address at an offset of 12 on entry to mvmul. The routine caches these addresses in the esi and ebx registers, respectively. The routine has a single loop that steps through the four rows of the matrix, using edx as the loop induction variable. On each iteration the inner product between the edxth row of the matrix and the vector v is computed. Register MM3 is used as a parallel accumulator, allowing the sum of the odd and even products to be formed with two multiplications and one add instruction. Prefetching is used on the matrix but not the vector fetches, since there is no next row for the vector. The 64-bit result is stored in in a local two-element vector vtmp, and the elements are added using scalar arithmetic instructions.

Between the vector arithmetic instructions and the scalar ones, it is necessary to plant an emms instruction to clear the MMX registers. Were this not done, a floating point exception would be reported. The floating point stack, which is aliased to the same state bits as the MMX registers, would be found to have been corrupted.

As the elements of the transformed vector are computed, they are stored in a temporary local four-element result vector, `rtmp`, to prevent the source vector being corrupted. At the end, `rtmp` is copied into `v` using MMX `movq` instructions.

```
GLOBAL mvmul
section .text
mvmul:enter 100,0
vtmp:equ -80
ttmp:equ -32
      xor edx,edx
      mov esi,DWORD[ebp+8]     ; esi gets addr of matrix
      mov ebx,DWORD[ebp+12]    ; ebx gets addr of vector
mvlooptop:cmp DWORD edx,3
          jg near mvloopend
          imul eax,DWORD edx,16
          lea eax,[eax+8]
          prefetch [esi+eax+8]
          movq MM3,[esi+eax]
          PFmul MM3,[ebx+8]
          imul eax,DWORD edx,16
          prefetch [esi+eax+8]
          movq MM2,[esi+eax]
          PFmul MM2,[ebx]
          PFadd MM3,MM2
          movq [ebp+vtmp],MM3 ; store pair in vtmp
          emms
          fld dword[ebp+vtmp]
          fadd DWORD[ebp+vtmp+4]
          fstp dword[ebp+edx*4+rtmp] ; dot product to rtmp[edx]
          lea edx,[edx+1]     ; inc edx
      jmp mvlooptop
mvloopend:
      mov edi,DWORD[ebp+12]    ; copy rtmp
      movq MM2,[ebp+rtmp]      ; to v
      movq [edi],MM2
      movq MM2,[ebp+8+rtmp]
      movq [edi+8],MM2
      leave
      emms
      ret 0
```

Algorithm 13. 3DNow routine to multiply a vector by a matrix.

3.7 Coordinate Transformations Using SSE Instructions

The SSE instructions were Intel's equivalent of 3DNow. Because new state bits were introduced to the CPU architecture, the 64-bit limit on vector registers was relaxed. SSE supports 128-bit long vector registers, sufficient to contain a four-element vector of floats. By way of contrast, let us look at how these instructions might be applied to the task of coordinate transformation performed by 3DNow code in Alg. 13.

The SSE variant closely parallels the 3DNow version. It is shown in Alg. 14. Since the assembly language uses the same mnemonic for a 128-bit vector register and for the 32-bit floating point scalar register, the listing distinguishes them by giving vector registers in capitals, XMM3, and scalar variants in lower

```
global mvmul
section .text
mvmul:enter 72,0
vtmp   equ -64
rtmp   equ -32
       mov ecx,0
       mov edi,DWORD[ebp+12]
       movups XMM4,[edi]
mvl1:  cmp ecx,3
       jg near mvl2
       mov edi,DWORD[ebp+8]
       imul esi,ecx,16
       movups XMM2,[edi+esi]
       mulps XMM2,XMM4
       movups [ebp+vtmp],XMM2
       movss xmm0,[ebp+vtmp]     ; sum the vector using
       movss xmm1,[ebp+vtmp+4]   ; scalar SSE instructions
       movss xmm2,[ebp+vtmp+8]
       addss xmm2,[ebp+vtmp+12]
       addss xmm1,xmm2
       addss xmm0,xmm1           ; dot product in xmm0
       movss [ebp+ecx*4+rtmp],xmm0
       inc ecx
       jmp mvl1
mvl2:  mov edi,DWORD[ebp+12]
       movups XMM3,[ebp+rtmp]
       movups [edi],XMM3
       leave
       ret 0
```

Algorithm 14. Matrix–vector multiplication using SSE code.

case, xmm3. The significant differences between the AMD and Intel variants are that in the Intel case:

1. The entire vector v can be cached in a register.
2. Only one multiply instruction is needed per row of the vector.
3. The scalar summation of the vector takes more instructions because of the vector register length.
4. No emms instructions have to be planted.

One might have expected that the SSE variant of the algorithm, using as it does a higher level of parallelism, would be faster. In fact, it is considerably slower than the AMD version. This is illustrated in Table 3.4, which shows their comparative performance. Despite the Intel code being run on a faster processor, it runs at only about half the speed of the AMD code. The difference is even more marked when we normalise for the effect of differences in clock speed. The AMD processor achieves three times as many floating point operations per cycle.

Another comparison is provided by the C version of mvmul, given in Alg. 15. This was compiled using gcc version 3.2 and the code produced uses no vector instructions. It can be seen that the Athlon is again markedly faster than the P4 when running the C code. Running C code, the Athlon achieved twice as many

Table 3.4. Comparative performance of the 3DNow and SSE versions of coordinate transformation

CPU	Clock (GHz)	C time	Assembler time	Relative gain	FOPs per cycle
Athlon	1.0	4.23	1.9	2.2×	0.16
P4	1.7	5.06	3.81	1.32×	0.05

Measurements for 10 million matrix to vector multiples. This amounts to 320 million floating point operations.

```
mvmulc(float *m, float *v)
{  float vtmp[4];
   int i,j;
   float t;
   for(i=0;i<4;i++)
   {
     t=0;
     for(j=0;j<4;j++) t=t+m[i*4+j]*v[j];
     vtmp[i]=t;
   }
   for(i=0;i<4;i++) v[i]=vtmp[i];
}
```

Algorithm 15. C variant of the matrix to vector multiply.

floating point operations per clock cycle. This probably indicates an inherently superior floating point unit on the Athlon.

However, the superiority of the 3DNow instruction architecture is brought out by comparing the relative speeds of C and assembler on each CPU. This comparison compensates for differences in clock speed and FPU speed, but we again see that gains from vectorisation are much more marked for the Athlon.

Intel SIMD Instructions

In the following sections we give a semi-formal definition of the multi-media instruction-sets used on Intel and AMD processors. For each instruction we provide a specification of its semantics and indicate the assembler syntax used. For all instructions we provide NASM syntax. The types used by the instructions and their semantics are defined in Pascal.

4.1 Types

The underlying types used by the architecture are defined first. These are comprised of :

1. a collection of base types
2. a collection of short vector types
3. types used to represent registers
4. types used in the store and recovery of machine state.

Base Types

We first define the underlying base types used by the multi-media instructions. The definitions of all types are given in Pascal syntax.

```
type
  int8 = -128..127;
  uint8 = 0..255;
  int16 = -32768..32767;
  uint16 = 0..65535;
  int32 = integer;
  int64 = -9223372036854775807..9223372036854775807;
  ieee32 = real;
  ieee64 = double;
```

Aggregates

We now define the short vector types used by the MMX, 3DNOW and SSE instructions.

MMX

```
int32vec2 = array [0..1] of int32;
int16vec4 = array [0..3] of int16;
```

	uint16vec4 = **array** [0..3] **of** uint16;
	int8vec8 = **array** [0..7] **of** int8;
	uint8vec8 = **array** [0..7] **of** uint8;
3DNOW	ieee32vec2 = **array** [0..1] **of** ieee32;
SSE	ieee32vec4 = **array** [0..3] **of** ieee32;
SSE2	ieee64vec2 = **array** [0..1] **of** ieee64;
	int64vec2 = **array** [0..1] **of** int64;
	int32vec4 = **array** [0..3] **of** int32;
	int16vec8 = **array** [0..8] **of** int16;
	uint16vec8 = **array** [0..8] **of** uint16;
	int8vec16 = **array** [0..15] **of** int8;
	uint8vec16 = **array** [0..15] **of** uint8;

Mnemonics for Lengths and Shifts

byte	formats = (b,
word	w,
dword	d,
qword	q,
dqword	dq);

We encode mnemonics for the three kinds of shifts, logical left and right, and arithmetic right.

shifts = (ll,ra,rl);

MMX Register Types

We define the MMX registers as variant records with multiple possible internal representations.

```
MMX = record
    case char of
        'a': (a:int64);
        'b': (b:int32vec2);
        'c': (c:int16vec4);
        'd': (d:uint16vec4);
        'e': (e:int8vec8);
        'f': (f:uint8vec8);
```
Only AMD
```
        'g': (g:ieee32vec2);
    end;
regid = 0..7;
```

SSE Register Types

We define the types of the SSE registers as a variant record allowing any of the formats supported in either SSE1 or SSE2 instruction-sets.

```
XMM = record
    case char of
```

SEE		'a': (a:ieee32vec4);
SEE2		'b': (b:ieee64vec2);
		'c': (c:int32vec4);
		'd': (d:int16vec8);
		'e': (e:uint16vec8);
		'f': (f:int8vec16);
		'g': (g:uint8vec16);
		'h': (h:int64vec2);
		end;

XMM and MMX Save State

This defines the type of data used when a save or restore is performed of the'entire SIMD state (see Sections 4.4.19 and 4.4.20). This block is 512 bytes long.

	fpu_reg_save = **record**
	mmr:MMX;
	exponent:int16;
	end;
	MMXpad = **array** [10..15] **of** *int8;*
	MMXsave = **record**
80 bit state	*data:fpu_reg_save;*
	pad:MMXpad;
	end;
	tMMXsaved = **array** [regid] **of** *MMXsave;*
	tMMXreg = **array** [regid] **of** *MMX;*
fpu exponents	*texponents* = **array** [regid] **of** *int16;*
	tXMMreg = **array** [regid] **of** *XMM;*
	tpad5 = **array** [1..14] **of** *XMM;*
	XMMstatus = **record**
fpu control word	*fcw:int16;*
fpu status word	*fsw:int16;*
	pad1:int8;
fpu tag word	*ftw:int8;*
fpu opcode	*fop:int8;*
fpu instruction addr	*fpuip:int32;*
code segment	*cs:int16;*
reserved	*pad2:int16;*
fpu data addr	*fpudp:int32;*
data segment	*ds:int16;*
reserved	*pad3:int16;*
MMX control reg	*mxcsr:int32;*
reserved	*pad4:int32;*
	MMXr:tMMXsaved;
	XMMr:tXMMreg;
	pad5:tpad5;
	end;

Define Memory

We define the memory both as an array of bytes and as an array of 16-byte vectors, because the SSE instructions have distinct aligned and unaligned memory load instructions. We also define the level 1 cache, (see Section 2.4.1).

<pre>
                    const
arbitrary   memsize = 16777216;
                    type
                        alignment = (IA32,SSE);
                        tbytemem = array [0..memsize − 1] of uint8;
                        tvecmem = array [0..memsize div 16 − 1] of XMM;
                    var
                        mem:record
                            case alignment of
                                IA32: (bytemem:tbytemem);
                                SSE: (vecmem:tvecmem);
                        end;
                        level1 : array [0..3] of array [0..31] of array [0..63] of uint8;
                        level2 : array [0..8] of array [0..511] of array [0..63] of uint8;
cache bank select   bank:integer;
</pre>

Define Register State

We give a partial description of the register state of the processor including all of the status vector that can be altered by the SIMD instruction-set.

<pre>
                    type
                        tgeneral = array [regid] of integer;
                    var
                        MMXreg:tMMXreg;
                        exponents:texponents;
                        XMMreg:tXMMreg;
general registers   general:tgeneral;
EFLAGS   ZF:boolean;
                        PF:boolean;
                        CF:boolean;
</pre>

Status and control registers:

<pre>
tag word   ftw:int8;
control word   fcw:int16;
status word   fsw:int16;
opcode   fop:int8;
instruction addr   fpuip:int32;
code segment   cs:int16;
data addr   fpudp:int32;
data segment   ds:int16;
MMx control reg   mxcsr:int32;
</pre>

Chapter 4 • Intel SIMD Instructions

Register Names

At the machine code level, all registers are simply numbered, but for historical reasons Intel associate names with the general registers. The mapping from register names to register numbers is

const
    eax = 0;
    ecx = 1;
    edx = 2;
    ebx = 3;
    esp = 4;
    ebp = 5;
    esi = 6;
    edi = 7;

4.2 shrl

Define shift right logical in arithmetic terms.

function *shrl (x:integer;c,w:integer):integer;*
begin
   shrl := **if** $c = 0$ **then** x **else** shrl$((x \div 2)$ **and not**$(2^{w-1}), c - 1, w)$
end;

4.3 saturate

function *saturate (x,low,high:integer) : integer;*

This function is used to define the effects of saturated arithmetic; it forces the output to be within the bounds low...high.

begin
    if $x >$ *high* **then** *saturate* $\leftarrow$ *high*
    else
      if $x <$ *low* **then** *saturate* $\leftarrow$ *low*
      else
         saturate $\leftarrow$ *x*
end;

4.4 Instructions

Each instruction is now presented as a procedure to give the semantics; along with this the NASM syntax for the instruction and the machines which support it are given. We also provide a star rating for how useful the instructions are:

    ***   indicates that the instruction is important, and is likely to be of general use in SIMD programming.

** indicates that the instruction is useful, either as a replacement for existing FPU instructions or in some specific SIMD contexts.

* indicates that the instruction is unlikely to be of use to the average SIMD programmer.

4.4.1 ADDPS

Instruction *ADDPS (d:regid;src:XMM);*

```
***   P3,P4,ATHLONXP
NASM  ADDPS XMMreg,r/m128
```

Add packed single-precision floating point. The source can be register or 16-byte aligned memory vector.

$XMMreg_d.a \leftarrow src.a + XMMreg_d.a$

4.4.2 ADDSS

Instruction *ADDSS (d:regid;src:XMM);*

```
**    P3,P4,ATHLONXP
NASM  ADDSS XMMreg,XMMreg/mem32
```

Scalar single floating point add. The source can be memory or XMM register. This instruction is useful if one wants to do floating-point scalar arithmetic without corrupting the MMX registers.

$XMMreg_d.a_0 \leftarrow src.a_0 + XMMreg_d.a_0$

4.4.3 ANDNPS

Instruction *ANDNPS (d:regid;src:XMM);*

```
**    P3,P4,ATHLONXP
NASM  ANDNPS XMMreg,r/m128
```

And negated, src is register or 16-byte aligned memory vector.

$XMMreg_d.g \leftarrow src.g \wedge$ **not** *$XMMreg_d.g$*

4.4.4 ANDPS

Instruction *ANDPS (d:regid;src:XMM);*

```
**    P3,P4,ATHLONXP
NASM  ANDPS XMMreg,r/m128
```

16-byte bitwise logical and.

$XMMreg_d.g \leftarrow src.g \wedge XMMreg_d.g$;

We define an enumerated type for comparison operations that can be done in parallel on packed floating-point values. These are passed as an 8-bit immediate field to the comparison opcode.

type
  $fcomp = (feq,$
  flt
  fle
  $funord$
  $fneq$
  $fnlt$
  $fnle$
  $ford);$

4.4.5 CMPPS

Instruction *CMPPS (d:regid;src:XMM;imm8:fcomp);*

```
**      P3,P4,ATHLONXP
NASM    CMPPS XMMreg,r/m128,imm8
```

Parallel single-precision floating-point comparison. Compares four pairs of floats and creates a Boolean mask as a result. Such masks can then be used to select results from other vectors. The src is either a register or a 16-byte aligned vector. When writing assembler pass in the ordinal value of fcomp typed field as a parameter.

var
  $i : 0..3;$
   for $i \leftarrow$ 0 **to** 3 **do**
    case *imm8* **of**

$$feq : XMMreg_d.c_i \leftarrow \begin{cases} -1 & \text{if } XMMreg_d.a_i = src.a_i \\ 0 & \text{otherwise} \end{cases};$$

$$flt : XMMreg_d.c_i \leftarrow \begin{cases} -1 & \text{if } XMMreg_d.a_i < src.a_i \\ 0 & \text{otherwise} \end{cases};$$

$$fle : XMMreg_d.c_i \leftarrow \begin{cases} -1 & \text{if } XMMreg_d.a_i \leq src.a_i \\ 0 & \text{otherwise} \end{cases};$$

$$fneq : XMMreg_d.c_i \leftarrow \begin{cases} 0 & \text{if } XMMreg_d.a_i = src.a_i \\ -1 & \text{otherwise} \end{cases};$$

$$fnlt : XMMreg_d.c_i \leftarrow \begin{cases} 0 & \text{if } XMMreg_d.a_i < src.a_i \\ -1 & \text{otherwise} \end{cases};$$

$$fnle : XMMreg_d.c_i \leftarrow \begin{cases} 0 & \text{if } XMMreg_d.a_i \leq src.a_i \\ -1 & \text{otherwise} \end{cases};$$

4.4.6 CMPSS

Instruction *CMPSS (d:regid;src:XMM;imm8:fcomp);*

```
**     P3,P4,ATHLONXP
NASM   CMPSS XMMreg,r/m32,imm8
```

Scalar single-precision floating-point comparison. Compares a pair of floats and creates a Boolean mask as a result.

The src is either a register or a memory location. There are no special alignment requirements.

case *imm8* **of**

$$feq : XMMreg_d.c_0 \leftarrow \begin{cases} -1 & \text{if } XMMreg_d.a_0 = src.a_0, \\ 0 & \text{otherwise} \end{cases}$$

$$flt : XMMreg_d.c_0 \leftarrow \begin{cases} -1 & \text{if } XMMreg_d.a_0 < src.a_0, \\ 0 & \text{otherwise} \end{cases}$$

$$fle : XMMreg_d.c_0 \leftarrow \begin{cases} -1 & \text{if } XMMreg_d.a_0 \leq src.a_0, \\ 0 & \text{otherwise} \end{cases}$$

$$fneq : XMMreg_d.c_0 \leftarrow \begin{cases} 0 & \text{if } XMMreg_d.a_0 = src.a_0, \\ -1 & \text{otherwise} \end{cases}$$

$$fnlt : XMMreg_d.c_0 \leftarrow \begin{cases} 0 & \text{if } XMMreg_d.a_0 < src.a_0, \\ -1 & \text{otherwise} \end{cases}$$

$$fnle : XMMreg_d.c_0 \leftarrow \begin{cases} 0 & \text{if } XMMreg_d.a_0 \leq src.a_0, \\ -1 & \text{otherwise} \end{cases}$$

4.4.7 COMISS

Instruction *COMISS (d:regid;src:XMM);*

```
**     P3,P4,ATHLONXP
NASM   COMISS XMMreg,r/m32
```

SSE Scalar Compare and Set EFLAGS. Compares single-precision floating-point numbers and set flags appropriately.

if *XMMreg$_d$.a$_0$ = src.a$_0$* **then**
begin
  ZF ← true;
  CF ← false;
  PF ← false
end
else
  if *XMMreg$_d$.a$_0$ > src.a$_0$* **then**
  begin
    ZF ← false;

… Chapter 4 • Intel SIMD Instructions

```
        CF ← false;
        PF ← false
      end
    else
      if XMMreg_d.a_0 < src.a_0 then
        begin
          ZF ← false;
          CF ← true;
          PF ← false
        end
      else
        begin
          ZF ← false;
          CF ← false;
          PF ← false
        end;
```

4.4.8 CVTPI2PS

Instruction *CVTPI2PS (d:regid;src:MMX);*

```
  *      P3,P4,ATHLONXP
NASM     CVTPI2PS XMMreg,r/m64
```

SSE Packed Integer to Floating-Point Conversion. Destination is lower two words of XMM register; source is an MMX register or memory location.

$XMMreg_d.a_0 \leftarrow src.b_0;$
$XMMreg_d.a_1 \leftarrow src.b_1;$

4.4.9 CVTPS2PI

Instruction *CVTPS2PI (d:regid;src:XMM);*

```
  *      P3,P4,ATHLONXP
NASM     CVTPS2PI MMXreg,r/m64
```

SSE Packed Floating-point to Integer Conversion with rounding: source is lower two words of XMM register or memory location; destination is an MMX register.

$MMXreg_d.b_0 \leftarrow$ **round** $(src.a_0);$
$MMXreg_d.b_1 \leftarrow$ **round** $(src.a_1);$

4.4.10 CVTTPS2PI

Instruction *CVTTPS2PI (d:regid;src:XMM);*

```
  **     P3,P4,ATHLONXP
NASM     CVTTPS2PI MMXreg,r/m64
```

SSE Packed Floating-point to Integer Conversion with truncation: source is lower two words of XMM register or memory location; destination is an MMX register.

$MMXreg_d.b_0 \leftarrow trunc\ (src.a_0);$
$MMXreg_d.b_1 \leftarrow trunc\ (src.a_1);$

4.4.11 CVTSI2SS

Instruction *CVTSI2SS (d:regid;src:integer);*

```
**     P3,P4,ATHLONXP
NASM   CVTSI2SS XMMreg,r/m32
```

SSE Scalar Integer to Floating-Point Conversion. Destination is lower word of XMM register; source is a general register or memory location.

$XMMreg_d.a_0 \leftarrow src;$

4.4.12 CVTSS2SI

Instruction *CVTSS2SI (d:regid;src:ieee32);*

```
**     P3,P4,ATHLONXP
NASM   CVTSS2SI reg32,XMMreg/mem32
```

SSE Scalar Floating-Point to Integer Conversion. Destination is a general register; source is lower word of XMM register or memory location.

$general_d \leftarrow$ **round** $(src);$

4.4.13 CVTTSS2SI

Instruction *CVTTSS2SI (d:regid;src:ieee32);*

```
**     P3,P4,ATHLONXP
NASM   CVTTSS2SI reg32,XMMreg/mem32
```

SSE Scalar Floating-Point to Integer Conversion with truncation. Destination is a general register; source is lower word of XMM register or memory location.

$general_d \leftarrow trunc(src);$

4.4.14 DIVPD

Instruction *DIVPD (d:regid;src:XMM);*

```
***    P4
NASM   DIVPD XMMreg,r/m128
```

Packed Double-Precision FP Divide. Destination is an XMM register; source is XMM register or memory location. Element by element division is performed.

var
  $i : 0..1;$
  for $i \leftarrow 0$ **to** 1 **do**
    $XMMreg_d.b_i \leftarrow \frac{XMMreg_d.b_i}{src.b_i};$

4.4.15 DIVPS

Instruction *DIVPS (d:regid;src:XMM);*

```
***    P3,P4,ATHLONXP
NASM   DIVPS XMMreg,r/m128
```

Packed Single-FP Divide. Destination is an XMM register; source is XMM register or memory location. Element by element division is performed.

var
  $i : 0..3;$
  for $i \leftarrow 0$ **to** 3 **do**
    $XMMreg_d.a_i \leftarrow \frac{XMMreg_d.a_i}{src.a_i};$

4.4.16 DIVSD

Instruction *DIVSD (d:regid;src:ieee64);*

```
**     P4
NASM   DIVSS XMMreg,XMMreg/mem64
```

Scalar Double-FP Divide. Destination is low word of an XMM register; source is XMM register low word or memory location. This is a useful alternative to the use of the FPU stack for real arithmetic since it removes resource contention between the FPU stack and the MMX registers.

$XMMreg_d.b_0 \leftarrow \frac{XMMreg_d.b_0}{src};$

4.4.17 DIVSS

Instruction *DIVSS (d:regid;src:ieee32);*

```
**     P3,P4,ATHLONXP
NASM   DIVSS XMMreg,XMMreg/mem32
```

Scalar Single-FP Divide. Destination is low word of an XMM register; source is XMM register low word or memory location.

$XMMreg_d.a_0 \leftarrow \frac{XMMreg_d.a_0}{src};$

4.4.18 EMMS

Instruction *EMMS;*

```
***    K6,MMX PENTIUM,Athlon,P3,P4,ATHLONXP
NASM   EMMS
```

Empty MMX State. This sets the FPU tag word (marking which floating-point registers are available) to all ones, meaning that all registers are available for the FPU to use. All other MMX instructions clear the FPU TagWord. This clearing of the tag word invalidates any values currently on the FPU stack, so that MMX instructions and FPU instructions cannot be mixed. EMMS should be used after executing MMX instructions and before executing any subsequent floating-point operations.

ftw ← $ff;

4.4.19 FXRSTOR

Instruction *FXRSTOR (src:XMMstatus)*;

```
*       P3,P4,ATHLONXP
NASM    FXRSTOR m512byte
```

Restore FP, MMX and SSE States. Loads the FP, MMX and XMM state from a memory area. Area should previously have been saved by FXSAVE (see Section 4.4.20).

var
  i:regid;
  fcw ← src.fcw;
  fsw ← src.fsw;
  ftw ← src.ftw;
  fop ← src.fop;
  fpuip ← src.fpuip;
  cs ← src.cs;
  fpudp ← src.fpudp;
  ds ← src.ds;
  mxcsr ← src.mxcsr;
  for *i ←* 0 **to** *7* **do**
  begin
    MMXreg$_i$ ← src.MMXr$_i$.data.mmr;
    exponents$_i$ ← src.MMXr$_i$.data.exponent;
    XMMreg$_i$ ← src.XMMr$_i$;
  end;

4.4.20 FXSAVE

Instruction *FXSAVE (var dest:XMMstatus)*;

```
*       P3,P4,ATHLONXP
NASM    FXSAVE m512byte
```

Save FP, MMX and SSE States. This is mainly of use in context switching and is unlikely to be used by applications coders. The processor retains the contents of the FP and MMX state and Streaming SIMD Extension state in the processor after the state has been saved. This instruction has been optimized to maximize floating-point save performance.

Chapter 4 • Intel SIMD Instructions

var
  i:regid;
dest.fcw ← *fcw*;
dest.fsw ← *fsw*;
dest.ftw ← *ftw*;
dest.fop ← *fop*;
dest.fpuip ← *fpuip*;
dest.cs ← *cs*;
dest.fpudp ← *fpudp*;
dest.ds ← *ds*;
dest.mxcsr ← *mxcsr*;
for *i* ← 0 **to** 7 **do**
begin
  dest.MMXr$_i$.data.mmr ← *MMXreg$_i$*;
  dest.MMXr$_i$.data.exponent ← *exponents$_i$*;
  dest.XMMr$_i$ ← *XMMreg$_i$*;
end;

4.4.21 MASKMOVQ

Instruction *MASKMOVQ (r1,r2:regid)*;

  ★   P4
NASM MASKMOVQ MMXreg,MMXrege

Byte Mask Write. This is analogous to the the x86 string move instructions in that it writes bytes in r1 under the byte mask provided by r2 to a destination specified by the (DS:) EDI register. This use of the EDI register as a destination register is somewhat old-fashioned but was probably chosen because of the need to provide a third operand to the instruction.

Note that this can be used in conjunction with comparison instructions that set vector register elements to either −1 or 0. It will work after wordwise or bytewise comparisons have been performed.

var
  i:integer;
for *i* ← 0 **to** 7 **do**
  if *MMXreg$_{r2}$.e$_i$* < 0 **then**
    mem.bytemem$_{general_{edi}+i}$ ← *MMXreg$_{r1}$.e$_i$*;

4.4.22 MAXPD

Instruction *MAXPD (d:regid;src:XMM)*;

  ★★   P4
NASM MAXPD XMMreg,r/m128

Packed Double-Precision FP Maximum. Destination is an XMM register; source is XMM register or memory location. Element by element comparison is performed.

```
var
  i : 0..1;
with XMMreg_d do
  for i ← 0 to 1 do
    if src.b_i > b_i then
      b_i ← src.b_i;
```

4.4.23 MAXPS

Instruction *MAXPS (d:regid;src:XMM);*

```
**      P3,P4,ATHLONXP
NASM    MAXPS XMMreg,r/m128
```

Packed Single-FP Maximum. Destination is an XMM register; source is XMM register or memory location. Element by element comparison is performed.

```
var
  i : 0..3;
with XMMreg_d do
  for i ← 0 to 3 do
    if a_i < src.a_i then
      a_i ← src.a_i;
```

4.4.24 MAXSD

Instruction *MAXSD (d:regid;src:ieee64);*

```
**      P4
NASM    MAXSS XMMreg,XMMreg/mem64
```

Scalar Double-FP Maximum. Destination is low word of an XMM register; source is XMM register low word or memory location.

$$XMMreg_d.b_0 \leftarrow \begin{cases} src & \text{if } (XMMreg_d.b_0) < src \\ XMMreg_d.b_0 & \text{otherwise} \end{cases};$$

4.4.25 MAXSS

Instruction *MAXSS (d:regid;src:ieee32);*

```
**      P3,P4,ATHLONXP
NASM    MAXSS XMMreg,XMMreg/mem32
```

Scalar Single-FP Maximum. Destination is low word of an XMM register; source is XMM register low word or memory location.

$$XMMreg_d.a_0 \leftarrow \begin{cases} src & \text{if } XMMreg_d.a_0 < src \\ XMMreg_d.a_0 & \text{otherwise} \end{cases};$$

4.4.26 MINPD

Instruction *MINPD (d:regid;src:XMM);*

```
**      P4
NASM    MINPD XMMreg,r/m128
```

Packed Double-Precision FP Minimum. Destination is an XMM register; source is XMM register or memory location. Element by element comparison is performed.

var
  $i : 0..1;$
with *XMMreg$_d$* **do**
  for $i \leftarrow 0$ **to** 1 **do**
    if $src.b_i < b_i$ **then**
      $b_i \leftarrow src.b_i;$

4.4.27 MINPS

Instruction *MINPS (d:regid;src:XMM);*

```
**      P3,P4,ATHLONXP
NASM    MINPS XMMreg,r/m128
```

Packed Single-FP Minimum. Destination is an XMM register; source is XMM register or memory location. Element by element comparison is performed.

var
  $i : 0..3;$
with *XMMreg$_d$* **do**
  for $i \leftarrow 0$ **to** 3 **do**
    if $a_i > src.a_i$ **then**
      $a_i \leftarrow src.a_i;$

4.4.28 MINSD

Instruction *MINSD (d:regid;src:ieee64);*

```
**      P4
NASM    MINSS XMMreg,XMMreg/mem64
```

Scalar Double-FP Minimum. Destination is low word of an XMM register; source is XMM register low word or memory location.

$$XMMreg_d.b_0 \leftarrow \begin{cases} src & \text{if } (XMMreg_d.b_0) > src \\ XMMreg_d.b_0 & \text{otherwise} \end{cases};$$

4.4.29 MINSS

Instruction *MINSS (d:regid;src:ieee32);*

```
**      P3,P4,ATHLONXP
NASM    MINSS XMMreg,XMMreg/mem32
```

Scalar Single-FP Minimum. Destination is low word of an XMM register; source is XMM register low word or memory location.

$$XMMreg_d.a_0 \leftarrow \begin{cases} src & \text{if } XMMreg_d.a_0 > src \\ XMMreg_d.a_0 & \text{otherwise} \end{cases};$$

4.4.30 MOVAPS_load

Instruction *MOVAPS_load* (*d:regid;src:XMM*);

```
**     P3,P4,ATHLONXP
NASM   MOVAPS XMMreg,r/m128
```

Packed Single-FP Aligned Load. Destination is an XMM register; source is XMM register or a 16-byte aligned memory location. For unaligned moves, use MOVUPS.

$XMMreg_d \leftarrow src$;

4.4.31 MOVAPS_store

Instruction *MOVAPS_store* (*d:regid;**var** dest:XMM*);

```
**     P3,P4,ATHLONXP
NASM   MOVAPS r/m128,XMMreg
```

Packed Single-FP Aligned Store. Source is an XMM register; destination is XMM register or a 16-byte aligned memory location. This shares its assembler mnemonic with MOVAPS_load (see Section 4.4.30).

$dest \leftarrow XMMreg_d$;

4.4.32 MOVD_load

Instruction *MOVD_load* (*d:regid;src:int32*);

```
**     Pentium MMX,K6,P3,P4,ATHLONXP
NASM   MOVD MMXreg,r/m32
```

32-Bit MMX Load. Destination is an MMX register, source is a general register or a memory location. It cannot be used to move words between MMX registers.

with *MMXreg_d* **do**
begin
  $b_0 \leftarrow src$;
  $b_1 \leftarrow 0$;

4.4.33 MOVD_store

Instruction *MOVD_store (d:regid;***var** *dest:int32);*

```
**      PentiumMMX,K6,P3,P4,ATHLONXP
NASM    MOVD r/m32,MMXreg
```

32-Bit MMX Store. Destination is a general register or a memory location; Source is low 32-bit word of an MMX register. It cannot be used to move words between MMX registers.

dest ← *MMXreg$_d$.b$_0$;*

4.4.34 MOVD_load_sse

Instruction *MOVD_load_sse (d:regid;src:int32);*

```
**      P4
NASM    MOVD XMMreg,r/m32
```

32-Bit XMM Load. Destination is an XMM register; source is a general register or a memory location. It cannot be used to move words between XMM registers.

with *XMMreg$_d$* **do**
begin
   c_0 ← *src;*
   c_1 ← 0;
   c_2 ← 0;
   c_3 ← 0;

4.4.35 MOVD_store_sse

Instruction *MOVD_store_sse (d:regid;***var** *dest:int32);*

```
**      P4
NASM    MOVD r/m32,XMMreg
```

32-Bit XMM Store. Destination is a general register or a memory location; source is low 32-bit word of an XMM register.

dest ← *XMMreg$_d$.c$_0$;*

4.4.36 MOVHLPS

Instruction *MOVHLPS (r1,r2:regid);*

```
**      P3,P4,ATHLONXP
NASM    MOVHLPS XMMreg,XMMreg
```

SSE Move High to Low. Moves top 8 bytes in r2 to bottom 8 bytes in r1. Both operands are XMM registers.

XMMreg$_{r1}$.a$_{0..1}$ ← *XMMreg$_{r2}$.a$_{2..3}$;*

4.4.37 MOVHPS_load

Instruction *MOVHPS_load (r1:regid;src:MMX);*

```
**      P3,P4,ATHLONXP
NASM    MMOVHPS XMMreg,mem64
```

SSE Move High Packed Single Precision. Moves two single-precision floats to the high pair of words in an XMM register. The lower two floats in the register do not change. Source is in memory.

$XMMreg_{r1}.a_{2..3} \leftarrow src.g_{0..1};$

4.4.38 MOVHPS_store

Instruction *MOVHPS_store (r1:regid;**var** dest:MMX);*

```
*       P3,P4,ATHLONXP
NASM    MOVHPS mem64,XMMreg
```

SSE Move High Packed Single Precision. Moves two single-precision floats from the high pair of words in an XMM register. Destination is in memory.

$dest.g_{0..1} \leftarrow XMMreg_{r1}.a_{2..3};$

4.4.39 MOVLHPS

Instruction *MOVLHPS (r1,r2:regid);*

```
*       P3,P4,ATHLONXP
NASM    MOVLHPS XMMreg,XMMreg
```

SSE Move High to Low. Moves bottom 8 bytes in r2 to top 8 bytes in r1. Both operands are XMM registers.

$XMMreg_{r1}.a_{2..3} \leftarrow XMMreg_{r2}.a_{0..1};$

4.4.40 MOVLPS_load

Instruction *MOVLPS_load (r1:regid;src:MMX);*

```
*       P3,P4,ATHLONXP
NASM    MMOVLPS XMMreg,mem64
```

SSE Move Low Packed Single Precision. Moves two single precision floats to the low pair of words in an XMM register. The lower two floats in the register do not change. Source is in memory.

$XMMreg_{r1}.a_{0..1} \leftarrow src.g_{0..1};$

4.4.41 MOVLPS_store

Instruction *MOVLPS_store (r1:regid;**var** dest:MMX);*

```
  *      P3,P4,ATHLONXP
NASM     MOVLPS mem64,XMMreg
```

SSE Move Low Packed Single Precision. Moves two single-precision floats from the low pair of words in an XMM register. Destination is in memory.

$dest.g_{0..1} \leftarrow XMMreg_{r1}.a_{0..1};$

4.4.42 MOVMSKPS

Instruction *MOVMSKPS (dest,src:regid);*

```
  **     P3,P4,ATHLONXP
NASM     MOVMSKPS r,XMMreg
```

Move Packed Single-Precision Mask Bits to Integer. Source is an XMM register; destination a general register. The bottom 4 bits of the general register are set to the signbits of the 32-bit integers in the XMM register.

var
  $i : 0..3;$
$general_{dest} \leftarrow 0;$
with $XMMreg_{src}$ **do**
  for $i \leftarrow 3$ **downto** 0 **do**
    if $c_i < 0$ **then**
      $general_{dest} \leftarrow general_{dest} + 2^i;$

4.4.43 MOVNTPS

Instruction *MOVNTPS (d:regid;var dest:XMM);*

```
  **     P3,P4,ATHLONXP
NASM     MOVNTPS mem128,XMMreg
```

Packed Single-FP Aligned Store without cache pollution. Source is an XMM register; destination is a 16-byte aligned memory location. The register is stored in memory directly without going into the cache.

$dest \leftarrow XMMreg_d;$

4.4.44 MOVNTQ

Instruction *MOVNTQ (s:regid;var dest:MMX);*

```
  **     P3,P4,ATHLONXP
NASM     MOVNTQ mem64,MMXreg
```

Quadword Store without cache pollution. Source is an MMX register; destination is a memory location. The register is stored in memory directly without going into the cache. No alignment restrictions are imposed on this instruction.

$dest \leftarrow MMXreg_s;$

4.4.45 MOVQ_load

Instruction *MOVQ_load* (*dest:regid;src:MMX*);

```
***    Pentium with MMX,K6,P3,P4,ATHLONXP
NASM   MOVQ MMXreg,r/m64
```

Move Quadword to MMX Register. Destination is an MMX register; source is either another MMX register or a memory location. This shares an assembler mnemonic with MOVQ_store.

$MMXreg_{dest} \leftarrow src$;

4.4.46 MOVQ_store

Instruction *MOVQ_store* (**var** *dest:MMX;src:regid*);

```
***    Pentium with MMX,K6,P3,P4,ATHLONXP
NASM   MOVQ r/m64,MMXreg
```

Move Quadword to MMX Register. Source is an MMX register; destination is either another MMX register or a memory location. This shares an assembler mnemonic with MOVQ_load.

$dest \leftarrow MMXreg_{src}$;

4.4.47 MOVSS_load

Instruction *MOVSS_load* (*dest:regid;src:ieee32*);

```
**     P3,P4,ATHLONXP
NASM   MOVSS XMMreg,r/m32
```

Move Quadword to MMX Register. Destination is the low 32-bit word of an XMM register; source is either another XMM register or a memory location. This shares an assembler mnemonic with MOVSS_store.

$XMMreg_{dest}.a_0 \leftarrow src$;

4.4.48 MOVSS_store

Instruction *MOVSS_store* (**var** *dest:ieee32;src:regid*);

```
**     Pentium with MMX,K6,P3,P4,ATHLONXP
NASM   MOVSS r/m32,XMMreg
```

Move Quadword to MMX Register. Source is a the low 32 bits of an XMM register; the destination is either another XMM register or a memory location. This shares an assembler mnemonic with MOVSS_load.

$dest \leftarrow XMMreg_{src}.a_0$;

4.4.49 MOVUPS_load

Instruction *MOVUPS_load (d:regid;src:XMM)*;

```
***    P3,P4,ATHLONXP
NASM   MOVUPS XMMreg,r/m128
```

Packed Single-FP Unaligned Load. Destination is an XMM register; source is XMM register or a 16-byte memory location. This is more generally useful than MOVAPS 4.4.30 but runs significantly slower. However, for many image processing applications it is impossible to ensure that the operands are 16-byte aligned. In this case MOVUPS should be used.

The performance overhead is sufficiently great that it often pays to use the MMX registers rather than the XMM registers if unaligned loads and stores must be used, since there are no alignment restrictions on the MOVQ instruction used to load the MMX registers.

$XMMreg_d \leftarrow src$;

4.4.50 MOVUPS_store

Instruction *MOVUPS_store (d:regid;**var** dest:XMM)*;

```
***    P3,P4,ATHLONXP
NASM   MOVUPS r/m128,XMMreg
```

Packed Single-FP Unaligned Store. Source is an XMM register; destination is XMM register or a 16-byte memory location. This shares its assembler mnemonic with MOVUPS_load (see Section 4.4.49).

$dest \leftarrow XMMreg_d$;

4.4.51 MULPD

Instruction *MULPD (d:regid;src:XMM)*;

```
**     P4
NASM   MULPD XMMreg,r/m128
```

Packed Double-Precision FP Multiply. Destination is an XMM register; source is XMM register or memory location. Element by element multiplication is performed. If unaligned access is used, this instruction has no performance advantage over the use of the FPU stack.

var
  $i : 0..1$;
for $i \leftarrow 0$ **to** 1 **do**
  $XMMreg_d.b_i \leftarrow (XMMreg_d.b_i) \times src.b_i$;

4.4.52 MULPS

Instruction *MULPS (d:regid;src:XMM)*;

```
***    P3,P4,ATHLONXP
NASM   MULPS XMMreg,r/m128
```

Packed Single-FP Multiply. Destination is an XMM register; source is XMM register or memory location. Element by element multiplication is performed. It is faster than the use of the FPU stack even when unaligned accesses are used.

var
  $i : 0..3$;
for $i \leftarrow 0$ **to** 3 **do**
  $XMMreg_d.a_i \leftarrow (XMMreg_d.a_i) \times src.a_i$;

4.4.53 MULSD

Instruction *MULSD (d:regid;src:ieee64)*;

```
**      P4
NASM    MULSS XMMreg,XMMreg/mem64
```

Scalar Double-FP Multiply. Destination is low word of an XMM register; source is XMM register low word or memory location. This is a useful alternative to the use of the FPU stack for real arithmetic since it removes resource contention between the FPU stack and the MMX registers.

$XMMreg_d.b_0 \leftarrow (XMMreg_d.b_0) \times src$;

4.4.54 MULSS

Instruction *MULSS (d:regid;src:ieee32)*;

```
**      P3,P4,ATHLONXP
NASM    MULSS XMMreg,XMMreg/mem32
```

Scalar Single-FP Multiply. Destination is low word of an XMM register; source is XMM register low word or memory location.

$XMMreg_d.a_0 \leftarrow (XMMreg_d.a_0) \times src$;

4.4.55 ORPS

Instruction *ORPS (d:regid;src:XMM)*;

```
**      P4
NASM    ORPS XMMreg,r/m128
```

128-Bit Or. Destination is an XMM register; source is XMM register or memory location. It is faster to use the MMX equivalent instruction POR when unaligned accesses are used.

var
  $i : 0..3$;
for $i \leftarrow 0$ **to** 3 **do**
  $XMMreg_d.c_i \leftarrow (XMMreg_d.c_i) \vee src.c_i$;

Chapter 4 • Intel SIMD Instructions

4.4.56 PACKSSDW

Instruction *PACKSSDW (dest:regid;src:MMX);*

```
**     PentiumMMX,K6,P3,P4,ATHLONXP
NASM   PACKSSDW MMXreg,r/m64;
```

Pack double to word with saturation. This takes a pair of 64-bit operands and packs the double words in the pair into the destination. It is useful for converting a vector of integers to a vector of shorts.

var
  c : **array** [0..3] **of** *int32*;
  i : 0..3;
$c_{0..1} \leftarrow MMXreg_{dest}.b_{0..1}$;
$c_{2..3} \leftarrow src.b_{0..1}$;
for $i \leftarrow 0$ **to** 3 **do**
  if $c_i > 32767$ **then** $MMXreg_{dest}.c_i \leftarrow 32767$
  else if $c_i < -32768$ **then** $MMXreg_{dest}.c_i \leftarrow -32768$
  else $MMXreg_{dest}.c_i \leftarrow c_i$;

4.4.57 PACKSSWB

Instruction *PACKSSWB (dest:regid;src:MMX);*

```
**     PentiumMMX,K6,P3,P4,ATHLONXP
NASM   PACKSSWB MMXreg,r/m64;
```

Pack word to byte with saturation. This takes a pair of 64-bit operands and packs the words in the pair into the destination. It is useful for converting a vector of shorts to a vector of signed bytes.

var
  d : **array** [0..7] **of** *int16*;
  i : 0..7;
$d_{0..3} \leftarrow MMXreg_{dest}.c_{0..3}$;
$d_{4..7} \leftarrow src.c_{0..3}$;
for $i \leftarrow 0$ **to** 7 **do**
  if $d_i > 127$ **then** $MMXreg_{dest}.e_i \leftarrow 127$
  else if $d_i < -128$ **then** $MMXreg_{dest}.e_i \leftarrow -128$
  else $MMXreg_{dest}.e_i \leftarrow d_i$;

4.4.58 PACKUSWB

Instruction *PACKUSWB (dest:regid;src:MMX);*

```
**     PentiumMMX,K6,P3,P4,ATHLONXP
NASM   PACKUSWB MMXreg,r/m64;
```

Pack word to unsigned byte with saturation. This takes a pair of 64-bit operands and packs the words in the pair into the destination. It is useful for converting a vector of shorts to a vector of unsigned bytes.

var
   d : **array** [0..7] **of** *int16*;
   i : 0..7;
$d_{0..3} \leftarrow MMXreg_{dest}.c_{0..3}$;
$d_{4..7} \leftarrow src.c_{0..3}$;
for $i \leftarrow$ 0 **to** 7 **do**
   if $d_i > 255$ **then** $MMXreg_{dest}.f_i \leftarrow 255$
   else if $d_i < 0$ **then** $MMXreg_{dest}.f_i \leftarrow 0$
   else $MMXreg_{dest}.f_i \leftarrow d_i$;

4.4.59 PADDB

Instruction *PADDB (dest:regid;src:MMX)*;

```
***     PentiumMMX,K6,P3,P4,ATHLONXP
NASM    PADDB MMXreg,r/m64;
```

Packed byte addition in MMX registers. Performs parallel element by element addition of all of the bytes in the source and destination. Source can be in memory.

var
   i : 0..7;
with $MMXreg_{dest}$ **do**
   for $i \leftarrow$ 0 **to** 7 **do** $f_i \leftarrow f_i + src.f_i$;

4.4.60 PADDB_sse

Instruction *PADDB_sse (dest:regid;src:XMM)*;

```
**      P4
NASM    PADDB XMMreg,r/m128;
```

Packed byte addition in XMM registers. Performs parallel element by element addition of all of the bytes in the source and destination. Extended version for XMM registers. Memory operands must be 16-byte aligned. It is not competitive in speed with the MMX version unless aligned memory operands are used, since unaligned use requires two instructions an unaligned load followed by the arithmetic operation.

var
   i : 0..15;
with $XMMreg_{dest}$ **do**
   for $i \leftarrow$ 0 **to** 15 **do** $f_i \leftarrow f_i + src.f_i$;

4.4.61 PADDW

Instruction *PADDW (dest:regid;src:MMX)*;

```
***     PentiumMMX,K6,P3,P4,ATHLONXP
NASM    PADDW MMXreg,r/m64;
```

Packed word addition in MMX registers. Performs parallel element by element addition of all of the words in the source and destination.

var
  $i : 0..3$;
with *MMXreg$_{dest}$* **do**
  for $i \leftarrow 0$ **to** 3 **do** $c_i \leftarrow c_i + src.c_i$;

4.4.62 PADDW_sse

Instruction *PADDW_ sse (dest:regid;src:XMM)*;

```
**      P4
NASM    PADDW XMMreg,r/m128;
```

Packed word addition in XMM registers. Performs parallel element by element addition of all of the words in the source and destination. Extended version for XMM registers. Memory operands must be 16-byte aligned. It is not competitive in speed with the MMX version unless aligned memory operands are used, since unaligned use requires two instructions an unaligned load followed by the arithmetic operation.

var
  $i : 0..7$;
with *XMMreg$_{dest}$* **do**
  for $i \leftarrow 0$ **to** 7 **do** $d_i \leftarrow d_i + src.d_i$;

4.4.63 PADDD

Instruction *PADDD (dest:regid;src:MMX)*;

```
***     PentiumMMX,K6,P3,P4,ATHLONXP
NASM    PADDD MMXreg,r/m64;
```

Packed doubleword addition in MMX registers. Performs parallel element by element addition of all of the 32-bit integers in the source and destination.

var
  $i : 0..3$;
begin
with *MMXreg$_{dest}$* **do**
  begin
    $b_0 \leftarrow b_0 + src.b_0$;
    $b_1 \leftarrow b_1 + src.b_1$;
  end;

4.4.64 PADDD_sse

Instruction *PADDD_sse (dest:regid;src:XMM)*;

```
**      P4
NASM    PADDD XMMreg,r/m128;
```

Packed double word addition in XMM registers. Performs parallel element by element addition of all of the 32-bit integers in the source and destination. Extended version for XMM registers. Memory operands must be 16-byte aligned. It is not competitive in speed with the MMX version unless aligned memory operands are used, since unaligned use requires two instructions an unaligned load followed by the arithmetic operation.

var
  $i : 0..3;$
with $XMMreg_{dest}$ **do**
  for $i \leftarrow$ 0 **to** 15 **do** $c_i \leftarrow c_i + src.c_i;$

4.4.65 PADDQ

Instruction *PADDQ (dest:regid;src:MMX);*

```
***    PentiumMMX,K6,P3,P4,ATHLONXP
NASM   PADDQ MMXreg,r/m64;
```

Quadword addition in MMX registers. Performs addition of the 64-bit integers in the source and destination. The EFLAGS are not set on overflow.

var
  $i : 0..3;$
with $MMXreg_{dest}$ **do** $a \leftarrow a + src.a;$

4.4.66 PADDQ_sse

Instruction *PADDQ_sse (dest:regid;src:XMM);*

```
**     P4
NASM   PADDQ XMMreg,r/m128;
```

Packed quadword addition in XMM registers. Performs parallel element by element addition of all of the 64-bit integers in the source and destination. Extended version for XMM registers. Memory operands must be 16-byte aligned. It is not competitive in speed with the MMX version unless aligned memory operands are used, since unaligned use requires two instructions an unaligned load followed by the arithmetic operation.

var
  $i : 0..1;$
with $XMMreg_{dest}$ **do**
  for $i \leftarrow$ 0 **to** 1 **do** $h_i \leftarrow h_i + src.h_i;$

4.4.67 PADDSB

Instruction *PADDSB (dest:regid;src:MMX);*

```
***    PentiumMMX,K6,P3,P4,ATHLONXP
NASM   PADDSB MMXreg,r/m64;
```

Packed byte addition in MMX registers with saturation. Performs parallel element by element addition of all of the bytes in the source and destination. Source can be in memory.

var
  $i : 0..7$;
with $MMXreg_{dest}$ **do**
  for $i \leftarrow 0$ **to** 7 **do**
    $e_i \leftarrow saturate\ ((e_i + src.e_i), -128, 127)$;

4.4.68 PADDSB_sse

Instruction *PADDSB_sse (dest:regid;src:XMM)*;

```
**      P4
NASM    PADDSB XMMreg,r/m128;
```

Packed saturated signed byte addition in XMM registers. Performs parallel element by element addition of all of the bytes in the source and destination. Extended version for XMM registers. Memory operands must be 16-byte aligned. It is not competitive in speed with the MMX version unless aligned memory operands are used, since unaligned use requires two instructions an unaligned load followed by the arithmetic operation.

var
  $i : 0..15$;
with $XMMreg_{dest}$ **do**
  for $i \leftarrow 0$ **to** 15 **do**
    $f_i \leftarrow saturate\ (f_i + src.f_i, -128, 127)$;

4.4.69 PADDUSB

Instruction *PADDUSB (dest:regid;src:MMX)*;

```
***     PentiumMMX,K6,P3,P4,ATHLONXP
NASM    PADDUSB MMXreg,r/m64;
```

Packed byte addition in MMX registers with unsigned saturation. Performs parallel element by element addition of all of the bytes in the source and destination. Source can be in memory.

var
  $i : 0..7$;
with $MMXreg_{dest}$ **do**
  for $i \leftarrow 0$ **to** 7 **do**
    $f_i \leftarrow saturate\ ((f_i + src.f_i), 0, 255)$;

4.4.70 PADDUSB_sse

Instruction *PADDUSB_sse (dest:regid;src:XMM);*

```
**      P4
NASM    PADDUSB XMMreg,r/m128;
```

Packed saturated unsigned byte addition in XMM registers. Performs parallel element by element addition of all of the bytes in the source and destination. Extended version for XMM registers. Memory operands must be 16-byte aligned. It is not competitive in speed with the MMX version unless aligned memory operands are used, since unaligned use requires two instructions an unaligned load followed by the arithmetic operation.

var
  $i : 0..15;$
with $XMMreg_{dest}$ **do**
  for $i \leftarrow 0$ **to** 15 **do**
    $g_i \leftarrow saturate\ (g_i + src.g_i,\ 0,\ 255);$

4.4.71 PAND

Instruction *PAND (dest:regid;src:MMX);*

```
***     PentiumMMX,K6,P3,P4,ATHLONXP
NASM    PAND MMXreg,r/m64;
```

Quadword and in MMX registers. Performs and of the 64-bit integers in the source and destination.

var
  $i : 0..3;$
with $MMXreg_{dest}$ **do**
  for $i \leftarrow 0$ **to** 3 **do**
    $d_i \leftarrow d_i \wedge src.d_i;$

4.4.72 PAND_sse

Instruction *PAND_sse (dest:regid;src:XMM);*

```
**      P4
NASM    PAND XMMreg,r/m128;
```

Packed quadword and in XMM registers. Performs parallel and of all of the bits in the source and destination. Extended version for XMM registers. Memory operands must be 16-byte aligned. It is not competitive in speed with the MMX version unless aligned memory operands are used, since unaligned use requires two instructions an unaligned load followed by the arithmetic operation.

var
  $i : 0..3$;
with $XMMreg_{dest}$ **do**
  for $i \leftarrow 0$ **to** 3 **do**
    $c_i \leftarrow c_i \wedge src.c_i$;

4.4.73 PANDN

Instruction *PANDN (dest:regid;src:MMX)*;

```
***    PentiumMMX,K6,P3,P4,ATHLONXP
NASM   PANDN MMXreg,r/m64;
```

Quadword and in MMX registers. Performs and of the bits in the source and the negated destination.

var
  $i : 0..1$;
for $i \leftarrow 0$ **to** 1 **do**
  with $MMXreg_{dest}$ **do** $b \leftarrow$ (**not** b) **and** $src.b$;

4.4.74 PANDN_sse

Instruction *PANDN_sse (dest:regid;src:XMM)*;

```
**     P4
NASM   PANDN XMMreg,r/m128;
```

Packed quadword and in XMM registers. Performs parallel element by element and of all of the bits in the source and the negated destination. Extended version for XMM registers. Memory operands must be 16-byte aligned. It is not competitive in speed with the MMX version unless aligned memory operands are used, since unaligned use requires two instructions an unaligned load followed by the arithmetic operation.

var
  $i : 0..3$;
with $XMMreg_{dest}$ **do**
  for $i \leftarrow 0$ **to** 3 **do** $c_i \leftarrow$ (**not** c_i) **and** $src.c_i$;

4.4.75 PAVGB

Instruction *PAVGB (dest:regid;src:MMX)*;

```
***    PentiumMMX,K6,P3,P4,ATHLONXP
NASM   PAVGB MMXreg,r/m64;
```

Packed byte unsigned average. Performs parallel element by element average of all of the pairs of bytes in the source and destination. Source can be in memory.

var
  $i : 0..7;$
with *MMXreg$_{dest}$* **do**
  for $i \leftarrow 0$ **to** 7 **do**
    $f_i \leftarrow (f_i + src.f_i);$

4.4.76 PAVGB_sse

Instruction *PAVGB_sse (dest:regid;src:XMM);*

```
**      P4
NASM    PAVGB XMMreg,r/m128;
```

Packed unsigned byte average in XMM registers. Performs parallel element by element average of all of the pairs of bytes in the source and destination. Extended version for XMM registers. Memory operands must be 16-byte aligned.

var
  $i : 0..15;$
with *XMMreg$_{dest}$* **do**
  for $i \leftarrow 0$ **to** 15 **do**
    $g_i \leftarrow \frac{g_i + src.g_i}{2};$

4.4.77 PAVGW

Instruction *PAVGW (dest:regid;src:MMX);*

```
***     PentiumMMX,K6,P3,P4,ATHLONXP
NASM    PAVGW MMXreg,r/m64;
```

Packed word unsigned average. Performs parallel element by element average of all of the pairs of words in the source and destination. Source can be in memory.

var
  $i : 0..3;$
with *MMXreg$_{dest}$* **do**
  for $i \leftarrow 0$ **to** 3 **do**
    $d_i \leftarrow \frac{d_i + src.d_i}{2};$

4.4.78 PAVGW_sse

Instruction *PAVGW_sse (dest:regid;src:XMM);*

```
**      P4
NASM    PAVGb XMMreg,r/m128;
```

Packed unsigned word average in XMM registers. Performs parallel element by element addition of all of the pairs of words in the source and destination. Extended version for XMM registers. Memory operands must be 16-byte aligned.

var
  $i : 0..7;$
with *XMMreg$_{dest}$* **do**
  for $i \leftarrow 0$ **to** 15 **do**
    $e_i \leftarrow \frac{e_i + src.e_i}{2};$

4.4.79 PCMPEQB

Instruction *PCMPEQB (dest:regid;src:MMX);*

    ***   PentiumMMX,K6,P3,P4,ATHLONXP
    NASM   PCMPEQB MMXreg,r/m64;

Packed byte comparison. Performs parallel element by element comparison of all of the pairs of bytes in the source and destination. Generates a vector of mask bytes with 0ff indicating true. Source can be in memory.

var
  $i : 0..7;$
with *MMXreg$_{dest}$* **do**
  for $i \leftarrow 0$ **to** 7 **do**
    $f_i \leftarrow \begin{cases} 255 & \text{if } (f_i = src.f_i) \\ 0 & \text{otherwise} \end{cases};$

4.4.80 PCMPEQB_sse

Instruction *PCMPEQB_sse (dest:regid;src:XMM);*

    **   P4
    NASM   PCMPEQB XMMreg,r/m128;

Packed byte comparison. Performs parallel element by element comparison of all of the pairs of bytes in the source and destination. Generates a vector of mask bytes with 0ff indicating true. Source can be in memory, but if so must be 16-byte aligned.

var
  $i : 0..15;$
with *XMMreg$_{dest}$* **do**
  for $i \leftarrow 0$ **to** 15 **do**
    $g_i \leftarrow \begin{cases} 255 & \text{if } (g_i = src.g_i) \\ 0 & \text{otherwise} \end{cases};$

4.4.81 PCMPEQW

Instruction *PCMPEQW (dest:regid;src:MMX);*

    ***   PentiumMMX,K6,P3,P4,ATHLONXP
    NASM   PCMPEQW MMXreg,r/m64;

Packed word comparison. Performs parallel element by element comparison of all of the pairs of bytes in the source and destination. Generates a vector of mask words with 0ffff indicating true. Source can be in memory.

var
    $i : 0..3;$
with *MMXreg$_{dest}$* **do**
    for $i \leftarrow 0$ **to** 3 **do**
        $c_i \leftarrow \begin{cases} -1 & \text{if } (c_i = src.c_i) \\ 0 & \text{otherwise} \end{cases};$

4.4.82 PCMPEQW_sse

Instruction *PCMPEQW_sse (dest:regid;src:XMM);*

```
**      P4
NASM    PCMPEQW XMMreg,r/m128;
```

Packed word comparison. Performs parallel element by element comparison of all of the pairs of words in the source and destination. Generates a vector of mask words with 0ffff indicating true. Source can be in memory, but if so must be 16-byte aligned.

var
    $i : 0..7;$
with *XMMreg$_{dest}$* **do**
    for $i \leftarrow 0$ **to** 7 **do**
        $d_i \leftarrow \begin{cases} -1 & \text{if } (d_i = src.d_i) \\ 0 & \text{otherwise} \end{cases};$

4.4.83 PCMPEQD

Instruction *PCMPEQD (dest:regid;src:MMX);*

```
***     PentiumMMX,K6,P3,P4,ATHLONXP
NASM    PCMPEQD MMXreg,r/m64;
```

Packed doubleword comparison. Performs parallel element by element comparison of all of the pairs of 32-bit words in the source and destination. Generates a vector of mask words with 0ffffffff indicating true. Source can be in memory.

var
    $i : 0..1;$
with *MMXreg$_{dest}$* **do**
    for $i \leftarrow 0$ **to** 1 **do**
        $b_i \leftarrow \begin{cases} -1 & \text{if } (b_i = src.b_i) \\ 0 & \text{otherwise;} \end{cases}$

4.4.84 PCMPEQD_sse

Instruction *PCMPEQD_sse (dest:regid;src:XMM);*

```
**      P4
NASM    PCMPEQD XMMreg,r/m128;
```

Packed doubleword comparison. Performs parallel element by element comparison of all of the pairs of 32-bit words in the source and destination. Generates a vector of mask words with 0ffffffff indicating true. Source can be in memory, but if so must be 16-byte aligned.

var
  $i : 0..3;$
with *XMMreg$_{dest}$* **do**
  for $i \leftarrow 0$ **to** 3 **do**
    $c_i \leftarrow \begin{cases} -1 & \text{if } (c_i = src.c_i) \\ 0 & \text{otherwise} \end{cases};$

4.4.85 PCMPGTB

Instruction *PCMPGTB (dest:regid;src:MMX);*

```
***     PentiumMMX,K6,P3,P4,ATHLONXP
NASM    PCMPGTB MMXreg,r/m64;
```

Packed byte comparison. Performs parallel element by element comparison of all of the pairs of bytes in the source and destination. Generates a vector of mask bytes with 0ff indicating true. Source can be in memory.

var
  $i : 0..7;$
with *MMXreg$_{dest}$* **do**
  for $i \leftarrow 0$ **to** 7 **do**
    $f_i \leftarrow \begin{cases} 255 & \text{if } (f_i > src.f_i) \\ 0 & \text{otherwise} \end{cases};$

4.4.86 PCMPGTB_sse

Instruction *PCMPGTB_sse (dest:regid;src:XMM);*

```
**      P4
NASM    PCMPGTB XMMreg,r/m128;
```

Packed byte comparison. Performs parallel element by element comparison of all of the pairs of bytes in the source and destination. Generates a vector of mask bytes with 0ff indicating true. Source can be in memory, but if so must be 16-byte aligned.

var
 $i : 0..15;$
with *XMMreg$_{dest}$* **do**
  for $i \leftarrow$ 0 **to** 15 **do**
   $g_i \leftarrow \begin{cases} 255 & \text{if } (g_i > src.g_i) \\ 0 & \text{otherwise} \end{cases};$

4.4.87 PCMPGTW

Instruction *PCMPGTW (dest:regid;src:MMX);*

```
***   PentiumMMX,K6,P3,P4,ATHLONXP
NASM  PCMPGTW MMXreg,r/m64;
```

Packed word comparison. Performs parallel element by element comparison of all of the pairs of bytes in the source and destination. Generates a vector of mask words with 0ffff indicating true. Source can be in memory.

var
 $i : 0..3;$
with *MMXreg$_{dest}$* **do**
  for $i \leftarrow$ 0 **to** 3 **do**
   $c_i \leftarrow \begin{cases} -1 & \text{if } (c_i > src.c_i) \\ 0 & \text{otherwise} \end{cases};$

4.4.88 PCMPGTW_sse

Instruction *PCMPGTW_sse (dest:regid;src:XMM);*

```
**    P4
NASM  PCMPGTW XMMreg,r/m128;
```

Packed word comparison. Performs parallel element by element comparison of all of the pairs of words in the source and destination. Generates a vector of mask words with 0ffff indicating true. Source can be in memory, but if so must be 16-byte aligned.

var
 $i : 0..7;$
with *XMMreg$_{dest}$* **do**
  for $i \leftarrow$ 0 **to** 7 **do**
   $d_i \leftarrow \begin{cases} -1 & \text{if } (d_i > src.d_i) \\ 0 & \text{otherwise} \end{cases};$

4.4.89 PCMPGTD

Instruction *PCMPGTD (dest:regid;src:MMX);*

```
***   PentiumMMX,K6,P3,P4,ATHLONXP
NASM  PCMPGTD MMXreg,r/m64;
```

Packed doubleword comparison. Performs parallel element by element comparison of all of the pairs of 32-bit words in the source and destination. Generates a vector of mask words with 0fffffff indicating true. Source can be in memory.

var
  $i : 0..1$;
with *MMXreg$_{dest}$* **do**
  for $i \leftarrow 0$ **to** 1 **do**
    $b_i \leftarrow \begin{cases} -1 & \text{if } (b_i > src.b_i) \\ 0 & \text{otherwise} \end{cases}$;

4.4.90 PCMPGTD_sse

Instruction *PCMPGTD_ sse (dest:regid;src:XMM)*;

```
**      P4
NASM    PCMPGTD XMMreg,r/m128;
```

Packed doubleword comparison. Performs parallel element by element comparison of all of the pairs of 32-bit words in the source and destination. Generates a vector of mask words with 0fffffff indicating true. Source can be in memory, but if so must be 16-byte aligned.

var
  $i : 0..3$;
with *XMMreg$_{dest}$* **do**
  for $i \leftarrow 0$ **to** 3 **do**
    $c_i \leftarrow \begin{cases} -1 & \text{if } (c_i = src.c_i) \\ 0 & \text{otherwise} \end{cases}$;

4.4.91 PEXTRW

Instruction *PEXTRW (r,m:regid;wordno:0..3)*;

```
**      P4
NASM    PEXTRW reg32,MMXreg,imm8;
```

Extract word from MMX register. The word in the MMX register m selected by wordno is copied to the general register r.

general$_r$ $\leftarrow$ MMXreg$_m$.d$_{wordno}$;

4.4.92 PEXTRW_sse

Instruction *PEXTRW_sse (r,x:regid;wordno:0..7)*;

```
**      P4
NASM    PEXTRW reg32,XMMreg,imm8;
```
Extract word from MMX register. The word in the XMM register x selected by wordno is copied to the general register r.

general$_r$ $\leftarrow$ XMMreg$_x$.e$_{wordno}$;

4.4.93 PINSRW

Instruction *PINSRW (r,x:regid;wordno:uint8);*

```
**      P4
NASM    PINSRW MMXreg,r/m16,imm8;
```
Insert word in MMX register. Copies bottom 16 bits of a general register into word of MMX register.

$MMXreg_x.e_{wordno} \leftarrow general_r;$

4.4.94 PMADDWD

Instruction *PMADDWD (dest:regid;src:MMX);*

```
**      Pentium MMX,K6,P3,P4,ATHLONXP
NASM    PMADDWD MMXreg,r/m64;
```

Packed Multiply accumulate. Used for computing inner product of two vectors of int16s. An example is given in Alg. 16. On entry we assume that two arrays x,y each contain $4n$ words, and that ecx is initialised to n. At exit the inner product is held in the bottom 32 bits of mm0.

```
lea esi,[x-8]
lea edi,[y-8]
pxor mm2,mm2              ; clear register
l1:movq mm0,[esi+ecx*8]   ; get first 4 ints from array x
pmaddwd mm0,[edi+ecx*8];
paddd mm2,mm0
loop l1                   ; loop for all sub vectors
movq mm0,mm2              ; copy subtotal
psrlq mm0,32              ; shift down high word
padd mm0,mm2              ; add high and low words
```
Algorithm 16. Inner product in assembler

var
  temp:mmx;
  i;
for $i \leftarrow 0$ **to** 1 **do**
begin
  $j \leftarrow 2 \times i;$
  $temp.b_i \leftarrow MMXreg_{dest}.c_j \times src.c_j + MMXreg_{dest}.c_{j+1} \times src.c_{j+1};$
end;
$MMXreg_{dest} \leftarrow temp;$

4.4.95 PMAXSW

Instruction *PMAXSW (d:regid;src:MMX);*

```
***     P4
NASM    PMAXSW MMXreg,r/m64
```

Packed 16-bit signed integer Maximum. Destination is an MMX register; source is MMX register or memory location. Element by element comparison is performed.

var
  i : 0..3;
with *MMXreg$_d$* **do**
  for $i \leftarrow$ 0 **to** 3 **do**
  if $c_i <$ *src.c$_i$* **then**
  $c_i \leftarrow$ *src.c$_i$*;

4.4.96 PMAXUB

Instruction *PMAXUB (d:regid;src:MMX)*;

```
***     P4
NASM    PMAXUB MMXreg,r/m64
```

Packed Unsigned Byte Maximum. Destination is an MMX register; source is MMX register or memory location. Element by element comparison is performed.

var
  i : 0..7;
with *MMXreg$_d$* **do**
  for $i \leftarrow$ 0 **to** 7 **do**
    if $f_i <$ *src.f$_i$* **then**
      $f_i \leftarrow$ *src.f$_i$*;

4.4.97 PMINSW

Instruction *PMINSW (d:regid;src:MMX)*;

```
***     P4
NASM    PMINSW MMXreg,r/m64
```

Packed 16-bit signed integer Minimum. Destination is an MMX register; source is MMX register or memory location. Element by element comparison is performed.

var
  i : 0..3;
with *MMXreg$_d$* **do**
  for $i \leftarrow$ 0 **to** 3 **do**
    if $c_i >$ *src.c$_i$* **then**
      $c_i \leftarrow$ *src.c$_i$*;

4.4.98 PMINUB

Instruction *PMINUB (d:regid;src:MMX);*

```
***     P4
NASM    PMINUB MMXreg,r/m64
```

Packed Unsigned Byte Minimum. Destination is an MMX register; source is MMX register or memory location. Element by element comparison is performed.

var
  $i : 0..7;$
with *MMXreg$_d$* **do**
  for $i \leftarrow 0$ **to** 7 **do**
    if $f_i > src.f_i$ **then**
      $f_i \leftarrow src.f_i;$

4.4.99 PMOVMSKB

Instruction *PMOVMSKB (d,m:regid);*

```
*       P4
NASM    PMOVMSKB reg32,MMXreg
```

Move Byte Mask to Integer Register. Source is an MMX register; destination a general register.

The sign bits of the bytes are put into a mask byte stored in a general register.

var
  $i : 0..7;$
  t:integer;
$t \leftarrow 0;$
with *MMXreg$_m$* **do**
  for $i \leftarrow 7$ **downto** 0 **do**
  begin
    if $e_i < 0$ **then**
      $t \leftarrow t + 1;$
    $t \leftarrow t \times 2;$
  end;
  general$_d$ $\leftarrow t;$

4.4.100 PMULHUW

Instruction *PMULHUW (dest:regid;src:MMX);*

```
**      P4
NASM    PMULHUW MMXreg,r/m64
```

Packed Multiply High Unsigned Word. Destination is an MMX register; source is MMX register or memory location. Element by element multiplication is performed and the top 16 bits of the results are retained.

var
  $i : 0..3$;
  t:integer;
with *MMXreg$_{dest}$* **do**
  for $i \leftarrow 0$ **to** 3 **do**
  begin
    $t \leftarrow d_i \times src.d_i$;
    $d_i \leftarrow t\ 16$;
  end;

4.4.101 PMULHW

Instruction *PMULHW (dest:regid;src:MMX)*;

```
***     PentiumMMX,K6,P3,P4,ATHLONXP
NASM    PMULHW MMXreg,r/m64
```

Packed Multiply High Signed Word. Destination is an MMX register; source is MMX register or memory location. Element by element multiplication is performed and the top 16 bits of the results are retained. This is ideal for multiplying together vectors of signed binary fractions or fixed point numbers represented as 16-bit integers.

var
  $i : 0..3$;
  t:integer;
with *MMXreg$_{dest}$* **do**
  for $i \leftarrow 0$ **to** 3 **do**
  begin
    $t \leftarrow d_i \times src.d_i$;
    $d_i \leftarrow t\ 16$;
  end;

4.4.102 PMULLW

Instruction *PMULLW (dest:regid;src:MMX)*;

```
**      PentiumMMX,K6,P3,P4,ATHLONXP
NASM    PMULLW MMXreg,r/m64
```

Packed Multiply High Signed Word. Destination is an MMX register; source is MMX register or memory location. Element by element multiplication is performed and the bottom 16 bits of the results are retained.

var
  $i : 0..3$;
  t:integer;
with *MMXreg$_{dest}$* **do**
  for $i \leftarrow 0$ **to** 3 **do**
  begin

$$t \leftarrow d_i \times src.d_i;$$
$$d_i \leftarrow t \wedge 65535;$$
end;

4.4.103 POR

Instruction *POR (dest:regid;src:MMX)*;

```
***    PentiumMMX,K6,P3,P4,ATHLONXP
NASM   POR MMXreg,r/m64;
```

Quadword OR in MMX registers. Performs OR of the 64-bit integers in the source and destination.

var
  $i : 0..3$;
with *MMXreg$_{dest}$* **do**
  for $i \leftarrow 0$ **to** 3 **do**
    $d_i \leftarrow d_i \vee src.d_i$;

4.4.104 PREFETCHNTA

Instruction *PREFETCHNTA (loc:integer)*;

```
**     P3,P4,ATHLONXP
NASM   PREFETCHNTA mem
```

Loads a cache line into the level 1 data cache. This is equivalent to the PREFETCH instruction used by AMD.

$level1_{bank,\ (loc\ 6) \wedge 31, 0..61} \leftarrow mem.bytemem_{loc..loc+63}$;
$bank \leftarrow (bank + 1) \bmod 4$;

4.4.105 PREFETCHT1

Instruction *PREFETCHT1 (loc:integer)*;

```
**     P3,P4,ATHLONXP
NASM   PREFETCHT1 mem
```

Loads a cache line into the level 2 data cache. It leaves level 1 unchanged.

$level2_{bank,\ (loc \div 64) \wedge 511, 0..61} \leftarrow mem.bytemem_{loc..loc+63}$;
$bank \leftarrow (bank + 1) \bmod 4$;

4.4.106 PREFETCHT0

Instruction *PREFETCHT0 (loc:integer)*;

```
**     P3,P4,ATHLONXP
NASM   PREFETCHT0 mem
```

Loads a cache line into the level 1 and level 2 data cache.

$level1_{bank,\ (loc \div 64) \wedge 31, 0..61} \leftarrow mem.bytemem_{loc..loc+63}$;
$level2_{bank,\ (loc \div 64) \wedge 511, 0..61} \leftarrow mem.bytemem_{loc..loc+63}$;
$bank \leftarrow (bank + 1)\ \textbf{mod}\ 4$;

4.4.107 PSADBW

Instruction *PSADBW (dest:regid;src:MMX)*;

```
**      P4
NASM    PSADBW MMXreg,r/m64;
```

Computes the sum of the absolute differences of the signed bytes in the destination register and those in the source operand. It then places this sum in the lowest word of the destination register and sets the three other words to zero.

begin
with *MMXreg*$_{dest}$ **do**
    begin
        $c_0 \leftarrow \sum \textbf{abs}(f_{i_0} - src.f_{i_0})$;
        $c_{1..3} \leftarrow 0$;
    end;
end;

4.4.108 PSHUFD

Instruction *PSHUFD (dest:regid;src:XMM;imm8:uint8)*;

```
**      P4
NASM    PSHUFD XMMreg,r/m128,imm8;
```

Performs a permutation of the 32-bit source words using the four 2-bit integer fields in the 8-bit immediate operand.

var
    p : **array** [0..3] **of** 0..3;
    i : 0..3;
$p_0 \leftarrow imm8\ \textbf{mod}\ 4$;
$p_1 \leftarrow (\frac{imm8}{4})\ \textbf{mod}\ 4$;
$p_2 \leftarrow (\frac{imm8}{16})\ \textbf{mod}\ 4$;
$p_3 \leftarrow (\frac{imm8}{64})\ \textbf{mod}\ 4$;
with *XMMreg*$_{dest}$ **do**
    for $i \leftarrow 0$ **to** 3 **do**
        $a_i \leftarrow src.a_{p_i}$;

4.4.109 PSHUFW

Instruction *PSHUFW (dest:regid;src:MMX;imm8:uint8)*;

```
**      P4
NASM    PSHUFW MMXreg,r/m64,imm8;
```

Performs a Permutation of the 16-bit source words using the four 2-bit integer fields in the 8-bit immediate operand.

var
  p: **array** [0..3] **of** 0..3;
  i : 0..3;
$p_0 \leftarrow$ imm8 **mod** 4;
$p_1 \leftarrow \left(\frac{imm8}{4}\right)$ **mod** 4;
$p_2 \leftarrow \left(\frac{imm8}{16}\right)$ **mod** 4;
$p_3 \leftarrow \left(\frac{imm8}{64}\right)$ **mod** 4;
with $MMXreg_{dest}$ **do**
  for $i \leftarrow$ 0 **to** 3 **do**
    $c_i \leftarrow src.c_{p_i}$;

4.4.110 PSxxf

Instruction *PSxxf (dest:regid;count:uint8;xx:shifts;f:formats);*

```
**      PentiumMMX,K6,P3,P4,ATHLONXP
NASM    PSLLW MMXreg,r/m64;
        PSLLW MMXreg,imm8;
        PSLLD MMXreg,r/m64;
        PSLLD MMXreg,imm8;
        PSLLQ MMXreg,r/m64;
        PSLLQ MMXreg,imm8;
        PSRAW MMXreg,r/m64;
        PSRAW MMXreg,imm8;
        PSRAD MMXreg,r/m64;
        PSRAD MMXreg,imm8;
        PSRLW MMXreg,r/m64;
        PSRLW MMXreg,imm8;
        PSRLD MMXreg,r/m64;
        PSRLD MMXreg,imm8;
        PSRLQ MMXreg,r/m64;
```

Packed shift instructions. The LL instructions shift left logically, the RL right logically shifting in 0. The RA shift right arithmetically, propagating the sign bit. The count can either be in an MMX register, in memory or in an immediate field.

var
  i:integer;
if $f = q$ **then**
  with $MMXreg_{dest}$
  do
    case xx **of**
      LL: $a \leftarrow a \times 2^{count}$;
      RA: $a \leftarrow \frac{a}{2^{count}}$;
      RL: $a \leftarrow shrl(a, count, 64)$;

```
            end
          else
            if f = d then
              with MMXreg_dest do
                for i ← 0 to 1 do
                  case xx of
                    LL: b_i ← b_i × 2^count;
                    RA: b_i ← b_i / 2^count;
                    RL: b_i ← shrl (b_i, count, 32);
                  end
                else
                  with MMXreg_dest do
                    for i ← 0 to 3 do
                      case xx of
                        LL: c_i ← c_i × 2^count;
                        RA : c_i ← c_i / 2^count;
                        RL: c_i ← shrl (c_i, count, 16);
                      end;
```

4.4.111 PSUBx

Instruction *PSUBx (dest:regid;src:MMX;x:formats);*

```
***     Pentium MMX,K6,P3,P4,ATHLONXP
NASM    PSUBW MMXreg,r/m64;
        PSUBD MMXreg,r/m64;
        PSUBW MMXreg,r/m64;
```

Perform signed unsaturated subtraction on two MMX register sized vectors.

var
  i:integer;
case *x* **of**
  b: **for** $i \leftarrow 0$
    $MMXreg_{dest}.e_i \leftarrow MMXreg_{test}.e_i - src.e_i$;
  w: **for** $i \leftarrow 0$
    $MMXreg_{dest}.c_i \leftarrow MMXreg_{dest}.c_i - src.c_i$;
  d: **for** $i \leftarrow 0$
    $MMXreg_{dest}.b_i \leftarrow MMXreg_{dest}.b_i - src.b_i$;
  end;

4.4.112 PSUBSx

Instruction *PSUBSx (dest:regid;src:MMX;x:formats);*

```
**           Pentium MMX,K6,P3,P4,ATHLONXP
Nasm Syntax  PSUBSB MMXreg,r/m64;
             PSUBSW MMXreg,r/m64;
```

Perform signed saturated subtraction on two MMX register sized vectors.

var
  i:integer;
case *x* **of**
  b: **for** $i \leftarrow 0$
    $MMXreg_{dest}.e_i \leftarrow saturate\ (MMXreg_{dest}.e_i - src.e_i, -128, 127);$
  w: **for** $i \leftarrow 0$
    $MMXreg_{dest}.c_i \leftarrow saturate(MMXreg_{dest}.c_i - src.c_i, -32768, 32767);$
end;

4.4.113 PSUBUSx

Instruction *PSUBUSx (dest:regid;src:MMX;x:formats);*

```
**      PentiumMMX,K6,P3,P4,ATHLONXP
NASM    PSUBUSB MMXreg,r/m64;
        PSUBUSW MMXreg,r/m64;
```

Perform unsigned saturated subtraction on two MMX register sized vectors.

var
  i:integer;
case *x* **of**
  b: **for** $i \leftarrow 0$
    $MMXreg_{dest}.f_i \leftarrow saturate(MMXreg_{dest}.f_i - src.f_i, 0, 255);$
  w: **for** $i \leftarrow 0$
    $MMXreg_{dest}.d_i \leftarrow saturate(MMXreg_{dest}.d_i - src.d_i, 0, 65535);$
end;

4.4.114 PSWAPD

Instruction *PSWAPD (dest:regid;src:MMX);*

```
**      PentiumMMX,K6,P3,P4,ATHLONXP
NASM    PSWAPD MMXreg,r/m64;
```

Packed Swap Doubleword. Copies the source operand to the destination register, swapping the upper and lower halves in the process.

$MMXreg_{dest}.b_0 \leftarrow src.b_1;$
$MMXreg_{dest}.b_1 \leftarrow src.b_0;$

4.4.115 PUNPCKHBW

Instruction *PUNPCKHBW (dest:regid;src:MMX);*

```
**      PentiumMMX,K6,P3,P4,ATHLONXP
NASM    PUNPCKHBW MMXreg,r/m64;
```

Packed interleave high bytes. Top 4 bytes from each operand are interleaved. If the first operand held `0x7A6A5A4A3A2A1A0A` and the second held `0x7B6B5B4B3B2B1B0B`, then `PUNPCKHBW` would return `0x7B7A6B6A5-B5A4B4A`.

var
   t:MMX;
   i:integer;
for *i* ← 0 **to** 3 **do**
begin
   $t.e_{i \times 2}$ ← $src.e_{i+4}$;
   $t.e_{i \times 2+1}$ ← $MMXreg_{dest}.e_{i+4}$;
end;
$MMXreg_{dest}$ ← *t*;

4.4.116 PUNPCKLBW

Instruction *PUNPCKLBW (dest:regid;src:MMX);*

```
**      PentiumMMX,K6,P3,P4,ATHLONXP
NASM    PUNPCKLBW MMXreg,r/m64;
```

Packed interleave low bytes. Bottom 4 bytes of each operand are interleaved.

var
   t:MMX;
   i:integer;
for *i* ← 0 **to** 3 **do**
begin
   $t.e_{i \times 2}$ ← $src.e_i$;
   $t.e_{i \times 2+1}$ ← $MMXreg_{dest}.e_i$;
end;
$MMXreg_{dest}$ ← *t*;

4.4.117 PUNPCKHWD

Instruction *PUNPCKHWD (dest:regid;src:MMX);*

```
**      PentiumMMX,K6,P3,P4,ATHLONXP
NASM    PUNPCKHWD MMXreg,r/m64;
```

Packed interleave high words. Top 2 words from each operand are interleaved.

var
   t:MMX;
   i:integer;
for *i* ← 0 **to** 1 **do**
begin
   $t.c_{i \times 2}$ ← $src.c_{i+2}$;
   $t.c_{i \times 2+1}$ ← $MMXreg_{dest}.c_{i+2}$;
$MMXreg_{dest}$ ← *t*;

4.4.118 PUNPCKLWD

Instruction *PUNPCKLWD (dest:regid;src:MMX);*

```
**      PentiumMMX,K6,P3,P4,ATHLONXP
NASM    PUNPCKLWD MMXreg,r/m64;
```

Packed interleave low words. Bottom 2 words of each operand are interleaved.

var
  t:MMX;
  i:integer;
for *i* ← 0 **to** 1 **do**
begin
  t.$c_{i \times 2}$ ← *src.c_i;*
  t.$c_{i \times 2+1}$ ← *MMXreg$_{dest}$.c_i;*
  MMXreg$_{dest}$ ← *t;*

4.4.119 PUNPCKHDQ

Instruction *PUNPCKHDQ (dest:regid;src:MMX);*

```
**       PentiumMMX,K6,P3,P4,ATHLONXP
NASM     PUNPCKHDQ MMXreg,r/m64;
```

Packed interleave high double words. Top double words from each operand are interleaved.

var
  t:MMX;
  i:integer;
t.b_0 ← *src.b_1;*
t.b_1 ← *MMXreg$_{dest}$.b_1;*
MMXreg$_{dest}$ ← *t;*

4.4.120 PUNPCKLDQ

Instruction *PUNPCKLDQ (dest:regid;src:MMX);*

```
**       PentiumMMX,K6,P3,P4,ATHLONXP
NASM     PUNPCKLDQ MMXreg,r/m64;
```

Packed interleave low double words. Bottom double words from each operand are interleaved.

var
  t:MMX;
  i:integer;
t.b_0 ← *src.b_0;*
t.b_1 ← *MMXreg$_{dest}$.b_0;*
MMXreg$_{dest}$ ← *t;*

4.4.121 PXOR

Instruction *PXOR (dest:regid;src:MMX);*

```
***      PentiumMMX,K6,P3,P4,ATHLONXP
NASM     PXOR MMXreg,r/m64;
```

Quadword XOR in MMX registers. Performs XOR of the 64-bit integers in the source and destination.

var
  $i : 0..3;$
with *MMXreg$_{dest}$* **do**
  for $i \leftarrow 0$ **to** 3 **do**
    $d_i \leftarrow (d_i \vee src.d_i) \wedge$ **not** $(d_i \wedge src.d_i);$

4.4.122 RCPPS

Instruction *RCPPS (dest:regid;src:XMM);*

    ***   P3,P4,ATHLONXP
    NASM   RCPPS XMMreg,r/m128;

SSE Packed Single-FP Reciprocal Approximation. For each of the four 32-bit floating-point numbers in the source operand RCPPS calculates an approximation of the reciprocal and stores it in the corresponding quarter of the destination register. The absolute value of the error for each of these approximations is at most 3/8192. It use is illustrated in Alg. 17.

var
  $i : 0..3;$
for $i \leftarrow 0$ **to** 3 **do**
  $XMMreg_{dest}.a_i \leftarrow \frac{1}{src.a_i};$

```
; for i:=0 to 3 do x[i]:=y[i]/z[i]
movdqu xmm0,[ebp+100]
movdqu xmm1,[ebp+116]
rcpps  xmm1,xmm1
mulps  xmm0,xmm1
movdqu [ebp+32],xmm0
```

Algorithm 17. Use of RCPPS.

4.4.123 RCPSS

Instruction *RCPSS (dest:regid;src:ieee32);*

    ***   P3,P4,ATHLONXP
    NASM   RCPSS XMMreg,XMMreg/mem32;

SSE Scalar Single-FP Reciprocal. This is a scalar equivalent to RCPPS.

$XMMreg_{dest}.a_0 \leftarrow \frac{1}{src};$

4.4.124 RSQRTPS

Instruction *RSQRTPS (dest:regid;src:XMM);*

    **   P3,P4,ATHLONXP
    NASM   RSQRTPS XMMreg,r/m128;

SSE Packed Single-FP Square Root Reciprocal Approximation. For each of the four 32-bit floating-point numbers x_i in the source operand RCPPS calculates an approximation of $1/\sqrt{x_i}$ and stores it in the corresponding quarter of the destination register. The absolute value of the error for each of these approximations is at most 3/8192.

var
  $i : 0..3;$
for $i \leftarrow 0$ **to** 3 **do**
  $XMMreg_{dest}.a_i \leftarrow \frac{1}{\sqrt{src.a_i}};$

4.4.125 RSQRTSS

Instruction *RSQRTSS (dest:regid;src:ieee32);*

```
***    P3,P4,ATHLONXP
NASM   RSQRTSS XMMreg,XMMreg/mem32;
```

SSE Scalar Single-FP Reciprocal Square Root. This is a scalar equivalent to RSQRTPS. It use is illustrated in Alg. 18. This normalises a four element single-precision vector, i.e. it takes an arbitrary vector in 4-space and projects it on to the unit hyper-sphere.

$XMMreg_{dest}.a_0 \leftarrow \frac{1}{\sqrt{src}};$

```
movdqu   xmm0,[ebp+100]         ; load vector
movdqu   xmm1,xmm0              ; copy it
mulps    xmm1,xmm1              ; square it
pshufd   xmm2,xmm1, 00001110b   ; move high words to low
addps    xmm1,xmm2              ; add top and bottom halves
pshufd   xmm2,xmm1, 00000001b   ; word[0]<-word[1]
addss    xmm1,xmm1              ; form sum of squares
rsqrtss  xmm1,xmm1              ; form sqrt
pshufd   xmm2,xmm1, 00000000b   ; replicate to vector
mulps    xmm0,xmm2              ; normalise
movdqu   [ebp+32],xmm0          ; store
```

Algorithm 18. Use of RSQRTSS to normalise a vector.

4.4.126 SFENCE

Instruction *SFENCE;*

```
**     P3,P4
NASM   SFENCE
```

SFENCE guarantees that all store instructions which precede it in the program order are globally visible before any store instructions which follow it. This relates to the use of the MOVNTPS instruction. The non-temporal store instruction minimizes cache pollution while writing data. The main difference between a non-temporal store and a regular cacheable store is in the write-allocation behaviour. With a normal store the processor will fetch the corresponding cache line into the cache hierarchy prior to performing the store. For a non-temporal store, if the data are not present in the cache hierarchy, the transaction will be weakly ordered; consequently, you are responsible for maintaining coherency. Non-temporal stores will not write allocate cache lines. Different implementations may choose to collapse and combine these stores inside the processor.

Since the cache may not have been updated, a subsequent fetch may obtain outdated copies of the data. Within well-defined assembler loops one may be able to guarantee that the data written with MOVNTPS will not be accessed again within your loop. When the assembler loop exits, however, then code outside the assembler loop may access the data so written. To ensure coherence, the SFENCE instruction should be issued after any sequence or loop that uses non-temporal stores.

4.4.127 SQRTPS

Instruction *SQRTPS (dest:regid;src:XMM);*

```
***    P3,P4,ATHLONXP
NASM   SQRTPS XMMreg,r/m128;
```

SSE Packed Single-FP Square Root. For each of the four 32-bit floating-point numbers x_i in the source operand RCPPS calculates $\sqrt{x_i}$ and stores it in the corresponding quarter of the destination register.

var
  $i : 0..3;$
for $i \leftarrow 0$ **to** 3 **do**
  $XMMreg_{dest}.a_i \leftarrow \sqrt{src.a_i};$

4.4.128 SQRTSS

Instruction *SQRTSS (dest:regid;src:ieee32);*

```
***    P3,P4,ATHLONXP
NASM   SQRTSS XMMreg,XMMreg/mem32;
```

SSE Scalar Single-FP Square Root. This is a scalar equivalent to SQRTPS.

$XMMreg_{dest}.a_0 \leftarrow \sqrt{src};$

4.4.129 SUBPS

Instruction *SUBPS (d:regid;src:XMM);*

```
***    P3,P4,ATHLONXP
NASM   SUBPS XMMreg,r/m128
```

Subtract packed single-precsion floating point. Source can be register or 16-byte aligned memory vector.

$XMMreg_d.a \leftarrow src.a - XMMreg_d.a$

4.4.130 SUBSS

Instruction *SUBSS (d:regid;src:XMM)*;

```
**      P3,P4,ATHLONXP
NASM    SUBSS XMMreg,XMMreg/mem32
```

Scalar single floating-point subtract. Source memory or XMM register. This instruction is useful if one wants to do floating-point scalar arithmetic without corrupting the MMX registers.

$XMMreg_d.a_0 \leftarrow src.a_0 - XMMreg_d.a_0$

4.4.131 UNPCKHPS

Instruction *UNPCKHPS (d:regid;src:XMM)*;

```
***     P3,P4,ATHLONXP
NASM    UNPCKHPS XMMreg,r/m128
```

Unpack High Packed Single-FP Data. Source can be register or 16-byte aligned memory vector.

begin
with $XMMreg_d$ **do**
begin
    $a_0 \leftarrow a_2$;
    $a_1 \leftarrow src.a_2$;
    $a_2 \leftarrow a_3$;
    $a_3 \leftarrow src.a_3$;
  end;
end;

4.4.132 UNPCLPS

Instruction *UNPCLPS (d:regid;src:XMM)*;

```
***     P3,P4,ATHLONXP
NASM    UNPCKLPS XMMreg,r/m128
```

Unpack Low Packed Single-FP Data. Source can be register or 16-byte aligned memory vector.

begin
with $XMMreg_d$ **do**
  begin
    $a_0 \leftarrow a_0$;
    $a_1 \leftarrow src.a_0$;
    $a_2 \leftarrow a_1$;
    $a_3 \leftarrow src.a_1$;
  end;
end;

4.4.133 XORPS

Instruction *XORPS (dest:regid;src:XMM);*

```
**    P4
NASM  XORPS XMMreg,r/m128;
```

Quadword XOR in MMX registers. Performs XOR of the 128-bit integers in the source and destination. Because the memory operand must be 16-byte aligned, use PXOR in preference to this. For most uses it will be faster.

var
  $i : 0..7;$
with *XMMreg$_{dest}$* **do**
  for $i \leftarrow 0$ **to** 7 **do**
    $d_i \leftarrow (d_i \vee src.d_i) \wedge$ **not**$(d_i \wedge src.d_i);$

3DNOW Instructions 5

These instructions assume the data structures declared in the previous chapter.

5.0.1 FEMMS

Instruction *FEMMS*;

```
*      K6,Athlon
NASM   FEMMS
```

Fast Empty MMX State. This is a faster AMD version of EMMS.

ftw ← $ff;

5.0.2 PF2ID

Instruction *PF2ID (dest:regid;src:MMX)*;

```
***    K6,Athlon
NASM   PF2ID MMXreg,r/m64;
```

3DNOW Packed floating point to integer. Converts two floating-point values to a pair of integers using truncation. Source can be in memory or a register.

with *MMXreg$_{dest}$* **do**
begin
  b_0 ← *trunc(src.g$_0$)*;
  b_1 ← *trunc(src.g$_1$)*;
end;

5.0.3 PFACC

Instruction *PFACC (dest:regid;src:MMX)*;

```
**     K6,Athlon
NASM   PFACC MMXreg,r/m64;
```

3DNOW Packed floating-point accumulate. This is useful in multiply accumulate sequences such as those involved in inner product operations, or in summing a vector.

with *MMXreg$_{dest}$* **do**
begin
  $g_0 \leftarrow g_0 + g_1$;
  $g_1 \leftarrow src.g_1 + src.g_0$;
end;

5.0.4 PFADD

Instruction *PFADD (dest:regid;src:MMX)*;

```
***    K6,Athlon
NASM   PFADD MMXreg,r/m64;
```

3DNOW Packed floating-point add. Parallel add of two floating-point values. Source can be in memory or a register.

with *MMXreg$_{dest}$* **do**
begin
  $g_0 \leftarrow g_0 + src.g_0$;
  $g_1 \leftarrow g_1 + src.g_1$;
end;

5.0.5 PFCMPEQ

Instruction *PFCMPEQ (dest:regid;src:MMX)*;

```
***    K6,Athlon
NASM   PFCMPEQ MMXreg,r/m64;
```

3DNOW Packed floating-point comparison. Element by element comparison of two pairs of floating-point numbers. If comparison succeeds destination set to 0ffffffff, otherwise set to 0. Source can be in memory or a register.

with *MMXreg$_{dest}$* **do**
begin
  $b_0 \leftarrow \begin{cases} -1 & \text{if } g_0 = src.g_0 \\ 0 & \text{otherwise} \end{cases}$;
  $b_1 \leftarrow \begin{cases} -1 & \text{if } g_1 = src.g_1 \\ 0 & \text{otherwise} \end{cases}$;
end;

5.0.6 PFCMPGT

Instruction *PFCMPGT (dest:regid;src:MMX)*;

```
***    K6,Athlon
NASM   PFCMPGT MMXreg,r/m64;
```

3DNOW Packed floating-point comparison. Element by element comparison of two pairs of floating-point numbers. If comparison succeeds destination set to 0ffffffff, otherwise set to 0. Source can be in memory or a register.

Chapter 5 • 3DNOW Instructions

with $MMXreg_{dest}$ **do**
begin

$$b_0 \leftarrow \begin{cases} -1 & \text{if } g_0 > src.g_0 \\ 0 & \text{otherwise} \end{cases};$$

$$b_1 \leftarrow \begin{cases} -1 & \text{if } g_1 > src.g_1 \\ 0 & \text{otherwise} \end{cases};$$

end;

5.0.7 PFCMPGE

Instruction *PFCMPGE (dest:regid;src:MMX)*;

```
***    K6,Athlon
NASM   PFCMPGE MMXreg,r/m64;
```

3DNOW Packed floating-point comparison. Element by element comparison of two pairs of floating-point numbers. If comparison succeeds destination set to 0ffffffff, otherwise set to 0. Source can be in memory or a register.

with $MMXreg_{dest}$ **do**
begin

$$b_0 \leftarrow \begin{cases} -1 & \text{if } g_0 \geq src.g_0 \\ 0 & \text{otherwise} \end{cases};$$

$$b_1 \leftarrow \begin{cases} -1 & \text{if } g_1 \geq src.g_1 \\ 0 & \text{otherwise} \end{cases};$$

end;

5.0.8 PFMAX

Instruction *PFMAX (dest:regid;src:MMX)*;

```
***    K6,Athlon
NASM   PFMAX MMXreg,r/m64;
```

3DNOW Packed floating-point maximum. Finds the greater of each of two pairs of floating-point values. Source can be in memory or a register.

with $MMXreg_{dest}$ **do**
begin

$$g_0 \leftarrow \begin{cases} g_0 & \text{if } g_0 > src.g_0 \\ src.g_0 & \text{otherwise} \end{cases};$$

$$g_1 \leftarrow \begin{cases} g_1 & \text{if } g_1 > src.g_1 \\ src.g_1 & \text{otherwise} \end{cases};$$

end;

5.0.9 PFMIN

Instruction *PFMIN (dest:regid;src:MMX)*;

```
***    K6,Athlon
NASM   PFMIN MMXreg,r/m64;
```

3DNOW Packed floating-point minimum. Finds the minimum of each of two pairs of floating-point values. Source can be in memory or a register.

with *MMXreg$_{dest}$* **do**
begin
$$g_0 \leftarrow \begin{cases} g_0 & \text{if } g_0 < src.g_0 \\ src.g_0 & \text{otherwise} \end{cases},$$
$$g_1 \leftarrow \begin{cases} g_1 & \text{if } g_1 < src.g_1 \\ src.g_1 & \text{otherwise} \end{cases},$$
end;

5.0.10 PFMUL

Instruction *PFMUL (dest:regid;src:MMX)*;

```
***     K6,Athlon
NASM    PFMUL MMXreg,r/m64;
```

3DNOW Packed floating-point multiply. Parallel mutiply of two floating-point values. Source can be in memory or a register.

with *MMXreg$_{dest}$* **do**
begin
  $g_0 \leftarrow g_0 \times src.g_0$;
  $g_1 \leftarrow g_1 \times src.g_1$;
end;

5.0.11 PFNACC

Instruction *PFNACC (dest:regid;src:MMX)*;

```
*       Athlon
NASM    PFNACC MMXreg,r/m64;
```

3DNOW Packed floating-point negative accumulate. This is the subtraction equivalent of PFACC; it is of little use.

with *MMXreg$_{dest}$* **do**
begin
  $g_0 \leftarrow g_0 - g_1$;
  $g_1 \leftarrow src.g_1 - src.g_0$;
end;

5.0.12 PFPNACC

Instruction *PFPNACC (dest:regid;src:MMX)*;

```
*       Athlon
NASM    PFPNACC MMXreg,r/m64;
```

3DNOW Packed floating-point negative accumulate. This is an odd mix of PFNACC and PFACC; it is of little use.

Chapter 5 • 3DNOW Instructions

with $MMXreg_{dest}$ **do**
begin
  $g_0 \leftarrow g_0 - g_1;$
  $g_1 \leftarrow src.g_1 + src.g_0;$
end;

5.0.13 PFRCP

Instruction *PFRCP (dest:regid;src:ieee32)*;

```
**      K6,Athlon
NASM    PFRCP MMXreg,r/m32;
```

3DNOW Floating point Reciprocal. The divide operation takes longer on computer hardware than other mathematical operators. Some high-performance machines avoid using a divide and substitute a reciprocal operation. The PFRCP operation computes a reciprocal approximation accurate to 14 bits. Note that unlike other 3DNOW instructions, this instruction takes a scalar argument. This is either a 32-bit memory operand or the lower 32 bits of an MMX register. The approximate reciprocal is stored in both halves of the result register.

This instruction has two deficiencies:

1. the fact that it operates on scalars rather than on vectors
2. its limited accuracy.

In combination, these make it difficult for a parallelising compiler to make use of it. It remains possible for hand coded instructions to use it, for instance in normalising a vector.

with $MMXreg_{dest}$ **do**
begin
  $g_0 \leftarrow \frac{1}{src};$
  $g_1 \leftarrow \frac{1}{src};$
end;

5.0.14 PFRCPIT

Instruction *PFRCPIT (dest:regid;src:ieee32)*;

```
**       K6,Athlon
Syntax   PFRCPIT1 MMXreg,r/m32;
         PFRCPIT2 MMXreg,r/m32;
```

3DNOW Floating-point Reciprocal Iteration step 1. This applies Newton–Raphson iteration to converge on the result of the floating-point reciprocal. Both PFRCPIT1 and PFRCPIT2 must be executed in succession. The iteration relation is

$$x_{i+1} = x_i(1 - b \times x_i)$$

to compute $1/b$. It can be used in conjunction with PFRCP to perform division as shown in Alg. 19 will perform the assignment $z \to \frac{y}{x}$. The first argument of the instruction must have been the source of a PFRCP instruction and the second argument must have been the output of the same PFRCP instruction.

```
movd mm0,[x]
pfrcp mm1,mm0
punpckldq mm0,mm0
pfrcpit1 mm0,mm1
pfrcpit2 mm0,mm1
movd mm0,[y]
pfmul mm0,mm2
movd [z],mm0
```

Algorithm 19. Use of PFRCP.

Newton–Raphson

var
   x: array $[0..1]$ of *ieee32*;
   b: *ieee32*;
begin
   $b \leftarrow MMXreg_{dest}.g_0$;
   $x_0 \leftarrow src$;
   $x_1 \leftarrow x_0 \times (2 - b \times x_0)$;
   with $MMXreg_{dest}$ **do**
   begin
      $g_0 \leftarrow x_1$;
      $g_1 \leftarrow x_1$;
   end;

5.0.15 PFSUB

Instruction *PFSUB (dest:regid;src:MMX)*;

   ***   K6,Athlon
   NASM   PFSUB MMXreg,r/m64;

3DNOW Packed floating-point subtract. Parallel subtraction of two floating-point values. Source can be in memory or a register.

with $MMXreg_{dest}$ **do**
begin
   $g_0 \leftarrow g_0 - src.g_0$;
   $g_1 \leftarrow g_1 - src.g_1$;
end;

5.0.16 PFSUBR

Instruction *PFSUBR (dest:regid;src:MMX)*;

   ***   K6,Athlon
   NASM   PFSUBR MMXreg,r/m64;

Chapter 5 • 3DNOW Instructions

3DNOW Packed floating-point reverse-order subtract. Parallel subtraction of two floating-point values. Source can be in memory or a register.

with *MMXreg$_{dest}$* **do**
begin
  $g_0 \leftarrow src.g_0 - g_0$;
  $g_1 \leftarrow src.g_1 - g_1$;
end;

5.0.17 PI2FD

Instruction *PI2FD (dest:regid;src:MMX)*;

```
***    K6,Athlon
NASM   PI2FD MMXreg,r/m64;
```

3DNOW Packed integer to floating-point conversion. Converts two integers to floating-point values. There may be a loss of precision. Source can be in memory or a register.

with *MMXreg$_{dest}$* **do**
begin
  $g_0 \leftarrow src.b_0$;
  $g_1 \leftarrow src.b_1$;
end;

5.0.18 PI2FW

Instruction *PI2FW (dest:regid;src:MMX)*;

```
***    Athlon
NASM   PI2FW MMXreg,r/m64;
```

3DNOW Packed int16 to floating-point conversion. Converts two 16-bit integers to floating-point values. Source can be in memory or a register.

with *MMXreg$_{dest}$* **do**
begin
  $g_0 \leftarrow src.c_0$;
  $g_1 \leftarrow src.c_2$;
end;

5.0.19 PREFETCH

Instruction *PREFETCH (loc:integer)*;

```
***    K6,Athlon
NASM   PREFETCH mem
```

Loads a cache line into the level 1 data cache. PREFETCHW does the same, but also marks the cache line as modified.

$level1_{bank,(loc\ 6) \wedge 31, 0..61} \leftarrow mem.bytemem_{loc..loc+63}$;
$bank \leftarrow (bank + 1) \bmod 4$;

Part II
SIMD Programming Languages
Paul Cockshott

Another Approach: Data Parallel Languages

6

There has been sustained research within the parallel programming community into the exploitation of SIMD parallelism on multi-processor architectures. Most work in this field has been driven by the needs of high-performance scientific processing, from finite element analysis to meteorology. In particular, there has been considerable interest in exploiting data parallelism in Fortran array processing, culminating in High Performance Fortran, Fortran 90 and F (Metcalf and Reid, 1996). Typically this involves two approaches. First, operators may be overloaded to allow array-valued expressions, similar to APL. Second, loops may be analysed to establish where it is possible to unroll loop bodies for parallel evaluation. Compilers embodying these techniques tend to be architecture specific to maximise performance and they have been aimed primarily at specialised super-computer architectures, even though contemporary general purpose microprocessors provide similar features, albeit on a far smaller scale.

In the period since SIMD programming was pioneered on super-computers, a set of well-defined programming abstractions has been developed to enable coders to take advantage of the parallelism offered by SIMD processors (Ewing et al., 1999):

- operations on whole arrays
- array slicing
- conditional operations
- reduction operations
- data reorganisation.

We will next consider these abstractions in more detail and look at their support in existing languages, in particular J, Fortran 90 (Ewing et al., 1999) and NESL (Blelloch, 1995). These languages are not currently available as tools to the MMX programmer, but it is instructive to see how they deal with array abstraction. J is an interpretive data parallel language which runs on PCs. Being interpretive, it is of interest not so much for its speed as for its conceptual model. Fortran 90 is a compiled language typically targeted at super-computers. NESL is a compiled functional language targeted at highly parallel machines.

6.1 Operations on Whole Arrays

The basic *conceptual* mechanism for whole array operations is the *map*, which takes an operator and one or more source arrays, and produces a result array by mapping the source(s) under the operator. Thus, if x, y are arrays of integers $k = x + y$ is the array of integers where $k_i = x_i + y_i$:

$$\boxed{3\;|\;5\;|\;9} = \boxed{2\;|\;3\;|\;5} + \boxed{1\;|\;2\;|\;4}$$

Similarly, if we have a unary operator $\mu:(T \to T)$ then we automatically have an operator $\mu:(T[\,] \to T[\,])$. Thus, $z = \mathrm{sqr}(x)$ is the array where $z_i = x_i^2$:

$$\boxed{4\;|\;9\;|\;25} = \mathrm{sqr}(\boxed{2\;|\;3\;|\;5})$$

Map replaces the *bounded iteration* or *for loop* abstraction of classical imperative languages. The map concept is simple, and maps over lists are widely used in functional programming. For array-based languages there are complications to do with the semantics of operations between arrays of different lengths and different dimensions. Iverson (1980) provided a consistent treatment of these. Recent languages built round this model are J, an interpretive language (Iverson, 1991, 2000; Burke, 1995), High Performance Fortran (Ewing et al., 1999), F (Metcalf and Reid, 1996) a modern Fortran subset and NESL an applicative data parallel language and ZPL (Snyder, 1999). In principle any language with array types can be extended in a similar way.

The map approach to data parallelism is machine independent. Depending on the target machine, a compiler can output sequential, SIMD or MIMD code for it. In particular map may be exploited through implementation-independent *algorithmic skeletons* (Cole, 1989) based on parallel templates for process farms which are instantiated with appropriate sequential arguments from the original source program (Michaelson et al., 2001).

Recent implementations of Fortran, such as Fortran 90, F and High Performance Fortran, provide direct support for whole array operations. Given that A,B are arrays with the same rank and same extents, the statements

1. `REAL,DIMENSION(64)::A,B`
2. `A=3.0`
3. `B=B+SQRT(A)*0.5`

would be legal, and would operate in a pointwise fashion on the whole arrays. Thus, line 1 initialises every element of array A to 3.0 and line 2 sets each element of array B to 0.5 times the corresponding element of A.

Intrinsic functions, such as SQRT, are defined to operate either on scalars or arrays, but are part of the language rather than part of a subroutine library. User-defined functions over scalars do not automatically extend to array arguments.

J[1] similarly allows direct implementation of array operations, although here the array dimensions are deduced at run time:

1. `> a=.1 2 3 5`
2. `> a`

---
[1] We will give examples from J rather than APL here for ease of representation in ASCII.

Chapter 6 • Another Approach: Data Parallel Languages

    3. 1 2 3 5
    4. > b=. 1 2 4 8
    5. > a+b
    6. 2 4 7 13

The pair =. is the assignment operator in J so line 1 initialises a new array a of length 4 and line 4 initialises a new array b of length 4. Line 2 displays the value of a and line 5 calculates and displays the array formed by summing corresponding elements of a and b.

Unlike Fortran, J automatically overloads user defined functions over arrays:

    7. > sqr=.^&2
    8. > c=. 1 2 4 8
    9. > c+(sqr a)*0.5
    10. 1.5 4 8.5 20.5

Here, line 7 defines a new monadic function sqr by partially applying the binary power function ^ to the exponent 2. Line 8 then initialises array c and line 9 calculates and displays the array formed by adding each element of c to half the square of the corresponding element of a.

The functional language NESL provides similar generality. The first J example above could be expressed as

    1. a+b: a in [1,2,3,5]; b in [1,2,4,8];
    2. $\Rightarrow$ [2,4,7,13] : [int]

and the second example as

    3. b+sqr(a)*0.5: a in [1,2,3,5]; b in [1,2,4,8];
    4. $\Rightarrow$ [1.5,4,8.5,20.5] : [float]

The Apply-to-Each construct, also known as comprehensions, are descended from the ZF notations used in SETL (Schwartz et al., 1986) and MIRANDA (Turner, 1986). Thus line 1 finds the sum of the successive elements of the *sequences* [1,2,3,5] bound to a and [1,2,4,8] bound to b. Similarly, line 3 finds the sum of successive elements of b and half the square of the successive elements of a.

Again, user-defined functions can be applied element-wise to sequences.

6.1.1 Array Slicing

It is advantageous for many applications to be able to specify sections of arrays as values in expression. The sections may be rows or columns in a matrix or a rectangular sub-range of the elements of an array, as shown in Figure 6.1. In image processing, such rectangular sub-regions of pixel arrays are called regions of interest. It may also be desirable to provide matrix diagonals (van der Meulen, 1977).

1	1	1	1
1	2	4	8
1	2	4	16
1	2	8	512

1	1	1	1
1	2	4	8
1	2	4	16
1	2	8	512

1	1	1	1
1	2	4	8
1	2	4	16
1	2	8	512

Figure 6.1. Different ways of slicing the same array.

The notion of array slicing was introduced to imperative languages by ALGOL 68 (Tannenbaum, 1976). In ALGOL 68 if x has been declared as [1:10]INT x, then x[2:6] would be a slice consisting of the second through the sixth elements inclusive that could be used on the right of an assignment or as an actual parameter.

Fortran 90 extends this notion to allow what it calls *triplet subscripts*, giving the start position end position and step at which elements are to be taken from arrays. For example:

```
REAL,DIMENSION(10,10)::A,B
A(2:9,1:8:2)=B(3:10,2:9:2)
```

would be equivalent to the loop nest

```
   DO 1,J=1,8,2
   DO 2,J=2,9
     A(I,J)=B(I+1,J+1)
 2 CONTINUE
 1 CONTINUE
```

J allows a similar operation to select subsequences. For example:

1. >a=.2*i.10
2. >a
3. 0 2 4 6 8 10 12 14 16 18
4. >3{a
5. 6

Here, i.n is a function which produces a list of the first n elements of an array starting with element 0. Line 1 constructs an array where each element is double its subscript. The symbol { is the sequence subscription operator so line 4 selects the element at index 3.

Selection of a subsequence is performed by forming a sequence of indices. For example:

```
6. >(2+i.3){a
7.    4 6 8
```

In line 6, the expression 2+i.3 forms the sequence 2 3 4 which then subscripts the array a.

NESL does not offer a direct equivalent to slicing.

6.1.2 Conditional Operations

Much data parallel programming is based on the application of some operation to a subset of the data selected through a mask. This can be thought of as providing a finer grain of selection than sub-slicing, allowing arbitrary combinations of array elements to be acted on. For example, one might want to replace all elements of an array A less than the corresponding element in array B with that element of B:

1	2	4	8	A
2	3	4	5	B
1	1	0	0	A < B
2	3	4	8	

Fortran 90 provides the WHERE statement to update selectively a section of an array under a logical mask:

```
REAL, DIMENSION(64)::A
REAL, DIMENSION(64)::B
WHERE (A>=B)
  A=A
ELSEWHERE
  A=B
ENDWHERE
```

The WHERE statement is analogous to ALGOL 68 and C conditional expressions, but extended to operate on arrays. It can be performed in parallel on all elements of an array and lends itself to evaluation under a mask on SIMD architectures.

NESL provides a generalised form of Apply-to-Each in which a sieve can be applied to the arguments. For example:

```
1. a+b : a in [ 1,2,3]; b in [4,3,2] | a<b
2. ⇒ [5,5] : [int]
```

In line 1, a and b are constrained by the requirement that each element of a must be less than the corresponding element of b.

Notice that in NESL, as in J, values are allocated dynamically from a heap so that the length of the sequence returned from a sieved Apply-to-Each can be less than that of the argument sequences in its expression part. In Fortran 90, the WHERE statement applies to an array whose size is known on entry to the statement.

6.1.3 Reduction Operations

In a reduction operation, a dyadic operator is injected between the elements of a vector or the rows or columns of a matrix to produces a result of lower rank. Examples include forming the sum or finding the maximum or minimum of a table. For example, + would reduce:

| 1 | 2 | 4 | 8 |

to $1 + 2 + 4 + 8 = 15$

The first systematic treatment of reduction operations in programming languages is due to Iverson (1962). His it reduction functional takes a dyadic operator and, by currying, generates a tailored reduction function. In APL and J the reduction functional is denoted by /. Thus +/ is the function which forms the sum of an array:

1. > a
2.   1 2 3 5
3. > +/a
4.   11

In line 3, the reduction +/a expands to $(1 + (2 + (3 + (4 + 0))))$.

The interpretation of reduction for non commutative operators is slightly less obvious. Consider:

5. > -/a
6. _3

In line 6, _3 is the J notation for -3, derived from the expansion of $(1 - (2 - (3 - 4(-0))))$ from -/a in line 5. In J as in APL, reduction applies uniformly to all binary operators.

Fortran 90, despite its debt to APL, is less general, providing a limited set of built-in reduction operators on commutative operators: SUM, PRODUCT, MAXVAL, MINVAL. NESL likewise provides a limited set of reduction functions sum, minval, maxval, any, all. where any and all are Boolean reductions: any returns true if at least one element of a sequence is true, i.e. disjunctive reduction; all returns true if they are all true, i.e. conjunctive reduction.

6.1.4 Data Reorganisation

In both linear algebra and image processing applications, it is often desirable to be able to perform bulk reorganisation of data arrays, for example to transpose a vector or matrix or to shift the elements of a vector.

For example, one can express the convolution of a vector with a three-element kernel in terms of multiplications, shifts and adds. Let $a =$ | 1 | 2 | 4 | 8 | be a

Chapter 6 • Another Approach: Data Parallel Languages

vector to be convolved with the kernel $k = \boxed{0.25 \mid 0.5 \mid 0.25}$. This can be expressed by defining two temporary vectors:

$$b = 0.25a = \boxed{0.25 \mid 0.5 \mid 1 \mid 2}$$

$$c = 0.5a = \boxed{0.5 \mid 1 \mid 2 \mid 4}$$

and then defining the result to the sum under shifts of b,c:

$$\boxed{1 \mid 2 \mid 4 \mid 8} \text{ convolve } \boxed{0.25 \mid 0.5 \mid 0.25} =$$

$$\begin{array}{cccc} 0.5 & 1 & 2 & 2 \\ 0.5 & 1 & 2 & 4 \\ 0.25 & 0.25 & 0.5 & 1 \\ \hline 1.25 & 2.25 & 4.5 & 7 \end{array} \quad \begin{array}{l} b \ll 1 \\ c \\ + \;\; b \gg 1 \end{array}$$

This example replicates the trailing value when shifting. In other circumstances, for example when dealing with cellular automata, it is convenient to be able to define circular shifts on data arrays.

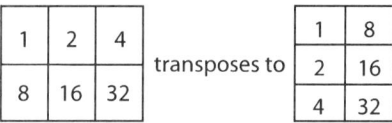

Figure 6.2. Reorganising by transposition.

Fortran 90 provides a rich set of functions to reshape, transpose and circularly shift arrays. For example, given a nine-element vector v, we can *reshape* it as a 3 by 3 matrix:

```
V=(/1,2,3,4,5,6,7,8,9/)
M=RESHAPE(V,(/3,3/))
```

to give the array

```
1 2 3
4 5 6
7 8 9
```

We can then cyclically shift this along a dimension

```
M2=CSHIFT(M,SHIFT=2,DIM=2)
```

to give

```
3 1 2
6 4 5
9 7 8
```

NESL provides similar operations on sequences to those provided on arrays by Fortran 90. For example, if

```
v=[1,2,3,4,5,6,7,8,9]
s=[3,3,3]
```

then

```
partition(v,s) ⇒ [[1,2,3][4,5,6][7,8,9]]
rotate(v,3)
⇒ [7,8,9,1,2,3,4,5,6]
```

is equivalent to the Fortran above.

6.2 Design Goals

In seeking to exploit new programming concepts, one may either design a new language or adapt an existing language. Designing a new language is high risk in terms of the effort to be expended in developing new tools and promoting a core community before any wider take-up is likely. There seems to be a strong case for the extension of popular programming languages to operate on vector data in a fashion that is processor independent. The constructs which make use of SIMD parallelism should appear as natural and simple extensions to the underlying language so that programmers who are already familiar with the language can immediately understand what is being computed.

Occam represents a salutary object lesson. This language was intended for a novel architecture, the Transputer, and had its own formal logic, CSP. However, Occam was never made adequately available on non-Transputer architectures, and the Transputer was overpriced and complex compared with the Intel/Motorola hegemony. Now only CSP survives, having found a niche as a language- and architecture-independent formal notation.

For data parallelism, APL (Iverson, 1962) and J (Iverson, 1991) represented radical breaks from their contemporaries, introducing novel notations. We think that this was an important factor in limiting their wider use. Overall, experience suggests that new concepts gain provenance if they are presented in a familiar guise and if their use involves low additional cost for the benefits they bring.

An existing language may be adapted through the introduction of new notation or through the overloading of existing notation. Both approaches involve modifications to existing language processors or the development of new ones. Furthermore, both approaches may lose backwards compatibility with the original. Finding a principled basis for adding a new notation to an extant language is problematic.

For example, the late 1980s and 1990s saw a variety of attempts to extend C and C++ with parallel programming concepts. Johnston (1995) lists

- CC++ with `par` and `parfor` constructs
- C** with aggregate classes and concurrent element nomination
- Mentat with aggregate classes and explicit parallel methods
- pC++ with concepts from High Performance Fortran.

Chapter 6 • Another Approach: Data Parallel Languages

In the same period. Lattice Logic Limited (3L) developed their Parallel C based on Occam-like constructs (3L Limited, 1995). All of these represent well-thought through extensions but none of these languages has gained widespread acceptance. We speculate that, in part, this was because the extensions did not build naturally on existing constructs.

NESL (Blelloch, 1995) was strongly grounded in the functional language tradition. For example, its sequences and Apply-to-Each are effectively overloadings of lists and list comprehensions. NESL has influenced recent research into extending Standard ML for data parallelism. However, because overall the functional paradigm is far less familiar than the imperative paradigm, functional languages in general have still to gain wider currency beyond their academic constituencies.

High Performance Fortran (HPF) (Ewing et al., 1999) and Fortran 90 are based on a a combination of overloading standard Fortran notation for arrays and operators, and the introduction of new notation, for example for conditional operations and slicing. HPF provides a relatively transparent extension to the widely used Fortran and represents the most successful SIMD language to date, enjoying wide use in the scientific and technical communities.

The language Vector Pascal has been designed to meet similar needs for high-performance computing on PCs. It takes as its base a well-known programming language, Pascal, for which many excellent implementations exist on PCs, and with which many programmers are already familiar. It extends the language through a few simple extensions of the type rules to allow the concise expression of data parallel operations. The data parallel operations can then be compiled either to scalar code on machines without SIMD instructions, or to parallel code on newer machines. Whether scalar or parallel code is generated, the source program itself is unchanged.

Alg. 20 shows the example program coded in Vector Pascal. Compared with the C++ code in Alg. 9:

- No non-standard types are used.
- No explicit iteration is used for the vector addition. Instead, it is simply written as `v3:=v1+v2`.
- It is much faster, at about 770 million operations per second (see Table 6.1).

Vector Pascal extends the array-type mechanism of Pascal to provide support for data parallel programming in general, and SIMD processing in particular.

```
PROGRAM vecadd;
VAR v1,v2,v3:ARRAY[0..6399] OF byte;
    i:integer;
BEGIN
    FOR i:=1 to 100000 DO v3:=v1+v2;
END.
```

Algorithm 20. Example program in Vector Pascal.

Table 6.1. Speeds of different implementations

Implementation	Elapsed time	Basic operations per second
C	72	8.9 million
C++ with SIMD classes	4.56	140 million
Vector Pascal	0.83	771 million
Assembler	0.77	831 million

Wherever possible, rather than introducing new constructs, we have sought to increase orthogonality in Strachey's sense (Strachey, 1967) by overloading extant notation. As most MMX extensions support arithmetic and logical operations over byte sequences, a central concern in choosing a host language was the degree to which the corresponding operators were already overloaded.

Pascal (Jensen and Wirth, 1978) was chosen as a base language over the alternatives C and Java. C overloads arithmetic operators to include address manipulation, often with implicit type coercions. Hence these operators could not also be used to express data parallelism over structures. Java overloads + both for string concatenation and to coerce other base types to string when they are +ed with strings. This precludes the use of + as a data parallel operation for combining, as opposed to joining, arrays.

Pascal has other advantages in providing additional notations which can be overloaded consistently for data parallelism. For example, the sub-range notation is a natural basis for slicing.

6.2.1 Target Machines

The aim was to produce a language and associated compiler technology that would target the machines that most programmers have on their desks. This essentially means PCs and Apples using the Intel and Motorola families of CPUs. This aim is different from that of the developers of HPF, who were targeting super-computers and highly parallel machines. Although it should be possible to develop Vector Pascal compilers for such machines, the main aim has been to provide a tool that would run on affordable, widely used, single-processor computers.

The initial development work was done with Intel and AMD processors in mind, because these are by far the most commonly used machines. Although these machines were the first target, Vector Pascal does not depend upon any machine-specific features. A processor does not need to have a SIMD instruction-set to run it. A Vector Pascal program can run correctly and efficiently on a classical SISD instruction-set such as the Intel 486 (see Table 13.1).

Processor technology develops fast, and software support for them typically lags well behind. A major design goal has been to develop a compiler technology that enables Vector Pascal to be re-targeted at new machines with minimal effort. Apple machines using the G4 processor were immediately identified as possible targets, as were the Alpha and SPARC chips. The aim was to provide along with Vector Pascal, a notation ILCG (see Appendix A) by which the instruction-sets of future machines, including their SIMD capabilities, could be described. Given a machine description in ILCG, the Vector Pascal compiler could automatically generate code for the new processor which made use of its data-parallel facilities.

Operating System Portability

Another aim of the language was that it should be readily portable between operating systems. Initially this meant portable between Microsoft operating systems and Linux. This has been achieved by implementing the compiler in Java, so that the Java environment allows a machine- and operating system-independent binary implementation of the compiler. Dynamic loading of code generator classes at run time then allows the code produced to be targeted at particular machines.

6.2.2 Backward Compatibility

There exists a large body of legacy code in Pascal. Some of this is in Standard Pascal, but a larger body of it is in Turbo Pascal. The Borland compilers for the PC probably did more to popularise Pascal than any prior implementation. Other compilers, such as TMT Pascal and Free-Pascal, have also supported the Turbo Pascal syntactic extensions, in particular the provision of Units for modular programming.

It was a design aim of Vector Pascal to allow such code to be compiled and run by the Vector Pascal compiler except in so far as it depends upon machine-specific MS-DOS calls.

Linkage Model

Turbo Pascal provides a very good model for type-safe linking together of Pascal units, but this is not enough. A language is much easier to use if it allows one to call out to other languages. This is particularly true if one is going to make use of graphics libraries. These are typically designed to be called from C with all that implies. Vector Pascal has thus chosen to make use of standard C linkers and C calling conventions. The syntactic notations used to import C procedures into Pascal code are those used in Turbo Pascal.

To reduce dependence on proprietary code, on current implementations the `gcc` linker is used to produce the final binaries.

6.2.3 Expressive Power

Compilers are there to make things easier for coders. Where possible they should allow the coder to say what they want done rather than how it should be done. It is the task of the compiler writer to automate the low-level details of programming, leaving the coder to concentrate on algorithm strategy. It has long been the claim of array programing language advocates that they improve programmer productivity by raising the expressive power of the language. Programmers using them learn to think differently. By thinking in a data-parallel way they hit upon strategies that might not occur to a coder used to the word at a time approach of C.

One way that the expressive power of a language can be raised is by the removal of restrictions. If the context-free grammar of the language seems to suggest that something should be allowed, but the type rules forbid it, then the lack of orthogonality reduces the power of the language. It forces the coder to use work-arounds to achieve their intention. For instance, Standard Pascal allows the expression a+b provided that the variables are scalars but not if they are arrays. For arrays a FOR loop has to be written.

Vector Pascal goes some way towards orthogonalising Standard Pascal.[2]

Another source of expressive power is the provision of type-complete operations. The only type-complete operations supported by Standard Pascal are assignment, parameter passing and array access. Vector Pascal provides a small number of additional type-complete syntactic forms, mostly associated with array manipulation. A concern at all times has been that orthogonalisations should be compatible with efficient implementation.

6.2.4 Run-time Efficiency

Syntactic extensions and orthogonalisations in Vector Pascal have been allowed, provided either that

- they can be provided at compile time with no run time cost, or
- they actually speed up run time code by making it easier to optimise, or
- their run time cost is no more than the equivalent hand-coded Pascal.

---

[2]There remain several non-orthogonal features, most obviously those associated with array index types. Pascal only allows finite sub-ranges types to be used as indices for arrays. This is both an implementation issue – allowing array access by address arithmetic – and a semantic issue. If infinite types were allowed as indices, then arrays would become partial maps rather than total maps, giving rise to the possibility of undefined values.

Basics of Vector Pascal

In this and following chapters we will present an introduction to the Vector Pascal programming language. The introduction will assume that the reader is familiar with imperative programming but not necessarily with Standard Pascal. Some space is therefore given to explaining Standard Pascal features. Marginal notes indicate the origin of features.

ISO-7185 — A paragraph marked thus describes a feature retained in Vector Pascal from Standard Pascal (Jensen and Wirth, 1978; ISO, 1991b).

ISO-10206 — A paragraph marked thus describes a feature introduced by Extended Pascal (ISO, 1991a) and retained in Vector Pascal.

TURBO — A paragraph marked thus describes a feature Vector Pascal inherits from the popular Turbo Pascal compiler.

VECTOR — A paragraph marked thus describes a feature introduced in Vector Pascal, but not used in Standard, Extended or Turbo Pascal. Some of these features are also implemented by yet other Pascal compilers.

7.1 Formating Rules

A Pascal program is made up of lexemes, spaces and and comments. Lexemes are either words, literal values, operators or punctuation characters.

7.1.1 Alphabet

Pascal is a comparatively old programming language, having been under development since the end of the 1960s (Jensen and Wirth, 1978). It was originally implemented on CDC mainframe computers that had a 60-bit word and that used a 6-bit character set which supported upper-case characters only.

ISO Pascal extended this to use an alphabet of symbols, all of which can be represented with ASCII. The most significant extension was to allow the use of lower-case letters and the bracket symbols { and }. Vector Pascal extends this further to use Unicode, which permits a far wider range of symbols to be used in programs.

Programs should be submitted to the compiler in UTF-8 encoded Unicode. Since the 7-bit ASCII is a subset of UTF-8, all valid ASCII-encoded Vector Pascal programs are also valid UTF-8 programs.

7.1.2 Reserved Words and Identifiers

ISO-7185

A word is either a reserved word or an identifier. In ISO Pascal all words have the same lexical form. They are sequences of characters, the first of which must be a letter; subsequent characters can be either letters or digits.

Thus the lexemes `begin`, `end`, `while`, `hope`, `x`, `a1`, `blue`, `blistering`, `barnacles` are all valid formats for reserved words or identifiers. On the other hand, `==toys`, `9b`, `?**!!!` are not.

In Vector Pascal, the rule for the formation of words is extended by

TURBO

1. Allowing the under-bar character to be used as a letter. Thus `blue_barnacles` is a valid identifier in Vector Pascal. An under-bar may even be used in the leading position of an identifier, as with `_ENDLINE`. This feature is provided only to allow compatibility with external libraries in C. Its use in Pascal is deprecated.

VECTOR

2. Allowing the use of several other Unicode alphabetic scripts: Greek, Cyrillic, Katakana or Hiagana characters in words.

VECTOR

3. Allowing the use of the Unicode unified Chinese, Japanese and Korean ideographs as characters in words.

A reserved word in the language has a pre-defined meaning which cannot be altered in a Pascal program. A list of the reserved words in Vector Pascal is provided in Table 7.1. An identifier is a word that, although it may be pre-defined in the language, can have its meaning defined or redefined within a program. Identifiers are typically used to name types, variables and procedures.

Table 7.1. Vector Pascal reserved words

English	Chinese	Unicode
ABS	绝对值	7EDD,5BF9,503C
ADDR	地址	5730,5740
AND	^	2227
ARRAY	数组	6570,7EC4
BEGIN	开始	5F00,59CB
BOOLEAN	布尔值	5E03,5C14,503C
BYTE2PIXEL	字转像	5B57,8F6C,50CF
CASE	个案	4E2A,6848
CHR	字符	5B61,7B26
CONST	常量	5E38,91CF
COS	余弦	4F59,5F26
DIA	判断	5224,65AD
DIV	÷	00F7
DO	开始	5FAA,73AF
DOWNTO	下至	4E0B,81F3
END	结束	7ED3,675F
ELSE	否则	5426,5219
EXIT	退出	9000,51FA
EXTERNAL	外部的	5916,90E8,7684
FALSE	错误	9534,8BEF
FILE	文件	6587,4EF6
FOR	当	4ECE
FUNCTION	函数	51FD,6570
GOTO	跳转	8DF3,8F6C
IF	如果	5982,679C

Table 7.1. (*Continued*)

English	Chinese	Unicode
IMPLEMENTATION	实现	5B9E,73B0
IN	∍	
INTERFACE	接口	63A5,53E3
LABEL	标签	6807,7B7E
LIBRARY	库	5E93
LN	自然对数	81EA,7136,5BF9,6570
MAX	最大值	6700,5927,503C
MIN	最小值	6700,5C0F,503C
MOD	%	0025
NAME	名称	540D,79F0
NEW	新建	65B0,5EFA
NOT	¬	00AC
OF	的	7684
OPERATOR	运算符	8FD0,7B97,7B26
OR	∧	2228
ORD	字转数	5B57,8F6C,6570
OTHERWISE	否则	5426,6570
PACKED	封装	5C01,88C5
PERM	排列	6392,5217
PIXEL2BYTE	像转字	50CF,8F6C,5B57
POINTER	指针	6307,9488
POW	幂	5E42
PRED	前移	524D,79FB
PROCEDURE	过程	8FDB,7A0B
PROGRAM	程序	7A0B,5E8F
PROTECTED	保护	4FDD,62A4
READ	读	8BFB
READLN	读行	8BFB,884C
REAL	实数	5B9E,6570
RECORD	记录	8BB0,5F55
REPEAT	重复	91CD,590D
ROUND	四舍五入	56DB,820D,4E94,5165
SET	集合	96C6,5408
SHL	左位移	5DE6,4F4D,79FB
SHR	右位移	53F3,4F4D,79FB
SIN	正弦	6B63,5F26
SIZEOF	长度	957F,5EA6
STRING	串	4E32
SQRT	√	221A
SUCC	后移	540E,79FB
TAN	正切	6B63,5207
THEN	那么	90A3,4E48
TO	到	5230
TRANS	距阵变换	8DDD,9635,53D8,6362
TRUE	真	771F
TYPE	类型	7C7B,578B
VAR	变量	53D8,91CF
WITH	与	4E0E
WHILE	当	5F53
WRITE	写	5199
WRITELN	写行	5199,884C
UNIT	单元	5355,5143
UNTIL	直到	76F4,5230
USES	使用	4F7F,7528

Both the English and Chinese variants are shown. The canonical Unicode representation of the Chinese variant is also shown.

7.1.3 Character Case

<small>ISO-7185</small>

Because of its original 6-bit character code, Pascal has the rule that case is not significant in variables or reserved words. Thus `begin`, `BEGIN` and `Begin` are equivalent forms for the one reserved word. Vector Pascal retains this convention and extends it to the Greek and Cyrillic alphabets, where character case is again disregarded, so that Δ is equivalent to δ, etc. In the example programs in this book, the reserved words are sometimes capitalised, but this is purely conventional and not necessary.

<small>VECTOR</small>

When writing identifiers in Pascal, it is a common convention to use the under-bar and/or capitalisation to mark any component words imported from natural languages, thus `Captain_Haddock`, `PinkCrabs`.

7.1.4 Spaces and Comments

<small>ISO-7185</small>

In Pascal, space characters are not significant between lexemes. The space characters are space, carriage return, newline and tab. This means that space characters can be freely inserted between word operators or literal values. Spaces cannot be inserted into words or into numbers.

It is conventional in Pascal to make judicious use of space characters to indent programs to improve their legibility.

Comments may be placed at will between lexemes. They take two forms:

```
{this is the first form of comment}
(* this is the other form of comment *)
```

<small>VECTOR</small>

A comment that starts with { includes all characters up to the next }. A comment that starts with (* includes all characters up to the next *). Thus a comment starting with { can be used to bracket out both text and comments starting with (* and vice versa. It is advantageous to stick to the use of one of these comment forms, allowing the other to be reserved for commenting out large blocks of code whilst developing programs.

It should be noted that this use of comments it not portable to Standard Pascal, where a comment starting with { can end with *) and vice versa.

A comment starting with (*! and ending with *) is treated as a TeX comment, that is, the body of the comment is passed through unmodified when the VPTeX literate programming tool is used (see Section 7.7).

7.1.5 Semicolons

<small>ISO-7185</small>

Since carriage returns are not significant in Pascal, statements are separated by semicolons. This is not the same as having semicolons terminate statements. A semicolon need not occur after the last statement in a block. However, placing a semicolon after the last statement has no ill effect, amounting to the insertion of a null or do nothing statement at the end of the block. No run time code is executed for the null statement. For example:

```
BEGIN
  x:=a+c;
```

```
  y:=x*pi  {no semicolon needed here}
END
```

whereas

```
BEGIN
  x:=a+c;
  y:=x*pi;  {null statement after ; here}
END
```

In the last example the second semicolon is not needed since there is no following statement before the END.

7.2 Base Types

7.2.1 Booleans

The Boolean type is the set {true, false}. The words true and false are reserved in Pascal. In Vector Pascal but not Standard Pascal the relation true<false holds. Internally in Vector Pascal true is held as the value -1, which in two's complement is a string of binary 1s.

7.2.2 Integer Numbers

The normal way to denote an integer constant in Pascal is to use a decimal integer. Thus 12, 012, -9, 999 are valid integer constants. For certain purposes it is convenient to work with other number bases, in particular binary, octal and hexadecimal. Vector Pascal allows the use of the based number format introduced in Extended Pascal (ISO, 1991a). In this a number base is given first, followed by a # sign, and then a number in that base. Thus, the decimal number 33 could be written in binary as 2#100001, in octal as 8#41 and in hexadecimal 16#21.

Less obviously, one could write 32#11, 20#1D or 17#1G.

The use of letters in based numbers is a generalisation of their use in hexadecimal numbers. 'A' stands for 10, 'B' for 11, ... 'Z' for 35. Lower-case letters can be substituted for upper-case letters. For backwards compatibility with Turbo Pascal it is also possible to write hexadecimal numbers preceded by a $ sign, e.g. 33 = $21. Integers written as hexadecimals must be within the range $00000000...$FFFFFFFF. The sign of an integer written in hexadecimal notation is determined by the leftmost (most significant) bit of its binary representation.

The largest integer supported on an implementation is given by the integer constant maxint. The smallest integer will be -maxint-1.

7.2.3 Real Numbers

Real numbers are denoted in standard floating point formats. Thus 12.0, 0.12, -9.9 are valid floating-point numbers. Exponent notation is allowed: 2 506 000 can be written as 2.506E6, meaning 2.506×10^6, or 0.12 can be denoted by 1.2E-1. The exponent character can be either a lower- or an upper-case E, and the exponent can be signed, thus 2.506E6 = 25.06e5 = 250.6e+4.

The largest real number supported on an implementation is given by the constant maxreal. The smallest real number greater than 0 that can be represented on an implementation is given by the constant minreal.

Since real numbers are stored in floating-point format with an exponent and a mantissa, they can span a huge range of numbers. However, when representing very large numbers the limited length of the mantissa means that whole ranges of large integers are mapped to the same real number. This can pose a problem in algorithms which are designed to converge numerically. Such algorithms typically define some small ϵ such that iteration continues until successive approximations differ by less than ϵ. The value of ϵ that is meaningful in such an algorithm depends upon the numerical accuracy with which real numbers are held. The constant epsreal can be used to determine this. If r is a real number then the smallest ϵ which when added to r will result in a value distinguishable from r is r*epsreal.

Complex Numbers

Complex numbers are supported by Vector Pascal; they are formed by invoking a constructor function cmplx. Thus cmplx(1.0,0.5) returns the complex number whose real part is 1.0 and imaginary part is 0.5.

7.2.4 Characters and Strings

Characters and strings in Pascal are enclosed in single quotes, thus the following are strings or characters: 'A', 'B', 'Book'. If the single quote character is to be included in a character literal or string it is indicated by two successive single quotes. Thus the character ' is written '''', and the string 'Joe''s' would print out as:

    Joe's

Discrete characters which have no printable denotation can be produced using the chr operator. Thus chr(13) is the ASCII newline character. However, unlike C, Standard Pascal does not allow such unprintable characters to be embedded in string literals.

The current Vector Pascal implementation uses 16-bit Unicode as its internal character set and allows any Unicode character to be embedded in a character string. Thus a newline is embedded in a string simply by running it over two lines (see Alg. 21). Hence Chinese and other characters can be embedded in Vector Pascal strings.

The ord operator returns the integer value of a character, thus ord('A') will return the integer value of the letter A in the current character set.

The lowest value character in the character set supported on an implementation is given by the constant minchar. The highest valued character in the character set supported on an implementation is given by the constant maxchar.

```
PROGRAM newlnstr;
CONST sl='a
new line';
BEGIN
   WRITELN(sl);
END.
```

outputs

```
a
new line
```

Algorithm 21. Illustrating the embedding of a newline in a string.

7.3 Variables and Constants

7.3.1 Declaration Order

Pascal was designed to be parsed by a single-pass compiler. Since the language is also strongly typed, this means that the compiler can only type check statements if all identifiers are declared before they are used. This contrasts with more recent languages such as Java, where the declaration of identifiers can follow their use. Although the Vector Pascal compiler has distinct syntax analysis and code generation passes, it retains the requirement that declaration of identifiers must precede use. Further, it is a requirement that all identifiers used in a program context must be declared before the first executable statement of that context.

Consider the example given in Alg. 22. Everything between the line starting CONST to the line finishing with END. makes up what is termed in Pascal a block. The block is made up of a declaration part, which goes from the line starting CONST to just before the BEGIN, and an execution part which goes from BEGIN to END.

Three user-defined identifiers, a, v, t, are used within the execution part. They are introduced in the declaration part. The declaration part is divided into two portions, one preceded by the word CONST, which introduces constants, a in this case, and the other preceded by the word VAR, which introduces variables, t, v in this case.

In Standard Pascal, the constant declaration must precede the variable declarations. The motivation for this is that the variable section may include arrays whose sizes are defined by constant identifiers. Hence the constant identifiers had to be introduced prior to the variable identifiers.

In Extended Pascal, this restriction was relaxed, allowing constant and variable declarations to be optionally interleaved in any order, so long as this does not cause any identifier to be used prior to its introduction. It remains good practice, however, to follow the standard ordering of constants and variables.

```
PROGRAM velocity;
CONST
        a=9.8;     {acceleration due to gravity}
VAR
        t,v:real;
BEGIN
        WRITE('How many seconds has the fall lasted');
        READLN(t);
        v:=0.5*a*t POW 2;
        WRITELN('Velocity =',v,'m/s');
END.
```

Algorithm 22. Program to compute the velocity of a falling body.

7.3.2 Constant Declarations

A constant is an identifier which denotes the same value throughout its existence. The identifier a in Alg. 22 is an example. The declaration associates an identifier with a value. The compiler deduces the type of the identifier from the type of the value. Here are some examples of constant declarations:

```
CONST
    Lo=0;                    {an integer constant}
    Hi=100;                  {an integer constant}
    Mean=(Lo+Hi) div 2;      {integer given by expression}
    Zed='Z';                 {a character constant}
    Err='Name too long';     {string constant}
    SecsPerYear=pi*1E7;      {real defined by expression}
```

TURBO

In Standard Pascal, the values associated with the identifiers have to be literal constants. In Vector Pascal, this restriction is relaxed to allow numeric expressions whose value can be calculated at compile time to occur in constant declarations. Thus a constant expression in Vector Pascal can include arithmetic operators, other previously declared constants and literal constants. In the example above, Mean and SecsPerYear are examples of constants intialised by compile time expressions.

In order to keep code readable and to simplify maintenance, Pascal programmers are encouraged to make wide use of constant identifiers to replace literal constants. If this is done, changing a single constant declaration will change all places in the code where the relevant constant is used.

There exists a notation for the declaration of array constants (see Section 7.5.1).

In addition to the predeclared constants associated with numeric precision, a floating-point approximation to π is available as the pre-declared constant pi.

7.3.3 Variable Declarations

All variables must be declared before use. A variable declaration consists of a comma-separated list of identifiers followed by a colon followed by a type and terminated by a semicolon. All the identifiers in the list are defined as having the same type. Additional variables of different types, or more of the same type, can follow in the same way until all the required identifiers have been declared. For example:

```
VAR
  boxlen,boxwidth,boxheight:real;
  boxcount:integer;
  isopen:boolean;
```

A variable when declared has an undefined value. The declaration merely reserves space for the variable. A program error is likely to occur if a variable is used before a value has been assigned to it.

7.3.4 Assignment

A variable can have its value set by the assignment operator := as shown in Alg. 22. The assignment operator is generic to all types. Arrays and records can be assigned to variables of the appropriate type by a single assignment operator.

7.3.5 Predefined Types

There exists in Pascal a system for declaring new types (see Chapter 9), but there exists a set of predefined types available to all programs. Six of these have already been introduced: `boolean`, `integer`, `real`, `complex`, `char`, `string`. Any of these can be used in a variable declaration.

In addition, there are a set of auxiliary types provided to allow the programmer to tailor the store used by variables to the arithmetic precision required by the algorithm. The auxiliary types should be used sparingly as their use hinders portability. The circumstances in which their use is advantageous are as follows:

1. When the numeric precision of an algorithm requires less accuracy than that provided by the standard types, and where economy in the use of memory is important. Under these circumstances, variables may be defined to be of type `byte`, `pixel` or `shortint`.
2. Where the range of numbers is sufficiently small and the programmer wants to take advantage of greater SIMD parallelism, types `byte`, `pixel` or `shortint` should be used.
3. Where the range of numbers being used is too great to represent as an integer or a real. Under these circumstances, a double-precision real `double`, or a 64-bit integer `int64`, representation may be stipulated.

7.4 Expressions and Operators

An expression is a sequence of identifiers, constants or bracketed expressions linked by operators. An expression is used to calculate new values from already existing ones.

```
a+b
5*a
x+y*z
4/b+c
```

are expressions.

7.4.1 Arithmetic

Pascal supports the basic arithmetic operations using the familiar operator symbols:

- `+` addition
- `−` subtraction
- `*` multiplication
- `×` Vector Pascal synonym for `*`   Unicode 2715
- `/` division with real or complex valued result

Expressions are evaluated such that multiplication and division are performed left to right before addition and subtraction. To ensure that the evaluation is as intended parentheses can be used.

`a/b+x/y*z`

is evaluated as

$$\frac{a}{b} + \left(\frac{x}{y} \times z\right)$$

which must be distinguished from

$$\frac{a}{b} + \frac{x}{y \times z}$$

to achieve which one would have had to write

`a/b+x/(y*z)`

Arithmetic is *not* allowed on characters. The + operator is allowed on strings where it is interpreted as string concatenation. Since single-character strings and individual characters have the same representation, + between characters is also interpreted as string concatenation. As a generalisation of multiplication being repeated addition, * is allowed between integers and strings, thus

```
expression      value
'abc'+'case'    'abccase'
```

Chapter 7 • Basics of Vector Pascal

```
'a'+'b'        'ab'
'abc'*3        'abcabcabc'
```

Pascal also supplies two further operators that operate exclusively on integer arithmetic:

ISO-7185

    MOD   remainder after division of integers
    DIV   truncated division of integers
    ÷   Vector Pascal synonym for DIV   Unicode 00f7

The effects of the various division operators are summarised below:

```
expression       value
16/5             3.2
16 div 5         3
16 mod 5         1
8 div 3*3        6
13-5 mod 3       11
```

`a/b+x div y*z`

is evaluated as

$$\frac{a}{b} + \left\lfloor \frac{x}{y} \right\rfloor \times z$$

which must be distinguished from

$$\frac{a}{b} + \left\lfloor \frac{x \times z}{y} \right\rfloor$$

for which one would have to write

`a/b+(x*z) div y`

since the effect of truncation will cause loss of precision in the first case.

Vector Pascal provides other dyadic operators on numbers which are not provided in Standard Pascal but which were introduced in subsequent systems. First there are the exponential operators:

    a**b   raises a to the fractional power b
    a POW b raises a to an integral power b

ISO-10206

16**0.5	4.0
4**1.5	8.0
16**−0.25	0.5
16 POW 2	256

The exponential operators have higher priority than any other dyadic operators.

There are also a set of operators that allow integers to be treated as bit vectors:

    a SHR b   shift the integer a right by b bits
    a SHL b   shift the integer a left by b bits

	a AND b	perform a bitwise and of a with b
	a OR b	perform a bitwise or of a with b

TURBO

Expression	Value
2#101 SHL 2	20
2#101 SHR 1	2
2#1100 AND 24	8
2#1100 OR 24	28

The operators AND and OR are also defined on Booleans. The shift operators can be used as alternatives for multiplication and division by powers of 2 so that:

a SHR n is equivalent to a DIV (2 POW n)

and

a SHL n is equivalent to a*(2 POW n)

It should not be assumed that the use of shift operators will necessarily be faster than the equivalent divide and multiply operators.

Finally, there are selection operators allowing the larger or smaller of two values to be chosen.

	a MIN b	returns the lesser of a, b
	a MAX b	returns the larger of a, b

VECTOR

7.4.2 Operations on Boolean Values

Boolean values can be manipulated using the operators AND, OR, NOT in addition to the comparison operators. The AND operator produces a TRUE result if and only if both operands are true. If a is TRUE and b is TRUE then (a AND b)=TRUE. The OR operator produces a TRUE result if *either* of its operands is TRUE. The NOT operators maps TRUE to FALSE and vice versa.

These results are summarised in the composite truth table:

a	b	a AND b	a OR b	NOT a
true	true	true	true	false
true	false	false	true	false
false	true	false	true	true
false	false	false	false	true

Vector Pascal allows single Unicode characters to be used for the boolean operators:

VECTOR

	Synonym	Unicode
NOT	¬	00ac
AND	∧	2227
OR	∨	2228

7.4.3 Equality Operators

The equality operator = takes two operands from a comparable type and returns a Boolean TRUE if the operands are the same. Otherwise it returns false. Equality is defined on integers, reals, Booleans, characters, strings, ordinals, sets (see Section 9.6) and pointers (see Section 9.5).

The not-equals operator <> takes two operands of a comparable type and returns TRUE if and only if the operands are not the same.

7.4.4 Ordered Comparison

Pascal provides the standard ordered comparison operators <, >, <=, >=, which can be applied between pairs of elements drawn any ordered type. That is, any pair of Booleans, any pair of integers or reals, any pair of characters, any pair of strings or a pair of elements drawn from the same ordinal type may be compared.

```
program compare;
const data:array[1..4] of string[4]=
          ('abc','abcd','Abc','aba');
begin
writeln('compare''abc'' to:');
write(' ',data,
      '<>',   'abc'<>data,
      '= ',   'abc'=data,
      '< ',   'abc'<data,
      '> ',   'abc'>data,
      '<=',   'abc'<=data,
      '>=',   'abc'>=data);{}
end.
```

Output produced:

```
compare 'abc' to:
           abc     abcd    Abc     aba
    <>     false   true    true    true
    =      true    false   false   false
    <      false   true    false   false
    >      false   false   true    true
    <=     true    true    false   false
    >=     true    false   true    true
```

Algorithm 23. Effect of string length and character values on string order.

When ordered comparisons are applied to strings both the character values and the lengths of the strings have to be taken into account. A string

```
PROGRAM truthtab;
CONST a:ARRAY[1..4] OF boolean=
        (true,true,false,false);
      b:ARRAY[1..4] OF boolean=
        (true,false,true,false);
BEGIN
WRITE('a',       a,
      'b',       b,
      'a and b', a AND b,
      'a or b',  a OR b,
      'a<>b',    a<>b,
      'a=b',     a=b,
      'a<b',     a<b,
      'a>b',     a>b,
      'a<=b',    a<=b,
      'a>=b',    a>=b);
END.
```

Output produced:

a	true	true	false	false
b	true	false	true	false
a and b	true	false	false	false
a or b	true	true	true	false
a<>b	false	true	true	false
a=b	true	false	false	true
a<b	false	true	false	false
a>b	false	false	true	false
a<=b	true	true	false	true
a>=b	true	false	true	true

Algorithm 24. truthtab, a program to print the truth tables for all of the dyadic Boolean operators.

is equal to another if it is the same length and has identical characters in all positions.

A string a is less than another string b if there exists a character in some position i in string b such that $a_j = b_j \, \forall j < i$ and either the length of a is less than i or $a_i < b_i$.

ISO-7185

The comparison operators when applied to Boolean types provide additional dyadic Boolean operators. The most useful of these are <>, which is the XOR operator when applied to Booleans and = which is equivalent to NOT XOR.

VECTOR

The ordered comparison operators give results that are not portable between Vector Pascal and ISO Pascal. The truth tables provided by all of the dyadic operators over the Booleans are shown in Alg. 24.

7.5 Matrix and Vector Operations

The most significant difference between Vector Pascal and other implementations of Pascal are the extensions that Vector Pascal provides to allow operations on simple variables to be transparently extended to work on arrays. Consider the program in Alg. 25. Invoking the program produces the following result:

C:\book>add1

```
(*
Program to Add 1 to the first 4 primes and then print
this, followed by twice the first 4 primes + 1
*)
PROGRAM Add1;
CONST   c:ARRAY[1..4] OF INTEGER=(1,2,3,5);
BEGIN
   WRITE(c,c+1,1+2*c);
END.
```

1	2	3	5
2	3	4	6
3	5	7	11

Algorithm 25. Simple example of array operations.

Add1 declares a constant array c to hold the first four primes. The program then prints out c, followed by the effect of adding 1 to each element of c, followed by the sum of the previous two lines.

7.5.1 Array Declarations

ISO-7185

Before any array is used, it must be declared. In Add1 the array c is a constant array. A similar variable array could be declared as

VAR v:ARRAY[1..4] OF integer;

However, the values of the variable array, as with any variable, are undefined when the program starts.

An array declaration specifies the range of the array, in this case 1...4 and the type of the array elements, in this case integer. The range specifies two things:

1. how many storage locations are to be allocated by the compiler for the array
2. the logical numbering of these storage elements.

ISO-7185

It is possible to declare multi-dimensional arrays. Thus

VAR mat:ARRAY[1..3,1..3] OF real;

declares a 3 by 3 matrix of locations to hold real numbers, whilst a constant matrix could be declared as

```
CONST ident:ARRAY[1..3,1..3] OF real=((1.0,0.0,0.0),
                                      (0.0,1.0,0.0),
                                      (0.0,0.0,1.0));
```

which is the 3 by 3 identity matrix. Note that when declaring a constant matrix, one must indicate the rows by brackets.

A two-dimensional array can conceptually be thought of as a single object with two dimensions, or as a one-dimensional array whose elements are themselves one-dimensional arrays. Pascal allows one to declare arrays in either of these formats but treats the two forms as synonymous. Hence the following two array variables are of identical type:

```
VAR v1:ARRAY[1..2,1..3] OF integer;
    v2:ARRAY[1..2] OF ARRAY[1..3] OF integer;
```

There will be an implementation-defined maximum number of array dimensions supported by any given Vector Pascal compiler. This is provided in the predefined constant `maxdims`.

7.5.2 Matrix and Vector Arithmetic

Basic Arithmetic

In the examples given in Algs 20, 25 and 30, arithmetic is performed on arrays in a fairly obvious and intuitive way. In a programming language however, simple intuition, although helpful, is not enough. One needs to know the precise meaning of a construct. Array arithmetic follows a set of consistent principles:

1. Vector Pascal allows any arithmetic operator that can be applied to a pair of elements of a data type t to be used between arrays of type t.
2. Vector Pascal performs array arithmetic on an element by element basis. Thus in Alg. 20, the zeroth element of `v1` is the sum of the zeroth elements of vectors `v2`, `v3`. This is precisely what is required for the addition and subtraction of vectors and matrics.

    Note that for multiplication and division this will not be the same as vector or matrix multiplication in linear algebra. Matrix multiplication is dealt with in Section 7.6.
3. When performing arithmetic on a pair of arrays, the bounds of the arrays must exactly match. An attempt to add an array whose bounds are 1...4 to an array whose bounds are 0...3 will give rise to either a compile time or a run time error.
4. The result of performing element by element array arithmetic is another array whose bounds will be the same as those of the arrays which gave rise to it.
5. A scalar x and an array y may be combined using dyadic operators. The result is an array whose bounds are those of y. This means that the scalar is

```
PROGRAM PrintIdent2;
CONST ident:ARRAY[1..3,1..3] OF integer=((1,0,0),
                                         (0,1,0),
                                         (0,0,1));
      factor:ARRAY[1..3] OF integer=(100,200,400);
BEGIN
   WRITE(factor*ident);
END.
```

this produces when invoked:

```
C:\book>printident2
            100           0           0
              0         200           0
              0           0         400
```

Algorithm 26. Element by element multiplication of each row of a matrix by a vector.

combined under the operator with every element in y. This form of construction is illustrated in Alg. 25. This implements the mathematical operation of multiplying a vector by a scalar. The same rule allows multiplication of a matrix by a scalar.

6. An array x of dimension n, and an array y of dimension m, where $n < m$, can be combined under a dyadic operator provided that the bounds of the rightmost n dimensions of each array match. This is illustrated in Alg. 26.
7. Assignment to an array is allowed if the value on the right-hand side of the assignment is an array of the same type.
8. Assignment to an array is allowed if the value on the right-hand side of the assignment is a scalar of the same type as the elements of the array or is castable to an element of the same type as the elements of an array [in some array languages this is called flood fill (Snyder, 1999)]. This is illustrated in Alg. 27, where 1 is cast to a real and used to fill y.
9. An array x of dimension n may be assigned to an array y of dimension m, where $n < m$ provided that the bounds of the rightmost n dimensions of each array match and that the elements of y are the same type as or implicitly castable to the type of those of x.

Reduction Operations: Forming Generalised Totals

The total of the numbers (1, 2, 3, 5) is formed by injecting the $+$ operator between them, thus $(1 + 2 + 3 + 5) = 11$. Similarly, the product of these numbers is formed by injecting the multiplication operator between them, thus $(1 \times 2 \times 3 \times 5) = 30$.

It is clear that this sort of operator injection is a general method by which a vector of numbers can be reduced to a scalar, forming in the process 'totals' that are parameterised by operators. In Vector Pascal and other array

```
PROGRAM flood;
VAR y:ARRAY[1..2,1..3] OF real;
BEGIN
    y:=1;
    WRITE(y);
END.
```

which produces on invocation:

```
C:\book>flood
        1.00000         1.00000         1.00000
        1.00000         1.00000         1.00000
```

Algorithm 27. Flood filling an array with a scalar.

```
(*! Program to find the arithmetic and
    geometric means of the first 4 primes *)
PROGRAM Mean1;
CONST c:ARRAY[1..4] OF integer=(1,2,3,5);
BEGIN
    WRITE((\+ c)/4,(\* c)**0.25);
END.
```

Algorithm 28. An example of operator reduction.

programming languages, this process is called a reduction operation.[1] An illustration is given in Alg. 28, which prints out 2.75 2.34035 as the means.

The arithmetic mean is computed by the expression (\+ c)/4. The key to this is the reserved word RDU or \, the reduction functional. This must be followed by a dyadic operator and an array expression. The operator is then injected between the elements of the rightmost dimension of the array delivering a result of rank one less than that of the array.

In the program Mean1 the + operator is injected forming a total which is then divided by 4 to give the mean. Analogously, the geometric mean is found by injecting the * operator between the elements of c and raising the result to the power of 0.25.

Reduction by any of the commutative operators yields the obvious results. For example, one can find the largest of four integers as shown in Alg. 29.

Care must be taken when performing reduction using non-commutative operators and operators whose result is not of the same type as their arguments. Consider what the expression RDU-c would mean in the program Mean1. At one level it obviously means $1 - 2 - 3 - 5$ but, depending on the bracketing convention used, this could either evaluate to $-9 = ((1 - 2) - 3) - 5$ or to $-3 = (1 - (2 - (3 - 5))) = 1 - 2 + 3 - 5$.

---

[1]The reduction functional was introduced in APL (Iverson, 1962), where it was written as /. For those who are familiar with APL, a form with similar flavour has been retained in Vector Pascal. Thus as an alternative to writing RDU+c one can write \+c.

```
(* Program to find the largest of 4 integers *)
PROGRAM Max1;
VAR x:ARRAY[1..4] OF integer;
BEGIN
    READ(x);
    WRITE(RDU MAX x);
END.
```

Given the input:
3 100 -9 99
this produces the output:

100

Algorithm 29. Reduction using MAX.

The convention used for reduction in Vector Pascal is the second. This is partly for compatibility with APL, but also because one of the few uses for reduction by - is in the evaluation of power series, where one wants just the alternation of positive and negative terms in the series, that evaluation of reduction from right to left gives.

When reducing by a relational operator such as =, one has to beware of generating type errors. If the array to which the reduction is applied is numeric, like c in Mean1, then RDU=c would translate as $1 = (2 = (3 = 5))$. This fails at compile on type consistency grounds, since $3 = 5$ generates a Boolean, which is then to be compared with 2, an integer.

The relational operators can only be used to reduce Boolean arrays. Thus RDU=b for b=(TRUE,TRUE,TRUE) will return TRUE.

7.5.3 Array Input/Output

When arrays are passed to a write statement as a parameter, the arrays are printed a row at a time, with newlines at the end of each dimension. Thus, when printing a two-dimensional array, each row is on a distinct line, followed by a blank line at the end of the array. This is illustrated by the code in Alg. 30, which when run prints

```
C:\book>printpowers
               1      2
               2      4

               2      4
               4      8

               3      9
               9     81

               9     81
              81   6561
```

```
PROGRAM PrintPowers;
CONST powers:ARRAY[1..2,1..2,1..2] OF integer=(((1,2),
                                                (2,4)),
                                               ((2,4),
                                                (4,8)));
VAR v:ARRAY[1..2,1..2,1..2] OF integer;
BEGIN
    WRITE(powers);
    v:=3 POW powers;
    WRITE(v);
END.
```

Algorithm 30. Illustration of how a multi-dimensional array is printed.

When reading data into an array, the elements of the array should be separated by spaces along the rows, and by newlines at the end of each dimension.

7.5.4 Array Slices

In many applications one wants to operate on parts of an array. For instance, in image processing there is the concept of a region of interest or a window, a rectangular sub-section of a two-dimensional array of pixels. Vector Pascal supports this with a syntax to refer to slices of arrays.

For instance, given the two-dimensional array dataset declared in Alg. 31, then WRITE(dataset[2..3]:3) will print out the second and third rows in fields three characters wide:

 11 13 17 19 23
 12 15 20 24 30

whereas WRITE(dataset[][3..5]:3) will output columns 3–5:

  3 5 7
 17 19 23
 20 24 30
 37 43 53
 57 67 83

and WRITE(dataset[2..3][3..5]:3) will output

 17 19 23
 20 24 30

We can select out a column with the syntax dataset[][2], which prints out as

  2
 13
 15
 28
 43

Chapter 7 • Basics of Vector Pascal

```
(* Demonstrate array slicing *)
PROGRAM slice;
CONST dataset:ARRAY[1..5,1..5] OF integer=
            (( 1, 2, 3, 5, 7),
             (11,13,17,19,23),
             (12,15,20,24,30),
             (23,28,37,43,53),
             (35,43,57,67,83));
BEGIN
  WRITELN('dataset');
  WRITE(dataset:3);
  WRITELN('dataset[2..3]');
  WRITE(dataset[2..3]:3);
  WRITELN('dataset[][3..5]');
  WRITE(dataset[][3..5]:3);
  WRITELN('dataset[2..3][3..5]');
  WRITE(dataset[2..3][3..5]:3);
  WRITELN('dataset[][2]');
  WRITE(dataset[][2]:3);
  WRITELN('dataset[2]');
  WRITE(dataset[2]:3);
  WRITELN('dataset[2,3]');
  WRITE(dataset[2][3]:3);
  WRITELN('dataset[2,3]');
  WRITE(dataset[2..2][3..3]:3);
END.
```

Algorithm 31. The use of array slices.

ISO-7185 and a row using `dataset[2]`, which prints out as

11 13 17 19 23

ISO-7185 or a single-array element with `dataset[2][3]`, which simply prints as

17

VECTOR as does the more complex `dataset[2..2][3..3]`.

Array selections can be used wherever entire variables can be used subject to type restrictions. It is worth taking care to understand the types of each of the selections above:

	Selection	Type
1	dataset	ARRAY[1..5] OF ARRAY[1..5] OF integer
2	dataset[2..3]	ARRAY[0..1] OF ARRAY[1..5] OF integer
3	dataset[2..3][3..5]	ARRAY[0..1] OF ARRAY[0..2] OF integer
4	dataset[][3..5]	ARRAY[0..4] OF ARRAY[0..2] OF integer
5	dataset[][2]	ARRAY[0..4] OF ARRAY[0..0] OF integer
6	dataset[2]	ARRAY[1..5] OF integer

```
7  dataset[2][3]        integer
8  dataset[2..2][3..3]  ARRAY[0..0] OF ARRAY[0..0] OF integer
```

Some of them select matrices, some vectors and one a scalar. In particular, one should distinguish between selecting a row and selecting a column. Row selection is like `dataset[2]` and column selection like `dataset[][2]`. A row is a one-dimensional array and a column is a two-dimensional array whose second dimension consists of arrays of length 1.

One should also distinguish between `dataset[2][3]`, an individual element of the array, and `dataset[2..2][3..3]`, a two-dimensional array each of whose dimensions is singular. Consider the following example assignments:

```
1  dataset[2][3] := 3                          valid
2  dataset[2..2][3..3] := 3                    valid, produces same effect
                                               as example 1
3  dataset[2..2][3..3] := dataset[1][2]        valid
4  dataset[2][3] := dataset[1..1][2..2]        invalid, rank on the right > left
```

In several cases the effect of selecting a singular array is identical with that of selecting an array element, but when an assignment is made, the expression on the right hand-side of the assignment must have rank lower than or equivalent to that on the left.

7.6 Vector and Matrix Products

In addition to the element by element arithmetic operations on vectors and matrices described above, Vector Pascal provides a vector and matrix product operator. This allows vectors to be multiplied by vectors, vectors to be multiplied by matrices or matrices to be multiplied by matrices.

7.6.1 Inner Product of Vectors

Given that v, w are one-dimensional arrays, then v.w is the scalar formed by the equation

$$\mathbf{v}.\mathbf{w} = \sum_{i=a}^{b} v_i \times w_i \qquad (7.1)$$

where a, b are the lower and upper bounds of the two arrays. This is referred to as the dot product or inner product of vectors. The inner product has direct geometric interpretations in computer graphics.

A first use of it is in computing the length of vectors. The length of a vector v written as $|v|$ is given by the generalisation of Pythagoras's equation:

$$\sqrt{\sum_{i=0}^{n} v_i^2} = |v| \qquad (7.2)$$

Chapter 7 • Basics of Vector Pascal

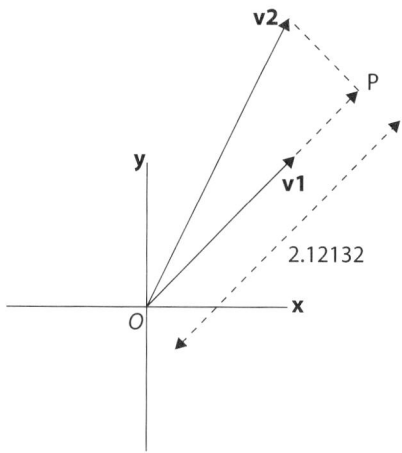

Figure 7.1. Projection of one vector on to another. In the example, v2 = (1,2), v1 = (1,1).

but

$$\sqrt{\mathbf{v}.\mathbf{v}} = \sqrt{\sum_{i=0}^{n} v_i^2} \qquad (7.3)$$

so the dot product operator is a key step in the calculation of vector lengths.

Another use is in measuring the projection of one vector against another. Consider Figure 7.1: suppose we want to measure how far **v2** extends in the direction of **v1**. Geometrically this can be done by constructing the right-angled triangle O, P, **v2** shown, and then measuring its base O, P. This is the *projection* of **v2** on to the extension of **v1**. The dot product operation is the computational key to this.

Given the vector **v2** = (1, 2), it is clear that its projections on to the x- and y-axes, respectively, are 1 and 2. If we define the unit vectors[2] **x** = (1, 0) and **y** = (0, 1), then by using the dot product operator we can measure the length of **v2** in the direction of **x** or **y**. This is shown in Alg. 32. More generally, if we have some vector **v** we can measure its length in the direction of some unit vector **r** by **r.v**. If we have some vector of arbitrary length (**v1** in Figure 7.1), we can measure the length of **v2** in the direction of **v1** by using the equation

$$\frac{\mathbf{v1}.\mathbf{v2}}{\sqrt{\mathbf{v1}.\mathbf{v1}}} = \frac{\mathbf{v1}.\mathbf{v2}}{|\mathbf{v1}|} = \frac{\mathbf{v1}}{|\mathbf{v1}|}.\mathbf{v2}$$

This can be considered as first normalising **v1** to produce the unit vector $\frac{\mathbf{v1}}{|\mathbf{v1}|}$, having the same direction as **v1**, and then projecting **v2** on to that normalised vector.

Note that in the Vector Pascal version of the equation:

```
dd:=(v2.v1)/sqrt(v1.v1);
```

---
[2] A unit vector has length 1.

```
program dotproduct;
type vec=array[0..1] of real;
const
  v1:vec=(1.0,1.0);
  v2:vec=(1.0,2.0);
  x:vec=(1.0,0.0);
  y:vec=(0.0,1.0);
var dx,dy,dd,l:real;norm45:vec;
begin
  dx:=v2.x;
  writeln('project',v2,'against x =',dx);
  dy:=v2.y;
  writeln('project',v2,'against y =',dy);
  dd:=(v2.v1)/sqrt(v1.v1);
  writeln('length',v2,'in direction',v1,' = ',dd);
end.
```

when executed this produces

```
project        1.00000    2.00000
against x =    1.00000
project        1.00000    2.00000
against y =    2.00000
    length     1.00000    2.00000
in direction   1.00000    1.00000
         =     2.12132
```

Algorithm 32. The dot product of two vectors. See Figure 7.1 for explanation.

the bracketing ensures that the division is scalar. This is more efficient than writing

```
v2.(v1/sqrt(v1.v2))
```

since in the latter case vector division has to be performed. For short vectors like these, it is not important, but for longer vectors the distinction is significant. For efficiency reasons one should rearrange equations to minimise the amount of vector arithmetic performed.

When compiled for a CPU with suitable vector instructions (see Table C.1 in Appendix C), the compiler will attempt translate the dot product of two vectors into vectorised code.

7.6.2 Dot Product of Non-real Typed Vectors

The example above describes the dot product operation in its classical mathematical form, where vectors or real numbers are multiplied together. The dot product operation can be decomposed into two components:

1. an element by element multiplication
2. a reduction step to form the total.

```
program overflow;
type bvec=array[0..7] of byte;
     ivec=array[0..7] of integer;
const b1:bvec=(1,2,4,8,16,32,16,8);
var t1,t2:integer;i1:ivec;
begin
   t1:=b1.b1;
   i1:=b1;
   t2:=i1.i1;
   writeln('byte dot product ',t1);
   writeln('int dot product ',t2);
end.
```

produces as output

```
byte  dot product      149
int   dot product     1685
```

note that 149 = (1685 mod 256)

Algorithm 33. The danger of overflow when computing dot products using limited precision.

VECTOR

As such, the expression v.w is equivalent to the Vector Pascal expression \+(v*w). It therefore has meaning for any types for which the operators + and * are defined. The integer interpretation of this is direct, but care has to be taken with the possibility of overflows occurring. The type of scalar result returned by the dot product operator is the same as the type of the elements of the arrays being multiplied. When working with integers, particularly integers of limited precision, this gives rise to the risk of the result being greater than can be represented in the available precision. Alg. 33 illustrates how a dot product of a vector of bytes is computed to only 8-bit precision, in contrast to the case where the same input values are represented as 32-bit integers.

It is also possible to perform the dot product operation between other types of vectors:

1. Vectors of complex numbers. In this case, the interpretation is in terms of complex addition and multiplication.
2. Vectors of sets (see Section 9.6). In this case, the interpretation is in terms of set union and intersection.
3. A vector of strings may multiply a vector of integers. In this case, the interpretation is in terms of concatenation and repetition. This is illustrated in Alg. 34.

7.6.3 Matrix to Vector Product

In Section 3.6, we discussed the use of matrix of the form given in Equation 3.3 to carry out generalised linear geometry transforms. We can do this in

```
program roman;
const rom:array[0..4] of string[1]=('C','L','X','V','I');
      numb:array[0..4] of integer  =( 2, 1, 1, 0, 3);
var s:string;
begin
  s:=numb.rom;
  writeln(s);
end.
```

produces output

```
[wpc@localhost tests]$ roman
CCLXIII
```

Algorithm 34. Use of the dot product operator to output the number 263 as the roman number CCLXIII.

VECTOR

Vector Pascal if a two-dimensional array is used to multiply a one-dimensional array, using the dot product operator. If M is a two-dimensional array and v a vector, M.v produces the transformed vector.

The program matvmult, shown in Alg. 35, shows the repeated application of a rotation and translation matrix to the unit x vector. When the matrix

$$\begin{pmatrix} \frac{1}{\sqrt{2}} & \frac{-1}{\sqrt{2}} & 0 & 0 \\ \frac{1}{\sqrt{2}} & \frac{1}{\sqrt{2}} & 0 & 0 \\ 0 & 0 & 1 & 0.2 \\ 0 & 0 & 0 & 1 \end{pmatrix}$$

is applied to a vector of the form $[x, y, z, 1]$, it rotates it by $45°$ and moves it up by 0.2.

7.6.4 Data-flow Hazards

Note that in Alg. 35, one cannot simply write v1:=M.v1; instead, one has to write

```
v2:=M.v1;
v1:=v2;
```

since the vector v1 might be changing whilst it was being read. Had the compiler encountered this statement, it would have generated the error messages:

```
compilation failed
17: Error assignment invalid
17: Error in primary expression started by m
17: Error attempting to reduce rank of variable
17: Error data hazard found. Destination v1 is used with
    an index permutation on right hand side of := which
    can cause it to be corrupted.
```

You can get round this by assigning to a temporary
array instead and then assigning the temporary to
destination v1

A check for data-flow hazards is applied to all array assignment statements. If array expressions could all be evaluated in parallel, then there would be no hazards. The problem arises because only simple array expressions can be evaluated entirely in parallel. In other cases the array assignment has to be

```
program matvmult;
type vec=array[0..3] of real;
     mat=array[0..3] of vec;
const
   rr2=0.7071067 ;              {1/sqrt(2)}
   M:mat=((rr2,-rr2,0.0,0.0),   {45degree spiral matrix}
          (rr2,rr2,0.0,0.0),
          (0.0,0.0,1.0,0.2),
          (0.0,0.0,0.0,1.0));
   v:vec=(1.0,0.0,0.0,1.0);
var v1,v2:vec;i:integer;
begin
   write(M,v);
   v1:=v;
   (* perform 8 45degree rotations *)
   for i:=1 to 8 do begin
      v2:=M.v1;
      v1:=v2;
      write(v1);
   end;
end.
```

produces as output

```
    0.70711    -0.70711    0.00000    0.00000
    0.70711     0.70711    0.00000    0.00000
    0.00000     0.00000    1.00000    0.20000
    0.00000     0.00000    0.00000    1.00000
    1.00000     0.00000    0.00000    1.00000
    0.70711     0.70711    0.20000    1.00000
    0.00000     1.00000    0.40000    1.00000
   -0.70711     0.70711    0.60000    1.00000
   -1.00000    -0.00000    0.80000    1.00000
   -0.70711    -0.70711    1.00000    1.00000
   -0.00000    -1.00000    1.20000    1.00000
    0.70711    -0.70711    1.40000    1.00000
    1.00000    -0.00000    1.60000    1.00000
```

Algorithm 35. Using a spiral rotation matrix to operate on the unit x vector.

broken down by the compiler into a sequence of steps. This gives rise to the danger that an array location may be altered by an early step prior to it being used a source of data by a subsequent step.

In most cases there will be no problem even where the destination vector appears on the right-hand side of an assignment. Thus:

```
M:=M+v;
```

for some matrix M and vector v is acceptable, since here each element of M depends only on its own prior value. However, for `v1:= M.v1`, we have the equations

$$v1_0 = \sum_{j=0}^{3} M_{0j} v1_j \qquad (7.4)$$

$$v1_1 = \sum_{j=0}^{3} M_{1j} v1_j \qquad (7.5)$$

Whatever the order in which the code for these equations is evaluated, either $v1_0$ or $v1_1$ will be altered before it is used in the other equation. Given that such hazards can arise in any language that allows parallel array assignments, there are two design approaches that can be taken to avoid them:

1. One can check for data-flow hazards at compile time and flag them as programming errors.
2. One can define the semantics of the language so that each array expression computes its full result before any assignment occurs.

Vector Pascal takes the first approach whereas APL NIAL and Fortran 90 take the second. For an interpretive language in which arrays are dynamically generated on the heap, such as APL and NIAL, this is the natural applicative semantics to adopt. For imperative languages where arrays are in the main statically allocated, there are advantages to each approach. The second approach gives rise to more natural semantics, requiring less thought on the part of the programmer, but it is less efficient. If each array expression generates a new array of values, then store must be allocated for this purpose. On modern machines one is not likely to be short of main memory, but frequent allocation of temporary buffers will have an impact on cache occupancy which might not have occurred in the equivalent sequential algorithm. In Vector Pascal, all array expressions are interpreted as loops around derived scalar expressions. The temporary store required by the scalar expressions can then be allocated in registers.

7.6.5 Matrix to Matrix Multiplication

The dot operator can be used between matrices to perform matrix multiplication as illustrated in Alg. 36. This applies the standard equation for matrix

```
program matmmult;
const
   A:array[1..2,1..3] of integer=((3,1,2),
                                  (2,1,3));
   B:array[1..3,1..2] of integer=((1,2),
                                  (3,1),
                                  (2,3));
var C:array[1..2,1..2] of integer;
begin
   C:=A.B;
   writeln(C);
end.
```

Produces output

```
     10          13
     11          14
```

Algorithm 36. Matrix by matrix multiplication.

multiplication:

$$c_{ik} = \sum_{s=1}^{p} a_{is} b_{sk} \qquad (7.6)$$

where A is of order $(m \times p)$ and B is of order $(p \times n)$ to give a resulting matrix C of order $(m \times n)$.

7.7 Typography of Vector Pascal Programs

Vector Pascal makes use of a number of other publicly available software tools. One of these is the TEX typesetting sytem.

There exists a canonical TEX representation of Vector Pascal programs, VPTEX. This representation can be obtained either by use of a compiler flag (the -L flag), which causes the compiler to output a program listing as a `.tex` file, or by using the VIPER Integrated Development Environment discussed in Sections 16.1–16.6. The program shown in Alg. 28 would look like Figure 7.2 once formated through VPTEX and LATEX.

> **program** *Mean1*;
> **const**
>   *c*:**array** $[1..4]$ **of** *integer* $= (1,2,3,5)$;
> **begin**
>   **write**($\frac{\Sigma c}{4}$,$(\Pi c)^{0.25}$);
> **end**.

Figure 7.2. Illustration of VPTEX formating applied to the program shown in Alg. 28 to find the mean of the first 4 primes.

```
program forms;
var a:array[1..4] of real;
    b:integer;
begin
    b:=3; {initialise b}
    a:=7/b;{flood fill}
    a[b]:=sqrt(a[b]*b);
    write(a);
end.
```

program *forms*;
var
   Let *a* ∈ array[1..4] of real;
   Let *b* ∈ integer;
begin
   b ← 3;
   $a \leftarrow \frac{7}{b}$;
   $a_b \leftarrow \sqrt{a_b \times b}$;
   write(*a*);
end.

initialise b
flood fill

Figure 7.3. The mapping from ASCII to TEX format.

In VPTEX the reserved words of Vector Pascal are rendered in bold sans-serif font. User-defined identifiers are rendered in italic sans-serif font.

Comments that are preceeded by a special comment opening sequence (*! are treated as LATEX source and passed directly to the .tex output file. By default these will be printed in roman face. Comments at the end of a line are printed by VPTEX as marginal notes. The example in Figure 7.3 of Vector Pascal in ASCII format shows some of the conversions performed when going to VPTEX format.

Note how array subscripting is printed using typographic subscripts and standard mathematical notation is used for square root. The VPTEX format is intended for both documentation and communication purposes, wherever the mathematical meaning of an algorithm has to be concisely expressed. The higher order operators in Vector Pascal lend themselves well to mathematical notation. In subsequent chapters VPTEX format will be used where it helps communicate algorithms and where the ASCII forms of the constructs used have already been introduced.

Algorithmic Features of Vector Pascal

Chapter 7 presented the key features of Vector Pascal's expression language. These allow it to be used as, in essence, a sophisticated calculator working on both scalars and arrays. In order to write general-purpose algorithms, one needs to add facilities for conditional evaluation and either recursion or unbounded iteration.

8.1 Conditional Evaluation

Vector Pascal reintroduces an old construct, the conditional expression. This was present in Algol-60 but was deleted from Pascal by Wirth because he considered that it could be bewildering (Wirth, 1996). It has been included in Vector Pascal because it is useful as a means of expressing conditional computation in a data-parallel way.

Suppose that we wish to grade some examination marks. All marks of 70 and above qualify for the first grade, all marks in the range 50 to 69 qualify for the second and those below for the third. Figure 8.1 shows a program that will grade an array of eight marks based on this rule. Invoking it produces the following results:

```
C:\book>grade
60  45  55  67  83  12  90  61
 2   3   2   2   1   3   1   2
```

```
PROGRAM grade;
VAR marks,grades:ARRAY[1..8] OF byte;
BEGIN
   READ(marks);
   grades:=IF marks>=70 THEN 1
           ELSE IF marks>=50 THEN 2
               ELSE 3;
   {format in 3 character wide fields}
   WRITE(GRADES:3);
END.
```

Figure 8.1. An example of conditional evaluation.

VECTOR

The conditional evaluation IF ... THEN ... ELSE takes a Boolean argument between IF and THEN and two arguments of matching type after the THEN and ELSE keywords. As shown in the example, conditional evaluation is allowed over array arguments provided that the normal rules for rank and dimensionality are met.

The conditional expression lends itself well to parallel evaluation on SIMD instruction-sets.

8.2 Functions

Functions are abstractions over expressions which allow certain terms of the expressions – the parameters – to be substituted in when the function is invoked. Vector Pascal provides a library of pre-given functions and prefix operators to perform common mathematical tasks; here we discuss user-written functions.

8.2.1 User-defined Functions

ISO-7185

A Pascal function has a name whose format follows the rules for identifiers, an optional parameter list and a return type. Within a context functions should be declared after constants and variables. Figure 8.2 illustrates three functions, one with no parameters, the second with one parameter and the third which recurses on its one parameter.

ISO-7185

Functions return their value by making an assignment to an implicit write-only variable with the same name as the function. The function does not return control to its calling environment on this assignment. This is different from languages such as C and Java where returning a value and returning control are done by the same construct.

ISO-10206

Vector Pascal allows any type, including array types, to be returned from a function. This contrasts with Standard Pascal, which limited function return types to scalars.

```
FUNCTION Pi4:real;
BEGIN
   Pi4:=pi/4
END;
(*Compute log_2(x)*)
FUNCTION Log2(x:real):real;
CONST Log2e=1.442695;   {log_2 of e}
BEGIN
   Log2:=ln(x)*log2e;
END;
FUNCTION Fact(i:integer):integer;
BEGIN
   Fact:=IF i<=1 THEN 1 ELSE Fact(i-1)*i
END;
```

Figure 8.2. Three functions.

Chapter 8 • Algorithmic Features of Vector Pascal

VECTOR

Vector Pascal has an extension to allow C style returning of values. The construct EXIT(x) would cause the current function to return with the value x.

Function declarations create a new scope within which new identifiers can be declared. These can be variables or constants used for temporary calculation within the function or other functions that perform a subtask within the function. Figure 8.3 illustrates this with a function that declares two local variables and two local functions for its computation.

Name Hiding

ISO-7185

If a function or procedure declares a local identifier, that local identifier has the effect of hiding any lexically equivalent identifiers declared outside the function.

Value Parameters

ISO-7185

The default parameter passing mechanism in Pascal is call by value. This means that when a parameter is passed into a function or procedure, a copy is made of the parameter. The parameter passed in is termed an actual parameter and the name declared in the parameter list is the formal parameter. Since the formal parameter is a copy of the actual one, any assignment to the formal parameter leaves the actual parameter unchanged.

Programmers should be aware of the efficiency considerations inherent in making copies of arrays passed as value parameters.

Var Parameters

ISO-7185

A parameter preceded by the keyword VAR is passed by reference. This means that an assignment to the formal parameter will have exactly the same effect as assigning to the corresponding actual parameter. An implication of this is that

```
CONST elems=100;
VAR   dataset:ARRAY[1..elems] OF real;
FUNCTION getrange:real;
{returns the range of values used in the dataset}
VAR top,bottom:real;
    FUNCTION highest:real;
      BEGIN highest:=RDU MAX dataset END;
    FUNCTION lowest:real;
      BEGIN lowest:=RDU MIN dataset END;
BEGIN
   top:=highest;
   bottom:=lowest;
   getrange:=top-bottom
END;
```

Figure 8.3. Use of local identifiers within a function.

```
(* scanb returns the index of the largest item in a
   and also updates big to hold the value of the largest
   item in a *)
FUNCTION scanb(VAR big:real;a:ARRAY[1..10] OF real):integer;
  FUNCTION find(i:integer);
  BEGIN
     find:=IF a[i]=big THEN i ELSE i+1;
  END;
BEGIN
   big:=RDU MAX a;
   scanb:=find(1);
END;
(* return the least element of a *)
FUNCTION scan(VAR a:ARRAY[1..10] OF real):real;
BEGIN
   scan:=RDU MIN a
END;
```

Figure 8.4. Two uses of var parameters.

the actual parameters must themselves be variables. It is an error to attempt to pass a constant or an expression as a var parameter.

Var parameters should be used in the following circumstances:

1. When a procedure or function needs to update its actual parameters. This is illustrated in function `scanb` in Figure 8.4, where two results are returned: the largest value in an array and its index.
2. For efficiency considerations when passing large parameters, in particular large arrays. Since only a reference to the array is passed in, this will typically be faster than copying the whole array. For example, see function `scan` in Figure 8.4.

It should be noted that whereas in implementations of Standard Pascal, array var parameters are typically passed as addresses, this is not necessarily true in Vector Pascal, where additional information may in some cases be passed concerning array bounds.

Protected Parameters

ISO-10206

A parameter declaration may be prefixed by the word PROTECTED. A protected parameter may not be assigned to within the body of the function. Protected parameters are useful for obtaining the semantic effect of a value parameter where efficiency considerations lead an array to be passed as a var parameter.

Parameter Types

Standard Pascal requires the types of parameters to be given by type names. Where arrays are passed as parameters they must be of user-defined array types

```
FUNCTION a(i:integer):real;FORWARD;

FUNCTION b(z:real):real
  BEGIN
    b:=IF z>5 THEN a(trunc(z)) ELSE 2*z;
  END;

FUNCTION a(i:integer):real;
  BEGIN
    a:=IF i>2 THEN 0.0 ELSE b(i/10);
  END;
```

Figure 8.5. Mutual recursion requires forward declaration.

(see Chapter 9). Vector Pascal allows array types to be explicitly given in the parameter declarations as in Figure 8.4.

Forward Declaration

Where two functions a and b are mutually recursive there is a potential clash with the Pascal rule that an identifier must be declared before it is used. To avoid a contradiction one of the functions must be declared as being FORWARD (Figure 8.5). A forward function has only its header given followed by the word FORWARD. Following this forward declaration, other functions can call it. At some later point in the program text the function is redeclared with its function body present this time.

8.2.2 Procedures

Functions provide a model of programming in which data are passed in through the parameters and a result is returned. A function that returns no result, which would be a void function in Java or C, is termed in Pascal a procedure. Declarations of procedures are similar to those of functions except that

1. The reserved word PROCEDURE substitutes for the word FUNCTION.
2. No return type is specified.
3. No assignment is allowed to the procedure name within the procedure.

Procedures communicate their effects preferably by means of var parameters. Alternatively, they may alter global variables, although this is regarded as a less ideologically sound practice.

Example Program to Compute Entropy

Let us now illustrate the use of the features introduced so far in a complete program.[1] The aim of the program is to compute the entropy H or mean

---
[1]This program, with modifications for Vector Pascal, is derived from Cherry (1980).

information per character of a source given p_i, the probabilities of occurrence of each character. The formula for information is given by Shannon (1948) as

$$H = \sum -p_i \log(p_i)$$

where each term of the series is actually positive since we know that $p_i < 1$ by the definition of a probability distribution, hence $\log(p_i) < 0$. If we use $\log_2$ instead of natural logarithms, then the measure comes out in bits. Thus, given a distribution defined over two possible measurement outcomes $\{0,1\}$ each of which is equally probable, we obtain the equation $-0.5\log_2(0.5) - 0.5\log_2(0.5) = -\log_2(0.5) = 1$, hence the conclusion of Shannon that one bit is the amount of information required to choose between two equally probable outcomes.

Let us assume that our program has to read in a table of probabilities, one for each character. The probabilities will be provided as real numbers in lexicographic order, one for each character in the character set which we shall assume to coincide with the Pascal type CHAR. The program outline, proceeding in a top-down fashion, might look as follows:

program *Shannon*;
var
   Let *P* ∈ ARRAY [char] OF real;
   Let *valid* ∈ boolean;
function *H* (**PROTECTED var** *P*:**array** [*char*] **of** *real*):*real*; (see Section 8.2.4)
procedure *ReadAndValidate* (**var** *P*:**array** [*char*] **of** *real*); (see Section 8.2.3)
begin
   ReadAndValidate (*P*);
   if *valid* **then WRITE**(*H* (*P*));
end.

8.2.3 Procedure ReadAndValidate

Let us defer the refinement of H until later, and concentrate on the code to read and validate. In Vector Pascal reading an array is trivial, but we need to check that

1. No $p_i > 1$, as this would validate the axioms of probability theory.
2. No $p_i < 0$, as this is again meaningless in probability theory.
3. No $p_i = 0$; although 0 is defined as a probability, $-p_i \log_2(p_i)$ is undefined at 0.
4. The sum of the probabilities is 1. If the sum is significantly different from 1 then this is probably an error in the input data. If it is slightly different then it is probably due to rounding errors and can be compensated for by renormalising the data.

Here is the refinement of *ReadAndValidate*:

procedure *ReadAndValidate* (**var** *P*:ARRAY$_{char}$ **of** *real*);
const
   tolerance = 0.005;

Chapter 8 • Algorithmic Features of Vector Pascal

normalise
```
var
  Let low,high,sum ∈ real;
begin
  read (P);
  low ← \min P;
  high ← \max P;
  sum ← ∑P;
  valid ← (low > 0) ∧ (high ≤ 1) ∧ (sum < 1 + tolerance) ∧ (sum > 1 − tolerance);
  if NOT valid then WRITE('data invalid');
  P ← P/sum;
end;
```

We compute the highest and lowest elements and the sum of the series. We update the Boolean variable valid depending on whether these values are within the valid ranges. We then renormalise the values to be within range taking into account minor errors in the precision of the source data.

8.2.4 Function H

We now provide a refinement of the function H. This uses a nested function to compute $\log_2(x)$, shown in Section 8.2.5.

function H (PROTECTED **var** P:ARRAY$_{char}$ **of** real):real;
function Log2 (x:real):real;(see Section 8.2.5)
begin
  $H \leftarrow \sum(-P \times Log2(P))$;
end;

8.2.5 Function Log2

We can convert from a logarithm to base e to a logarithm to base 2 by multiplying the natural logarithm of a number by the logarithm of 2 to the base e.

function Log2 (x:real):real;
const
  Log2e = 1.442695;
begin
  Log2 ← ln(x) × log2e;
end;

8.3 Branching

8.3.1 Two-way Branches

We have already looked at the use of the IF ... THEN ... ELSE ... construct in conditional expressions. In that case a Boolean variable is used to determine which of two alternative expressions is to be returned as a result. It can also be used in conditional statements to control whether a statement is executed. We have given a simple example of the If statement in the program Shannon, where it was used to guard Write statements. The general form with an ELSE is illustrated in

```
IF valid THEN WRITE(H(P))
ELSE WRITE('No result computed');
```

Dangling Else

It is important to realise that in Pascal the keyword ELSE binds with the closest preceding THEN. This rule means that code has to be read with care to determine its meaning. Consider the following:

```
IF b1 THEN
   IF b2 THEN
     WRITE('both true')
   ELSE write('b1 false');
```

From the indentation and messages it is clear that the coder wanted the message b1 false to be printed out if b1 was false. In fact nothing will be printed, as the compiler interprets this as:

```
IF b1 THEN BEGIN
   IF b2 THEN
     WRITE('both true')
   ELSE write('b1 false');
END;
```

To achieve the desired end, the coder should have written

```
IF b1 THEN BEGIN
   IF b2 THEN
     WRITE('both true')
   END
ELSE write('b1 false');
```

8.3.2 Multi-way Branches

The following structure:

```
IF b1 THEN statement1
ELSE IF b2 THEN statement2
ELSE IF b3 THEN statement3
 ....
ELSE statementN
```

selects one of n alternatives based on $n-1$ Boolean expressions. This is the most general form of multi-way branch but it is composed of a sequence of two way branches which use Booleans, a bivalent type, as the selector.

Pascal also allows multi-way branching on subrange and ordinal types using the case statement

```
CASE errcode OF
1,7    : WRITE('divide by zero');
2      : WRITE('Log of negative number');
3..6,8 : WRITE('bounds error');
END;
```

The example above shows a classical Pascal case statement. There is a selection expression, `errcode`, and a series of statements, each of which is preceded by a list of guards. The guards are either values or ranges of values. At run time control is passed to that statement, if any, whose guards include the value of the selection expression. After this statement has executed, control passes to the statement following the `END`. C and Java programmers should note that no `break` is required following the cases, unlike the analogous `switch` statement.

ISO-10206

Vector Pascal supports the `OTHERWISE` construct in case statements:

```
CASE c OF
'a'..'z'  : WRITE('lower case');
'A'..'Z'  : WRITE('upper case');
OTHERWISE   WRITE('not a letter');
END;
```

The statement guarded by `OTHERWISE` receives control for all selections other than those for which an explicit guard is provided.

TURBO

For compatibility with code written for Turbo Pascal, the word `ELSE` may substitute for `OTHERWISE`.

As shown in the example above, the guards need not be integers, but they must be scalars known at compile time. There will be an implementation-defined limit to the range of the types that can be used in case selections in Vector Pascal, which will be accessible to programmers using the predefined constant `maxcaseswitch`.

VECTOR

8.4 Unbounded Iteration

An unbounded iteration construct allows a statement to be iterated for a number of times that is determined by the iteration process itself. The number of iterations cannot in general be predicted at compile time. Pascal provides two unbounded iteration constructs, `WHILE` and `REPEAT` statements.

8.4.1 While

ISO-7185

The while loop is probably the most frequently used structure for controlling iteration. The general form of the while statement is

```
WHILE b DO s;
```

where b is a Boolean expression and s is a statement. It is evaluated as run time as follows:

1. When the while statement is first encountered the processor evaluates b.
2. If it is false, execution continues with the first statement after the while statement.
3. If b is true, the processor executes s.
4. After executing s the processor re-evaluates b and goes to step 2 above.

The while statement should be used when the number of repetitions to be executed is not only unknown at compile time but also may be zero.

While statements can have compound statements for their bodies:

```
WHILE remainder>=divisor DO
BEGIN
  remainder:=remainder-divisor;
  quotient :=quotient+1
END;
```

8.4.2 Repeat

The second form of unbounded repetition, the REPEAT statement, should be used when the number of iterations is a priori unknown but is known to be at least one. Consider the example

```
{skip blanks}
REPEAT
  read(ch)
UNTIL ch <> ' ';
```

ISO-7185

The repeat statement has the general form

REPEAT s1; s2; ... UNTIL b;

where s1, s2, ... are statements and b is a Boolean expression. It is evaluated as follows:

1. Statements s1, s2, ... are executed.
2. Expression b is evaluated.
3. If b is false, control passes to the first statement after the repeat statement. Otherwise the processor goes back to step 1.

The unbounded repetition statements are particularly useful when dealing with potentially infinite data types, for instance files and input streams. Whereas in Vector Pascal the sum of an array a can be written RDU+a, to obtain the sum of a file of numbers one needs unbounded iteration. Figures 8.6 and 8.7 show how repeat and while loops could be used to provide the total of all the integers in a file up to and including the first zero value. The number of non-zero values is not initially known.

```
program sumfile (input,output);
var
    Let total, x ∈ integer;
begin
    total ← 0;
    repeat
        read(x);
        total ← total + x;
    until x = 0;
end.
```

Figure 8.6. Use of unbounded iteration to sum the integers in a file up to the first 0 value.

```
program sumfile2 (input,output);
var
    Let total, x ∈ integer;
begin
    read(total);
    x ← total;
    while x ≠ 0 do
    begin
        total ← total + x;
        read(x);
    end;
end.
```

Figure 8.7. Use of a while loop to achieve the same result as in Figure 8.6.

Note that these programs include parameters `input` and `output` for the standard i/o streams in the program header. The use of these is now relatively obsolete, since in most Pascal implementations predeclare these files, allowing them to be elided as in previous examples. This form is shown for compatibility with the usage in older Standard Pascal implementations.

8.5 Bounded Iteration

Bounded iteration involves a number of repetitions of an action that is predetermined before the action starts. It can either be determined at compile time or determined by calculations performed by the program before the iteration commences.

8.5.1 For to

The most commonly used bounded iteration construct in Pascal is the FOR ... TO loop. It has the general form

ISO-7185

FOR i := x TO y DO s

```
const
    maximum = 10;
var
    Let a ∈ ARRAY[1.. maximum] OF real;
    {typical Vector Pascal}
    function newsum:real;
    begin
        newsum ← ∑a
    end;
    {typical Pascal}
    function oldsum:real;
    var
        Let i ∈ integer;
        Let t ∈ real;
    begin
        t ← 0;
        for i ← 1 to maximum do
            t ← t + aᵢ;
        oldsum ← t;
    end;
```

Figure 8.8. The use of a for loop to perform operations on an array contrasted with the use of explicit array arithmetic.

where i is a variable drawn from some integer or other scalar type t; x and y are expressions of type t, and s is a statement. When a FOR ... TO statement is encountered the processor performs the following actions:

1. The expression x is evaluated and assigned to i.
2. The value of i is compared with that of y and if it is greater control passes to the first statement after the FOR statement.
3. The statement s is evaluated.
4. x is assigned the value succ(x).
5. The processor goes back to step 2.

In Standard Pascal the most common use of for loops is to iterate over arrays whose size is known. In Vector Pascal the provision of array arithmetic makes this less necessary. Figure 8.8 contrasts the preferred Vector Pascal construct for summing the elements of an array with the preferred Standard Pascal construct which uses a FOR ... TO loop.

8.5.2 For Downto

A second form of the FOR statement iterates down through a range. It has the same general form as the FOR ... TO statement except that the word DOWNTO is substituted for the word To. In this case the iteration variable is decremented as it steps through the range. In this case the starting value

```
const
    maximum = 10;
var
    let a ∈ ARRAY[1..maximum] OF real;
    {find number with biggest integer absolute reciprocal}
    function recipmax:integer;
    label 99;
    var
        Let i, r ∈ integer;
        Let ok ∈ boolean;
    begin
        r ← 0;
        ok ← false;
        for i ← 1 to maximum do
        begin
            if A_i = 0 then goto 99;
            r ← r MAX ROUND (1/abs(a_i));
        end;
        recipmax ← r;
        ok ← true;
        99: if NOT ok then recipmax ← maxint
    end;
```

Figure 8.9. The use of GOTO to escape from an error condition.

must be greater than or equal to the finishing value if the statement s is to be executed one or more times.

8.6 Goto

Pascal allows unconditional transfers between points in a program. A goto statement has the form GOTO n; where n is a decimal integer termed a label. Individual statements can be labeled by prefixing them by a label. Although labels take the format of decimal integers, there is no need for the order in which labels occur in the source to be ascending.

Labels must be declared at the head of the program or procedure in which they occur.

The most common use of goto statements is to escape from a an error condition to the end of a procedure, bypassing any intervening statements. GOTOs should only be used to perform jumps within a procedure.[2]

Figure 8.9 illustrates this by using a goto to escape from a potential divide by zero error. The presence of a zero in the input data causes the function to escape to a line which returns the largest supported integer as a proxy for infinity.

---

[2]In Vector Pascal, a goto that jumps to an enclosing scope will transfer control but will not unwind the stack. This can lead to unpredictable error conditions.

9 User-defined Types

Thus far we have seen that data in Pascal can be of types integer, real, Boolean, character or string. In addition, Pascal provides a rich set of type constructors that allow user-defined types to be declared. A user-defined type is given a name which follows the normal scope rules of the language. It associates an identifier with the set of possible values that a variable of that type may take on at run time.

The general syntactic form of a type declaration is

TYPE $i = t$;

where i is a well-formed identifier and t is a type expression. These type expressions are built up using several organising principles:

1. A type may be drawn from a range of values.
2. A type may be a specialisation of the real numbers.
3. It may be formed as some form of array.
4. Several types can be joined to form a composite type.
5. A type can be defined as a power-set of some range.
6. A type may be a pointer or reference to another type.

9.1 Scalar Types

ISO-7185

A scalar type in Pascal is a set that is homomorphic to a subrange of the natural numbers. The types Boolean and char are predefined scalar types.

A value of a scalar type can range over this set. A scalar type is defined in terms of an ordered list of identifiers. The identifiers introduced in the ordered list must be unique within the scope of definition. For example:

```
TYPE day=(sunday,monday,tuesday,wednesday,
         thursday,friday,saturday);
     colour=(red,green,blue);
```

This introduces eight identifiers: day, a type identifier, and seven constants, sunday ... saturday, all of type day. Given the type definition for day, variables of this type can now be declared:

```
VAR today:day;
```

Assignments can be made to these variables provided that the value being assigned is drawn from the appropriate set of identifiers. Thus,

```
today:=monday;
```

is valid but

```
today:=1;
```

is not.

The complete set of comparison operators are implicitly defined over all scalar types, as are the operators `MIN` and `MAX`.

9.1.1 SUCC and PRED

There is a pair of built-in operators, `SUCC` and `PRED`, defined over every scalar type t such that $x = $ `SUCC PRED`$x \forall x \in t$ and $y = $ `PRED SUCC`$y \forall y \in t$.

This definition of the successor and predecessor functions differs from that given in the Pascal standard, which defines `SUCC` as follows:

succ(x)

The function shall yield a value whose ordinal number is one greater than that of the expression *x*, if such a value exists. It shall be an error if such a value does not exist (ISO, 1991b, p. 45).

The implication of these definitions is that in Vector Pascal the successor function operates in a modulo fashion. As one steps through a scalar type with the successor function, one eventually gets back to the starting point. This is illustrated in Figure 9.1.

The intention of the ISO definition is to ensure that the result of performing the successor or predecessor functions is always a member of the type of its

program *ordinals*;
type
    day = (*sunday,monday,tuesday,wednesday,*
    thursday,friday,saturday);
var
    Let *today,tomorrow,day2* ∈ *day*;
begin
    today ← *friday* **MAX** *saturday*;
    tomorrow ← **SUCC** *today*;
    day2 ← **SUCC**(*sunday*,2);
    writeln(*today,tomorrow,today* < *friday,day2* < *friday*);
end.

output generated:

    saturday   sunday   false   true

Figure 9.1. A program illustrating both the comparability of user-defined scalar types and their cyclical nature.

argument. The Vector Pascal approach of using modulo arithmetic achieves the same result in a different way. It has certain advantages:

- For certain data types, for example the days of the week, it leads to a more natural approach.
- It is congruous with the general restrictions of finite length computer integer arithmetic, which is inherently modular. In this way scalar types which typically have small ranges are brought into conformity with the semantics of the integer data type. For example, the program

program *wrap*;
var
   Let $i \in$ integer;
begin
   $i \leftarrow$ *maxint*;
   write$(i, j + 1)$;
end.

will on most Pascal systems print out the largest and smallest integers handled by the processor. This is permitted under the Pascal standard, which states (ISO, 1991b, p. 49):

> Any dyadic operation on two integers in the same interval shall be correctly performed according the mathematical rules for integer arithmetic provided that the result is also in this interval.

Since `maxint+1` is outside the defined interval for integer arithmetic, the default modular arithmetic performed by most computer hardware is allowed by the standard.

- The rule that an error will arise if SUCC is applied to the top element of the type forces the compiler to plant range checking code. This is typically slower than performing a modulus operation.

Conformity with the Standard

Where backward compatibility demands it, the Vector Pascal compiler can perform the successor and predecessor functions in the way required by the standard. To do this the compiler directive `{$m-}` is inserted into the body of the program. This switches off modular arithmetic until the obverse directive `{$m+}` is inserted.

When modular arithmetic is switched off, then range checks will be placed after each invocation of SUCC or PRED.

The placement of range checks can itself be controlled by the compiler directives `{$r-}` and `{$r+}` as shown in Table 9.1. The default state of the range checking switches is on.

Extended Syntax for SUCC

ISO-10206

Extended Pascal allows a second parameter to be supplied to SUCC and PRED. The second parameter is an integer which specifies the size of the increment or

Table 9.1. Effect of the compiler directives $m and $r

$m	$r	Means
+	+	Default status, use modular arithmetic and array bounds checks
+	−	Use modular arithmetic, but no array bounds checks
−	+	Bounds checks on arrays, succ and pred
−	−	Neither range checks nor modular arithmetic

```
FUNCTION tolower(c:char):char;
BEGIN
  tolower:=CHR(ORD(c)-ORD('Z')+ORD('z'));
end;
```

Figure 9.2. Illustrating how the ORD function can be used to allow arithmetic on a scalar type, in this case char.

decrement to be performed. Thus given the definition of day above, the line

```
WRITE(SUCC(sunday,2));
```

will produce the output tuesday. This extended syntax is supported in Vector Pascal. As with the single-parameter format, the default in Vector Pascal is for the increment or decrement to be performed by modular arithmetic.

9.1.2 ORD

ISO-7185

There is an operator ORD which returns the integer corresponding to a member of a scalar type. Figure 9.2 illustrates how the ORD operator can be used in calculations to convert letters to lower case.

9.1.3 Input/Output of Scalars

VECTOR

Standard Pascal does not support the reading and writing of scalars to and from text files. Vector Pascal does. A scalar type is printed out as the equivalent string of characters. A read operation whose target is a variable of scalar type will:

1. read in the next identifier in the text file
2. check it against the valid members of the scalar type
3. generate an error condition if the identifier is not or the right type
4. convert the textual form of the identifier into the appropriate binary code.

9.1.4 Representation

Scalar types in Vector Pascal will be stored using either octets, halfwords or words, depending on the range of the type.

```
PROGRAM increment;
{Program to read in a string of decimal digits
 convert it to an integer, increment it
 and print the result.
}
TYPE
    decimalchar='0'..'9';
    decimalint = 0..9;
VAR line:string;

FUNCTION s2int(s:string):integer;
  LABEL 99;
  VAR c:char; i,t:integer;
   FUNCTION toint(d:decimalchar):decimalint;
   BEGIN
    toint:=ORD(d)-ORD('0')
   END;
  BEGIN
     i:=1; t:=0;
     WHILE i<length(s) DO
     BEGIN
        c:=s[i];
        IF (c<'0') OR (c>'9') THEN GOTO 99;
        t:=10*t+toint(c);
        i:=i+1;
     END;
     99: s2int:=t
  END;
BEGIN
   READLN(line);
   WRITELN(s2int(line)+1);
END.
```

Figure 9.3. The use of sub-range types.

9.2 Sub-range Types

A type can be defined to be a sub-range of another integer or scalar type:

```
TYPE weekday=monday..friday;
     decimalchar='0'..'9';
     decimalint = 0..9;
```

A sub-range type inherits its signature of operators from the type of which it is a sub-range. Thus, the type decimalchar in the example above can have comparison operations, ORD, PRED and SUCC, on its values. The type decimalint, on the other hand, can take part in arithmetic operations. The use of these types is illustrated in Figure 9.3.

9.2.1 Representation

Sub-range types in Vector Pascal will be stored using either octets, halfwords or words, depending on the range of the type.

Numeric sub-range types whose ranges fall within the range $-128\ldots 127$ are represented as signed octets. Numeric types whose lower bound is zero or greater and whose upper bound is in the range $128\ldots 255$ are represented as unsigned octets.

Numeric sub-range types whose upper bound is in the range $2^8\ldots 2^{15}-1$ and whose lower bound is greater than or equal to -2^{15} will be stored in signed 16-bit integers.

Numeric sub-range types whose upper bound is in the range $2^{15}\ldots 2^{16}-1$ and whose lower bound is zero or positive will be stored in unsigned 16-bit integers.

Other numeric subranges are stored as signed 32-bit numbers. As always when working with finite precision arithmetic, care has to be taken with arithmetic operations on sub-range types which could potentially take them out of bounds.

9.3 Dimensioned Numbers

One use of types in programming languages is to divide up our universe of discourse into different categories which are incommensurable. It does not make sense to compare days of the week with colours. By allocating a set of distinct names to days of the week and to colours using scalar types, one can prevent a programmer inadvertently assigning values proper to one type to variables of another.

A variable of type `day` and a variable of type `colour` will both occupy one octet, and thus from the format standpoint one could be copied into another. Semantically it would be nonsense. Strong typing protects us from even attempting it.

There is another sort of error which it would be nice to avoid, one captured in the aphorism that one cannot add apples to oranges. This type of error relates to performing arithmetic between quantities of things that are themselves incommensurable. Numbers are used in two senses. In the one sense they are abstract mathematical objects whose production and manipulation is governed by formal laws. The finite numerical representations used on computers along with the arithmetic hardware of the processor provide a partial model for these abstract numbers. However, in addition to this Platonic existence, numbers have a more mundane use in measurement. In commerce people work with quantities such as £35.2, $12.5, 2.3 barrels Brent Crude, where the number is paired with a unit of currency or a commodity. These quantities have to be kept distinct. Adding barrels of oil to dollars does not make sense. Conceptually, quantities of oil and quantities of dollars are measurements along orthogonal axes.

Standard Pascal provides no means of distinguishing between these types of numbers, but Vector Pascal provides a way of specialising the type `real` so

Chapter 9 • User-defined Types

that it can represent real valued measurements along such conceptually orthogonal axes. These specialisations of the real numbers are termed dimensioned numbers.

Let us consider the coding in Vector Pascal of a fragment of program to handle currency conversions and oil price bids in several currencies. Let us assume that the trading takes place in UK currency, US currency and EU currency and that there is only one type of oil being traded. Our system of measurement is thus arranged along four axes. In Pascal, the standard way to represent a fixed size collection of entities such as these axes is to use a scalar type:

```
TYPE commodity=(oil,UKcurrency,EUcurrency,UScurrency);
```

The type `commodity` now provides us with a set of labels for our axes of measurement. We can use them to define a collection of further types for quantities of each of these currencies.

```
barrels=real OF oil;
pounds =real OF UKcurrency;
euros  =real OF EUcurrency;
dollars=real OF UScurrency;
```

The part of the defintion after the word `OF` gives the *dimension* of the type. The scalar type from which the dimension name is taken is termed the *basis* of the dimensioned type set. A dimensioned type set is a set of numeric types that share a basis.

Suppose we now want to write a function to quote, for instance, in euros for a certain number of barrels of oil. In generalised commodity trading with n commodities, there is a matrix of n^2 possible inter-commodity exchanges or relative values. However, in an ideal consistent system of commodity exchange these n^2 relative values are degenerate. By using one commodity as a numeraire or universal equivalent (Marx, 1976), one can derive the entire matrix from $n-1$ prices in terms of this universal equivalent.

If we fix Sterling to be our universal equivalent, then we can use the Sterling price of oil and of EU currency to quote oil in euros. We therefore need three variables to hold the exchange rates of the other commodities against Sterling. What should the types of these variables be?

The dollar rate for Sterling is typically specified as some number x of dollars per pound. We can write this as $x\$/£$, or borrowing the conventions of the physical sciences, $x\$£^{-1}$; x is thus a real number whose dimension can be expressed in more verbose Pascal terms as `UScurrency*UKcurrency POW -1`. We can therefore specify our exchange ratios as

```
VAR
  dollarRate:real OF UScurrency*UKcurrency POW -1;
  euroRate   :real OF EUcurrency*UKcurrency POW -1;
  oilRate    :real OF oil*UKcurrency POW -1;
```

Here the dimension is given as a product of sub-dimensions each raised to a power. All of the sub-dimensions must be drawn from the same basis.

We can now write a function that will quote a price in euros for a quantity of oil (see Figure 9.4).

function *oilInEuros(b:barrels):euros;*
begin
    oilInEuros ← $\frac{b \times euroRate}{oilrate}$;
end;

Figure 9.4. Function oilInEuros.

Let us look at the expression used to calculate the function. The parameter b is of dimension oil, and euroRate is of dimension EUcurrency per UKcurrency. Hence the expression b*euroRate is of dimension oil times EUcurrency per UKcurrency. If we divide this by the oilrate, which is of dimension oil per UKcurrency, then the dimensions oil and UKcurrency cancel out, leaving the dimension EUcurrency, which is what we want.

Now suppose we want to read from the keyboard a quantity of oil and print out the euro price. We immediately have a problem, since the built-in read procedure only supports the system real type. We can read the quantity of oil wanted into a real valued variable, but how do we pass it to the function oilInEuros?

```
VAR oilwanted:real;
BEGIN
  READ(oilwanted);
  WRITE(oilInEuros(oilwanted));
```

will not work for two reasons:

1. The system real type is dimensionally incompatible with the type barrels wanted by the function oilInEuros.
2. The type euros returned by the function is incompatible with the types supported by the system write routine.

The answer to these problems is provided by the use of dimensioned constants to encode units of measurement. Suppose we have the constants shown in Figure 9.5. By multiplying the variable oilwanted in procedure euroquote by the constant barrel it is converted to the type barrels. Similarly, by dividing the price variable through by the constant euro, it is converted from a dimensioned real constant to a dimensionless constant suitable for printing.

The dimensioned constants can also be used to initialise the relative prices using statements of the form

```
dollarRate:=1.45*dollar/pound;
```

One should note that the relationship between the names dollars and dollar is purely conventional. What matters from the standpoint of the compiler is that the name of the dimensioned constant denoting the unit of account is distinct from the name of the type of the unit of account. This is illustrated by the declaration of the constant cent (see Figure 9.5), which shares the type dollars but has a different value.

Chapter 9 • User-defined Types

```
program trade;
type
    commodity = (oil,UKcurrency,EUcurrency,UScurrency);
    barrels = real of oil;
    pounds = real of UKcurrency;
    euros = real of EUcurrency;
    dollars = real of UScurrency;
const
    barrel:barrels =1.0;
    megabarrel:barrels =1E6;
    dollar:dollars =1.0;
    cent:dollars = 0.01;
    pound:pounds =1.0;
    euro:euros =1;
var
    Let dollarRate ∈ real OF UScurrency * UKcurrency POW −1;
    Let euroRate ∈ real OF EUcurrency * UKcurrency POW −1;
    Let oilRate ∈ real OF oil * UKcurrency POW −1;
function oilInEuros (b:barrels):euros; (see Figure 9.4)
procedure euroquote; (see Figure 9.6)
begin
```

$dollarRate \leftarrow \frac{1.45 \times dollar}{pound}$;
$eurorate \leftarrow \frac{1.62 \times euro}{pound}$;
$oilRate \leftarrow \frac{0.04 \times barrel}{pound}$;
$euroquote$;

end.

Figure 9.5. A simple program which uses dimensioned types in the context of a commodity trading problem.

```
procedure euroquote;
var
    Let oilwanted ∈ real;
    Let price ∈ euros;
begin
    WRITE('Oil in barrels:');
    readln(oilwanted);
    price ← oilInEuros(oilwanted × barrel);
    WRITELN(chr($ee), price/euro);
end;
```

Figure 9.6. Procedure euroquote.

9.3.1 Arithmetic on Dimensioned Numbers

At compile time, a vector of integers is associated with each dimensioned number type. The dimension vector is indexed by the basis of the dimensional type set.

Dimensioned values can be added or subtracted provided that they have the same basis and the same values in their dimension vectors. Dimensionless numbers cannot be added to or subtracted from dimensioned numbers.

Dimensioned values can be multiplied by dimensionless numbers. The operation leaves the dimensions unchanged. Two-dimensioned numbers may be multiplied provided that they share the same basis. The result type's dimension vector is the sum of the dimension vectors of the types being multiplied.

Dimensioned values can be raised to an integer power n using the POW operator. In the statement b:=a POW n, let a_i denote the ith element of the dimension vector of the type of a and b_i the corresponding element of the dimension vector of the type of b. Then the rules of dimensional algebra require that $b_i = na_i$.

Dimensioned quantities can be divided by dimensionless numbers. Such division leaves the dimensions unchanged. Dimensioned quantities can be divided provided that they share the same basis. Consider c:=a/b, then using the same notation as before, $c_i = a_i - b_i$.

9.3.2 Handling Different Units of Measurement

Consider the problem that arises when working with different systems of measurement, for example the metric system of kilograms, and metres and the American or imperial system of pounds and feet. Serious errors can arise if quantities in one system are confused with those in the other. Dimensioned numbers provide a way of avoiding this danger, but there are some potential pitfalls in using them.

One approach would be to use two distinct enumerated types as the bases for the systems of measurement:

```
TYPE Imperial=(lbs,ft,secs);
     Metric=(kgs,mtrs,secs);
```

This falls foul of the rule that the identifier secs cannot be a member of two distinct scalar types. One might alternatively try defining a composite scalar type that includes identifiers for both imperial and metric units:

```
TYPE measurements=(kgs,mtrs,secs,lbs,ft);
```

This will work, and would provide a basis for the definition of dimensioned numbers for the different units:

```
kilograms=REAL OF kks;
meters   =REAL OF mtrs;
seconds  =REAL OF secs;
pounds   =REAL OF lbs;
feet     =REAL OF ft;
```

This type system is secure, in the sense that it is as impossible to assign a quantity of type pounds to a variable of type kilograms as it is to assign a variable of type feet to one of type pounds. This approach, however, fails to model accurately the properties of the real-world measurement systems that we are using. The difference between feet and pounds is of a different order to

Chapter 9 • User-defined Types

that between kilograms and pounds. Kilograms and pounds are both units of mass whereas the foot is a unit of length. In terms of dimensional analysis, kilograms and pounds are dimensionally identical but differ in scale, whereas pounds and feet are dimensionally distinct. If we fail to make this distinction we are forced into making a needless duplication of dimensional types. For instance, we would need to define two types for acceleration:

```
metricacc=REAL OF mtrs*secs POW -2;
imperacc =REAL OF ft*secs POW -2;
```

A function to compute velocity from acceleration and time would work for metric or imperial units but not both, since its formal parameters would only be consistent with one of the types of acceleration.

The preferred approach to the problem is first to define the basis of the dimensioned type system in a way that is independent of our measuring rods as illustrated in Figure 9.7. We then go on to define a number of different measuring rods. Using these constants, one can initalise variables of type length with expressions such as 3.0 * miles or 7 * mtrs. The expressions directly express what is done when we measure a distance, the laying out of a measuring rod a certain number of times. Using the same approach, we define a set of standard intervals for time: seconds, hours, days, weeks, etc. A function to compute distance traveled will now work whichever dimensionally correct units we use to supply its parameters:

```
FUNCTION compD(a:acceleration; t:interval):length;
BEGIN
    compD:=(a*t*t)/2.0;
END;

BEGIN
  WRITE(compd(9.8*metersPerSecond/secs,3*hrs)/miles);
  WRITELN(compd(2*miles/(hrs*hrs),1*yrs)/mtrs);
END.
```

9.4 Records

ISO-7185

A record type defines a set of similar data structures. Each member of this set, a record instance, is a Cartesian product of number of components or *fields* specified in the record type definition. Each field has an identifier and a type. The scope of these identifiers is the record itself:

```
TYPE monthname=(jan,feb,mar,apr,may,jun,
                jul,aug,sep,oct,nov,dec);
    date = RECORD
                year:integer;
                month:monthname;
                day:1..31;
            END;
```

type
    measure = (matter,space,time);
    *length = REAL **of** space;*
    *interval = REAL **of** time;*
    *mass = REAL **of** matter;*
    *acceleration = REAL **of** space * time **pow** -2;*
    *velocity = REAL **of** space * time **pow** -1;*
    *force = REAL **of** matter * space * time **pow** -2;*
const
    {- measures of space}
    cmlen = 0.01;
    inchlen =2.54 * cmlen;
    footlen = 12 * inchlen;
    kilometerlen = 1000;
    milelen = 1760 * 3 * footlen;
    mtrs:length = 1.0;
    cms:length = cmlen;
    ins:length = inchlen;
    ft:length = footlen;
    kms:length = kilometerlen;
    miles:length = milelen;
    {- measures of time}
    minutelen = 60.0;
    hourlen = 60 * minutelen;
    daylen = 24 * hourlen;
    yearlen = 365.25 * daylen;
    secs:interval = 1.0;
    mins:interval = minutelen;
    hrs:interval = hourlen;
    yrs:interval = yearlen;
    {- measures of velocity}
    metersPerSecond:velocity = 1;
    milesPerHour:velocity = milelen/hourlen;

Figure 9.7. The preferred approach to using dimensioned numbers to handle different units of measure.

`Date` is now the name for a type each of whose elements has a `year`, `month` and a `day` field. The type can be used to declare variables in the usual way:

`VAR today,eid:date;`

Record variables can be assigned just like any other:

`today:=eid;`

ISO-7185

The names of the fields of the record are hidden until a record variable is subscripted using the full-stop operator. This allows the fields to be addressed as component parts of the entire variable:

`today.day:=succ(today.day);`

```
IF today.day = 1 THEN today.month:=succ(today.month);
IF today.month = jan THEN today.year:= today.year+1;
```

ISO-7185

A record type may have as a final component a *variant part*. The variant part, if a variant part exists, is a union of several variants, each of which may itself be a Cartesian product of a set of fields. If a variant part exists there may be a tag field whose value indicates which variant is assumed by the record instance:

```
TYPE valcode=(strval,numval,textval,rangeval);
     value=RECORD
             seqnum:integer;
             CASE valdist:valcode OF
             strval,textval:(thestring:string[20];);
             numval         :(thenum:real;);
             rangeval       :(first,last:integer;);
           END;
```

ISO-7185

All field identifiers, even if they occur within different variant parts, must be unique within the record type. The variant parts, where they exist, will typically be aliased to the same store locations. Assignment to one of the variants will typically corrupt all of the others.

9.5 Pointers

Variable names in Pascal are tokens for storage addresses in computer memory. The compiler associates with the name a type and a statically defined formula for calculating the address at which that variable will reside at run time. Store for variables is allocated either on the run time stack or in a global data segment. In order that the compiler can calculate where these addresses will be, Pascal requires that all variables, including array variables, have a predefined size. A benefit of this strategy is that variable accesses, including array accesses, can be translated into very efficient machine code. The obvious disadvantage is that the memory requirements of algorithms may not be known at compile time.

Suppose that we want to read a list of names in from a file and sort them. We could allocate an array that we thought would be large enough, read the file into the array and sort it as shown in Figure 9.8.

If we use a fixed-size buffer, we have to be sure that the data will fit into the buffer. This encourages us to make the buffer substantially larger than we expect to need, just for safety. The consequence is that in a large program with many buffers a great deal of space is wasted.

Pascal provides a mechanism for store to be dynamically allocated at run time in a distinct area of memory termed the heap. The built-in procedure NEW will allocate a buffer and return a typed pointer to it.

The type constructor ^ can be used to define the type of a pointer to a buffer. Suppose we have the definition

```
TYPE pint=^integer;
```

```
PROGRAM sortf;
{Program to sort a file of lines alphabetically}
CONST maxsize=100;
TYPE  t=STRING[80];
      index=1..maxsize;
      dataarray=ARRAY[1..maxsize] OF t;
VAR buf:dataarray;
    count,i:integer;

PROCEDURE bubblesort(VAR a:dataarray; n:index);
 VAR i,j:integer;
     temp:t;
 BEGIN
       FOR i:=1 TO n-1 DO
        FOR j:=1 TO n-1 DO
         IF a[j]>a[j+1] THEN BEGIN {swap pair}
            temp:=a[j]; a[j]:=a[j+1]; a[j+1]:=temp;
          END;
 END;
{Read lines up until a blank line}
PROCEDURE readdata(VAR a:dataarray; var n:integer);
 VAR s:t;
 BEGIN
      n:=0;
      REPEAT
       READLN(s);
       IF s<>'' THEN BEGIN
         n:=SUCC(n);
         a[n]:=s;
        END
       UNTIL (s='') OR (n=maxsize);
  END;
BEGIN
      readdata(buf,count);
      IF count>0 THEN bubblesort(buf,count);
      FOR i:=1 TO count DO WRITELN(buf[i]);
END.
```

Figure 9.8. An approach to sorting a file using a fixed-size buffer. It should be noted that the inefficient bubble sort procedure is presented just for simplicity.

then we can declare a pointer variable:

VAR p:pint;

The variable p is initially undefined. It does not point at a buffer until NEW(p) is called. After the call, p contains the address of a buffer large enough to hold an integer. The buffer can be accessed to by *de-referencing* the pointer variable thus:

```
p^:=7;
write(p^+1);
```

The type of the expression p^ is integer, and more generally if *x* is of type ^*t* then the expression *x*^ is of type *t*.

The main use of dynamically allocated buffers is to hold data structures made up of inter-linked records. We can illustrate this with an alternative sorting program. This will both make use of dynamically allocated buffers and be more efficient than the example in Figure 9.8. It will create a sorted binary tree of records, each of which holds a string. As lines are read in they will be inserted into the appropriate position in the tree. At the end, the tree will be traversed to print the lines out in sorted order.

Our basic data types are

```
TYPE pnode=^node;
     node=record line:string[80]; l,r: pnode end;
```

The nodes will form a tree with the rule that any node reached by the field l must hold a string less than the current string, and any node reached by the field r must hold a string greater than or equal to the current string. The type pnode is declared as a pointer to the as yet undefined type node. This is the only exception to the Pascal rule that an identifier must be declared before it is used. The exception is necessary if one is to have recursive data types.

9.5.1 Pointer Idioms

The program in Figure 9.9 illustrates a number of common idioms used in programming with pointers. Some of these are matters of style and some illustrate syntactic features of Pascal designed to facilitate programming with pointers.

Constructor Functions

It is good practice to write *constructor* functions to handle heap allocation and buffer initialisation. Thus we have a function newnode which calls new and allocates values to all fields of the record buffer.

The Value nil

The insert function ensures that whenever a new string is inserted into the tree it is in the appropriate position. Given a null tree indicated by the pointer taking on the reserved value nil, the function updates its parameter to point to a new buffer. The value nil can be assigned to any pointer type and should be used as a placeholder to indicate the ends of lists or pointers which do not yet have a buffer allocated to them. The new buffer created by insert has both of its pointer fields initialised to nil.

```
PROGRAM Tsort;
TYPE pnode=^node;
    textline=string[80];
    node=RECORD line:textline; l,r:pnode END;
VAR l:textline;
    t:pnode;
FUNCTION newnode(line:textline; l,r:pnode):pnode;
 VAR p:pnode;
 BEGIN
     NEW(p);
     p^.line:=line; p^.l:=l; p^.r:=r;
     newnode:=p
 END;
PROCEDURE insert(s:textline; VAR p:pnode);
 BEGIN
     IF p=nil THEN p:=newnode(s,nil,nil)
     ELSE IF s<p^.line THEN insert(s,p^.l)
     insert(s,p^.r)
 END;
PROCEDURE print(p:pnode);
 BEGIN
     IF p<>nil THEN WITH p^ DO BEGIN
        print(l);writeln(line);print(r);
      END;
 END;
BEGIN
    t:=nil; {an empty tree}
    REPEAT
        READLN(l);
        IF l<>'' THEN insert(l,t);
    UNTIL l='';
    print(t); {output in sorted order}
END.
```

Figure 9.9. A more efficient sorting program than in Figure 9.8, one which, moreover, makes use of dynamic storage allocation from the heap.

Pointer Comparison

ISO-7185

Pointer values can be compared for equality and inequality, but the ordered comparison operators >, <, >= and <= are not allowed on pointers.

The WITH Construct

The fields in a record normally have to be accessed by explicit subscripting, using the . operator. When one has to operate on several fields of a record in sequence, it is useful to dispense with the explicit subscripting. The reserved

Chapter 9 • User-defined Types

ISO-7185

word `WITH`, illustrated in the phrase

`WITH p^ DO`

in the procedure `print` allows the fields of the buffer record pointed to by `p` to be referred to as local variables. Thus the field identifiers `line`, `l`, `r` are used in the following compound statement as if they were normal variables.

9.5.2 Freeing Storage

In the example above, the file is read into memory once, printed and then the program terminates. So long as the computer has enough memory to store the file in RAM, the program will run. If a program keeps on allocating buffers then it will eventually run out of memory. The following small program will cause problems:

```
PROGRAM evernew;
TYPE t=string[80];
    pt=^t;
VAR p:pt;
BEGIN
  WHILE true DO new(p);
END.
```

Repeated calls will be made on the operating system to allocate more buffer space. Eventually it will run out of store to handle it, causing a crash in a system-dependent fashion.

ISO-7185

Buffers that are not needed can be returned to the system by the predefined Pascal procedure `dispose`. This is called with a single pointer parameter thus:

`dispose(p);`

The buffer pointed to by `p` is returned to the system and can be re-allocated on subsequent calls to `new`.

Allocation Using `getmem`

The procedure `new` will always allocate a buffer at least big enough for the data type referred to by its parameter. There may be occasions when this is inefficient. In the program `tsort`, the nodes contained buffers big enough to hold 80 character strings, although most lines would be much shorter.

TURBO

Turbo Pascal introduced an alternative store allocator, `getmem`, for such situations. It allows one to control explicitly the number of bytes of store allocated. Doing this is potentially dangerous, for several reasons:

1. It can reduce portability.
2. It requires the programmer to have a detailed knowledge of the layout of data types such as strings.
3. If mistakes are made in the sizes of buffers allocated, then the type system is subverted and no protection is provided against memory corruption.

For compatibility, `getmem` is also provided in Vector Pascal.

Garbage Collection

In most Pascal implementations, all de-allocation from the heap has to be done explicitly using `dispose`. There is no reason in principle why Pascal cannot be made to run with an automatic storage recovery system and some implementations have them. For instance, the Delphi system uses reference counts to handle automatic freeing of long strings held on the heap.

<small>VECTOR</small>

Vector Pascal has the option of being linked using the Boehm conservative garbage collector. When using this option, `dispose` can still be called and will free the buffer it is passed. If, however, there are either deliberate or inadvertent memory leaks, the garbage collector will be eventually be invoked to recover unused buffers.

9.6 Set Types

Pascal is rather unusual as imperative languages go in that it includes sets as a built-in data type. A set type y is declared using the syntactic form $y = \text{SET OF } t$, where t is some type. This would appear to allow one to construct sets of any predeclared type. Russell's paradox is avoided since the set type y is itself undeclared at this point. In practice, compiler writers have found sets hard to implement, so the Pascal standard only requires simplified versions in which the type t must be an ordinal type.[1]

<small>ISO-7185</small>

Thus one can declare a set of characters but not a set of records. Some compilers also restrict the maximum size of the sets supported to be no larger than the character set.[2]

9.6.1 Set Literals

Suppose we have the type `day` defined in Figure 9.1. We can define a set of days and declare variables of that type:

```
TYPE dayset=SET OF day;
VAR  days:dayset;
```

One can then assign set literals to the variable as in

```
days:=[monday,friday,tuesday];
```

A set literal is either:

1. the null set, written [ ]

---

[1] The term ordinal types describes a collection of types which have a common property: they are either numeric integers, or they can be mapped on to integers (their 'ordinal values'), and are indeed represented internally by these ordinal values. Some predefined types are ordinal types, in particular integer and integer sub-ranges such as word, char (character type). Other ordinal types are defined within the program: enumerated types, specified sub-ranges of ordinal types.
[2] The Borland Turbo Pascal compiler did this.

Chapter 9 • User-defined Types

Table 9.2. The set operators

		Returns a	Meaning
ISO-7185	$a + b$	Set	a, b:sets, union of a with b
ISO-7185	$a - b$	Set	a, b:sets, members of a not in b
ISO-7185	$a * b$	Set	a, b:sets, intersection of a with b
ISO-10206	$a >< b$	Set	a, b:sets, symmetric difference $=(a+b)-(a*b)$
ISO-7185	a IN b	Boolean	a:scalar, b:set, set membership
ISO-7185	$a = b$	Boolean	a, b:sets, set equality
ISO-7185	$a <> b$	Boolean	a, b:sets, set inequality
ISO-7185	$a <= b$	Boolean	a, b:sets, a subset of b
ISO-7185	$a >= b$	Boolean	a, b:sets, b subset of a

2. a singleton set, written [today]
3. a comma-separated list of elements as in [monday,friday,tuesday]
4. or it may be defined in terms of sub-ranges as in [monday..thursday, sunday].

Note that whereas the ordinal type over which a set is defined is ordered, the elements of a set do not have to be listed in any particular order.

9.6.2 Operations on Sets

The set operators are summarised in Table 9.2. They broadly follow the operators for arithmetic with the addition of the symmetric difference operator ><, introduced in the ISO standard (ISO, 1991a), and with the elimination of and > and < operators. The priorities of the operators follow those which they have in Pascal numeric arithmetic.

The semantics of the set operators are illustrated in Figure 9.10. Two other features of set use are brought out in this example.

1. There is no built-in way of printing or reading sets in Pascal. Instead, it has to be explicitly programmed.
2. In the example, the procedure pset is used to print sets of char. The procedure uses an extension to the for statement for use with sets, FOR i IN

ISO-10206
s DO. In this, i iterates over s's members in the ascending order provided by the base type of s.

9.7 String Types

Vector Pascal's treatment of strings follows that of Turbo Pascal. A string is a pair consisting of a length field followed by an array of char with lower bound 1 and a type-specific upper bound. Strings constitute a family of types differentiated by their upper bound. Thus, in

```
TYPE textline=string[80];
    namefield=string[64];
    longstring=string[200];
```

```
PROGRAM setcomp (output);
TYPE chs=SET OF char;
(* Print the set s*)
PROCEDURE pset(VAR s:chs);
VAR c:char;
BEGIN
     FOR c IN s DO WRITE(c);
END;
{print s1 op s2 '='}
PROCEDURE ptrip(VAR s1,s2:chs;op:string);
BEGIN
  pset(s1);WRITE(op:3);pset(s2);WRITE('= ':3);
END;
VAR v,v1,v2,v3:chs;
BEGIN
  v:=['a'..'f'];
  v1:=['A'..'M'];
  v2:=v+v1;
  WRITE('v =':12);pset(v);WRITELN;
  WRITE('v1=':12);pset(v1);WRITELN;
  WRITE('v2=':12);pset(v2);WRITELN;
  v3:=v2-v1;
  WRITE('v2-v1=':12);pset(v3);WRITELN;
  v3:=(v2)*['A'..'c'];
  WRITE('v2*[A..c]=':12);pset(v3);WRITELN;
  ptrip(v1,v2,' =');WRITELN(v1=v2:6);
  ptrip(v1,v2,' <>');WRITELN(v1<>v2:6);
  ptrip(v1,v2,' <=');WRITELN(v1<=v2:6);
  ptrip(v1,v2,' >=');WRITELN(v1>=v2:6);
  v3:=v2><v;
  ptrip(v2,v,' ><');pset(v3);WRITELN;
END.
```

Output produced:

```
         v =abcdef
         v1=ABCDEFGHIJKLM
         v2=ABCDEFGHIJKLMabcdef
     v2-v1=abcdef
 v2*[A..c]=ABCDEFGHIJKLMabc
  ABCDEFGHIJKLM =ABCDEFGHIJKLMabcdef=false
  ABCDEFGHIJKLM<>ABCDEFGHIJKLMabcdef= true
  ABCDEFGHIJKLM<=ABCDEFGHIJKLMabcdef= true
  ABCDEFGHIJKLM>=ABCDEFGHIJKLMabcdef=false
  ABCDEFGHIJKLMabcdef><abcdef=ABCDEFGHIJKLM
```

Figure 9.10. A program which illustrates the effect of the set operators.

three distinct types of string are defined. `Textline` is a string type whose characters are numbered 1...80, `longstring` has characters numbered 1...200, etc.

There is a distinction between the upper bound of the string and the current *length* of the string. The upper bound of a string type defines how much space is allocated for character storage in the string. The length indicates how many of the characters are currently valid. The length cannot exceed the upper bound. There is an implementation defined constant `maxstring` which specifies the maximum upper bound with which a string type can be declared.

Individual characters of a string can be obtained by indexing the string as a one-dimensional array. Thus:

```
var s:textline;
begin
  s:='sammy snake';
  write(s[1],s[3],length(s));
end;
```

would produce the output

```
sm    11
```

TURBO

Note that the length field of the string is being found using a predefined function[3] `length`. The characters of a string can also be assigned to using array index notation:

```
s[2]:='i'; s[3]:='l'; s[4]:='l';
write(s);
```

will produce the output

```
silly snake
```

Or one can assign to whole slices of a string at once:

```
b:='Billy King';
s[1..4]:=b[1..4];
writeln(s);
```

will produce the output

```
Billy snake
```

It is important to note that the type of `s[1..4]` in the above is `ARRAY [1..4] OF char` and not `STRING[4]`. Thus the following assignments would

---

[3]If the implementation is such that the value of `maxstring` is known to be 255, then the length field will be held as a single byte as in Turbo Pascal and the length could be obtained by the expression `ord(s[0])`. This usage is not portable between implementations with different maximum string lengths.

be rejected by the compiler:

```
s[1..4]:='bill';
s:=b[1..4];
```

Each is an invalid combination of an array of char and a string.[4]

To obtain a string containing the first four characters of b we would have to call the system function substring:

```
s:=substring(b,1,4);
write(s);
```

Whereas the assignment s[1..4]:=b[1..4] leaves the length of s unchanged, assigning a string to s, as the example above does, changes the length. The use of a distinct length field for the string has advantages over the C convention of null-terminating strings:

1. The length of a string can be found faster since no search has to be done for null.
2. The string can contain null characters, which is usefull when dealing with encoded strings.

Between strings the + operator is interpreted as concatenation. The comparison operators give results as shown in Alg. 23. No other operators are valid on strings.

---

[4]This is a deviation from the Pascal standard which allows assignments of string constants to arrays of char, requiring the constant to be blank padded up to the length of the array.

10 Input and Output

10.1 File Types

ISO-7185

Pascal provides the word FILE as a type constructor. For any type t then FILE OF t is the type of an extensible n-tuple whose elements are of type t. Associated with each such n-tuple is a file cursor which defines the point within the tuple at which data can be read or written. Variables may be declared to have file types.

Whereas other variables are *volatile*, file variables allow Pascal programs access to the persistent store provided by the underlying operating system.[1]

10.1.1 Binary Files

A file type may be declared as, for instance, a file of integers or as a file of some record type:

```
TYPE intfile=FILE OF integer;
    gender=(male,female);
    person=RECORD
      name:string[50];
      sex :gender;
    END;
    pfile=FILE OF person;
```

Files such as these are termed *binary files*. The persistent data stored in them have a format which is implementation dependent. The arrangement of binary digits in the persistent store mirrors that of the bits in the volatile store. As such, the format of a FILE OF t created by a program running on an Intel processor may differ from that of a FILE OF t created on a Motorola processor because of differences in the internal binary formats used on the machines. This can give rise to difficulties when binary files are transported between different processors.

Binary files are also unsuitable for human consumption.

---

[1] The persistent store is often thought of as the disk and the volatile store as the RAM of the computer. This is not strictly accurate, as on some operating systems both will be mapped to the computer's virtual memory and reside either on disk or in RAM depending on frequency of use.

10.1.2 Text Files

Pascal also provides a predeclared type identifier text which is defined to be equal to `FILE OF char`. A file of type `text`, as the name implies, is made up of a sequence of characters. Text files can be read by people, and also provide a relatively machine-independent[2] means of recording and transferring numerical information. This is because numbers are represented in text files in terms of their decimal expansion.

10.1.3 Operating System Files

When originally released (Jensen and Wirth, 1978), Pascal provided no clearly defined mechanism for associating file variables with operating system files. This led to divergent approaches by implementors. In some systems file variables could only be accessed if they had first been associated with a persistent operating system file. In others, for instance DEC Pascal, a temporary file was created on disk whenever control entered a scope containing a file variable, and this file was automatically bound to the file variable.

The Turbo Pascal compiler adopted the former approach, and provided procedures to associate file variables with operating system files which were later adopted as a de facto standard by the implementors of most other Pascal systems for the PC.

The Pascal standardisation community recognised that there was a need for a standard way of binding file variables to operating system files. When the Extended Pascal standard, ISO-10206, was released in 1991 (ISO, 1991a), it introduced the concept of a *bindable* variable. A bindable variable in a Pascal program is a symbol or reference to something outside the program itself. ISO-10206 says that file variables are bindable. Procedures are defined for carrying out the bindings between file variables and operating system files.

The concept of a bindable variable is elegant and can potentially be used for things other than file variables, such as graphics contexts or mice. But because the procedures provided for file binding in ISO-10206 are incompatible with those derived from Turbo Pascal, and because the latter are used by almost all Pascal programs that have written for the PC and Linux platforms, the author has chosen not to implement the ISO-10206 file binding mechanism. Instead, Vector Pascal derives its library of file binding routines from those introduced in Turbo Pascal.

Assign

Before a file variable is used, a call must be made to the system procedure `assign` to bind it to a named operating system file. `Assign` takes a file variable and an operating system file name as parameters. The file name should follow the naming conventions of the operating system on which the program is running.

---

[2]Not absolutely machine independent, because in principle Pascal implementations may use EBCDIC, ISO or other character sets.

Example

```
assign(f, 'c:\myfiles\src\alpha.txt');
```

Although `assign` established a binding with the operating system file, it does not open the file, which must be done using one of the following procedures.

Append

TURBO

If the file already exists, is sequential in nature, and one wants to add to it, it is opened with `append`. Provided that the file variable has been bound to an operating system file, this will open it for writing with the file cursor indicating the end of the file.

Example

```
assign(f, 'c:\myfiles\src\alpha.txt');
append(f);
```

Rewrite

ISO-7185

If a file is to be written for the first time or is to be overwritten, the procedure `rewrite` is called. `Rewrite` can also be called if it is necessary to move the file cursor back to the start of the file at any point during the writing of an already opened file.

Example

```
assign(f, 'c:\myfiles\src\data.txt');
rewrite(f);
```

Reset

ISO-7185

If a file is to be opened for reading, or if an already open file is to be re-read, then the procedure `reset` must be called. It positions the file cursor at the start of the file.

Example

```
assign(n, 'people/names.src');
reset(n);
```

Close

TURBO

When a file variable is no longer in use, the procedure `close` should be called. Calling this causes any buffers to be flushed to disk. After a call to `close` the file variable still has the operating system file name associated with it and allowing a further call to `append`, `reset` or `rewrite`.

Example

```
assign(n,'people/names.src');
rewrite(n);
write(n,namelist);
close(n);
reset(n);
read(n,othernames);
```

10.2 Output

ISO-7185

Pascal defines two standard output procedures, `write` and `writeln`. Unlike other procedures, these may take a variable number of arguments of variable type. Furthermore, their names are reserved and cannot be redefined. `Write` works on both text and binary files, `writeln` only on the former.

10.2.1 Binary File Output

To write to a binary file, two formats can be used:

1. `write(`f,e_0`);` where f : FILE OF t, and e_0 : t.
2. `write(`$f,e_1,e_2,\ldots,e_n$`);` where f : FILE OF t, and e_i : t.

The values of the expressions e_i are transferred to the file in the order in which they are listed and the file cursor moved to point immediately beyond the file.
  Expressions of any type may be validly written to a binary file.

10.2.2 Text File Output

When outputting to a text file, there are four variants in which `write` can be called and six in which `writeln` can be called. All these variants can be defined in terms of the two canonical forms 1.a and 2.a, in the enumeration below.

1. (a) `write(`f,e_0`);` where f : FILE OF char, and e_0 : t and t is an integer, real, string, ordinal or array type. This outputs an appropriately formated representation of e_0 to the file f.
   (b) `write(`e_0`);` This is equivalent to `write(output,`e_0`);`.
   (c) `write(`$f,e_1,e_2,\ldots,e_n$`);` where f : FILE OF char, and each t_i is an integer, real, string, ordinal or array type. This is equivalent to `write(`f,e_1`); write(`f,e_2`) ... write(`f,e_n`);`.
   (d) `write(`$e_1,e_2,\ldots,e_n$`);` This is equivalent to `write(output,`$e_1,e_2,\ldots,e_n$`);`.
2. (a) `writeln(`f`);` This outputs a newline to the file f. The sequence of characters output will vary between operating systems. On Linux it will

be a line feed character[3] whereas on Windows it will be a carriage return, line feed sequence.[4]
(b) `writeln`; This is shorthand for `writeln(output);`.
(c) `writeln(f,`e_0`)`; This is shorthand for `write(f,`e_0`)`; `writeln(f);`.
(d) `writeln(`e_0`)`; This is equivalent to `write(`e_0`)`; `writeln;`.
(e) `writeln(`$e_1,e_2,\ldots,e_n$`)`; This is equivalent to `write(`$e_1,e_2,\ldots,e_n$`)`; `writeln;`.
(f) `writeln(f,`$e_1,e_2,\ldots,e_n$`)`; This is shorthand for `write(f,`$e_1,e_2,\ldots,e_n$`)`; `writeln(f);`.

Example

```
VAR a:string[30];
    b,c:integer;
BEGIN
  b:=9+12;
  c:=20;
  a:='too much';
  WRITE('total',a);
  WRITELN;
  WRITELN(output,b,b>c);
  WRITELN(c,1/c);
  WRITE(c*c);
  WRITELN(' is c raised to the power 2');
END;
```

which produces the output

```
total   too much
   21       true
   20       0.05
  400 is c raised to the power 2
```

Formating Output in Columns

The example above shows that the default behaviour of the `write` procedure for text files is to write the data out in columns of equal width. The standard width of these columns is 12 for all types other than characters for which the standard column width is one character.

If the textual representation of a value is shorter than the column width, the output field is left-padded with space characters. If the output width is greater then the column width, then the field overflows the column to the right. Where the default widths are unsuitable, Pascal provides a means by which column widths can be altered.

---
[3]chr(10).
[4]chr(13)chr(10).

Output of Integers

ISO-7185

For integer output one can follow the integer expression with a colon and then another integer expression giving the column width to be used. The decimal expansion of the integer is printed right justified in the column. Thus, to print the integer x out in a field six characters wide, one writes

```
write(x:6);
```

Output of Reals

ISO-7185

For real numbers you can specify both the the width of the field and the number of digits after the decimal point. Thus:

```
write(x:8:2);
```

Output of Characters

ISO-7185

When a character variable is printed, it is output in binary with no modifications to the text file. If the optional width field is present, the character is left padded with spaces before output, in a manner analogous to integers (see above).

```
{Chin_prog01}
{Print a Cosine graph going across the screen}
{26/11/2002}
程序 Graph(output);
    变量
        d:0..95;
        y:real;
    开始{BEGIN}
        写行; {Writeln}
        写行; {Writeln}
        写行('********COSINE GRAPH********'); {Writeln('COSINE GRAPH')}
        d:=0;
        当 d<=90 循环   {while d<=90 do}
            开始   {begin}
            y:= 余弦 (d*Π/180)*30; {y:=cos(d*pi/180)*30}
            如果 四舍五入(y)=0 {if round(y)=0}
            那么 写行('*')         {then writeln('*')}
            否则 写行(' ':四舍五入(y), '*'); {else writeln(' ':round(y), '*');
            d:=d+5;
        结束;  {end;}
结束.{END.}
```

Algorithm 37. The use of formatted output and also the use of Chinese characters in reserved words. The equivalent Standard Pascal program commands are shown as comments.

Chapter 10 • Input and Output

Output of Scalars

<small>VECTOR</small>

When a scalar variable is printed, the lower-case form of the element of the enumerated type is output to the text file. The field is left-padded by the optional width field in the same way as integers are.

Output of Strings

A string is printed without enclosing quotes. Semantically `write(s)` is equivalent to

<small>TURBO</small>

```
for i:=1 to length(s) do write(s[i])
```

10.2.3 Generic Array Output

<small>VECTOR</small>

In Standard Pascal, any type including an array can be written to a binary file, but output to text files must be of simple types or string types. Vector Pascal, in conformity with the general overloading of operations on arrays, extends `write` to operate on arrays. A one-dimensional array is written as a sequence of values on a line. Thus, for a one-dimensional array a with bounds $l \ldots u$, the statement `write(a);` would be equivalent to

```
FOR i:=l TO u DO write(a[i]);
```

where i is a temporary integer variable. If the array b has more than one dimension, and the bounds of the leftmost dimension are $m \ldots n$ then the expansion is

```
FOR j:=m TO n DO writeln(b[j]);
```

In conjunction with the re-write rules given in Section 10.2.2, this gives an unambiguous definition of `write` for arrays. The effect is that dimensions of the arrays are separated by newlines. These rules are illustrated in Figure 10.1.

10.3 Input

<small>ISO-7185</small>

Pascal defines two standard input procedures, `read` and `readln`. Like the standard output procedures but unlike other procedures, these may take a variable number of arguments of variable type. Again, their names are reserved and cannot be redefined. Read works on both text and binary files, `readln` only on the former.

Other than the optional leading file variable, all parameters to a `read` call must be variables.

10.3.1 Generic Array Input

In Standard Pascal, any type including an array can be read from a binary file, but input from text files must be of simple types or string types. Just as Vector Pascal extends write operations to arrays, so it extends read operations in such

```
PROGRAM ARRAYOUT(OUTPUT);
CONST a:ARRAY[1..2,1..2,1..3] OF integer=
        (((1,2,3),
          (2,4,6)),
         ((99,2,97),
          (98,4,94)));
BEGIN
write(a);
END.
```

produces the output

```
           1       2       3
           2       4       6

          99       2      97
          98       4      94
```

Figure 10.1. The formating rules for output of multi-dimensional arrays.

VECTOR

a way as to ensure that if an array a is written to a file f with the call `write`(f,a) then it can be read by the call `read`(f,a). The expected input format for arrays is hence that which would have been produced by the array having been written by a Vector Pascal program (see Section 10.2.3).

10.3.2 Binary File Input

Input from a binary file involves direct binary transfers of the bytes of the binary representation from the file to the variable.

10.3.3 Text File Input

When performing input from a text file representational, conversions are performed between number and scalar types' ASCII text representation and their memory representation. The semantic expansion rules for `read` and for `readln` mirror those for `write` and `writeln` shown in Section 10.2.2, but with the substitution of `read` wherever `write` occurs in the rules and the substitution of the file variable `input` wherever the file variable `output` is referred to in Section 10.2.3.

`Readln` simply reads the next newline sequence from its input file.

Input of Integers or Reals

ISO-7185

On a call of `read`(f,n) with text file f and numeric variable n, the spaces in the text file are skipped up to the first decimal digit. Decimal to binary conversion is then performed on the number and the result placed in n.

Input of Characters

ISO-7185

No format conversion is performed on character input. The character is read in binary form from the text file and transfered to the character variable parameter.

Input of Scalars

Spaces are skipped up until the first letter. Letters and digits are then read up until the first non-alphanumeric character. The alphanumeric sequence is then converted to lower case and compared with the legitimate lower-case representations of the identifiers in the enumerated scalar type. If one is found then the ordinal value of the identifier within the scalar type is returned.

VECTOR

Input of Strings

TURBO

Characters are read into the string variable up until either the first newline is encountered in the input file or the maximum length of the string is reached.

10.4 File Predicates

ISO-7185

Two file predicates, `eof(f)` and `eoln(f)`, are provided to test the position of the file cursor. `eof` tests for end of file and `eoln` tests for end of line.

10.5 Random Access to Files

For database applications, it is necessary to be able to read and write records at random positions in a file.

10.5.1 Seek

UNIX

The file cursor in a binary file may be positioned at any place in the file using the function `seek`. Its form is

`function seek(var f:fileptr;pos,mode:integer):integer;`

The type fileptr is a generic type for any binary file type. The parameter `pos` specifies the position to seek to in the file. The `mode` parameter should be one of:

SEEK_SET	pos is relative to start of file
SEEK_CUR	pos is relative to current file cursor
SEEK_END	pos is relative to the end of the file.

10.5.2 filepos

TURBO

The current position of the cursor within a binary file can be obtained using the function `filepos`, the form of which is

`function filepos(var f:fileptr):integer;`

10.5.3 Untyped i/o

There are two procedures, `blockread` and `blockwrite`, available to perform untyped i/o of sequences of bytes with the forms

```
procedure blockread(var f:fileptr;
                    var buf;
                        count:integer;
                    var resultcount:integer);
procedure blockwrite(var f:fileptr;
                     var buf;
                         count:integer;
                     var rcount:integer);
```

where `f` is any binary file, `buf` is any variable (where an array is to be transferred the first element of the array should be passed), `count` is the number of bytes to transfer and `resultcount` as a post-condition holds the number of bytes actually transferred.

10.6 Error Conditions

When performing i/o operations, error conditions can arise owing to factors external to the program, such as the non-existence of files or files containing unexpected content. These can set an internal system io-error flag. If an i/o operation is performed whilst the io-error flag is set the program will abort.

TURBO

The flag can be queried using the `ioresult` function, which has the form `function ioresult:integer;`. It returns a non-zero value if the io-error flag is set. Calling the function has the side effect of clearing the flag. It is good practice to check the io-error status after each call to file the opening procedures `reset` and `rewrite`, as shown in Figure 10.2.

          program *iocheck*;
          var
             Let $\phi \in$ text;
             Let $S \in$ string;
          begin
             assign (ϕ, 'message');
             reset (ϕ);
             if *ioresult* = 0 **then**

file exists
             begin
                read(ϕ,S);
                write('Message is:' , S);
             end
             else

error in opening file
                write('Could not open message file');
          end.

Figure 10.2. The use of `ioresult` to check the validity of file open calls.

Permutations and Polymorphism

11

Standard Pascal allows the assignment of whole arrays. As we have seen in Section 7.5, Vector Pascal extends this to allow the consistent use of mixed-rank expressions on the right-hand side of an assignment. For example, given

```
r1:real; r1:array[0..7]of real;
r2:array[0..7,0..7]of real
```

then we can write

1. `r1:= 1/2;`
2. `r2:= r1*3;`
3. `r1:= \+ r2;`
4. `r1:= r1+r2[1];`

Line 1 assigns `0.5` to each element of `r1`. Line 2 assigns `1.5` to every element of `r2`. In line 3, `r1` gets the totals along the rows of `r2`. In line 4, `r1` is incremented with the corresponding elements of row 1 of `r2`.

These may be translated directly to standard Pascal through iteration:

1. `for i:=0 to 7 do r1[i]:=1/2;`
2. `for i:=0 to 7 do for j:=0 to 7 do r2[i,j]:=r1[j]*3;`
3. `for i:=0 to 7 do begin`
   `t:=0;`
   `for j:=7 downto 0 do t:=r2[i,j]+t;`
   `r1[i]:=t;`
   `end;`
4. `for i:=0 to 7 do r1[i]:=r1[i]+r2[1,i];`

The compiler has to generate an implicit loop over the elements of the array being assigned to and over the elements of the array acting as the data source. In the above, `i`, `j`, `t` are assumed to be temporary variables not referred to anywhere else in the program. The loop variables are called implicit indices.

The variable on the left-hand side of an assignment defines an array context within which expressions on the right-hand side are evaluated. Each array context has a rank given by the number of dimensions of the array on the left-hand side. A scalar variable has rank 0. Variables occurring in expressions with an array context of rank r must have r or fewer dimensions. The n bounds of any n-dimensional array variable, with $n \leq r$ occurring within an expression evaluated in an array context of rank r, must match with the rightmost n bounds of the array on the left-hand side of the assignment statement.

Where a variable is of lower rank than its array context, the variable is replicated to fill the array context. This is shown in the examples above. Because the rank of any assignment is constrained by the variable on the left-hand side, no temporary arrays, other than machine registers, need be allocated to store the intermediate array results of expressions.

Maps are implicitly and promiscuously defined on both monadic operators and unary functions. If f is a function or unary operator mapping from type r to type t, then if x is an array of r then a:=f(x) assigns an array of t such that a[i]=f(x[i]).

11.1 Array Reorganisation

Array reorganisation involves *conservative operations* which preserve the number of elements in the original array. If the shape of the array is also conserved, we have an element permutation operation. If the shape of the array is not conserved but its rank and extents are, we have a permutation of the array dimensions. If the rank is not conserved we have a flattening or reshaping of the array.

Vector Pascal provides syntactic forms to access and manipulate the implicit indices used in maps and reductions. These forms allow the concise expression of many conservative array reorganisations.

When an assignment is performed to an array, the compiler creates implicit index variables with which to perform the iterations. These index variables may be accessed using the syntactic form iota i, where i is an integer.[1] iota i returns the ith current implicit index. Thus, the sequence

```
v1:array[1..3] of integer;
v2:array[0..4] of integer;
...
v1:= iota 0;
v2:= iota 0*2;
```

would set v1 and v2 to

```
v1 =1   2   3
v2 =0   2   4   6   8
```

In contrast, given the sequence

```
m1:array[1..3,0..4] of integer;
m2:array[0..4,1..3] of integer;
m2:= iota 0 + 2*iota 1;
```

---

[1] The reserved word ndx is a synonym for iota.

Chapter 11 • Permutations and Polymorphism

would set m2 to:

```
m2=  2   4   6
     3   5   7
     4   6   8
     5   7   9
     6   8  10
```

The argument to iota must be an integer known at compile time within the range of implicit indices in the current context.

A generalised permutation of the implicit indices is performed using the syntactic form

```
perm[index-sel[,index-sel]*]expression
```

The *index-sel*s are integers known at compile time which specify a permutation on the implicit indices. Thus in *e* evaluated in context perm[*i,j,k*]*e*, then

```
iota 0 = iota i, iota 1 = iota j, iota 2 = iota k
```

This is particularly useful in converting between different image formats. Hardware frame buffers typically represent images with the pixels in the red, green, blue and alpha channels adjacent in memory. For image processing it is convenient to hold them in distinct planes. The perm operator provides a concise notation for translation between these formats:

```
type rowindex=0..479;
     colindex=0..639;
var channel=red..alpha;
    screen:array[rowindex,colindex,channel] of pixel;
    img:array[channel,colindex,rowindex] of pixel;
...
screen:=perm[2,0,1]img;
```

trans and diag provide shorthand notions for expressions in terms of perm. Thus, in an assignment context of rank 2, trans = perm[1,0] and diag = perm[0,0].

The form trans x transposes a vector, matrix, or tensor.[2] It achieves this by cyclic rotation of the implicit indices. Thus, if trans e for some expression e is evaluated in a context with implicit indices:

```
iota 0 .. iota n
```

then the expression e is evaluated in a context with implicit indices:

```
iota'0 .. iota'n
```

where

```
iota' x = iota((x+1) mod n+1)
```

It should be noted that transposition is generalised to arrays of rank greater than 2.

---

[2] Note that trans is not strictly an operator, as there exists no Pascal type corresponding to a column vector.

For example, given the definitions used above, the program fragment

```
m1:=(trans v1)*v2;
m2:=trans m1;
```

will set m1 and m2:

```
m1=  0    2    4    6    8
     0    4    8   12   16
     0    6   12   18   24
m2=  0    0    0
     2    4    6
     4    8   12
     6   12   18
     8   16   24
```

11.1.1 An Example

The program in Figure 11.1 illustrates the use of implicit indices and their manipulation.

1. α, an array of $1\ldots 5$, is initialised to the numbers $1\ldots 5$.
2. t, a two-dimensional array, is then organised to form a times table by multiplying α with α^T.
3. b then gets the sum down the columns of the table.
4. c is initialised to successive powers of 2, i.e. $2^{1\ldots 5}$.
5. d gets the diagonal of t, which of course contains $(1\ldots 5)^2$.
6. t is reassigned a new times table whose elements are $\iota_0^2 \times 2^{\iota_0}$.

11.1.2 Array Shifts

Shifts and rotations of arrays are not supported by any explicit Vector Pascal operator, although one can use a combination of other features to achieve them. For example, given

```
var a,b:array[0..n-1] of integer;
```

a left rotation can achieved as

```
a:=b[(1+iota 0) mod n];
```

and a reversal by

```
a:=b[n-1-iota 0];
```

11.1.3 Element Permutation

Permutations are widely used in APL and J programming, an example being sorting an array a into descending order using the J expression \:a{a. This uses the operator \: to produce a permutation of the indices of a in descending order, and then uses { to index a with this permutation vector. The use of analogous constructs requires the ability to index one array by another. If

```
program tables;
var
    Let α,b,c,d ∈ array[1..5] of integer;
    t :array [1..5,1..5] of integer;
begin
    α ← ι₀;
    t ← α × α^T;
    write(t);

    b ← Σt^T;
    writeln(b);
    c ← 2^ι₀;
    d ← diag t;
    t ← c × d^T;
    writeln(c,d);
```

times tables

sum of columns
powers of two
squares up to 25

output table of $i^2 \times 2^i$

```
    write(t);
end.
```

Program output:

1	2	3	4	5
2	4	6	8	10
3	6	9	12	15
4	8	12	16	20
5	10	15	20	25
15	30	45	60	75
2	4	8	16	32
1	4	9	16	25
2	4	8	16	32
8	16	32	64	128
18	36	72	144	288
32	64	128	256	512
50	100	200	400	800

Figure 11.1. Demonstration of the use of transpose to produce tables: VPTEXed program. For the original Pascal source, see Figure 11.2.

`x:array[t0] of t1` and `y:array[t1] of t2`, then in Vector Pascal, `y[x]` denotes the virtual array of type `array[t0] of t2` such that `y[x][i]= y[x[i]]`.

For example, given the sequence

`const per:array[0..3] of integer=(3,1,2,0);`

```
program tables;
var alpha,b,c,d:array[1..5] of integer;
    t:array[1..5,1..5] of integer;
begin
    alpha:=iota 0;
    t:=alpha*trans alpha;
    write(t); {times tables}
    b:=\+trans t;
    writeln(b); {sum of columns}
    c:=2 pow iota 0; {powers of two}
    d:=diag t;       {squares up to 25}
    t:=c*trans d;
    writeln(c,d);
    (*! output table of $i^2\times2^i$ *)
    write(t);
end.
```

Figure 11.2. Demonstration of the use of transpose to produce tables: the original Pascal source.

```
var ma,m0:array[0..3] of integer;
...
m0:=(iota 0)+1;
ma:=m0[per];
```

would set the variables such that

m0	=	1	2	3	4
per	=	3	1	2	0
ma	=	4	2	3	1

11.1.4 Efficiency Considerations

Expressions involving transposed vectors, matrix diagonals and permuted vectors, or indexing by expressions involving modular arithmetic on iota, do not parallelise well on SIMD architectures such as the MMX. These depend on the fetching of blocks of adjacent elements into the vector registers, which requires that element addresses be adjacent and monotonically increasing. Assignments involving re-mapped vectors are usually handled by scalar registers

11.2 Dynamic Arrays

Pascal implementations typically use three areas of store for variables. Global variables are allocated space in a static area of memory allocated before computation starts. Variables local to procedures are dynamically allocated space on the stack whenever the procedure is entered. Variables accessed via pointers are allocated space on the heap at run time by calls to the procedure new. For global and local variables, the compiler has to know the offset of the

Chapter 11 • Permutations and Polymorphism

```
FUNCTION mkim(rows,cols:integer):pimage;
VAR tim:pimage;
BEGIN
   getmem(tim,rows*sizeof(prow));
   WHILE rows>0 DO
   BEGIN
      rows:=rows-1;
      getmem(tim^[rows],cols);
   END;
   mkim:=tim;
END;
```

Figure 11.3. Use of getmem to allocate dynamically a two-dimensional array for image data.

variables relative either to the base of the global segment, or relative to a base register that points at the current procedure context on the stack. This is the reason why in Standard Pascal the bounds of all arrays must be known at compile time.

This restriction can be inconvenient for many algorithms which require arrays whose size needs to be determined at run time. An example is when a program reads in an image file from disk, where prior to reading the file the size of the pixel array needed is unknown. A number of ways round this restriction have been experimented with in Pascal implementations.

In Turbo Pascal, the usual approach was to declare an image array as follows:

```
TYPE row   =ARRAY[0..maxcol] OF byte;
     prow  =^ row;
     image =ARRAY[0..maxline] OF prow;
     pimage=^image;
VAR im:pimage;
```

The constants `maxcol` and `maxline` are defined to be much larger than the largest number of rows and columns with which we expect to have to deal. Once the file header has been read in, store is explicitly allocated for `im` using a procedure `getmem`, which has the form

TURBO

`procedure getmem(var p:pointertype; bytes:integer);`

and then space is allocated for the rows of the image. The initialisation might be done using the function `mkim` shown in Figure 11.3. The elements of the array are then accessed using pointer dereferencing thus:

`im^[i]^[j];`

Whilst this technique works, and is still supported in Vector Pascal, it is inelegant and means that array bounds checking is dispensed with.

11.2.1 Schematic Arrays

Extended Pascal provided a notation that allowed dynamically sized multi-dimensional arrays to be declared. This involved the declaration of *schema types*.

In the previous problem we could have declared a schema type for images:

```
TYPE image(maxrow,maxcol:integer)=
    ARRAY[0..maxrow,0..maxcol] OF byte;
    pimage=^image;
VAR im:pimage;
```

The image array can be allocated space on the heap using an extended form of `new`:

```
new(im,rows,cols);
```

where `rows`, `cols` are variables initialised at run time.

Access to the array now involves only one level of indirection as in `im^[i,j]`. This probably makes little difference to performance on modern processors with large caches. Four memory accesses are still required to determine the array element's address, one each for `i` and `j`, one for `im` and one for a hidden descriptor field specifying the length of the rows. However, it is conceptually neater and allows array bounds checking to be enforced by the compiler.

11.3 Polymorphic Functions

Standard Pascal provides some limited support for polymorphism in its `read` and `write` functions. Vector Pascal allows the writing of polymorphic functions and procedures through the use of parametric units.

TURBO

The unit is a concept introduced in Turbo Pascal to support separate compilation. Vector Pascal supports Turbo Pascal type units and an example is given in Section 13.2. Here we are concerned only with the extensions provided by parametric units.

VECTOR

Consider the issue of writing a sort routine such that shown in Figure 9.8. In Standard Pascal this has to be written to sort items of some given type `t` – in the case of Figure 9.8, it sorted strings. If we want a routine to sort integers, we could modify the source of the program `sortf` to redefine `t` so that

```
t=integer;
```

Since the only operation other than assignment that `bubblesort` carries out on values of type `t` is to compare them, it follows that we could have declared `t` to be any comparable type. However, there is no way in Standard Pascal to do this without altering the program source. Vector Pascal gets round this restriction by allowing type parameters to be passed to compilation units. We can therefore write a generalised sort unit, that has a type `t` passed into it. This is shown in Figure 11.4.

The algorithm used is identical with that in Figure 9.8, except that `t` is unspecified. If we are to use the unit `genericsort`, we must instantiate it with a specific type. An instantiation to sort integers is given by

unit *intsort*;
    interface
    in *genericsort* (*integer*);

Chapter 11 • Permutations and Polymorphism

unit *genericsort(t)*;
interface
type
    dataarray (n,m:integer) = **array** [*n..m*] **of** *t*;
procedure *sort* (**var** *a:dataarray*); (see Figure 11.5)

implementation

procedure *sort* (**var** *a:dataarray*); (see Figure 11.5)
begin
end.

Figure 11.4. A polymorphic sorting unit.

procedure *sort* (**var** *a:dataarray*);
var
    Let $i,j \in$ integer;
    Let *temp* $\in t$;
begin
    for $i \leftarrow a.n$ **to** $a.m - 1$ **do**
        for $j \leftarrow a.n$ **to** $a.m - 1$ **do**
        if $a_j > a_{j+1}$ **then** *begin* **begin**
            temp $\leftarrow a_j$;
            $a_j \leftarrow a_{j+1}$;
            $a_{j+1} \leftarrow$ *temp*;
        end;
end;

Figure 11.5. Procedure sort.

which, when compiled, creates a compiled unit called `intsort` whose interface and body are provided by `genericsort` where all references to type `t` are interpreted as meaning `integer`.

The unit `intsort` can now be included in the program shown in Figure 11.6, where `sort` is passed an array of integers to sort.

11.3.1 Multiple Uses of Parametric Units

Suppose we have a program that needs sort both integers and arrays of dates.

We have given a declaration for dates in Section 9.4, but for dates to be sortable we need to have the > operator defined on them. This can readily be done using the operator definition facility of Vector Pascal. The unit `calendar`, shown in Figure 11.7, exports both the type date and the operator > over dates.

```
program sort;
uses intsort;
const
   a:array [1..5] of integer = (2,8,3,4,7);
var
   Let b ∈ ARRAY[1..5] of integer;
begin
   b ← a;
   sort (b_{1..4});
   write(a,b);
end.
```

program output:

2	8	3	4	7
2	3	4	8	7

Figure 11.6. A program that uses the integer sorting unit.

```
unit calendar;
interface
  type
     monthname = (jan,feb,mar,apr,may,jun,
     jul,aug,sep,oct,nov,dec);
     date = record
        year:integer;
        month:monthname;
        day:1..31;
     end;
  function dategt (a,b:date):boolean; (see Section 11.3.2)
     OPERATOR >= dategt;
implementation
function dategt (a,b:date):boolean; (see Section 11.3.2)
begin
end.
```

Figure 11.7. A unit to export dates and their order.

Chapter 11 • Permutations and Polymorphism

```
program sort2;
uses calendar,datesort,intsort;
const
    a:array [1..5] of integer = (2,8,3,4,7);
var
    Let b ∈ array[1..5] of integer;
    Let c ∈ array[1..3] of date;
    Let i,d ∈ integer;
begin
    b ← a;
    sort (b₁..₄);
    WRITE(a,b);
    for i ← 1 to 3 do
    begin
        read(d);
        cᵢ.day ← d;
        readln(c[i].month,c[i].year);
    end;
    sort (c₁..₃);
    for i ← 1 to 3 do writeln(cᵢ.day,cᵢ.month,cᵢ.year);
end.
```

Given the input:

```
11   sep   2002
16   mar   1952
4    jan   2002
```

this produces the output:

```
        2    8    3    4    7
        2    3    4    8    7
       16   mar   1952
        4   jan   2002
       11   sep   2002
```

Figure 11.8. The use of two instantiations of the same parametric unit within one program.

11.3.2   Function dategt

The ordering of dates is done taking years as more significant than months, which are more significant than days:

function *dategt (a,b:date):boolean;*
begin
  if *a.year > b.year* **then**
    dategt ← true

else if (*a.year* = *b.year*) **and** (*a.month* > *b.month*) **then**
   dategt ← *true*
else if (*a.year* = *b.year*) **and** (*a.month* = *b.month*) **and** (*a.day* > *b.day*) **then**
   dategt ← *true*
else *dategt* ← *false*;
end;

Using this, we can create another instantiation of `genericsort` to sort dates:

unit *datesort*;
interface uses *calendar*;
   in *genericsort* (*date*);

Both sorting units are then imported into program `sort2` shown in Figure 11.8. The compiler uses the type of the parameter to decide which instance of the generic function is to be called. This is a limited form of procedure overloading. It allows mutiple instantiations of a generic function to share the same name. All instances of a generic function have the same number of parameters, only their types differ.

Part III
Programming Examples
Paul Cockshott

Advanced Set Programming   12

12.1 Use of Sets to Find Prime Numbers

Let us look at a simple but practical algorithm that uses sets. The algorithm is a very old one for finding prime numbers and is shown in Alg. 38.

To find all primes less than or equal to `maxlim`, it removes successive multiples of each prime number from a set intialised to include all integers from 2 to `maxlim`. A non-prime is a multiple of primes. Hence once we have removed all multiples of primes, the set of integers we are left with must be the

```
program seive (output);
const
    maxlim = 100;
type
    range = 1..maxlim;
    intset = set of range;
var
    Let primes ∈ intset;
    Let i, k, j ∈ integer;
begin
    primes ← [2..maxlim];
    k ← 1;
    for i in primes do
    begin
        j ← i × (k + 1);
        while j ≤ maxlim do
        begin
            primes ← primes − [j];
            j ← j + i;
        end;
    end;
    primes ← primes + [1];
    for i in primes do WRITELN(i);
end.
```

Algorithm 38. The sieve of Eratosthenes, coded using sets.

primes. When removing the multiples of prime i, we can ignore all multiples less than or equal to $i \times p$, where p is the highest prime less than i, since we have already removed all multiples of p from the set. The basic step of removing numbers from the set of primes is done with the line

```
primes:=primes-[j];
```

which subtracts the set containing only the integer j from the set primes. Note that we cannot in Pascal write

```
primes:=primes-j;
```

without giving a rise to a type error, since j is an integer and primes is a set.

12.1.1 Set Implementation

Like other Pascal compilers, Vector Pascal implements ordinal sets as bitmaps. A Pascal set is defined over an ordinal type. Associated with each element of the ordinal type, the compiler allocates one bit in a bitmap to indicate membership of the set. This representation is efficient and compact for dense sets. For sparse sets it can be wasteful of space. It is usually better to represent very sparse sets as explicitly programmed linked lists or trees rather than using the built-in set types. If the occupancy of the sets is likely to be less than 1% of the range over which the set type is defined, then more space-efficient representations can usually be explicitly programmed.

If space efficiency is not of key importance, the bitmap representation used in Pascal has considerable speed advantages. On machines with a wide word length such as the MMX, the basic set operations can be performed at high speed, as they translate into AND and OR operations on machine words.

The overall efficiency of set algorithms also depends crucially on the efficiency of the set insertion and deletion operations. These are expressed in Pascal in terms of addition or subtraction of singleton sets. Unless these are recognised as special cases, the compiler will generate code to perform Boolean operations on what can be large bitmaps. If the addition or subtraction of singleton sets is recognised as a special case, then the compiler can generate code to toggle an individual bit, which will be much faster for large bitmaps.

Vector Pascal performs such optimisations. Their presence not only makes set operations very fast compared with other Pascal implementations, but also alters the complexity order of algorithms. Table 12.1 compares the run times on sieve of two Pascal compilers: Vector Pascal and Prospero Extended Pascal.[1] It can be seen that Vector Pascal is between 40 and 300 times faster than Prospero Pascal. Column 4 of the table shows that for Vector Pascal the algorithm is $< \mathbf{O}n$, whereas column 5 shows that for Prospero Pascal it is $\approx \mathbf{O}n^2$.

---

[1] Prospero Pascal is probably the only complete implementation of ISO-10206 available for Intel processors. Other Pascal compilers for PCs will generally not handle sets of arbitrary size as required by the program.

Table 12.1. Comparative performances of different Pascal implementations on the Sieve program as a function of set size

Maxlim	1	2	3	4	5
	Seconds		Ratio	Microseconds per integer	
	Vector	Prospero		Vector	Prospero
20000	0.73	42	57:1	0.1217	6.96
25000	0.91	63	69:1	0.1213	8.40
40000	1.30	315	242:1	0.1083	26.25

Measurements taken using a 700 MHz Trans-Meta Crusoe processor. Vector Pascal compiled to the MMX instruction-set. Columns 1 and 2 give total run time in seconds to find the primes excluding time to print them. Column 3 shows the speed ratio between the two compilers. Columns 4 and 5 show how the time to process each integer changes as the set size grows.

12.2 Ordered Sets

Standard Pascal supports only sets of *ordinal* types. Vector Pascal allows sets of any *ordered* type. Thus Vector Pascal allows one to define sets of strings or sets of reals. Since the maximum cardinality of such sets is not known until run time, dynamic data structures are used. One consequence of this is that any program using dynamic sets should be compiled with garbage collection enabled to prevent memory leaks.

Dynamic sets are implemented in terms of balanced binary trees. Since binary trees are a sorted data structure, they require an ordering relationship between the elements stored in the nodes of the tree. Hence it is possible to declare sets of any type over which the operators $<, >, =$ are declared. Among the predeclared types, sets of string or real numbered types will be implemented dynamically.

When a dynamic set type SET OF x is declared, the compiler loads a generic set unit parameterised by the type x. It then code generates a library of routines specialised to handling sets of x.

One adverse consequence of the use of tree structures for dynamic sets is that they cannot be written out to a binary file as a single operation. Input and output of sets has to proceed by iterating through the set.

As an example of the use of dynamic sets, we will consider a program that reads two documents and sends to the standard output channel a list of all words that occur in both documents.

The data type used will be a set of lexemes, where a lexeme is a string of up to wordmax characters. Words of more than wordmax characters will be ignored. The strategy is to form a set of lexemes for each file, form the intersection of these and then print the intersection.

We will define a valid lexeme to be a sequence of adjacent alphabetic characters. All other sequences of characters will be skipped over.

The main program, shown in Alg. 39, reads in the files to sets, intersects them and then lists the result.

For instance the command

```
D:\WPC\documents\ilcg\book\tests>uniquewords norm.pas
roman.pas
```

produces the list of words

```
array
of
program
var
writeln
```

The contents of the two files can be determined by using the cat command:

```
D:\WPC\documents\ilcg\book\tests>cat roman.pas norm.pas
program roman;
const rom:array[0..4] of string[1]=('C','L','X','V','I');
numb:array[0..4] of integer=(2,1,1,0,3);
var s:string;
begin
   s:=numb.rom;
```

program *uniquewords*;
const
    wordmax =20;
type
    lexeme =**string** [*wordmax*];
    lexset =**set of** *lexeme*;

var
    files: **array** [1..2] **of** *text*;
    words: **array** [1..2] **of** *lexset*;
    Let *i* ∈ integer;
    Let *commonwords* ∈ lexset;
    Let *aword* ∈ lexeme;
function *openfiles:boolean*; (see Section 12.2.1)

procedure *loadset*(**var** *f:text*;**var** *words:lexset*); (see Section 12.2.2)

begin
    if *openfiles*
    then
    begin
        for *i* ← 1 **to** 2 **do** *loadset* (*files$_i$*,*words$_i$*);
        commonwords ← *words$_1$* × *words$_2$*;
        for *aword* **in** *commonwords* **do**
            writeln(*aword*);
    end
    else writeln('Usage:uniquewords file1 file2');
end.

Algorithm 39. Main program for unique words.

Chapter 12 • Advanced Set Programming

```
       writeln(s);
end.

program norm;
type vec=array[0..3] of real;
function n(var v:vec):real;
begin
   n:=sqrt(\+(v*v));
end;
var v:vec;  r:real;
begin
   v:=iota 0;
   r:=n(v);
   writeln(v,r);
end.
```

On the other hand, we can find all of the unique words in a single file by intersecting it with itself thus:

```
D:\WPC\documents\ilcg\book\tests>uniquewords norm.pas
norm.pas
array
function
iota
n
norm
of
program
r
real
sqrt
type
v
var
vec
writeln
```

12.2.1 openfiles

function *openfiles:boolean;*

This returns true if it has suceeded in opening both files. Two possible error conditions can arise:

1. The number of filenames supplied to the program may be wrong. This is tested using the integer valued function **paramcount** which is provided in the System Unit. This returns the number of parameters provided to the program on the command line.

2. The names provided may not correspond to valid files. This is tested by attempting to reset the files for writing and then testing the ioresult function. To use this one must disable the automatic i/o checks provided on resetting a file which would otherwise cause the program to abort with a run time error. This is done with the compiler directive {$i-}. The previous presence of this directive allows the ioresult function to be used to test whether file opening failed.

label 99;
var
   Let $i \in$ integer;
begin
   openfiles ← *false*;
   if *paramcount* < 2
   then goto 99;
   for $i \leftarrow$ 1 **to** 2 **do**
   begin
      assign (*files$_i$,paramstr(i)*);
      {$i-checks off}
      reset (*files$_i$*);
      if *ioresult* $\neq$ 0
      then goto 99;
      {$i+checks on}
   end ;
   openfiles ← *true*;
   99:
end;

12.2.2 loadset

procedure *loadset* (**var** *f:text*;**var** *words:lexset*);

This procedure finds all the unique words in a file and returns them in lexset. This module is responsible for all of the parsing of the input files. It declares the set `letters` used in discriminating words from other text:

const
   a = 'a';
   z = 'z';
var
   Let *letters* $\in$ set of char;
type
   state = (*inword,skipping*);
var
   Let $c \in$ char;
   Let $s \in$ state;
   Let *theword* $\in$ lexeme;
function *getch:char*; (see Section 12.2.2)

Chapter 12 • Advanced Set Programming

procedure *getlex* (**var** *l:lexeme*); (see Section 12.2.2)
begin
  s ← *skipping*;
  words ← [ ];
  letters ← ['a' .. 'z', 'A' .. 'Z'];
  repeat
    getlex (*theword*);
    words ← *words* + [*theword*];
  until *theword* = ' ';
of loadset   **end**;

getch

function *getch:char*;

Read in a character from the current file, return the null character on end of file. This function has to deal with the problems of

1. Ends of lines, which in Pascal are detected by the **eoln** function. These are dealt with by returning the ASCII CR character 13.
2. End of file, detected by the **eof** function. This is dealt with by returning the ASCII NUL character 0. The occurence of NUL characters is dealt with at the next higher level of processing to ensure that termination occurs.

var
  Let *local* ∈ char;
begin
  if *eoln* (*f*) **then**
  begin
    readln (*f*);
    getch ← **chr**(13);
  end
  else
  begin
    if *eof* (*f*) **then**
    begin
      getch ← **chr**(0);
    end
    else
    begin
      read (*f,local*);
      getch ← *local*;
    end;
  end;
of getch   **end**;

getlex

procedure *getlex* (**var** *l:lexeme*);

This procedure parses the input stream for the next word. It then returns it in l. It operates as a simple finite state machine that can be in one of two states:

1. skipping: the machine is in this state between words whilst it moves over non letter characters.
2. inword: the machine is in this state whilst it parses a word.

The special case of the occurrence of the null character causes a branch to label 99, ensuring that a null string is returned by the procedure. This is used at the next higher level as a termination condition. Labels, although deprecated in structured programming, remain a useful construct for escaping from loops. Note that membership of the character in the set of letters is used to switch between the two states of the parser. This is an entirely orthodox use of sets in Pascal.

label 99;
begin
  $l \leftarrow$ '';
  while $s = $ *skipping* **do**
  begin
    $c \leftarrow $ *getch*;
    if c **in** *letters* **then** $s \leftarrow $ *inword*;
    if $c = $ **chr**(0) **then goto** 99;
  end;
  while $s = $ *inword* **do**
  begin
    if *length* (l) $= $ *wordmax*
    then goto 99;
    $l \leftarrow l + c$;
    $c \leftarrow $ *getch*;
    if c **in** *letters* **then** $s \leftarrow $ *inword* **else** $s \leftarrow $ *skipping*;
    if $c = $ **chr**(0) **then goto** 99;
  end;
  99:
end; *of getlex*

12.3 Sets of Records

One can also define sets over record types provided that appropriate equality and ordering operators have been defined. Although Vector Pascal does not support persistence, this can still provide a useful mechanism for implementing in-memory databases, provided that one writes the routines to load and store the sets of records.

Let us consider the case of a simple name, address and telephone number database. We can define an appropriate record type as follows:

```
person=record
  id:string[80];
```

Chapter 12 • Advanced Set Programming

```
    address:string;
    home,mobile:string[30];
end;
```

Let us choose to treat the id as a primary key for the database, that is, we will define two records to be identical if they have the same primary keys. The address and telephone number fields will be ignored for identity purposes. The consequence is that each person in the set will have a unique address and pair of telephone numbers.

To do this, we need to define ordering operators over persons:

```
operator = = personeq;
operator < = personlt;
```

and then define the appropriate ordering functions:

```
function personlt(p1,p2:person):boolean;
begin
  personlt:=p1.id<p2.id;
end;
function personeq(p1,p2:person):boolean;
begin
  personeq:=p1.id=p2.id;
end;
```

12.3.1 Retrieval Operations

Given a set of person records in db, we can add a person by the operation

```
db:=db+[p];
```

Less obviously, we can query the set to look up a person given their name.

```
p.id:=id;
res:=db*[p];
for p in res do;
```

The operation x*y returns the set of elements in x that also occur in y. In the case of db*[p] it selects the singleton set comprising the record in db whose id field matched the id field of p. This is then loaded into p by the following for .. in loop. The address and telephone number fields of the record p will now be those last stored in the set.

12.4 Use of Sets in Text Indexing

Our next example will address text retrieval. Suppose one wants to search for the occurrence of a word in a number of files. Most operating systems provide tools to do this, either on the command line or through the file manager. The simplest such tool is probably the Unix grep command. One might try to discover which of one's Pascal files were units by entering

```
$ grep ''unit'' *.pas
```

and obtain the response

```
bloomfilter.pas:unit bloomfilter;
bmp.pas:unit bmp;
bmp.pas:This unit provides a library to access and manipulate
bmp.pas: in .bmp files. It is used internally in the unit BMP
calendar.pas:unit calendar;
datesort.pas:unit datesort;
intsort.pas:unit intsort;
metricunits.pas:PROGRAM metricunits;
personrecs.pas:unit personrecs;
System.pas:unit system;
```

Then `grep` would search all of the files with the .pas suffix for the sequence 'unit', finding in the process all of one's units plus some other files.

The technique involves reading the entire files to find any occurence of the requested word. Although fast enough for searching within one directory, it is slow when applied to a whole directory tree. For faster access one wants some sort of index, which, when given a word, will return all the files containing that word. This index would either have to associate with each word a set of files that contain it, or associate with each file a set of the words that it contains. We will take the latter approach.

If we assume that the index will be held on disk, performance is likely to be constrained either by disk seek times for a random access structure, or by disk throughput if an index is read in a single pass. If we are storing a set of words with each file, we have to access each set of words once. There will be many such sets. We can either design the sets on disk in such a way that the entire set is read in with a single DMA transfer, or represent each set as some sort of tree on disk that we navigate with random access reads. Since disks achieve the highest bandwidth on sequential accesses, and since the number of sets to be queried will be large, the best strategy is to read each entire set in turn. This implies that the performance constraint will be provided by disk bandwidth rather than by disk seek times. In order to make the best use of bandwidth, we shall try to use a relatively compact set representation.

The sets of ordinal type are stored very compactly as a bitmap. However, we have a problem, since textual words do not constitute an ordinal type. They can be stored in ordered sets as shown in Section 12.2, but these sets, being implemented as trees, cannot be written to direct access files. However, there is a way to use ordinal sets to act as surrogates of sets of words. Suppose we have a hash function that will assign an ordinal to each possible word, then the words can be stored in an ordinal set using their hashed images (Figure 12.1). So if we define an ordinal type with, let us say, a range of 1000 elements, we can take a word such as 'cat' and hash it into this range and store the corresponding ordinal in the set.

If we prepare one such an ordinal set for each text file, such that the hashed images of the words in the file have been added to the set, we could use it for indexing. Let us call these sets *index-sets*. To check which files might contain a word, we need only check for the presence of its hashed ordinal in each of these index-sets. If the hashed ordinal is not present, we know that the file will not contain the word.

Chapter 12 • Advanced Set Programming

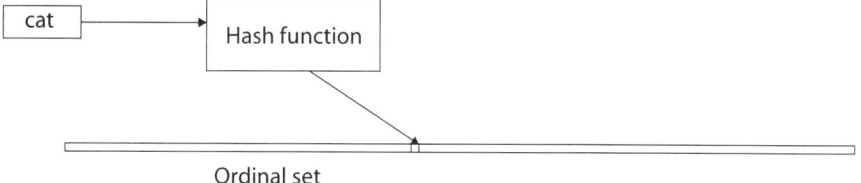

Figure 12.1. Use of a hash function to store words in an ordinal set.

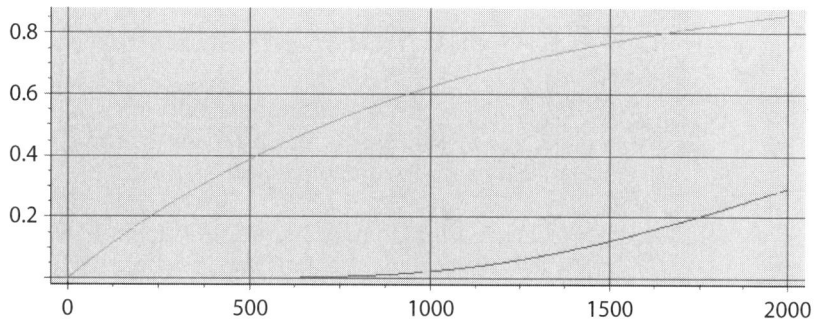

Figure 12.2. The upper line shows the probability of false positives with a set in the range 0...1023 as the number of unique words stored in it rises. The lower line shows the probability of false positives if unanimous results must be obtained from eight independently hashed sets.

However, like any hashing process, this will suffer from collisions, where two words hash to the same ordinal, prevents us from being able to deduce unambiguously the presence of a word in a file from the presence of its ordinal in the index-set.

Let our hash function be uniform and the cardinality of our index sets be m. Then, if a file contains n distinct words, what is the probability of obtaining a false positive when we test for set membership?

Define a function $u(n)$ which gives the expected number of members of the index set as a function of the words inserted, we have $u(0) = 0$, and the recurrence relation

$$u(n) = u(n-1) + 1 - \frac{u(n-1)}{m}$$

Clearly, the probablity of a false positive is given by $\frac{u(n)}{m}$. Figure 12.2 shows how this probability rises with the number of hashed words inserted into the set goes up. Clearly, as the number of words stored approaches half the range of the index set, the selectivity of the index becomes poor. At a 50% loading we have just under a 40% false-positive probability. If we assume that the index is used as a filter to supply filenames to a text searching program such as `grep`, this may still be worthwhile.

However, we can greatly inprove the selectivity of the index by using multiple independently hashed sets. Suppose that instead of a single set we have p of them, then the probability of false positives becomes $\left[\frac{u(n)}{m}\right]^p$; in words, the probability of false positives falls exponentially with the number of independently hashed index-sets that we use.

Let us give an example. If we have a single index-set ranging over $0\ldots 1023$, then the false-positive rate with a loading of 512 entries is 39.4%, but with eight independent index-sets each of the same size, the false-positive rate falls to 0.06%. An alternative approach might be simply to use a single set that was eight times as big, but this is much less effective. It would give a false-positive rate of 6% at the same loading, 100 times less selective than the use of multiple sets.

12.5 Constructing an Indexing Program

Let us now construct a program that will construct an index of all of the words in all of the files in the current directory tree. We can break the design of the program into three component parts:

1. Parsing text files to find the words in them. This problem has basically been solved in a previous example (see Section 12.2.2).
2. Traversing a directory tree to find all the files in it. This is a new problem for us and we will examine it below (see Section 12.5.1).
3. Constructing and manipulating the index sets. This will be dealt with in the unit bloomfilter (see Section 12.6).

12.5.1 dirlist: A Program for Traversing a Directory Tree

We start by constructing a program that simply lists a directory tree. We can then use this as a framework to do something to each file in a directory tree. The logic of the program is simple; the main novelty consists in the introduction of a number of sugared Linux system calls for accessing directories. The same calls work under Windows.

program *dirlist*;

This program takes a single parameter: a directory name. It traverses the directory tree listing all of the filenames found.

const
  above = '..';
  this = '.';

The constants are used to refer to the Unix and Windows representations of the current and superior directory.

var
  Let $s \in$ string;
procedure *intodir* (*s*:**string**;*level*:*integer*); (see Section 12.5.2)
begin
  $s \leftarrow paramstr$ (1);
  intodir (*s*,0);
end.

12.5.2 intodir

procedure *intodir* (*s*:**string**;*level*:*integer*);

This procedure recursively traverses the directory whose name is passed as a parameter. All files encountered are listed to the standard output stream. The body of the function is shown in Alg. 40. A major complication is the need to convert between Unicode strings used internally and the ASCII filenames used by Linux. It uses the following variables:

var
   buf: **array** [0..100] **of** *ascii*;
   Let $n \in$ pchar;
   Let *un* $\in$ string;
   Let *thedir* $\in$ pdir;
   Let *theentry* $\in$ pdirentry;

Type ascii is an internal representation of ASCII characters, stored one per byte. It is declared in the system unit. The type pchar is a pointer to an ASCII character. This is the standard way in which strings are passed in C and it is needed to converse with the Linux or Windows file system. Types pdir and pdirentry are types declared in the system unit for traversing operating system directories. The function also makes use of a group of system procedures or

begin
   unicodestring2ascii(*s*,*buf*$_0$);
   thedir := *opendir*(@*buf*);
   if *thedir* $\neq$ *nil* **then**
   begin
      chdir(@*buf*);
      theentry $\leftarrow$ *readdir*(*thedir*);
      while (*theentry* $\neq$ *nil*) **do**
      begin
         n $\leftarrow$ *entryname*(*theentry*);
         un $\leftarrow$ *strpas*(*n*);
         writeln(*un*);
         if *isdir*(*n*) **then**
            if *un* $\neq$ *above* **then**
               if *un* $\neq$ *this* **then**
                  intodir(*un*,*level*+1);
         theentry $\leftarrow$ *readdir*(*thedir*);
   end;
   unicodestring2ascii(*above*,*buf*$_0$);
   chdir(@*buf*);
   end;
end;

Algorithm 40. Body of the function intodir.

functions:

- The procedure unicodestring2ascii takes a Vector Pascal string and copies it into an array of ASCII characters, appending the requisite null character expected by C.
- The function opendir must be passed the address of an ASCII string and returns a directory handle.
- The chdir procedure changes the current directory to the one specified by the ASCII string provided in its parameter.
- The function readdir reads the next directory entry from the directory directory specified by the handle passed to it.
- The function entryname returns a pointer to an ASCII string which has to be converted to a Pascal string using the function strpas.

12.6 bloomfilter

unit *bloomfilter*;

This unit provides a set of library routines for creating and manipulating index-sets for indexing the words in documents.

interface
  const
    maxhash = 1023;
    bloomdepth = 8;

The above constants control the overall dimensions of the index-sets. Maxhash defines highest ordinal number in the set and bloomdepth defines how many index sets are to be used for each file.

  type
    hashcode = 0..*maxhash*;
    bloomrange = 1..*bloomdepth*;
    filter = **set of** *hashcode*;

A filter is a single index-set. These are then grouped into a

    bloom = **array** [*bloomrange*] **of** *filter*;

A lexeme will be hashed to a hash vector, a vector of independently computed hash codes:

    hashvector = **array** [*bloomrange*] **of** *integer*;

Each text file is then described by a filefilter which encodes information about the words in the file along with the filename:

    filefilter = **record**
      wordset:*bloom*;
      filename:*string*;
    end;

Chapter 12 • Advanced Set Programming

procedure *hashword* (**var** *theword*:**string**;**var** *codes:hashvector*); (see Section 12.6.1)
procedure *setfilter* (**var** *theword*:**string**;**var** *f:bloom*); (see Section 12.6.2)
function *testfilter* (**var** *theword*:**string**;**var** *f:bloom*):*boolean*; (see Section 12.6.3)
implementation

12.6.1 hashword

procedure *hashword* (**var** *theword*:**string**;**var** *codes:hashvector*);

This procedure performs parallel hashes on theword to yield a a vector of hash codes in codes. It uses for this purpose the vector of prime numbers:

const
   primes: **array** [*bloomrange*] **of** *integer* = (7,11,13,17,19,23,29,31);
var
   Let $i,l \in$ integer;
   Let $j \in$ hashcode;
begin
   $l \leftarrow$ *length* (*theword*);
   codes $\leftarrow$ 0;
   for $i \leftarrow 1$ **to** *l* **do**
   begin
      $j \leftarrow$ **ord**(*theword$_i$*);

The following line has the effect of computing the polynomials:

$$c_1 p_1^{l-1} + c_2 p_1^{l-2} \cdots + c_{l-1} p_1 + c_l$$

$$c_1 p_2^{l-1} + c_2 p_2^{l-2} \cdots + c_{l-1} p_2 + c_l$$

$$c_1 p_3^{l-1} + c_2 p_3^{l-2} \cdots + c_{l-1} p_3 + c_l$$

etc., where c_j is the *j*th character in the string and p_i is the *i*th prime in the vector of primes. Where the instruction-sets allow, it will be computed in parallel.

     codes $\leftarrow$ *codes* $\times$ *primes* + *j*;
   end;

Constrains the result to be in the appropriate range.

   codes $\leftarrow$ *codes* $\wedge$ *maxhash*;
end;

12.6.2 setfilter

Computes the hash vector for the word and inserts the hashed elements into all of the filters in the bloom. Note that the assignment context of the second statement is an array of sets; this has the effect of causing the array identifier `codes` to be indexed in the set on the right-hand side.

```
procedure setfilter (var theword:string;var f:bloom);
var
  Let codes ∈ hashvector;
  Let i ∈ integer;
begin
  hashword (theword,codes);
  f ← f + [codes];
end;
```

12.6.3 testfilter

Computes the hash vector for the word and tests if the coresponding elements are present in all the filters of the bloom. Note the use of and-reduction on the vector of Booleans that results from the expression `codes in f`.

```
function testfilter (var theword:string;var f:bloom):boolean;
var
  Let codes ∈ hashvector;
begin
  hashword (theword,codes);
  testfilter ← \∧ (codes ∈ f);
end;
```

12.7 The Main Program to Index Files

This uses a slightly modified version of intodir to traverse the tree. The new version of intodir calls the procedure **processfile** for every file encountered. In consequence, indexes are built for every file in the directory tree and the index records all written to the index file.

The usage of the program involves issuing the command

```
indexfiles
```

which causes the current directory and all sub-directories to be scanned and an index of all the words found to be stored in the file `wordindex.ind`.

```
program indexfiles;
uses bloomfilter;
const
  dirsep = '\' ;
  wordmax = 25;
  above = '..';
  this = '.';
type
  lexeme = string;
var
  Let index ∈ file of filefilter;
procedure loadset (var f:text;var words:bloom);
  (see Section 12.2.2 for something similar.)
```

procedure *processfile* (*fn,path*:**string**); (see Section 12.7.1)
procedure *intodir* (*s*:**string**;*prefix*:**string**);
  (see Section 12.5.2 for something similar.)
begin
  assign (*index*, 'wordindex.ind');
  rewrite (*index*);
  intodir ('.' , '.');
  close (*index*);
end.

12.7.1   processfile

This builds an index for file fn and adds it to the index. It uses a Standard Pascal file of records to write the index records to disk. It associates with each index record the full file path that was used to find the file. This is built up by the intodir procedure as it traverses the directory tree.

procedure *processfile* (*fn,path*:**string**);
var
  Let *ff* ∈ filefilter;
  Let *f* ∈ text;
begin
  writeln(*path*);
  assign (*f,fn*);
  {$i-}
  reset (*f*);
  if *ioresult* = 0 **then**
  begin
    {$i+}
    ff.wordset ←;
    loadset (*f,ff.wordset*);
    ff.filename ← *path*;
    write(*index,ff*);
  end
  else writeln('cant open', *fn*, ':', *path*);
  close (*f*);
end;

12.7.2   A Retrieval Program

The retrieval program searchindex scans the index file for a word and prints the names of the files that are likely to contain the word. For example:

    searchindex bird

will list all the files containing the word 'bird'. The index file is assumed to be in the current directory and called `wordindex.ind`.

program *searchindex*;
uses *bloomfilter*;
  label 99;

```
var
  Let index ∈ file of filefilter;
  Let entry ∈ filefilter;
  Let i ∈ integer;
begin
  else
  begin
    assign (index, 'wordindex.ind');
    {$i-}
    reset (index);
    if ioresult = 0 then
      while not eof (index) do
      begin
        read (index,entry);
        if ioresult ≠ 0 then goto 99;
        if testfilter(paramstr(1),entry.wordset) then
          writeln(entry.filename);
      end;
      99:close (index);
  end;
end.
```

As an example, `indexfiles` was used to construct an index over the gcc include directory. The times taken to search for the files containing the word printf using `searchindex` and `grep` were then compared. The statistics below indicate that `searchindex` was approximately 100 times faster than using `grep`.

Number of files	712
Size of data	3.8 Mbyte
Size of index	980 K
Time using `searchindex`	0.04 s
Time using `grep` -R	4.06 s

The files in this case were relatively small, so the index file was relatively large compared with the data being indexed. This could have been reduced by

1. Using a shorter string to hold the file names in the bloom records. With the current design, the filenames occupy 510 bytes, which is excessive.
2. Using smaller sets, the set data currently occupy 1024 bytes per file. This could be reduced if most of the files being indexed are small.

It will be understood that the data structures in this example are not highly optimised for storage efficiency, being designed instead for ease of understanding in a textbook. They do, however, indicate how comparatively simple set structures can give significant performance boosts in text retrieval.

Parallel Image Processing

13.1 Declaring an Image Data Type

Vector Pascal does not have a predeclared image data type. However, one can readily declare one. There are two common approaches to representing full-colour image data. In both of them the colour is represented as three components, each of 8-bit precision.

1. Display manufactures for PCs usually store the information as two-dimensional arrays of 24- or 32-bit pixels, made up of red, green and blue fields with an optional alpha field for colour blending. The fields typically contain 8-bit unsigned numbers with 0 representing minimum brightness of the colour and 255 representing the maximum brightness. This approach simplifies display design but is not so suitable for image processing.
2. The alternative approach separates the colour information out into distinct planes, so that a colour picture is manipulated as three'distinct'monochrome images, one of which represents the red component, one the green and one the blue. This approach allows image-processing procedures designed to operate on monochrome images to be applied unmodified to each of the planes of a colour image.

In what follows we use the colour plane model for images:[1]

```
type
    image(maxplane,maxrow,maxcol:integer)=
      array[0..maxplane,0..maxrow,0..maxcol]of pixel;
```

This declares an image to be a parameterised data type with a variable number of image colour planes and a variable number of rows and columns. Although this definition will store also pixels in an 8-bit representation, it is as a signed 8-bit binary fraction in the range $-1\ldots 1$, instead of as 8-bit unsigned integers.

13.2 Brightness and Contrast Adjustment

The signed fractional representation of pixels lends itself well to image-processing applications where arithmetic is done on pixels. We frequently want

---

[1]The definitions of the image type along with several of the functions over images are given in **Unit Bmp** in Section 13.12.

```
program contrast;
uses bmp;
var
    Let im,outim ∈ pimage;
begin
    if loadbmpfile('grey1.bmp',im) then
    begin
        new(outim,im ^.maxplane,im ^.maxrow,im ^.maxcol);
        outim↑ ← im↑ × −1.0;
        storebmpfile('neg.bmp',outim↑);
        outim↑ ← im↑ × 0.5;
        storebmpfile('half.bmp',outim↑);
        outim↑ ← im↑ + 0.3;
        storebmpfile('bright.bmp',outim↑);
    end
    else writeln('failed to load file');
end.
```

negate image

halve contrast

brighten

Algorithm 41. Simple manipulations of image contrasts and brightnesses. The type pimage used is a pointer to an image.

to subtract images from one another. Doing this can give rise to negative-valued pixels. Using an unsigned format, negative pixels have no natural representation. Using signed pixels, 0 represents mid grey, −1 represents black and 1 white. This representation allows the contrast of an image to be adjusted simply by multiplying by a constant. Thus, if we multiply an image by 0.5 we halve its contrast; if we multiply it by −1, we convert it to an negative image, etc.

13.2.1 Efficiency in Image Code

Alg. 41 illustrates how easy it is to alter the brightness/contrast of an image by adding/multiplying it with a real value. Although concise, this does not necessarily produce the fastest code. The rules used in expression evaluation mean $im\uparrow \times 0.5$ is expanded out to $im\uparrow_{\iota_0,\iota_1,\iota_2} \times 0.5$, which is a multiplication of a pixel by a real. Since reals are of higher precision, the pixel has to be promoted to a real before the multiplication. This effectively prevents the original array expression being vectorised.

A more efficient approach is seen in the procedure **adjustcontrast** shown in Alg. 42, where a vector of pixels is initialised to hold the adjustment factor. By holding it as a vector of fixed-point numbers, the operation can be effectively vectorised on MMX-based processors.[2] Since the fixed-point pixel format only works for $|f| \leq 1$, it is necessary to use floating-point multiplication when increasing the image contrast.

---

[2] It is a weakness of the Intel MMX instruction-set that it does not support scalar to vector operations. There are no instructions to operate between a signed byte and a vector of signed bytes. Motorola processors do not suffer from this weakness.

Chapter 13 • Parallel Image Processing

procedure *adjustcontrast(f:real;* **var** *src,dest:image);*
var
   Let $l \in$ ^line;
   Let $r \in$ real;
begin
  new(*l,src.maxcol*);
  { $r− }
  $l\uparrow \leftarrow f$;
  if (**abs**(*f*) < 1) **then** *dest* ← *src* × $l\uparrow$
  else *dest* ← *src* × *f*;
  { $r− }
  dispose (*l*);
end;

Algorithm 42. A more efficient way of adjusting contrast. Note that in this example the type line refers to a vector of pixels.

Recall that pixels are represented as signed 8-bit numbers, with the conceptual value 1.0 being encoded as $+127$ and the conceptual value -1.0 being encoded as -128. Multiplication of pixels proceeds by

1. multiplying the 8-bit numbers to give a 16-bit result
2. shifting the result right arithmetically by seven places
3. selecting the bottom 8 bits of the result

The 8-bit signed format contains 7 bits of significance plus the sign bit and the 16-bit result contains 14 bits of significance plus two replicated sign bits. It is clear that this format cannot represent multiplication by a number greater than 1.

13.3 Image Filtering

As another practical example of Vector Pascal, we will look at an image-filtering algorithm. In particular we will look at applying a separable three-element convolution kernel to an image. We shall initially present the algorithm in Standard Pascal and then look at how one might re-express it in Vector Pascal. The entire program is shown in Alg. 45 and then developed in Algs 44 and 46.

Convolution of an image by a matrix of real numbers can be used to smooth or sharpen an image, depending on the matrix used. If A is an output image, K a convolution matrix, then if B is the convolved image:

$$B_{y,x} = \sum_i \sum_j A_{y+i,x+j} K_{i,j}$$

A separable convolution kernel is a vector of real numbers that can be applied independently to the rows and columns of an image to provide filtering. It is a specialisation of the more general convolution matrix, but is

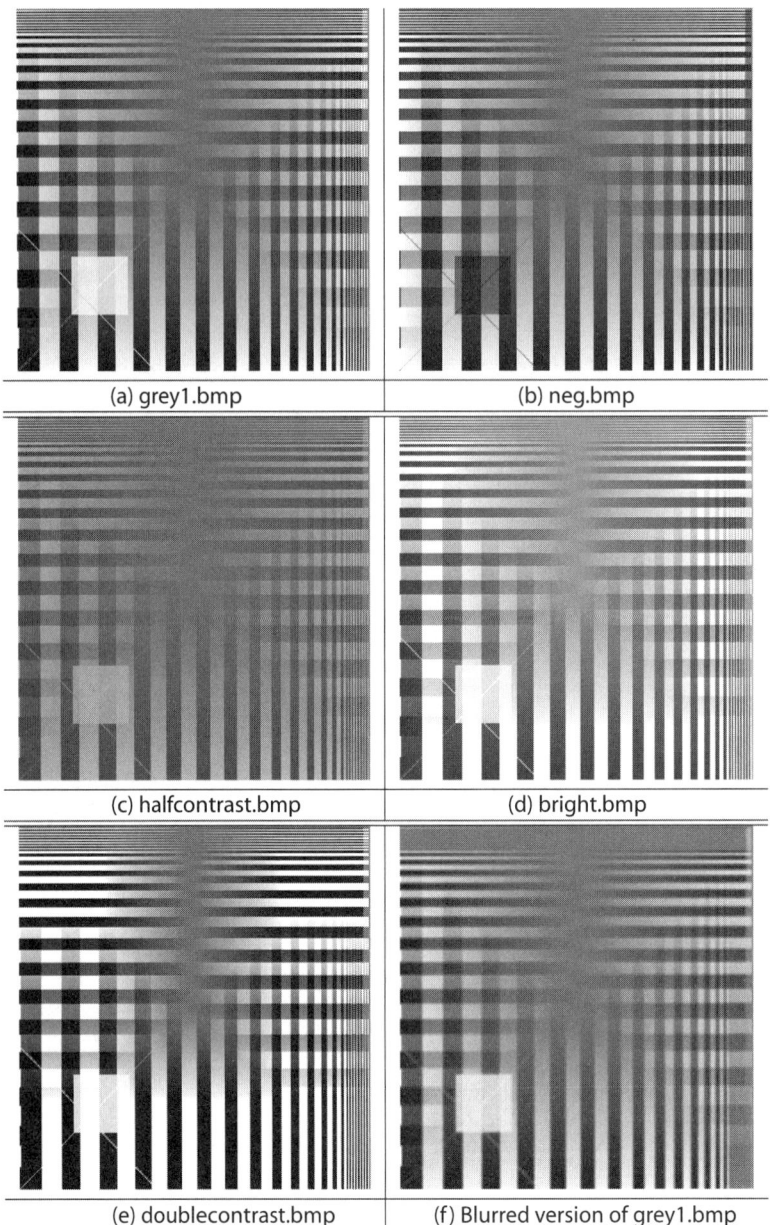

Figure 13.1. Test images used to illustrate brightness, contrast adjustment and filtering. The images (a)–(e) were produced by the program graphio.

algorithmically more efficient to implement. If **k** is a convolution vector, then the corresponding matrix K is such that $K_{i,j} = \mathbf{k}_i \mathbf{k}_j$.

Given a starting image A as a two-dimensional array of pixels, and a three-element kernel c_1, c_2, c_3, the algorithm first forms a temporary array T whose

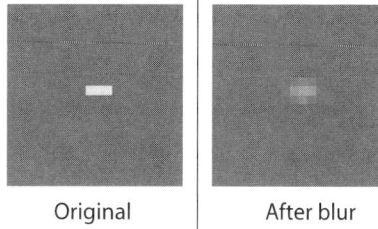

Figure 13.2. The effect of a blurring filter on a finite impulse.

elements are the weighted sum of adjacent rows: $T_{y,x} = c_1 A_{y-1,x} + c_2 A_{y,x} + c_3 A_{y+1,x}$. Then in a second phase it sets the original image to be the weighted sum of the columns of the temporary array: $A_{y,x} = c_1 T_{y,x-1} + c_2 T_{y,x} + c_3 T_{y,x+1}$. Clearly, the outer edges of the image are a special case, since the convolution is defined over the neighbours of the pixel, and the pixels along the boundaries are missing one neighbour. A number of solutions are available for this, but for simplicity we will perform only vertical convolutions on the left and right edges and horizontal convolutions on the top and bottom lines of the image.

13.3.1 Blurring

An image can be blurred using the separable filter (0.25,0.5,0.25). Consider that this implies each row in the output image is formed by a mixture of itself and the rows above and below, with half the amplitude of the signal coming from the current row and half from the adjacent rows. Similarly, each column is made up of half from the current column and half from the adjacent column. The net result is that a pixel's influence spreads out over a 3 × 3 grid. We can examine the effect of the filter on a point source. Here a single pixel that stands out against a uniform background in the initial image shows how the initial pixel spreads out to affect the region around. This is shown in Figure 13.2.

Figure 13.3 shows the effect of using this filter on the classical "Mandrill" test image.

13.3.2 Sharpening

If we use a filter that has negative weights away from the centre, the effect is to sharpen an image. Suppose we apply the filter (−0.25,1.0,−0.25) to an image, what will be the result?

The first thing to note is that this filter is non-unitary, that is, its coefficients do not add up to 1. If we use a unitary filter such as the blur (0.25,0.5,0.25), the mean contrast of the image is unchanged.

Since the coefficients of our sharpening filter sum to 0.5 and since the filter is applied twice, once vertically and once horizontally the net effect is to reduce the mean contrast to one-quarter of what it was originally. This is shown in

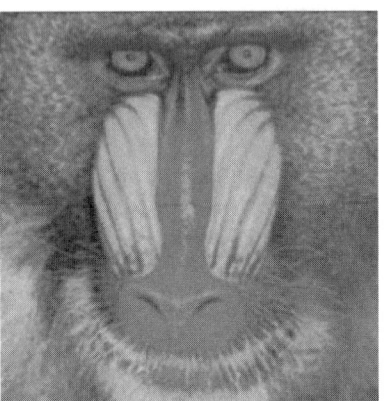 

Figure 13.3. The image at the top is the original. The bottom left image has been subjected to a blurring filter (0.25,0.5,0.25) and that on the right to a sharpening filter.

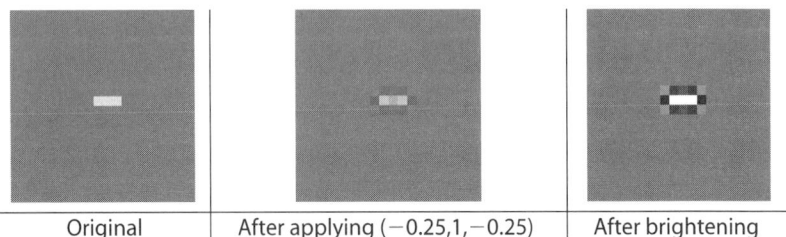

Figure 13.4. Effect of a sharpening filter on a finite impulse.

Figure 13.4. To compensate, we must multiply the image by 4.0 to restore the original contrast, as shown in Alg. 43. Note the characteristic "ringing" induced in the image by sharpening filters. Figure 13.3 shows how the picture of a Mandrill can be sharpened. Note that over the fur, the effect of sharpening is

Chapter 13 • Parallel Image Processing

procedure *sharpen*(**var** *im:image*);
var
   Let *i* ∈ integer;
begin
   i ← 1;
   pconv(im, −0.25,0.998, −0.25*)*;
end;

Algorithm 43. The sharpening method.

just to introduce noise. This is for two reasons:

1. This algorithm results in the loss of 2 bits of precision when the multiplication by 4 takes place; the effect is to introduce additional quantization noise.
2. Sharpening is only visually effective where an feature with high spatial frequency occurs against a background with lower spatial frequency. The hair area is all of high spatial frequency. In consequence, the ringing produced by sharpening overlaps with other hairs, occluding them.

13.3.3 Comparing Implementations

Alg. 44 shows `conv`, an implementation of the convolution in Standard Pascal. The pixel data type has to be explicitly introduced as the sub-range $-128\ldots 127$. Explicit checks have to be in place to prevent range errors, since the result of a convolution may, depending on the kernel used, be outside the bounds of valid pixels. Arithmetic is done in floating point and then rounded.

Because ISO Pascal does not support dynamic arrays, the image sizes in both this version and the parallel version are statically declared.

Image-processing algorithms lend themselves particularly well to data-parallel expression, working as they do on arrays of data subject to uniform operations. Alg. 47 shows a data-parallel version of the algorithm `pconv` implemented in Vector Pascal. Note that all explicit loops disappear in this version, being replaced by assignments of array slices. The first line of the algorithm initialises three vectors `p1`, `p2`, `p3` of pixels to hold the replicated copies of the kernel coefficients `c1`, `c2`, `c3` in fixed-point format. These vectors are then used to multiply rows of the image to build up the convolution. The notation `theim[][1...maxpix-1]` denotes columns `1...maxpix-1` of all rows of the image. Because the built-in pixel data type is used, all range checking is handled by the compiler. Since fixed-point arithmetic is used throughout, there will be slight rounding errors not encountered with the previous algorithm, but these are acceptable in most image-processing applications. Fixed-point pixel arithmetic has the advantage that it can be efficiently implemented in parallel using multi-media instructions.

It is clear that the data-parallel implementation is more concise than the sequential one, 12 lines with 505 characters compared with 26 lines with 952 characters. It also runs considerably faster, as shown in Table 13.1. This expresses the performance of different implementations in millions of effective

procedure *conv(c1,c2,c3:real)*;
var
  tim:**array**[0..m ,0..m] **of** *pixel*;
  Let *quarter, half, temp* ∈ real;
  Let *i,j* ∈ integer;
begin
  for *i* ← 1 **to** *m* −1 **do**
    for *j* ← 0 **to** *m* **do**
    begin
      temp ← *theim*$_{i-1,j}$ × *c1* + *theim*$_{i,j}$ × *c2* + *theim*$_{i+1,j}$ × *c3*;
      if *temp* >127 **then** *temp* ← 127 **else**
        if *temp* < −128 **then** *temp* ← −128;
      tim$_{i,j}$ ← **round**(*temp*);
    end;
    for *j* ← 0 **to** *m* **do**
    begin
      tim$_{0,j}$ ← *theim*$_{0,j}$;
      tim$_{m,j}$ ← *theim*$_{m,j}$;
    end;
    for *i* ← 0 **to** *m* **do**
    begin
      for *j* ← 1 **to** m −1 **do**
      begin
        temp ← *tim*$_{i,j-1}$ × *c1* + *tim*$_{i,j+1}$ × *c3* + *tim*$_{i,j}$ × *c2*;
        if *temp* > 127 **then** *temp* ← 127 **else**
          if *temp* < −128 **then** *temp* ← −128;
        tim$_{i,j}$ ← **round**(*temp*);
      end;
      theim$_{i,0}$ ← *tim*$_{i,0}$;
      theim$_{i,m}$ ← *tim*$_{i,m}$;
    end;
end;

Algorithm 44. Standard Pascal implementation of the convolution.

arithmetic operations per second. It is assumed that the basic algorithm requires six multiplications and six adds per pixel processed. The data-parallel algorithm runs 12 times faster than the serial one when both are compiled using Vector Pascal and targeted at the MMX instruction-set. The `pconv` also runs one-third faster than `conv` when it is targeted at the 486 instruction-set, which in effect serialises the code.

For comparison, `conv` was run on other Pascal compilers,[3] DevPascal 1.9, Borland Pascal and its successor Delphi.[4] These are extended implementations,

---

[3] In addition to those shown, the tests were performed on PascalX, which failed either to compile or to run the benchmarks. TMT Pascal failed to run the convolution test.
[4] Version 4.

Chapter 13 • Parallel Image Processing

```
program dconv;
const
    m = 255;
    repeats = 400;
type
    pixel = −128..127;
    tplain = array[0..m,0..m] of pixel;
var
    Let theim,theres ∈ tplain;
    Let i ∈ integer;
    Let oldtime,ops ∈ real;
procedure showtime; (see Alogrithm 46)
procedure conv (c1,c2,c3:real); (see Alogrithm 44)

begin
    oldtime ← secs;
    ops ← 12 × (m +1) × (m +1) × repeats;
    for i ← 1 to repeats do conv (0.2, 0.6, 0.2);
    showtime;
    writeln('done',secs);
end.
```

Algorithm 45. The program dconv, a test harness for image convolution written to work under several Pascal compilers.

```
procedure showtime;
var
    Let sec,duration,rate ∈ real;
begin
    sec ← secs;
    duration ← sec − oldtime;
    write(duration,' ');
    rate ← ops/duration;
    write(rate/1000000,'M ops per sec');
    oldtime ← sec;
end;
```

Algorithm 46. The procedure showtime.

but with no support for vector arithmetic. Delphi is a state-of-the-art commercial compiler, as Borland Pascal was when released in 1992. DevPas is a recent free compiler. In all cases range checking was enabled for consistency with Vector Pascal. The only other change was to define the type pixel as equivalent to the system type shortint to force implementation as a signed byte. Delphi runs `conv` 40% faster than Vector Pascal does, whereas Borland Pascal runs it at only 7% of the speed, and DevPascal is roughly comparable to Vector Pascal.

procedure *pconv*(**var** *theim:tplain;c1,c2,c3:real*);
var
    tim:**array**[0..m,0..m] **of** pixel;
    Let *p1,p2,p3* ∈ array[0..m] **of** pixel;
begin
    p1 ← *c1*;
    p2 ← *c2*;
    p3 ← *c3*;
    $tim_{1..m-1}$ ← $theim_{0..m-2} \times p1 + theim_{1..m-1} \times p2 + theim_{2..m} \times p3$;
    tim_0 ← $theim_0$;
    tim_m ← $theim_m$;
    $theim_{0..m,1..m-1}$ ← $tim_{0..m,0..m-2} \times p1 + tim_{0..m,2..m} \times p3 + tim_{0..m,1..m-1} \times p2$;
    $theim_{0..m,0}$ ← $tim_{0..m,0}$;
    $theim_{0..m,m}$ ← $tim_{0..m,m}$;
end;

Algorithm 47. Vector Pascal implementation of the convolution.

Table 13.1. Comparative performance on convolution

Algorithm	Implementation	Target processor	Million operations per second
conv	Borland Pascal	286 + 287	6
	Vector Pascal	Pentium + MMX	61
	DevPascal	486	62
	Delphi 4	486	86
pconv	Vector Pascal	486	80
	Vector Pascal	Pentium + MMX	820

Measurements done on a 1 GHz Athlon, running Windows 2000.

13.4 genconv

The convolution algorithms presented so far use one-dimensional kernels and work by being applied successively in vertical and horizontal directions. As such, they are unable to deal with asymmetrical kernels – ones which blur in one direction and sharpen in another, for instance. They also, because they use 8-bit pixel multiplication, suffer from rounding errors when using sharpening convolutions.

We will now present

procedure *genconv*(**var** *p:image*;**var** *K:matrix*);

which computes a general convolution on an image *p* producing a modified image *q* such that if

$$q_{i,j,k} = \sum_x \sum_y p_{i,j+y-a,k+x-b} \times K_{x,y}$$

where $a = (K.rows)\,div\,2$ and $b = (K.cols)\,div\,2$. At the end *p* is updated with *q*.

function *dup(i,j :integer)*:*boolean*; (see Section 13.4.1)
function *prev(i,j :integer)*:*pimage*; (see Section 13.4.2)
function *pm(i,j :integer)*:*pimage*; (see Section 13.4.3)
procedure *doedges*; (see Section 13.4.4)
procedure *freestore*; (see Section 13.4.5)
begin
   new(f,K.rows,K.cols);
   f↑ ← nil;
   new(flags,K.rows,K.cols);
   flags↑ ← false;

   for i ← 1 **to** K.rows **do**
     for j ← 1 **to** K.cols **do**
     else f↑[i,j] ← pm(i,j);

The loops above perform the premultiplication of the input image to form the matrix of images. If item $K_{i,j}$ is a duplicate then we use a previous premultiply or else we perform the premultiply now.

   $a \leftarrow \frac{K.rows}{2}$;
   $b \leftarrow \frac{K.cols}{2}$;
   p[][a..p.maxrow − a,b..p.maxcol − b] :=0;
   for i← 1 **to** K.rows **do**
     for j ← 1 **to** K.cols **do**
       p[][a..p.maxrow − a,b..p.maxcol −b] :=
       p[][a..p.maxrow − a,b..p.maxcol − b] + f^[i,j]
       ^[**iota** 0,i + **iota** 1 − a,j + **iota**2 − b];

The above line forms the convolution by replacing the central region of the image with the sum of the shifted premultiplied images.

   doedges;

   freestore;
end;

Algorithm 48. Main body of the generalised convolution.

Genconv allows an image to be convolved with an arbitrary two-dimensional matrix of real numbers. If one performs this operation naively with an $n \times n$ matrix of reals against an image of dimensions $r \times c$, then the algorithmic complexity will be $\mathbf{O}rcn^2$, since each output pixel is the result of multiplying n^2 input pixels by kernel components.

However, it is worth observing that for most practical convolutions there are repeated matrix elements in the kernel. A nine-element matrix might contain only four distinct values. We can take advantage of this by analysing the matrix to determine how many unique components it has and then forming premultiplied copies of the input image, one for each unique matrix

function *dup(i,j:integer):boolean*;
var
    Let $c,d,l,m \in$ integer;
    Let $b \in$ boolean;
begin
    $c \leftarrow K.cols$;
    $d \leftarrow j + i \times c$;
    $b \leftarrow false$;
    for $l \leftarrow 1$ **to** c **do**   **for** $m \leftarrow 1$ **to** $k.rows$ **do**
        $b \leftarrow b \vee (K_{i,j} = K_{m,l}) \wedge (m + c \times l < d)$;
    $dup \leftarrow b$
    {dup:=\or\or((K[i,j]=K)and(iota 1+c*iota 0<d));}

The Vector Pascal statement is more or less a direct translation of the mathematical formulation of the problem. We use or-reduction over both axes of the matrix to search for duplicates.
end;

    Algorithm 49. The function which checks for duplicate kernel elements.

element in the kernel. Appropriate selection from these premultiplied copies allows us to compute the convolution.

Let us define a couple of types and a variable to help with this:

type
    premult(rows,cols:*integer*) = **array** [1..*rows*,1..*cols*] **of** *pimage*;
    tflag(rows,cols:*integer*) = **array** [1..*rows*,1..*cols*] **of** *boolean*;
var
    Let $f \in \hat{}$ premult;
    Let $a,b,i,j \in$ integer;
    Let $flags \in \hat{}$ tflag;

We will use f to hold the premultiplied versions of the image such that $f_{i,j} = p \times K_{i,j}$. The algorithm for constructing the premultiplied matrix of images will avoid carrying out redundant multiplications.

a,b store the steps away from the centre of the kernel.

flags[i,j] is true if f[i,j] holds the first pointer to a premultiplied image.

13.4.1 dup

This function returns true if there exists an m,n such that

$$n + m \times K.cols < j + i \times K.cols$$

and

$$K_{m,n} = K_{i,j}$$

in other words, if the matrix element $K_{i,j}$ is preceded in the matrix by an identical element. If that is true, then the element $K_{i,j}$ is a duplicate and this fact can be taken advantage of in reducing the amount of premultiplication required to perform the convolution.

13.4.2 prev

For duplicated matrix elements, $K_{i,j}$ function prev returns the premultiplied version of the image that was previously computed for this value of the matrix element.

This uses classical Pascal constructs to search the matrix for the position of the premultiplied duplicate and then assigns the duplicate to the return value of the function. Note that the function does not return when the assignment is made.

13.4.3 pm

The function pm (shown in Alg. 51) premultiplies the image by the real valued coefficient $K_{i,j}$ returning a new image. The fact that a new premultiplied image has been created is recorded in the flags matrix.

function prev (i,j:integer):pimage;
var
    Let $m,n \in$ integer;
    Let $s \in$ real;
begin
    $s \leftarrow k_{i,j}$;
    for $m \leftarrow 1$ **to** $i-1$ **do**
        for $n \leftarrow 1$ **to** K.cols **do**
            if $K_{m,n} = s$ **then**
                prev $\leftarrow f\uparrow[m,n]$;
    for $n \leftarrow 1$ **to** $j-1$ **do**
        if $K_{i,n} = s$ **then**
            prev $\leftarrow f\uparrow[i,n]$;
end;

Algorithm 50. Function to find a previous instance of a kernel element.

function pm(i,j:integer):pimage;
var
    Let $x \in$ pimage;
begin
    new(x,p.maxplane,p.maxrow,p.maxcol);
    adjustcontrast($K_{i,j}$,p, $x\uparrow$);
    flags$\uparrow[i,j] \leftarrow$ true;
    pm $\leftarrow x$;
end;

Algorithm 51. The premultiplication function.

13.4.4 doedges

When performing a convolution on an image, the edges always pose a problem. The convolution operation determines the value of each output image from the corresponding neighbourhood in the input image. Around the edges only part of this neigbourhood exists. Some strategies that can be adopted here are as follows:

1. One can treat the image as being topologically equivalent to a torus so that upper the neighbourhood of pixel on the top line of the image continues on to bottom lines of the image. This approach is computationally easy: when finding the neighbours of pixel $p_{i,j}$ we would normally do this by using the expression $p_{i+y,j+x}$ iterating over a range of values of x and y. To treat the image as a torus we substitute the indexing expression p[(i+y)mod p.rows,(j+x)mod p.cols]. Although this is computationally easy, it does not make a great deal of sense, since it allows output pixels to be influenced by input pixels in the parts of the picture that are furthest away from it.
2. One can mirror the original image around all four edges so that on, for instance, the top edge the upper neighbour of a pixel is the same as its lower neighbour. This makes more sense than using a toroidal topology, and will work well for where the edge of the image is intersected by a feature that runs a right angles to the edge.
3. One can assume that the edge pixels themselves are replicated to an arbitrary degree beyond the edge itself, and compute the edge convolution on this basis. This is the most parsimonious assumption, and is the one we use here.

If we have a 5×5 convolution matrix and a 100×100 image, then we will have a central sub-region of the output image: q[2..97,2..97], which can be evaluated from the full convolution matrix. The 2-pixel wide vertical margins can be expressed a sum of columns of images within the premultiplied image matrix. Thus the zeroth output column is the sum of the zeroth image columns within the first three columns of the premultiplication matrix plus the first image column of the fourth column of the premultiplied image matrix and the second image column of the fifth column of the premultiplied image matrix, etc. Processing the edges takes many more lines of code because it is a mass of special cases.

13.4.5 freestore

The first occurrence of an image in the premultiplied image matrix is disposed of. The record in the flags matrix, initialised when premultiplication occurred, is used to keep track of this.

13.5 Digital Half-toning

Printing images on paper requires that they be converted into a dot pattern since it is not practical to print with ink of varying shades of grey. Since a

Chapter 13 • Parallel Image Processing

```
                    procedure doedges;
                    var
                        Let i,j,l,m,n,row,col ∈ integer;
                        Let r ∈ pimage;
$r-                 begin
                        j ← k.rows/2;
                        i ← k.cols/2;
                        p[][0..j − 1] := 0;
                        p[][][0..i − 1] := 0;
                        p[][1 + p.maxrow − j..p.maxrow] := 0;
                        p[][][1 + p.maxcol − i..p.maxcol] := 0;
iterate through the     for n ← 0 to p.maxplane do
planes                      for l ← 1 to k.rows do
                                for m ← 1 to k.cols do
                                begin
                                    r ← f↑[l,m];
top                             for row ← 0 to j − 1 do
                                    p_{n,row} ← p_{n,row} + r↑[n,(row + l − j − 1)];
```

The line above computes the convolution for the top edge, so that the neighbours above the top are replaced by the correspoding elements of the permultiplied top scan-line.

```
                                for row ← p.maxrow j + 1 to p.maxrow do
bottom                              p_{n,row} ← p_{n,row} + r↑[n,(row + l − j − 1)];
                                for col ← 0 to i − 1 do  for row ← 0 to p.maxrow do begin begin
left                                p_{n,row,col} ← r↑[n,row,(col + 1 + m − i)] + p_{n,row,col};
                                end;
```

Using a similar technique we compute the convolution for the left edge. Note that the construct p[n] [] [col] means of planes n select the column col from all rows.

```
                                for col ← 1 + p.maxcol − i to p.maxcol
                                    do for row ← 0 to p.maxrow do begin
right                                   begin
                                            p_{n,row,col} ← p_{n,row,col} + r↑[n];
                                        end;
                                        {$r+}
                                end;
                    end.
```

Algorithm 52. The edge processing algorithm.

digital image may have a range of grey values, one has to map these to dots in such a way that the average darkness of the dots over a small area of the paper is the same as the average darkness of the corresponding area of the image. In this section we present two algorithms to achieve this, one parallel and the other inherently sequential.

procedure *freestore*;
var
　Let *i,j* ∈ integer;
begin
　for *i* ← 1 **to** *K.rows* **do**
　　for *j* ← 1 **to** *K.cols* **do**
　　　if *flags*↑[*i,j*]
　　　then dispose(*f*↑[*i,j*]);
end;

Algorithm 53. The release of temporary store.

Figure 13.5. Effect of applying a diagonal edge detection filter to Mandrill.

13.5.1 Parallel Half-tone

Alg. 54 is a parallel technique for half toning. It involves defining a mask of pixels of varying brightnesses and comparing the image with this mask. If a pixel is darker than the corresponding mask position it is printed as black and otherwise as white. The effect is shown in Figure 13.6. The mask is chosen to be 8 bytes long to ensure that the operation will parallelise in the MMX registers. The mask is combined with the picture using modular arithmetic on the indices ι_0, ι_1.

Chapter 13 • Parallel Image Processing

Figure 13.6 Mandrill rendered with a 4 × 8 mask.

procedure *halftone*(**var** *src,dest:image*);
const
    black:pixel = −1.0;
    white:pixel = 1.0;
    pattern: **array** [0..3,0..7] **of** *pixel* = ((0.75,−0.95,0.0,0.5,−0.3,0.33,−0.2,−0.7),
    (0.62,−0.75,−0.1,−0.45,0.8,0.25,0.95,−0.6),
    (−0.15,0.3,0.4,−0.8,−0.9,−0.5,0.15,0.17),
    (−0.25,0.9,0.7,−0.33,−0.4,0.2,0.1,−0.82));
begin
    dest ← *pattern*$_{\iota_1 \bmod 4, \iota_2 \bmod 8}$;

    dest ← $\begin{cases} white \text{ if } src > dest \\ black \text{ otherwise} \end{cases}$;
end;

Algorithm 54. Parallel half-toning using a fixed mask.

13.5.2 errordifuse

It is clear that simply masking, although quick, yields annoying artifacts since the human eye is well able to pick out the repetitive motifs embedded within the mask. Another disadvantage is that the mask will approximate the brightness of the picture with a spatial wavelength equivalent to twice the size of the mask itself. It therefore responds poorly to sharp edges.

If one is willing to sacrifice parallelism, error diffusion techniques yield a much better result, as is shown in Figure 13.7.

Alg. 55 compensates for the quantization errors by adjusting the likelihood of using black or white for neighbouring pixels. Once it has decided whether to render a pixel in black or white, it computes the quantization error in `e1`. This error term is then spread around the pixels to the right and below by subtracting weighted components of it to a temporary source image.

When the corresponding pixels in the temporary source come to be processed, the likelihood of their being rendered black or white is now biased away from its original value by this error term.

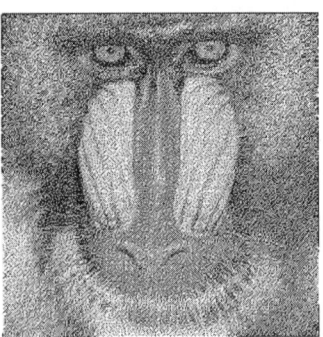

Figure 13.7. Mandrill rendered using error diffusion.

procedure *errordifuse*(**var** *src,dest:image*);
var
    Let *temp* ∈ ^image;
    Let *i,j,k* ∈ integer;
    Let *black,white* ∈ pixel;
    Let *e1,e2,e3* ∈ real;
    Let *r1,r2* ∈ integer;
begin
    black ← −1.0;
    white ← 1.0;
    new(*temp,src.maxplane,src.maxrow,src.maxcol*);
$$dest \leftarrow \begin{cases} 1.0 & \text{if } src > 0 \\ -1.0 & \text{otherwise} \end{cases};$$
    temp↑ ← *src*;
    for *k* ← 0 **to** *src.maxplane* **do**
        for *i* ← 1 **to** *src.maxrow* −1 **do**   **for** *j* ← 1 **to** *src.maxcol* −1 **do**
        begin
            r1 ← *random*;
            r2 ← *random*;
$$e3 \leftarrow \begin{cases} 0.2 & \text{if } r1 > r2 \\ -0.2 & \text{otherwise} \end{cases};$$
$$dest_{k,i,j} \leftarrow \begin{cases} white & \text{if } temp\uparrow[k,i,j] > 0.0 \\ black & \text{otherwise} \end{cases};$$
            e1 ← $dest_{k,i,j}$ − *temp*↑[k,i,j];
            temp↑[k,i,j +1] ← *temp*↑[k,i,j +1] −(0.45−*e3*) × *e1*;
            temp↑[k,i +1,j] ← *temp*↑[k,i +1,j] −(*e3* + 0.375) × *e1*;
            temp↑[k,i +1,j − 1] ← *temp*↑[k,i +1,j −1] −(0.125) × *e1*;
        end;
        dispose(*temp*);
end;

Algorithm 55. Classical error diffusion, non-parallel code.

Suppose a pixel had the value 0.2 and was rendered as 1.0. The error term e1 would be 0.8, which would be subtracted from the surrounding pixels. Sufficient might be added to the pixel to the right to trip it from its original rendering as white to a rendering as black.

The way in which the errors are distributed is randomised using the term e3. In the absence of this random term one obtains visually intrusive "brain coral" patterns in the half toning.

13.6 Image Resizing

A very common operation in dealing with images is to resize them, making them larger or smaller. This may be done either uniformly – preserving their aspect ratio – or unevenly so that both the shape and size of the image change.

In a naive resizing algorithm we simply scale the indices of the pixels in the source image by the ratio of the images sizes. Suppose we wanted to halve the size of an image, then we could simply select every second pixel. As can be seen in Figure 13.8, a number of unpleasant artifacts occur with this method. When shrinking an image, thin lines can lose pixels, or even vanish. When enlarging an image, what were originally square pixels become oblong, something which is particularly disconcerting when looking at text. Collectively these errors are called aliasing.

The removal of these artifacts is termed anti-aliasing. The artifacts arise because of the spatial frequencies possible in pictures of different sizes. The notion of spatial frequency is illustrated by the test image shown in Figure 13.1. These show horizontal and vertical gratings of varying spatial frequency. The Nyquist theorem states that the maximum spatial frequency, measured in oscillations per inch, that can be supported by an image is half the number of pixels per inch. The highest frequency in the images shown in Figure 13.1 corresponds to this limit. If we apply the blurring convolution [0.25,0.5,0.25] to the test image in Figure 13.1.a to produce the image in Figure 13.1.f, we have the effect of making the highest spatial frequency invisible. Thus the blurring convolution can be viewed as a subtractive spatial frequency filter that selectively removes the highest frequency information.

Now consider what happens when one increases the size of an image. The effect is to introduce new spatial frequency bands into the image. Since these

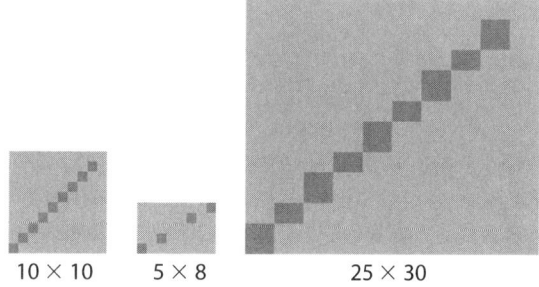

Figure 13.8. Naive resampling used to scale pictures introduces artifacts.

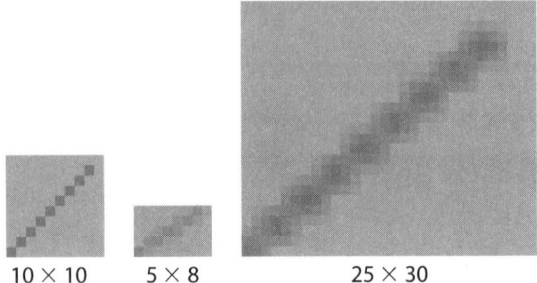

Figure 13.9. Anti-aliased rescaling using blurring and interpolation reduces artifacts.

frequencies are higher than any that we have had up to now, what will occupy them?

If we use a naive sampling algorithm, simply replicating each original pixel, the higher frequency bands are populated with Moiré fringe noise, generated by the interference between the old Nyquist limit frequency and the new Nyquist limit frequency. What we want instead is for these wavebands to be empty. We can achieve this by using an interpolation procedure which fills in new pixel positions as a weighted average of the neighbouring pixel positions.

Conversely, if one reduces the size of an image, one removes certain possible spatial frequencies. But if one uses a naive approach, some of the original high-frequency information is erroneously transferred to lower frequencies. The answer in this case is to apply a blurring filter first to remove the high-frequency information before sampling. Figure 13.9 shows the effect of blurring before shrinking and of interpolating when expanding.

If we resize an image, we have to take into account the possibility that the scaling in the horizontal and vertical directions will differ; it is therefore desirable to resize it in two steps, once in each direction. Consider first the problem of expanding an image. Horizontal interpolation involves the process shown in Figure 13.10.

Here we introduce a new sample point r between two existing sample points p, q. The value of r should be a weighted average of the values at the known points. If r is close to p then p should predominate and vice versa for r. The simplest equation that achieves this is

$$r = p\frac{\delta(p,r)}{\delta(p,q)} + q\left(1 - \frac{\delta(p,r)}{\delta(p,q)}\right)$$

where $\delta(a,b)$ is the horizontal distance between points a,b.

It is clear that in the general case of horizontal resizing, the weights $\delta(p,r)/\delta(p,q)$ will differ for sequential pixels. As such, horizontal rescaling lends itself poorly to SIMD parallelization. Vertical rescaling can be parallelized, since we can compute a complete new scan line as the weighted average of two original scan lines. It is therefore important to perform expansion in the horizontal direction first followed by rescaling in the vertical direction. This maximises the share of the work that can be run in parallel. Alg. 56 illustrates this.

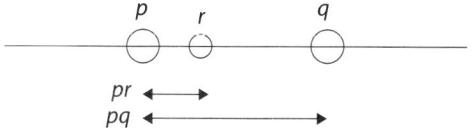

Figure 13.10. Horizontal interpolation of a new pixel position *r* between existing pixel positions *p* and *q*.

procedure *resize*(**var** *src,dest:image*);

This invokes the horizontal and vertical resize functions to do the effective work. Since vertical interpolation is run in parallel whereas horizontal interpolation must run sequentially, we want to do as much work as possible in the vertical resizing. If we are making a picture higher then it is quicker to resize horizontally and then resize vertically. If we are reducing the height of a picture the reverse holds.

var
   Let *t* ∈ pimage;
begin
  if *(src.maxrow < dest.maxrow)* **then**
  begin
    new(*t,src.maxplane,src.maxrow,dest.maxcol*);
    resizeh(src,t↑);
    resizev(t↑,dest);
    dispose(*t*);
  end
  else
  begin
    new(*t,src.maxplane,dest.maxrow,src.maxcol*);
    resizev(src,t↑);
    resizeh(t↑,dest);
    dispose(*t*);
  end
end;

Algorithm 56. Resize an image.

13.7 Horizontal Resize

This is done with the procedure

procedure *resizeh*(**var** *src,dest:image*);

This will change the size of an image in the horizontal direction. *Dest* must be same height as *src*. Its internal operation is shown in Alg. 57.

var
    Let $n \in$ real;
    Let $t, av \in$ pimage;
    Let $i \in$ integer;
begin
    $n \leftarrow \frac{1+src.maxcol}{1+dest.maxcol}$;
    if $n < 1$
    else
        if $n = 1$
        then $dest \leftarrow src$
        else
            if $n \leq 2$
            then
            begin

We cannot simply select every nth pixel on a row, since this would allow high-frequency noise to penetrate the reduced image. We have to filter out this noise first. The way we do it is by first forming a new image each of whose pixels is the average of the corresponding two horizontally adjacent pixels in the source.

        new(*t,src.maxplane,src.maxrow,src.maxcol*);
        new(*av,src.maxplane,src.maxrow,src.maxcol*);
        adjustcontrast(0.5,*src,t*↑);

        av↑ ← *t*↑;
        av^[][*src.maxcol*] := *src*[][*src.maxcol*];

av now contains a horizontally blurred version of the source.

        dispose(*t*);
        interpolateh(*av*↑,*dest*);
        dispose(*av*);
        end
        else
        begin
            ;

Apply the shrinking recursively to get down to a shrinkage factor < 2.

by 2
by n/2

        new(*t,src.maxplane,src.maxrow,*(1+*src.maxcol*)**div** 2+−1);
        resizeh(*src,t*↑);
        resizeh(*t*↑.*dest*);
        dispose(*t*);
        end
end;

Algorithm 57. Horizontal resize an image.

13.8 Horizontal Interpolation

This is performed by procedure

procedure *Interpolateh*(**var** *src,dest:image*);

This will interpolate an image in the horizontal direction. *Src* and *dest* must differ in size only in the horizontal direction.
This is an inherently serial procedure and as such used classical Pascal loops. Its internals are shown in Alg. 59.

13.9 Interpolate Vertically

This is performed by the procedure

procedure *Interpolatev* (**var** *src,dest:image*);

This interpolates in the vertical direction. *Src* and *dest* must differ in size only in the vertical direction. This is parallel code, and uses array expressions. The internals of the procedure are given in Alg. 60.

13.10 Displaying Images

In all of the examples up to now we have concentrated on the internals of image processing. We have relegated the job of making the images visible to other utilities by writing the images out to .bmp files that we can look at in some image viewer.

It is, of course, possible to write a Vector Pascal program that will output an image to the screen, but to do this we need to call libraries that interface between Vector Pascal and the display hardware of the machine on which the program runs. A good library for this purpose is the Simple Direct Media Layer, or SDL library. This is targeted at games designers and is portable between Linux and Windows, allowing 2D graphics programs to be similarly portable. SDL is incorporated into many Linux distributions, and for other system it is available from www.libsdl.org.

SDL uses an abstraction termed a surface to represent both the display and images. Image files can be loaded into these surfaces and blitted to the display. The surfaces allow us to abstract from the pixel formats used in the display hardware. One can specify the bit depth and organisation of the pixels to be used on a surface and SDL will translate these to the format used by the display hardware behind the scenes.

13.10.1 demoimg – An Example Image Display Program

We take as an example a program that loads an image file into a three-dimensional array of pixels, the standard Vector Pascal image type in other

procedure *resizev*(**var** *src.dest:image*);

Change the size of an image in the vertical direction. *Dest* must be same width as *src*.

var
    Let *n* ∈ real;
    Let *t,av* ∈ pimage;
    Let *rows* ∈ integer;
begin
    $n \leftarrow \frac{1+src.maxrow}{1+dest.maxrow}$;
    else
        if *n* =1 **then** *dest* ← *src*
        else
            if *n* ≤ 2
            then
            begin

This filters in the vertical direction.

        new(*t,src.maxplane,src.maxrow,src.maxcol*);
        new(*av,src.maxplane,src.maxrow,src.maxcol*);
        adjustcontrast(0.5.*src.t*↑);
        for *rows* ← 0 **to** *src.maxrow* − 1 **do**
            av↑← *t*↑;
        av^[][*src.maxrow*] := *src*[][*src.maxrow*];

av now contains a vertically blurred version of the source.

        dispose(*t*);
        interpolatev(*av*↑*dest*);
        dispose(*av*);
    end
    else
    begin

Apply the shrinking recursively to get down to a shrinkage factor <2.

        rows ← $\frac{src.maxrow}{2}$;
        new(*t,src.maxplane,rows,*(*src.maxcol*));
by 2   *resizev*(*src,t*↑);
by *n*/2   *resizev*(*t*↑,*dest*);
        dispose(*t*);
    end
end;

Algorithm 58. Vertical resize routine.

Chapter 13 • Parallel Image Processing

```
var
    Let ratio,p,q ∈ real;
    Let i,j,k,l ∈ integer;
begin
```
$$ratio \leftarrow \frac{1+src.maxcol}{1+dest.maxcol};$$
```
    for j ← 0 to dest.maxrow do
    begin
        for k ← 0 to dest.maxcol do
        begin
            p ← k × ratio;
```

p holds the horizontal position in the source from which the data must come.

$$l \leftarrow trunc(p);$$

l holds the sample point below p and $l + 1$ holds the position above it.

$$q \leftarrow p - l;$$

q holds the distance away from l, that p was.

```
            if l + 1 > src.maxcol then dest [][j,k] := rc [][j,l]
            else
                dest [][j,k] := src [][j,l] * (1−q)+src [][j,1+l] * q;
```

Interpolate in the horizontal direction using linear weighting.

```
        end;
    end;
end;
```

Algorithm 59. Horizontal interpolation routine.

words. It then performs some image processing on it and displays it on the screen.

The new problems to be dealt with here concern:

1. Linking to SDL.
2. Initialising the SDL sub-system.
3. Converting the images into a format recognised by SDL.

Linking to SDL

A program that is going to use SDL must start with the compiler directives:

```
{$l SDL}
{$l pthread}
{$c sdl_rwops.c}
```

```
var
    Let l ∈ ^line;
    Let pp ∈ pixel;
    Let i,j,k ∈ integer;
    Let ratio, p,q ∈ real;
begin
    new (l,dest.maxcol);
    ratio ← (1+src.maxrow)/(dest.maxrow+1);
    for j ← 0 to dest.maxrow do
    begin
        p ← j × ratio;
        k ← trunc(p);
        q ← p − k;
        pp ← q;
```

Convert weight to pixel.

$$l\uparrow \leftarrow pp;$$

Replicate to a line to allow efficient vectorisation.

```
        for i ← 0 to src.maxplane do  if k + 1 > src.maxrow then dest_{i,j} ← src_{i,k} × l↑
        else
            dest_{i,j} ← src_{i,1+k} × l↑;
        pp ← 1− q;
        l↑ ← pp;
        for i ← 0 to src.maxplane do dest_{i,j} ← dest_{i,j} + src_{i,k} × l↑;
    end;
    dispose(l);
end;
```

Algorithm 60. Vertical interpolation of image lines.

The first two lines specify the compiled SDL and system libraries that are needed. The last line specifies the name of a C stub file that contains some auxiliary routines needed to interface Vector Pascal to the standard SDL library. The library routines will be located on the standard library path. The file `sdl_rwops.c` should be located in the current directory.

In addition, the program must include the Pascal unit *SDL* in its uses list. This unit contains the Pascal declarations of all of the routines in the SDL library.

Initialisation

The key steps here are initialising the SDL video sub-system and creating a surface to represent the display screen.

At 253 × 169   Original 512 × 512   At 598 × 756

Figure 13.11. Effect of applying resize to Barbara.bmp.

Pixel Conversion

Pixel conversion involves two translations. First, we must change the data from 8-bit signed numbers to 8-bit unsigned numbers. The operator **pixel2byte** will do this. Next we have to reorganise the data from the planar organisation used for image processing applications to the adjacent pixel format used in the display hardware, and which is assumed by SDL. This can be achieved in a single Vector Pascal statement. We then have to create an SDL surface that uses our array of unsigned bytes as its pixel store.

The program is as follows:

```
{$l SDL}
{$l pthread}
{$c sdl_rwops.c}
program demoimg;
{Demonstration program designed to test the SDL video subsystem
with Vector Pascal. Written by Ben Watt}
uses SDL, bmp;
const
  {Resolution}
  width = 250;
  height = 250;
  colordepth = 16;
  toppixel = 2;
type

  unsignedRGBimage(row,col,depth:integer) = array [0..row,0..col,0..depth]
  of byte;

  punsignedRGBimage = ^unsignedRGBimage;
var
  Let caption ∈ pasciiarray;
  Let screen,bg,ghost ∈ PSDL_Surface;
  Let colorkey ∈ UInt32;
  Let src,dest ∈ SDL_Rect;
```

```
Let background ∈ pimage;
Let unsignedbackground ∈ punsignedRGBimage;
begin
  src.x ← 0;
  src.y ← 0;
  src.w ← 180;
  src.h ← 180;
  dest ← src;
  {Initialisation}
  SDL_Init(SDL_INIT_VIDEO);
  screen ← SDL_SetVideoMode(width, height, colordepth, SDL_DOUBLEBUF);
  if screen = nil then
  begin
    writeln ('Couldn' 't initialise video mode at ', width , 'x' ,
    height ,'x', colordepth ,'bpp');
  end
  else
  begin
    {Set the window caption}
    new (caption);
    string2pasciiarray('Vector Pascal Demo', caption);
    SDL_WM_SetCaption(caption, nil);
    dispose(caption);
```

Load an image. This will be stored as planes of signed pixels, which is suitable for image processing but not for display. Immediately after loading we apply an image processing operation to it, calling the *sharpen* procedure from the *bmp* unit.

loadbmpfile('bg.bmp', *background*);
  sharpen(*background*↑);

Create a buffer of unsigned bytes to hold the image for display purposes. This has the colours packed into 24-bit pixels. We then copy the image into the buffer, permuting the indices as we do.

new(*unsignedbackground*,*background*^.*maxrow*,*background*^.*maxcol*,2);
  unsignedbackground ↑ ←**pixel2byte**(*background*↑[ι_2,ι_0,ι_1]);

Create an SDL surface from the buffer passing in a description of its dimensions and the location of the pixel fields.

	bg := *SDL_CreateRGBSurfaceFrom*(@*unsignedbackground*^[0,0,0],
width	*background*↑.*maxcol* + 1
height	*background*↑.*maxrow* + 1
bit pixels	24,
pitch	3*(*background*^.*maxcol* +1),
RED MASK	$ff,
green	$ff00,

blue $ff0000,
alpha   0
alpha   );

We now use SDL to load in another .bmp file directly into an SDL surface. We will not do image manipulation on this image in order to show SDL's ability to directly load and display .bmp files.

> *Ghost ← SDL_LoadBMP*('ghost.bmp');
> **if** (*bg=nil*) ∨(*Ghost=nil*) **then**
> **begin**
>   **WriteIn**('Could not load image');
>   *SDL_Quit*;
>   *Halt*(1);
> **end**
> **else**
> **begin**

Draw Background, copying the background surface to the screen.

> *SDL_BlitSurface(bg,@src,screen,@dest)*;
> *src.w ← 32*;
> *src.h ← 32*;

Draw the Ghost Image on the screen.

> *dest.x ← 20*;
> *dest.y ← 20*;
> *SDL_BlitSurface(Ghost,@src,screen,@dest)*;

Make sure that the hardware display is updated.

> *SDL_UpdateRect(screen, 0, 0, 0, 0)*;
>   **end**;
>   (* Wait 6 seconds before closing. *)
>   *SDL_Delay(6000)*;
>   *SDL_FreeSurface(ghost)*;
>   *SDL_FreeSurface(bg)*;
>   *SDL_Quit*;
>   **end**;
> **end**.

13.11   The Unit BMP

What follows is a Vector Pascal source unit converted to LaTeX and formatted using the VPTeX system:

unit *bmp*;

This unit provides a library to access and manipulate bitmap images provided in Microsoft .bmp file format.

> **interface**

The module exports an image type as a three-dimensional array of pixels in which the first dimension identifies the colour plane, the second dimension indicates the row and the third dimension indicates the column of the pixel.

type

image(maxplane,maxrow,maxcol:integer) =
array [0..*maxplane*,0..*maxrow*,0..*maxcol*] **of** *pixel*;
pimage = ˜*image*;
filename = **string** [79];

procedure *storebmpfile(s:***string**;**var** *im:image)*; (see Section 13.12.2)

This procedure will store an image im as a Microsoft .bmp file with name s:

function *loadbmpfile(s:filename;***var** *im:pimage):boolean*; (see Section 13.12.3)

This function returns true if it has sucessfully loaded the .bmp file s. The image pointer im is initialised to point to an image on the heap. The program should explicitly discard the image after use by calling dispose.

procedure *adjustcontrast(f:real;***var** *im:image)*; (see Section 13.12.4)

This procedure takes a real number as a parameter and adjusts the contrast of an image to by that factor. If $f = 2$ then contrast is doubled; if $f = 0.5$ then contrast is halved.

procedure *pconv(***var** *im:image;c1,c2,c3:real)*; (see Section 13.12.5)

This procedure performs a data parallel separable convolution of width 3 on the image

implementation
type

The following data structures are defined by Microsoft for their bitmap files (.BMP)

> *bitmapfileheader* = **packed record**
> *bftype* : *array*$_{1..2}$ **of** *byte*;
> *bfsize* : *integer*;
> *res1* : *array*$_{0..3}$ **of** *byte*;
> *bfoffbits* : *integer*;
> **end**;

Note that in the bitmapfileheader the bftype field has been defined in terms of bytes rather than as char since Vector Pascal uses 16-bit UNICODE internal representation of characters, whereas the file format expects 8-bit ASCII.

A BitmapInfoHeader is the internal data structure used by microsoft Windows to handle device independent bitmaps (DIBs). We only need this structure to interpret the data in a .BMP file.

> *TBitmapInfoHeader* = *record*
> *biSize* : *integer*;
> *biWidth* : *integer*;

biHeight : *integer*;
biPlanes : *Word*;
biBitCount : *Word*;
biCompression : *integer*;
biSizeImage : *integer*;
biXPelsPerMeter : *integer*;
biYPelsPerMeter : *integer*;
biClrUsed : *integer*;
biClrImportant : *integer*;
end;

This data structure can optionally include a colour table, but this library does not support reading .bmp files with colour tables:

TBitmapInfo = *record*
   bmiHeader : *TBitmapInfoHeader*;

end;

The start of a .bmp file has a file header followed by information about the bitmap itself:

bmpfile = **packed** *record*
   fileheader : *bitmapfileheader*;
   filedata : *tbitmapinfo*;
end;
pbmpfile =↑*bmpfile*;

This data type is the format in which lines of pixels are stored in .bmp files. It is used internally in the unit BMP to load and store images to files. This process involves translating between internal and external representations.

imageline(mincol,maxcol,minplane,maxplane:integer) =
array [*mincol..maxcol,minplane..maxplane*] **of** *byte*;

procedure *initbmpheader*(**var** *header:bmpfile*;**var** *im:image*); (see Section 13.11.1)

procedure *storebmpfile*(*s*:**string**;**var** *im:image*); (see Section 13.11.2)

function *loadbmpfile*(*s:filename*;**var** *im:pimage*):*boolean*; (see Section 13.11.3)

type
line (*high:integer*) = **array** [*0..high*] **of** *pixel*;

procedure *adjustcontrast*(*f:real*;**var** *im:image*); (see Section 13.11.4)

procedure *pconv*(**var** *im:image;c1,c2,c3:real*); (see Section 13.11.5)

begin

end.

13.11.1 Procedure initbmpheader

procedure *initbmpheader*(**var** *header:bmpfile;***var** *im:image*);

This procedure has the task of initialising a Window's BMP file header in a way conformant with the dimensions of the image passed as a parameter:

begin

FileHeader BMP files have the letters BM at the start followed by a 32-bit integer giving the file size, 4 reserved bytes and then a 32-bit integer giving the offset into the file at which the bitmap data start.

header.fileheader.bftype$_1$ ← **ord** (*'B'*);
header.fileheader.bftype$_2$ ← **ord** (*'M'*);
header.fileheader.bfsize ← **sizeof**(*bmpfile*) +
(*im.maxcol* + 1) ×
(*im.maxplane* + 1) ×
(*im.maxrow* + 1);
header.fileheader.res1 ← 0;
header.fileheader.bfoffbits ← **sizeof**(*bmpfile*);

Bitmap info Next comes a bitmap info header which gives details about the bitmap itself. The fields of this are as follows:

bisize This gives the size of the entire bitmap info header as a 32-bit integer.

biwidth This 32-bit integer gives the number of columns in the image, which can be determined from the bounds of the pixel array provided.

biheight Another 32-bit integer which gives the number of scan lines in the image, which can again be determined from the bounds of the image array.

biplanes This gives the number of planes in the image as a 16-bit integer. This defaults to 1.

bibitcount Gives the number of bits per pixel; we only support 8- and 24-bit versions at present.

bicompression The meaning of this field is not clear, it seems to be 0 in most files.

biXPelsPerMeter, biYPelsPerMeter These specify the printable spacing of pixels. The author uses the value $ec4 that is observed in a number of .bmp files.

biClrUsed, biClrImportant These fields are only used in images with colour maps; set them to zero for now.

with *header.filedata.bmiheader* **do** *begin* **begin**
    bisize ← **sizeof**(*tbitmapinfo*);
    biwidth ← *im.maxcol* + 1;
    biheight ← *im.maxrow* + 1;
    biplanes ← 1;
    bibitcount ← 8 × (*im.maxplane* + 1);
    bicompression ← 0;

$biXPelsPerMeter \leftarrow$ \\$ec4;
$biYPelsPerMeter \leftarrow$ \\$ec4;
$biClrUsed \leftarrow 0$;
$biClrImportant \leftarrow 0$;
        end;

end;

13.11.2 Procedure storebmpfile

procedure *storebmpfile* (*s*:**string**;**var** *im*:*image*);
This function writes an image in Vector Pascal format to a microsoft .BMP file. It is designed only to work with one or three plane images.

type
    lines(*rows,cols,planes*:*integer*) = **array** [0..*rows*,0..*cols*,0..*planes*] **of** *byte*;
var
    Let $f \in$ file;
    Let *fsize,i,index,j,k,m,row,res* $\in$ integer;
    Let *pf* $\in$ bmpfile;
    Let *la* $\in$ ˆ*lines*;
    Let *b* $\in$ byte;
begin
    assign(*f,s*);
    rewrite(*f*);
setup header   *initbmpheader*(*pf,im*);
write it   *blockwrite*(*f,pf*,**sizeof**(*bmpfile*),*res*);
get buffer   **new**(*la,im.maxrow,im.maxcol,im.maxplane*);

Convert the data from the planar signed fixed point format used in Vector Pascal to the interleaved unsigned byte format used in Windows:

$la \uparrow \leftarrow$ **perm** [2,0,1] **pixel2byte**(*im*);

Compute the size of the data part of the resulting file and write it out with a single block write operation:

$fsize \leftarrow (im.maxplane + 1) \times (im.maxrow + 1) \times (im.maxcol + 1)$;
write data   *blockwrite* (*f,la*↑[0,0,0],*fsize,res*);
free buffer   **dispose** (*la*);
                close (*f*);
end;

13.11.3 Function loadbmpfile

function *loadbmpfile* (*s*:*filename*;**var** *im*:*pimage*):*boolean*;
var
    Let $f \in$ file of byte;
    Let *fsize,i,index,j,k,m,row,res* $\in$ integer;
    Let *la* $\in$ ˆ*imageline*;
    Let *pf* $\in$ bmpfile;

```
begin
  loadbmpfile ← false;
  assign (f,s);
  reset (f);
  if ioresult ≠ 0 then loadbmpfile ← false false
  else
  begin
    fsize ← filesize (f);
    i ← sizeof(bmpfile);
    blockread (f,pf,i,res);
    with pf.filedata.bmiheader do
    begin
      new(im,2,biheight -1,biwidth -1);
      new(la,0,biwidth -1,0,2);
      if bibitcount = 8 then loadbmpfile ← false false
      else if bibitcount = 24 then
      begin
```

Read in the file one line at a time, translating it as we go into signed fixed-point format

```
        for i ← 0 to biheight − 1 do
        begin
          blockread(f,la↑[0,0],3 × biwidth,res);
          for k ← 0 to biwidth − 1 do
            for m ← 0 to 2 do
              im↑[m,i,k] ← byte2pixel(la↑[k,m]);
        end;
        loadbmpfile ← true;
      end;
      dispose(la);
      close(f);
    end;
  end;
end;
```

13.11.4 Procedure adjustcontrast

```
procedure adjustcontrast (f:real;var im:image);
var
  Let l ∈ˆline;
begin
  new(l,im.maxcol);
  {$r-}
  l↑ ← f;
  if (abs (f) < 1) then im ← im × l↑ else im ← im × f;
  {$r+}
  dispose (l);
end;
```

13.11.5 Procedure pconv

procedure pconv(**var** im:image;c1,c2,c3:real);

Convolution of an image by a matrix of real numbers can be used to smooth or sharpen an image, depending on the matrix used. If A is an output image and K a convolution matrix, then if B is the convolved image

$$B_{y,x} = \sum_i \sum_j A_{y+i,x+j} K_{i,j}$$

A separable convolution kernel is a vector of real numbers that can be applied independently to the rows and columns of an image to provide filtering. It is a specialisation of the more general convolution matrix, but is algorithmically more efficient to implement.

If **k** is a convolution vector, then the corresponding matrix K is such that $K_{i,j} = \mathbf{k}_i \mathbf{k}_j$.

Given a starting image A as a two-dimensional array of pixels and a three-element kernel c_1, c_2, c_3, the algorithm first forms a temporary array T whose elements are the weighted sum of adjacent rows: $T_{y,x} = c_1 A_{y-1,x} + c_2 A_{y,x} + c_3 A_{y+1,x}$. Then in a second phase it sets the original image to be the weighted sum of the columns of the temporary array: $A_{y,x} = c_1 T_{y,x-1} + c_2 T_{y,x} + c_3 T_{y,x+1}$.

Clearly, the outer edges of the image are a special case, since the convolution is defined over the neighbours of the pixel, and the pixels along the boundaries are missing one neighbour. A number of solutions are available for this, but for simplicity we will perform only vertical convolutions on the left and right edges and horizontal convolutions on the top and bottom lines of the image.

type
    plane(rows,cols:integer) = **array** [0..rows,0..cols] **of** pixel;

var
    Let T,l ∈ ^plane;
    Let i ∈ integer;
procedure convp(**var** p,l,T:plane); (see Section 13.12.6)

begin

This allocates a temporary buffer to hold a plane, and three temporary buffers to hold the convolution coordinates as lines of pixels.

    new(T,im.maxrow,im.maxcol);
    new(l,3,im.maxcol);
    l↑ [0] ← c1;
    l↑ [1] ← c2;
    l↑ [2] ← c3;

Perform convolution on each of the planes of the image. This has to be done with an explicit loop as array maps only work with functions, not with procedures.

    for i ← 0 **to** im.maxplane **do** convp(im$_i$,l↑,T↑);

This sequence frees the temporary buffers used in the convolution process.

dispose(*l*);
dispose(*T*);
end;

13.11.6 Procedure convp

procedure *convp*(**var** *p,l,T:plane*);
This convolves a plane by applying the vertical and horizontal convolutions in turn.

var
    Let $r,c \in$ integer;
begin

This sequence performs a vertical convolution of the rows of the plane p and places the result in the temporary plane T. It uses the lines of pixels $l[i]$ as convolution weights. Use of lines of pixels rather than the floating-point numbers for the kernel weights allows the computation to proceed 8 pixels at a time in parallel.

```
{$r-}{disable range checks}
```
$r \leftarrow p.\text{rows}$;
$T_{1..r-1} \leftarrow p_{0..r-2} \times l_0 + p_{1..r-1} \times l_1 + p_{2..r} \times l_2$;
$T_0 \leftarrow p_0$;
$T_r \leftarrow p_r$;

Now perform a horizontal convolution of the plane T and place the result in p.

$c \leftarrow p.\text{cols}$;
$p_{0..r,1..c-1} \leftarrow T_{0..r,0..c-2} \times l_0 + T_{0..r,2..c} \times l_2 + T_{0..r,1..c-1} \times l_1$;
$p_{0..r,0} \leftarrow T_{0..r,0}$;
$p_{0..r,c} \leftarrow T_{0..r,c}$;
```
{$r+}{enable range checks}
```
end;

Pattern Recognition and Image Compression   14

Our next examples of SIMD programming will be drawn from image compression. The encoding and decoding of compressed images were one of the original target applications of the MMX architecture. In this chapter we will give some theoretical background to image compression for those unfamiliar with it, and then go on to examine an example compressor–decompressor (CODEC) that makes use of SIMD parallelism.

14.1 Principles of Image Compression

14.1.1 Data Compression in General

Data compression is the name for techniques which take files or streams of data and transform them in some way so that they can be represented in fewer bits than they originally used. For data compression to be useful, there must be a reverse process, decompression, which takes the compressed representation and transforms it back into the original format. Let us call the data prior to compression the *source*, the data after compression the *encoding* and the data after decompression the *decode*. Compression techniques are generally expressed as being either lossy or lossless.

In a lossy technique, the decode is similar to but not identical with the source. For instance, an MPEG encoded film will decode to a sequence of video frames which, to the human eye, look almost the same as the original film. The functionally important measure of similarity in these cases is almost always in terms of human perception. However, objective metrics based on signal to noise ratios are also widely used to assess the quality of compression techniques.

In a lossless technique, the decode is identical with the source. A well-known example is the LZW encoding process used in .zip files. Lossless techniques depend on the fact that the most commonly used data representations of text or computer programs are redundant – that is, the source contains more bits than information.

In computer programming, one generally thinks of a bit as simply a binary digit, but in information theory it has a more technical meaning as the amount of information required to decide between two equally probable outcomes. Consider a text file sent as 7-bit ASCII stored in 8-bit bytes. It is evident that the most significant bit conveys no information, since it will always be zero.

It is less evident that the remaining seven binary digits will generally contain less than 7 bits of information.

One binary digit can encode two possible messages, seven binary digits can obviously encode 128 or 2^7 distinct messages. Where an ASCII stream to have no redundancy, where it to contain 8 bits of information per byte, it would be the case that each successive bit of a byte distinguished between equally probable outcomes, each bit was as likely to be a 1 as it was to be a 0. Each possible ASCII character would have to occur with equal frequency.

This does not occur in practical text streams; letters and spaces occur more frequently than most control characters, for instance. Within the letters there is a range of frequency of occurrence, with e occurring much more often than z. A net reduction in file size can be achieved if the representation is changed to one in which frequently occurring letters are encoded in less than 7 bits whilst less frequent ones are stored in more than 7 bits. Because the shorter codes occur more often, the savings here outway the cost of more bits for less frequent letters. This is an example of a lossless encoding technique.

When compressing text files, lossless encodings are the only acceptable choice, since any corruption of decoded text is immediately apparent. The underlying reason for this is that text files have relatively little redundancy, certainly when compared with the spoken word. By writing text down we abstract from all personal variations in voice, or the emotional inflection that speech carries. This abstraction corresponds to a loss of redundancy.

14.1.2 Image Compression

Data compression is an essential feature of our nervous system. The function of a nervous system is to capture environmental stimulae, categorise them and activate motor programs that will enhance survival in the environment that generated the stimulae. The number of possible motor programs is much less than the number of configurations of stimulae that an animal will encounter. In mapping a large set of input messages to a smaller set of responses, the nervous system is doing compression.

In an animal such as ourselves, this compression is done by multiple layers of neurons. Consider vision. There are fewer neurons in the optic nerve than receptor cells in the retina, and it takes the input from many optic nerve cells to make a cell in the primary visual cortex fire. By the time a scene has been processed by the primary visual cortex, it has been represented in terms of salient features, edges with particular orientations, intensity gradients, etc. Image compression software can fool the brain into thinking it is seeing the source image to the extent that the decoded image is composed of those features that the visual cortex is anyway tuned to recognise.

14.1.3 Vector Quantisation of Images

We shall present an example based on an image compression technique known as vector quantisation. This differs from techniques such as MPEG and H261, which are based on the discrete cosine transform (DCT). Vector quantisation is better suited to very low bandwidth channels, for instance, sending video

Chapter 14 • Pattern Recognition and Image Compression

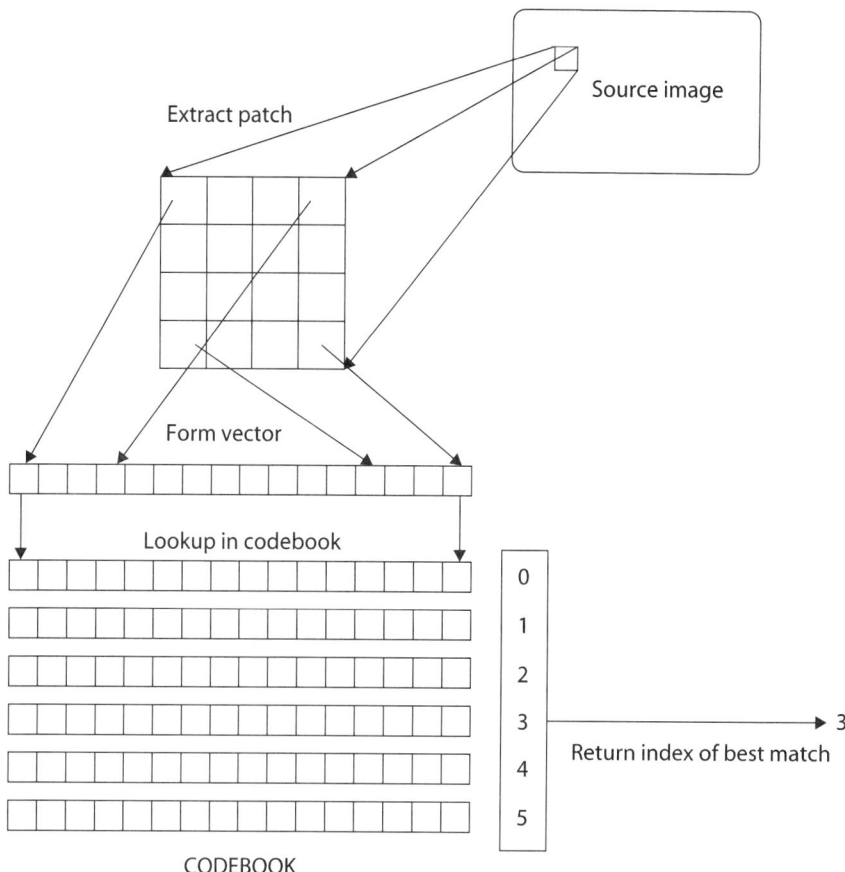

Figure 14.1. Outline of the vector quantisation process. Patches from the image are unwound into vectors and these are then looked up in a codebook of vectors to find the best match. Then the index of the best match is output as a surrogate for the patch.

over mobile telephone links. What we can present as a textbook example involves considerable simplification when compared with a functional video CODEC, but we can show both the key principles of vector quantisation and how SIMD techniques can accelerate the process.

An outline of the compression process is shown in Figure 14.1. The original image is divided into rectangular patches. The pixels in these patches are then formed into vectors. Each such vector is looked up in a codebook to find a codebook entry that is similar to it. The entire patch is then encoded using the row number in the codebook. At the decode end the reverse process takes place: the row number is used to fetch a row from the codebook. This is then formed into a patch which is placed in the image. This is illustrated in Figure 14.2.

When compressing an image, each patch must be compared with each entry in the codebook to find the closest match. If we have n pixels in the image and m rows in the codebook, the algorithmic complexity will be $\mathbf{O}mn$. Decompression is much more efficient, being done simply by indexing the codebook to

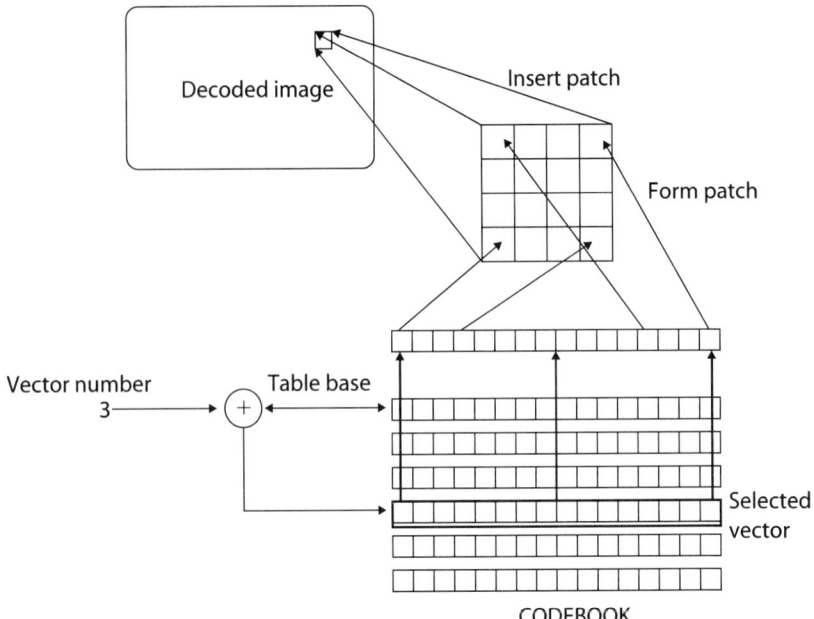

Figure 14.2. The process of decoding a VQ image is inherently faster than encoding since the codebook searching used during encoding is replaced by a fetch from a calculated offset into the codebook. The vector found is formed into a patch and placed in the image.

find the relevant row, giving a complexity of **O**n. This does not matter much for compressing a single image, but when compressing a video stream, there is a need to accelerate the search. It is possible to do this by using indexing algorithms, using techniques such as Hierarchical Vector Quantisation (HVQ), but these can result in non-optimal entries being selected from the codebook. SIMD parallelism is ideal for accelerating codebook lookup.

We will give a very simplified image compressor example. It will use 4×4 pixel patches which will be compressed using a codebook with 256 rows. The net effect will be to perform 16:1 compression on the image file. This is a relatively low compression ratio. Higher compression ratios can be obtained by using larger patches. So 8×8 patches would give a 64:1 compression, etc. Many compressors use some form of adaptive vector quantisation, so that large patches are used in areas of the image with low detail and smaller patches where the details are finer. This allows a higher overall level of compression to be obtained without too much detail being lost. We leave such refinements out of our example.

14.1.4 Data Structures

Let us first look at the data structures we may use for compressing image files. We need to define the basic parameters of our compression process, the patch size, the length of the vectors used in the codebook and how many symbols there will be in our code alphabet. We will declare all of this in a unit *vq*.

unit *vq*;
interface
  const
    patchsize = 4;
    vectorlen = *patchsize* * *patchsize*;
    maxcode = 255;

Following this, we declare the type of the code vectors. We declare them as vectors of pixels, but we also declare a type which is a similar vector of reals. We do this because although we will want to use a codebook of pixels for decode purposes, this is inadequate for encoding. The limited precision of 8-bit pixels means that we obtain prohibitive rounding errors if we do our compression calculations to only 8-bit accuracy. The encoder therefore uses real valued code vectors.

type
codevec = **array** [0..*vectorlen* −1] **of** *pixel*;
rcodevec = **array** [0..*vectorlen* −1] **of** *real*;
codeword = 0..*maxcode*;
book = **record**
  rows.cols:word;
  tab: array [*codeword*] of *codevec*;
end;
codefileheader = record
    imwidth,imheight:word;
    colourplanes:1..10;
    table:*book*;
end;
var
Let *cbk* ∈ book;
rtab: array [*codeword*] of *rcodevec*;

The type declarations also include declarations of the records to be used as file headers for compressed files. These define the parameters of the image being compressed: its height, width and number of colour planes. Following this in the file comes the codebook, which is also self-describing.

14.1.5 encode

The one function exported by *vq* is the encoder shown as Alg. 61. This iteratively computes the squared distance between the source vector and each vector in the real-valued version of the codebook. The key expression is the line

$$d \leftarrow \sum (rv - rtab_i) \times (rv - rtab_i);$$

```
function encode(var v:codevec):codeword;
var
    Let i,j,k ∈ integer;
    Let d,least ∈ real;
    Let rv ∈ rcodevec;
    Let dv ∈ codevec;
begin
    rv ← v;
    j ← 0;
    least ← 2 × vectorlen;
    for i ← 0 to maxcode do
    begin
        d ← Σ(rv − rtab_i) × (rv − rtab_i);
        if d < least then
        begin
            j ← i;
            least ← d;
        end
    end;
    encode ← j;
end;
```

Algorithm 61. The vector quantisation routine proper. This takes a vector and searches the codebook for the vector with the closest Euclidean distance to the source vector and returns the index of the closest matching vector.

or in source format

```
d:=\+(rv-rtab[i])*(rv-rtab[i]);
```

Our aim is to select the vector which is closest to the source vector, that is, we want to minimize the distance $\delta(\mathbf{v},i) = \sqrt{\Sigma_j(\mathbf{v}_j - \mathbf{C}_{i,j})^2}$, where $\mathbf{v}$ is the source vector and $\mathbf{C}$ is the codebook matrix. However, since the ordering of squared distances will be the same as the ordering of the distances, it is unnecessary to compute the square roots. It is very important that the calculations here are done to sufficient precision. We cannot use pixels since they are saturated to 8-bit precision, and the subtraction of two pixels can fall outside the range that can be represented by 8-bit signed numbers. This will lead to gross errors in distance calculations if we use 8-bit accuracy. The use of reals obviates this problem. The pixels vector passed to the routine is converted to a vector of reals at before searching takes place. All subsequent calculations are done in reals. This somewhat reduces the effective parallelism. On a bare-bones MMX instruction-set such as that supported by Meta-data on the Crusoe, there is no effective parallelism, but on recent Intel processors we can take advantage of 4-fold parallelism even when working with reals.

The decode program is much simpler, involving no more than copying pixels from the codebook into the appropriate places in the image. It is shown in Alg. 62.

```
program vqdecode;
uses vq,bmp;
const
    q = patchsize - 1;
var
    Let p ∈ pimage;
    Let f ∈ file;
    Let header ∈ codefileheader;
    Let i,j,k,l ∈ integer;
    Let index ∈ codeword;
begin
    assign (f,paramstr(1) + '.vq');
    {$i-}
    reset (f);
    if ioresult = 0 then
    begin
        blockread (f,header,sizeof(codefileheader),l);
        cbk ← header.table;
        new (p,header.colourplanes - 1,header.imheight - 1,header.imwidth - 1);
        for i ← 0 to p↑.maxplane do
            for j ← 0 to p↑.maxrow/patchsize do
                for k ← 0 to p↑.maxrow/patchsize do
                begin
                    blockread (f,index,sizeof(codeword),l);
                    (* Copy codevector into patch *)
                    p^[i,j*patchsize..j*patchsize + q,k*patchsize..k*patchsize + q] :=
                    cbk.tab$_{index,\iota_1 \times patchsize + \iota_2}$;
                end;
        storebmpfile (paramstr(2),p↑);
    end
    else writeln('cant open ', paramstr(1) + '.vq');
end.
```

Algorithm 62. The program `vqdecode`. This takes two parameters, a filename without extension for the encoded file and a filename with extension as the destination file. Input is assumed to be in the format generated by the `vqencode` program and output is a Windows BMP file.

14.2 The *K* Means Algorithm

The quality of the compressed image that we will obtain using a codebook depends on how well the entries in the codebook represent the spread of image patches found in the original image. The rows in the codebook matrix are all potentially estimators of the source vectors. They will be a good set of estimators if there is a good chance that one will be close to each source vector.

Vector quantizers can either use a universal codebook, designed to be suitable for a wide range of images, or a tailored codebook that has estimators based on the image being compressed. The process of forming such a codebook is referred to as training the codebook on the image.

The Concept of Mean

Suppose we have a collection of numbers and we must select a single estimator for them; the best number to choose is their average. The average or mean of a set of numbers is their expected value. It is the estimate which minimises error between it and the observations.

Suppose instead of being allowed a single number to represent a set of scalar observations we are allowed two. Suppose we wish to reconstruct the observations with minimal error at a remote site, and that for each observation we are allowed to send 1 bit. On the basis of this bit we select one of the two estimators. By analogy with the concept of the single mean of a set of observations, these two numbers are termed the two means of the observations.

Consider the five numbers 1, 2, 3, 5, 7. Their mean, given by the equation $\mu = \frac{\sum_{i=1}^{n} o_i}{n}$, is $\frac{18}{5} = 3.6$, but the two means which best approximate the distribution are 2 and 6.

If we used the single mean to estimate the observations, we would have the following errors:

o_i	μ	$o_i - \mu$	$(o_i - \mu)^2$
1	3.6	−2.6	6.76
2	3.6	−1.6	2.56
3	3.6	−0.6	0.36
5	3.6	1.4	1.96
7	3.6	3.4	11.56
Totals 18	18	0	23.2

Note that the sum of errors will be zero for the mean, but the sum of squared errors will in general be non-zero. Let us look at the situation where we have two means:

o_i	μ_j	$o_i - \mu_j$	$(o_i - \mu_j)^2$
1	2	−1	1
2	2	0	0
3	2	1	1
5	6	−1	1
7	6	1	1
Totals 18	18	0	5

Again the sum of errors is zero but the sum of squared errors is markedly reduced. In data compression literature one typically evaluates estimators in terms of the peak signal to noise ratio (PSNR) that they give. The peak signal energy is measured as the square of the maximum swing between low and high values in the signal. For instance, if the numbers in our example above were encoded in 3 bits, then they would have a swing of 7, and peak signal energy for a single observation would be 49, and for a sequence of five numbers it would be 245. The ratio between this and the sum of the squared errors errors gives the PSNR. PSNR is typically expressed logarithmically as decibels.[1] If we had only the mean to go on, our signal to noise ratio would be $\frac{245}{23.2}$, or 10.2 decibels. If we have two estimators the PSNR increases to 49, or 16.9 decibels.

As the number of estimators rises so should the PSNR, provided that our estimators are appropriately chosen to minimise the squared error.

Outline of the K Means Algorithm

How can we choose our estimators? One way to do so is with the following algorithm:

1. Select K distinct initial values for the K means.
2. Partition the observations into K disjoint sets associated with the means, such that each observation is assigned to the set proper to the mean that best approximates it.
3. Recalculate each mean as the mean of its proper subset.
4. If any mean has changed as a result of this process, go back to step 2.

Consider the operation of the algorithm with data 1,2,3,5,7 and $K = 2$. Let the initial values of the means be 0,2. The algorithm proceeds as shown:

Means	Partitions
0,2	{1},{2,3,5,7}
1,4.25	{1,2},{3,5,7}
1.5,5	{1,2,3},{5,7}
2,6	{1,2,3},{5,7}

The K means algorithm extends naturally from scalars to vectors. The single mean μ of a matrix **M** is the row vector which minimises the sum of squared distances between μ and the rows of **M**, as follows:

1		−1	
2	1	−1	
3	2	2	
6	3	0	Totals
2	1	0	Average vector

Given the encode procedure defined in Alg. 61, we can implement the vector version of K means as shown in Alg. 63. This basic training step is iterated in the main compression program as shown in Alg. 64.

---

[1] To express the ratio in decibels we take its logarithm to the base 10 and multiply by 10.

procedure *trainstep*(**var** *im:image*);
var
   accum: **array**[*codeword*,0..*vectorlen* − 1] **of** *real*;
   n: **array**[*codeword*] **of** *integer*;
   Let *i,j,k,l* ∈ integer;
   Let *patch* ∈ codevec;
   Let *index* ∈ codeword;
begin
   $n \leftarrow 1$;
   $accum \leftarrow cbk.tab$;
   for $i \leftarrow 0$ **to** *im.maxplane* **do**
     for $j \leftarrow 0$ **to** $\frac{im.maxrow}{patchsize}$ **do**
       for $k \leftarrow 0$ **to** $\frac{im.maxcol}{patchsize}$ **do**
       begin
          $patch \leftarrow im_{i, j \times patchsize + \iota_0 \div patchsize, k \times patchsize + \iota_0 \bmod patchsize}$;
          $index \leftarrow encode(patch)$;
          $accum_{index} \leftarrow accum_{index} + patch$;
          $n_{index} \leftarrow n_{index} + 1$;
       end;
   $cbk.tab \leftarrow \frac{accum}{n_{\iota_0}}$;
   $rtab \leftarrow cbk.tab$;
end;

Algorithm 63. Basic training step of the vector *K* means algorithm.

program *vqencode*;
uses *vq,bmp*;
var
   Let *i* ∈ integer;
   Let *p* ∈ pimage;
   Let *f* ∈ file;
procedure *trainstep*(**var** *im:image*); (see Alg. 63)
procedure *encodeimage*(**var** *im:image*;**var** *f*:**file**); (see Alg. 65)
begin
   if *loadbmpfile*(*paramstr*(1) + '.bmp', *p*) **then**
   begin
     for $i \leftarrow 1$ **to** 5 **do**
       trainstep(*p*↑);
     assign(*f*,*paramstr*(1) + '.vq');
     rewrite(*f*);
     encodeimage(*p*↑,*f*);
     close(*f*);
   end;
end.

Algorithm 64. The main image encode program.

Chapter 14 • Pattern Recognition and Image Compression

procedure *encodeimage*(**var** *im:image*; **var** *f* :**file**);

Encode an image, writing it out to the file with the appropriate header information. The file is written out as a sequence of planes each of which is a sequence of rows, each of which is a sequence of codewords.

var
    Let *header* ∈ codefileheader;
    Let *i,j,k,l* ∈ integer;
    Let *patch* ∈ codevec;
    Let *index* ∈ codeword;
begin
    header.imwidth ← *im.maxcol* + 1;
    header.imheight ← *im.maxrow* + 1;
    header.table ← *cbk*;
    header.colourplanes ← *im.maxplane* + 1;
    blockwrite (*f*,*header*,**sizeof**(*codefileheader*),*i*);
    for *i* ← 0 **to** *im.maxplane* **do**
        for *j* ← 0 **to** $\frac{im.maxrow}{patchsize}$ **do**
            for *k* ← 0 **to** $\frac{im.maxcol}{patchsize}$ **do**
            begin
                patch ← $im_{i,j \times patchsize + \iota_0 \div patchsize, k \times patchsize + \iota_0 \bmod patchsize}$;
                index ← *encode* (*patch*);
                blockwrite (*f*,*index*,**sizeof**(*codeword*),*l*);
            end;
end;

Algorithm 65. Encodes an image given the codebook.

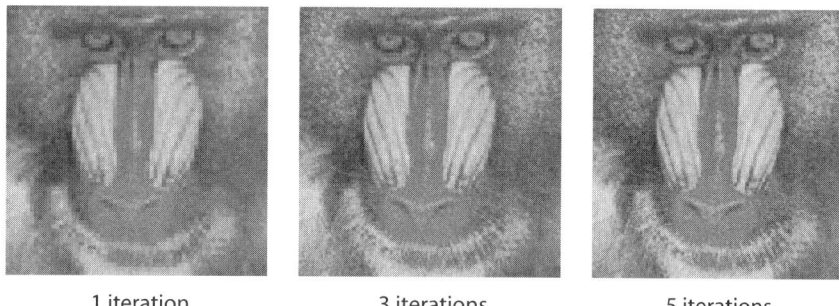

1 iteration   3 iterations   5 iterations

Figure 14.3. Effect of increasing number of iterations of the *K* means on image quality. All images have been compressed to 16K from an 192K original, using the program `vqencode`, and then decoded using `vqdecode`. Compare these with the images in Figure 13.3.

We can see the effect of the *K* means algorithm in Figure 14.3, which shows how the image quality improves with more iterations of the basic training step. Initially there is little detail within the 4 × 4 blocks, but as the computation progresses more detail appears. This is shown more clearly in Figure 14.4.

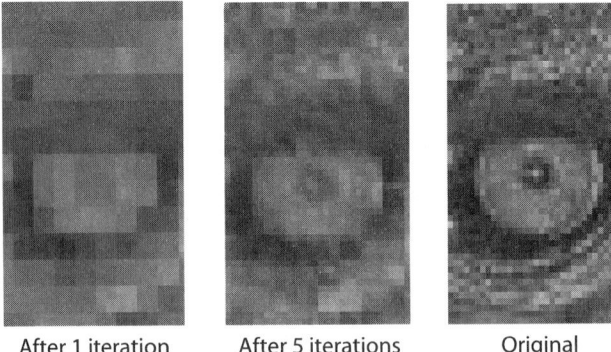

After 1 iteration   After 5 iterations   Original

Figure 14.4. This shows how detail becomes apparent within the image blocks as iterations of the K means algorithm progress.

It is apparent that the algorithm is a categorizer and pattern recognizer. It discovers commonly occurring patterns of pixels and categorizes incoming vectors against these patterns. Although we are using it for image processing, the general algorithm is applicable to other domains in which the input data can be mapped to a vector.

Performance

The kernel of the K means implementation is the encode function, which searches for the closest matching vector in the codebook. As discussed above (Section 14.1.5), the need to maintain accuracy during calculations forces us to perform the distance calculations using reals rather than 8-bit fixed-point notation. This constrains the parallelism achievable to a factor of 4 – the width of the floating-point vector registers in the SSE instructions.

What we observe when we run the algorithm compiled for a P4 is roughly a doubling of performance relative to compiling the code for a Pentium and executing it on a P4. The time is to perform five iterations of the K means algorithm and one encoding of the Mandrill picture.

Target CPU	Actual CPU	Clock speed (GHz)	Time (s)	Vectorisation gain (%)
P4	P4	1.7	5.1	107
P2	P4	1.7	10.6	0

This is slightly disappointing, but when considering results such as these we have to take into account the effect of Amdahl's law. Suppose that just under one-third of the instructions executed by the P2 were inherently serial, then the effect of Amdahl's law alone would limit us to a doubling of program speed. The fact that the acceleration is not greater is probably due both to a residuum of serial instructions and to the fact that Intel processors cannot in general dispatch four floating point operations per clock cycle.

14.2.1 Vector Quantisation of Colour Images

Another use for the K means algorithm is in selecting an optimal colour palette for images. If we want to represent a colour image using only 8 bits per pixel, one can either encode the colour within the 8 bits, allocating perhaps 3 bits for red and green and 2 for blue, or one can try and find 256 representative colours. One can view the process of finding representative colours for a palette as a form of vector quantisation – carried out over the colour space with vectors of length 3.

This form of compression gives one a reduction in file size of about 3 to 1. An alternative approach is to utilise the correlation that exists between different colour planes and use codebook vectors that extend over all planes. For example, one could use vectors of length 48 instead of 16 in our compression program with the vectors drawn from corresponding 4×4 patches on each plane. This will give a very high compression, but at the cost of a noticeable degradation of quality.

3D Graphics 15

We said earlier that the handling of 3D graphics transforms was a key motivation for AMD's introduction of 3DNow instructions and for Intel's Streaming SIMD instructions. In Section 3.6 we discussed the theory behind 3D coordinate transformations and gave assembler routines to carry out some of the key operations with AMD and Intel instructions. These routines, it was clear, were machine specific. We will now look at a complete example program written in Vector Pascal that displays a twirling 3D model on the screen. The program will, when compiled with the appropriate CPU flags, take advantage of the SSE or 3DNow instructions, but will also work correctly, albeit somewhat slower, using the Pentium instructions.

Since we are concentrating on 3D graphics transforms, and since these remain the same whether one is drawing a wire-frame or a shaded model, our example will deal with the graphics pipeline for wire-frame models. This pipeline goes from an internal representation of an object to an image on the screen as shown in Figure 15.1.

In our example we assume that there is minimal hardware support for graphics, with a simple screen buffer being the only resource available. Clearly, on many machines the line or triangle drawing and the 3D transforms might also be handled in the display card. In that case one would interface to them via OpenGL or some similar library. In our example we want to demonstrate how one can use the CPU itself to do the graphics transforms. This is in any case what one is forced to do if one is wanting to manipulate a graphical data structure for non-display purposes, since display cards do not work on data in main memory.

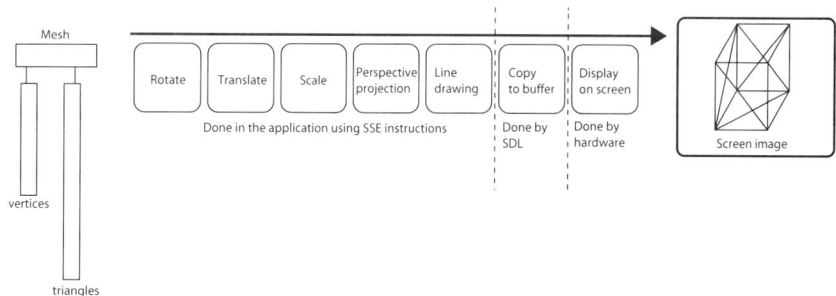

Figure 15.1. The graphics pipeline used in this chapter.

15.1 Mesh Representation

The first thing we have to decide upon is how to represent 3D objects internally. A common way is as a triangulated mesh. For instance, VRML (Virtual Reality Markup Language) uses an indexed face set notation for surface meshes. Here is an example of a VRML mesh definition:

```
DEF wrist01-ROOT Transform {
   translation 0.4645 60.36 0.5294
   children [
      Shape {
         appearance Appearance {
            material Material {
               diffuseColor 0.6082 0.1463 0.2895
               shininess 0.4
               transparency 0
            }
         }
         geometry DEF wrist01-FACES IndexedFaceSet {
            ccw TRUE
            solid TRUE
```

It is divided into a list of vertices, followed by a list of polygons. Within a VRML file the list of points is provided as a list of triples of fixed-point decimal numbers. These define coordinates in metres. The range of accuracy demanded by the VRML specification corresponds to a 128-bit binary number with 63 bits in front of the binary point and 64 bits after it. This is sufficient to represent distance ranging from the galactic to sub-atomic scales.

```
            coord DEF wrist01-COORD Coordinate { point [
-1.564 -0.6776 26.61,
-1.128 -0.8732 26.56,
-0.9983 -0.9498 26.95,
            -1.731 -0.1768 26.63,
. . . . . . .
            -0.9016 -0.7997 -27.03]
         }
```

These are then linked into polygons by a list of coordinate indices. Each polygon is terminated by a -1.

```
coordIndex [
     0, 1, 2, -1,
     3, 0, 4, -1, 5, 6, 3, -1, 7, 8, 9, -1, 10, 9, 11, -1,
     12, 13, 11, -1, 14, 12, 15, -1, 16, 14, 17, -1, 18, 16, 19, -1,
     20, 18, 21, -1, 22, 20, 23, -1, 2, 1, 22, -1, 8, 7, 6, -1,
```

A suitable Pascal unit declaring the mesh data type is

unit *mesh*;
interface
  type
    vervec(topver:*integer*) = **array** [0..*topver*,0..3] **of** *real*;
    tvervec(topver:*integer*) = **array** [0..*topver*,0..2] **of** *real*;
    trivec(toptri:*integer*) = **array**[0..*toptri*,0..2] **of** *integer*;
    pvervec =^*vervec*;
    ptrivec =^*trivec*;
    trimesh = **record**
      vertices:pvervec;
      triangles:ptrivec;
    end;
  function *mktrimesh* (**var** *vert:tvervec*;**var** *tri:trivec*):*trimesh*;
implementation
  function *mktrimesh* (**var** *vert:vervec*;**var** *tri:trivec*):*trimesh*; (see Alg. 66)
begin
end.

The representation that we use in Pascal is based on this VRML one, with certain modifications:

1. We restrict our polygons to being triangles, since these are guaranteed to be planar.
2. Consequently, the triangles do not have to be terminated by -1.
3. We represent the vertices in homogeneous coordinates, as four-element vectors, for the reasons discussed in Section 3.6.

A generator function is provided to convert mesh data in 3D vectors to 4D homogeneous coordinates.

function *mktrimesh* (**var** *vert:vervec*;**var** *tri:trivec*):*trimesh*;
var
  Let $m \in$ trimesh;
begin

with *m* **do** *begin* **begin**
    new (*vertices,vert.topver*);
    vertices↑ ← *vert*;
    vertices↑ ← 1;
    new (*triangles,tri.toptri*);
    triangles↑ ← *tri*;
  end;
  mktrimesh ← *m*;
end;

Algorithm 66. The generator function for triangle meshes.

15.2 linedemo: An Illustration of 3D Projection

We will now look at a demonstration program to display a mesh in wire-frame format. It puts the mesh up in a window and then rotates it.

The program also demonstrates a number of useful graphics concepts coded in Vector Pascal:

1. The use of the SDL interface for display purposes (see Section 15.3.2).
2. Line drawing using Bresenham's algorithm (see Section 15.6).
3. Graphics transformations for rotation of a 3D object (see Sections 15.4 and 15.3.2).
4. Graphics transforms for the projection of a 3D object on to a view-screen (see Section 15.5).

```
{$l SDL}
{$l pthread}
{$c sdl_rwops.c}
```
program linedemo;
uses SDL,mesh,paul;
const

Constants are used to define the screen setup. We use a full colour screen which allows us to use integers as pixels.

>   width = 400;
>   height = width;
>   colourdepth = 32;
>   toppixel = 3;
>   red = 0;
>   green = 1;
>   blue = 2;
>   alpha = 3;

We now declare some constants which are used to set up the viewing parameters.

>   zoom = 7 * width;
>   zoffset = 2.5;

type
>   unsignedRGBimage(row,col:*integer*) = **array** [0..row,0..col] **of** *integer*;
>   punsignedRGBimage = ^ *unsignedRGBimage*;
>   transform = **array** [0..3,0..3] **of** *real*;

It is useful to define the identity matrix or null transform first, since other transforms can be built up from these.

const
>   *identity:transform* = ((1.0, 0.0, 0.0, 0.0),
>   (0.0, 1.0, 0.0, 0.0),
>   (0.0, 0.0, 1.0, 0.0),
>   (0.0, 0.0, 0.0, 1.0));

var
  Let *unsignedbackground* ∈ punsignedRGBimage;
procedure *rotmat* (*radians:real;d:integer;***var** *t:transform*); (see Section 15.4)
procedure *BresenhamLine* (*x0,y0,x1,y1,Color:integer*); (see Section 15.6)
procedure *drawline* (*x1,y1,x2,y2:real;col:integer*); (see Section 15.5.1)
procedure *draw* (*m:trimesh;t:transform;col:integer*); (see Section 15.5)
procedure *demo3d*; (see Section 15.3)
begin
  demo3d;
end.

The program uses a dual buffer strategy with an internal buffer on which drawing takes place *bg* and a screen buffer used for display purposes *screen*. The internal buffer will be aliased to the two-dimensional array pointed to by *unsignedbackground*. The screen buffer will be aliased by SDL to the actual screen hardware. The use of two buffers ensures that the drawing and display of an image appear to the user as an atomic operation, even though it actually occurs in two phases.

15.3 demo3d: Main Procedure of linedemo

procedure *demo3d*;
var
  Let *caption,filename* ∈ pasciiarray;
  Let *screen,bg,ghost* ∈ PSDL_Surface;
  Let *colorkey* ∈ UInt32;
  Let *src,dest* ∈ SDL_Rect;
  Let *i* ∈ integer;

  Let *t,t3,t4,t5* ∈ transform;
begin

The first task is to set up the SDL regions of interest in the internal buffer and in the screen buffer. These are held as the rectangles *src* and *dest*.

src.x ← 0;
src.y ← 0;
src.w ← *width*;
src.h ← *height*;
dest ← *src*;
t ← 0;

15.3.1 Viewing Matrices

We now set up the viewing projection matrix *t* to have the form

$$t = \begin{matrix} zoom & 0 & 0 & 0 \\ 0 & -zoom & 0 & 0 \\ 0 & 0 & 1 & zoffset \\ 0 & 0 & 0 & 1 \end{matrix}$$

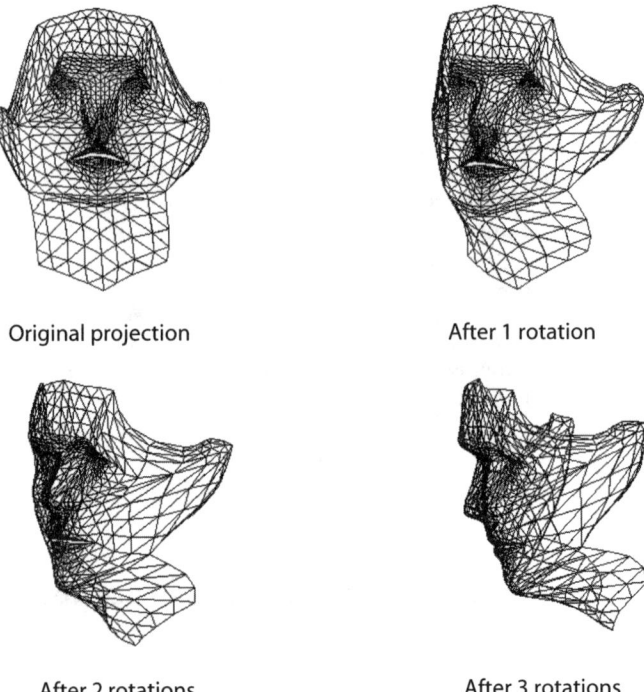

Figure 15.2. A sequence of four frames drawn by LineDemo.

and an initially null (identity) rotation transform

$$t3 = \begin{matrix} 1 & 0 & 0 & 0 \\ 0 & 1 & 0 & 0 \\ 0 & 0 & 1 & 0 \\ 0 & 0 & 0 & 1 \end{matrix}$$

$t_{0,0} \leftarrow zoom;$
$t_{1,1} \leftarrow -zoom;$
$t_{2,2} \leftarrow 1;$
$t_{3,3} \leftarrow 1;$
$t_{2,3} \leftarrow zoffset;$
$t3 \leftarrow identity;$

To understand the function of these matrices, we need to look at the virtual camera model being used. We are simulating the effect of looking at the object being modeled through a pinhole camera as shown in Figure 15.3.

An object is imaged through a pinhole on to an imaging plane, upon which an inverted version of the object will be projected. The screen of the computer is then mapped logically to a region of the image plane of the logical camera. Let us assume that all measurements are done in metres. The size of the image

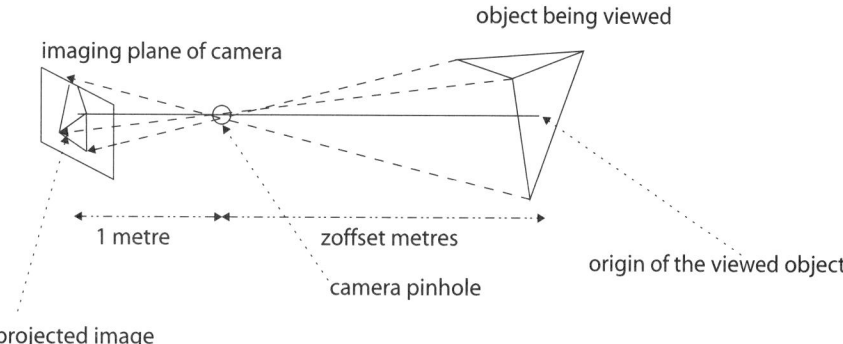

Figure 15.3. The pinhole camera model.

that will be shown on the screen varies as follows:

1. The size will vary directly with the number of pixels per metre in the imaging plane of the camera.
2. The size will vary directly with the distance between the pinhole and the imaging plane.
3. The size will vary inversely with the distance between the pinhole and the object being viewed.

We can simplify this by assuming that the image plane is at a fixed distance of 1 m from the pinhole, in which case there are only two factors influencing the scale: the distance to the object and the pixels per metre of the imaging plane. These are incorporated into the parameters *zoom* and *zoffset* in the projection matrix. The matrix mimics the effect of the pinhole by inverting around the *x*-axis, whilst scaling by *zoom* and shifting the object away from the pinhole by *zoffset*.

15.3.2 SDL Initialisation

The next section of the program is concerned with setting up the SDL interface that will display 2D images on to the screen once the 3D structure has been rendered to 2D.

SDL_Init (SDL_INIT_VIDEO);
screen ← SDL_SetVideoMode (width,height,colourdepth,SDL_DOUBLEBUF);
if *screen = nil* **then**
begin
　writeln (*'Couldn' 't initialise video mode at'* , *width*, *'x'*,
　height, *'x'*, *colourdepth*, *'bpp'*);
end
else
begin
　{Set the window caption}

```
new (caption);
string2pasciiarray ('Vector Pascal 3d Demo', caption);
SDL_WM_SetCaption (caption,nil);
dispose (caption);
```

Create a buffer of unsigned bytes to hold the image for display purposes. This has the colours packed into 32-bit pixels. We then copy the image into the buffer, permuting the indices as we do so.

```
new (unsignedbackground,height − 1,width − 1);
unsignedbackground↑ ← −1;
```

Create an SDL surface from the buffer passing in a description of its dimensions and the location of the pixel fields.

```
bg := SDL_CreateRGBSurfaceFrom (@unsignedbackground ^[0,0],
width
height
colourdepth
4 * width,
$ff,
$ff00,
$ff0000,
0
);
new (filename);
```

```
string2pasciiarray ('face00.bmp', filename);
for i ← 0 to 3 do begin begin
```

Create rotations around the y- and x-axes. This is explained more fully in Section 15.4. The rotations are selected to ensure that the images cycle with a period of 16 frames.

$$rotmat\ (\tfrac{i\times\pi}{8},1,t3);$$
$$rotmat\ (\tfrac{i\times\pi}{16},0,t4);$$

Compose the rotations into a single rotation matrix.

$$t5 \leftarrow t3.t4;$$

Combine with the viewing transform, and draw the mesh (see Section 15.5.1).

$$t4 \leftarrow t.t5;$$
```
draw (themesh,t4,0);
```

Copy the internal buffer to the screen.

```
SDL_BlitSurface (bg,@src,screen,@dest);
```

Make sure that the hardware display is updated.

```
SDL_UpdateRect (screen,0,0,0,0);
filename↑ [5] ← i + 49;
SDL_SaveBMP (bg,filename);
```

Clear the local display buffer.

        unsignedbackground↑ ← −1;
    end;
    SDL_FreeSurface (bg);
    SDL_Quit;
  end;
end;

15.4 Create a Rotation Matrix

This function produces a rotation matrix in *t* which can be used to rotate a homogeneous coordinate vector through the specified number of radians.

procedure *rotmat (radians:real;d:integer;***var** *t:transform);*

d must be in the range 0–2 to specify the rotation axis

$$\begin{matrix} 0 & \text{x axis} \\ 1 & \text{y axis} \\ 2 & \text{z axis} \end{matrix}$$

The matrix will be of the form

$$\begin{pmatrix} 1 & 0 & 0 & 0 \\ 0 & \cos\theta & -\sin\theta & 0 \\ 0 & \sin\theta & \cos\theta & 0 \\ 0 & 0 & 0 & 1 \end{pmatrix}$$

for the *x*-axis rotations, of the form

$$\begin{pmatrix} \cos\theta & -\sin\theta & 0 & 0 \\ \sin\theta & \cos\theta & 0 & 0 \\ 0 & 0 & 1 & 0 \\ 0 & 0 & 0 & 1 \end{pmatrix}$$

for the *z*-axis and of the form

$$\begin{pmatrix} \cos\theta & 0 & \sin\theta & 0 \\ 0 & 1 & 0 & 0 \\ -\sin\theta & 0 & \cos\theta & 0 \\ 0 & 0 & 0 & 1 \end{pmatrix}$$

for rotations about the *y*-axis.

var
  Let *sint,cost* ∈ real;
function *m3 (i:integer):integer;* (see Section 15.4.1)
begin
  sint ← sin(radians);

if $d = 1$ **then** *sint* ← $-sint$;
cost ← cos(*radians*);
t ← *identity*;
$t_{m3(d),m3(d)}$ ← *cost*;
$t_{m3(d+1),m3(d+1)}$ ← *cost*;
$t_{m3(d),m3(d+1)}$ ← $-sint$;
$t_{m3(d+1),m3(d)}$ ← *sint*;
end;

15.4.1 Calculate x mod 3

function *m3* (*i:integer*):*integer*;
begin *m3* := $(1 + i)$ **mod** 3;
end;

15.5 2D Projection

The procedure draw performs the 3D to 2D rendering function. The process involves taking the 3D coordinates of the vertices and determining the *x* and *y* coordinates that these will be projected to by the combined rotation, translation and viewing matrix passed into the draw function.

To do this we create a new vector of vertices *dest* to which the source vertices will be mapped.

procedure *draw* (*m:trimesh;t:transform;col:integer*);
var
  Let *dest* ∈^*vervec*;
  tri: **array** [0..2] **of** *integer*;
  Let *i,j,k,l* ∈ integer;
  newpos: **array** [0..3] **of** *real*;
begin
with *m* **do begin**
   new (*dest,vertices^.topver*);

Project to the screen coordinates using the composite transform matrix. Multiplying each vertex by the matrix will rotate it and then move it *zoffset* away from the pinhole and then scale the *x* and *y* coordinates from metres to pixels. The resultant vector is stored in *newpos*. We then store in *dest* the *x* and *y* coordinates of the point divided by the distance of the transformed point from the pinhole. As Figure 15.4 shows, this has the effect of appropriately scaling the *x,y* coordinates to take into account perspective.

   for *i* ← 0 **to** *vertices↑.topver* **do begin**
       newpos ← *t.(vertices↑[i])*;
       dest↑ [*i*,0..1] ← $\frac{newpos}{newpos_2}$;
       dest↑ [*i*,2] ← $newpos_2$;
   end;
   for *i* ← 0 **to** *triangles↑.toptri* **do**
   begin

Chapter 15 • 3D Graphics

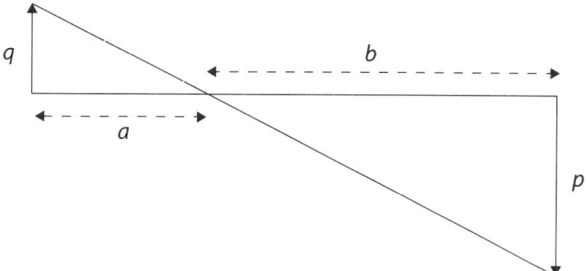

Figure 15.4. The projection triangles. p is a vector in object space and q is its image under pinhole projection. We can treat p as either the x or y component of a point in camera coordinates. a is the focal length of the virtual camera and b is the distance from the pinhole to the base of the vector. $\frac{q}{a} = \frac{p}{b}$ by similarity of triangles, thus $q = p\frac{a}{b}$ and where $a = 1$, then $q = \frac{p}{b}$.

Look up the vertices to be drawn and store them locally.

> $j \leftarrow triangles\uparrow[i,0]$;
> $k \leftarrow triangles\uparrow[i,1]$;
> $l \leftarrow triangles\uparrow[i,2]$;

Check that everything to be drawn is in front of the pinhole and then draw the three lines of the triangle using *drawline* (see Section 15.5.1).

>   **if** $(dest\uparrow[l,2] > 0)$ **and** $(dest\uparrow[j, 2] > 0)$ **and** $(dest\uparrow[k,2] > 0)$ **then**
>   **begin**
>   *drawline* $(dest\uparrow[j,0],dest\uparrow[j,1],dest\uparrow[k,0],dest\uparrow[k,1],col)$;
>   *drawline* $(dest\uparrow[k,0],dest\uparrow[k,1],dest\uparrow[l,0],dest\uparrow[l,1],col)$;
>   *drawline* $(dest\uparrow[l,0],dest\uparrow[l,1],dest\uparrow[j,0],dest\uparrow[j,1],col)$;
>   **end**;
> **end**;
> **dispose** (*dest*);
> **end**;
end;

15.5.1 Entry Point to Line Drawing

procedure *drawline* (*x1,y1,x2,y2:real;col:integer*);

Take a pair of points specified in 2D real coordinates and draw the line with the 2D origin centred on the middle of the screen. The actual drawing is done using Bresenham's algorithm.

begin
> $x1 \leftarrow x1 + \frac{width}{2}$;
> $y1 \leftarrow y1 + \frac{height}{2}$;
> $x2 \leftarrow x2 + \frac{width}{2}$;
> $y2 \leftarrow y2 + \frac{height}{2}$;
> **if** $(x1 \geq 0)$ **and** $(y1 \geq 0)$ **and** $(x2 \geq 0)$ **and** $(y2 \geq 0)$ **and**

then
  BresenhamLine (**round**(*x1*),**round**(*y1*),**round**(*x2*),**round**(*y2*),*col*);
end;

15.6 Bresenham Line Drawing Procedure

We use a fast and efficient line drawing algorithm due to Bresenham. This involves only adding and subtracting in its inner loop.

Consider drawing a line on a raster grid where we restrict the allowable slopes of the line m to the range $0 \leq m \leq 1$. We restrict the procedure so that it always increments x as it goes. After drawing a point at (x,y), there are two choices for the next point on the line:

1. point $(x+1, y)$
2. point $(x+1, y+1)$.

Hence, when working in the first positive octant of the plane, line drawing becomes a matter of deciding between two possibilities at each step. Each time we plot a point on the raster grid we make an error ϵ in the y direction relative to the real-valued point determined by the equation of the line. We will choose to plot $(x+1, y)$ if ϵ is less than 0.5, otherwise we will plot $(x+1, y+1)$. This will minimise the total error between the mathematical line and what is drawn.

let $\delta_x = x1 - x0$
let $\delta_y = y2 - y1$
with $\delta_x \geq \delta_y$

All other types of lines can be derived from this type. First perform the following initialisation:

```
x:=x0;
y:=y0;
d:=(2*deltay)-deltax;
```

Loop from $x0$ to $x1$ and for each loop perform the following operations for each x position: all multiplications are by 2. If we pre-multiply dx and dy by 2, we can remove all multiplications from the inner loop. The complete procedure is given in Alg. 67.

```
PutPixel(x,y); {Draw a pixel at the current point}
if d<0 then
d:=d+(2*deltay)
else
d:=d+2*(deltay-deltax);
y:=y+1;
end;
x:=x+1;
```

```
procedure BresenhamLine (x0,y0, x1,y1,Color:integer);
var
    Let dy,dx,stepx,stepy,fraction ∈ integer;
begin
    dy ← y1 − y0;
    dx ← x1 − x0;
    if dy < 0 then
    begin
        dy ← −dy;
        stepy ← −1;
    end
    else stepy ← 1;
    if dx < 0 then
    begin
        dx ← −dx;
        stepx ← −1;
    end
    else stepx ← 1;
    dy ← dy × 2;
    dx ← dx × 2;
    (* Set pixel at x0, y0*}
    unsignedbackground↑[y0,x0] ← color;
    if dx > dy then
    begin
        fraction ← dy − (dx 1);
        while x0 ≠ x1 do
        begin
            if fraction ≥ 0 then
            begin
                y0 ← y0 + stepy;
                fraction ← fraction − dx;
            end;
            x0 ← x0 + stepx;
            fraction ← fraction + dy;
            unsignedbackground↑[y0,x0] ← color;
        end
    end
    else
    begin
        fraction ← dx − (dy 1);
        while y0 ≠ y1 do
        begin
            if fraction ≥ 0 then
            begin
                x0 ← x0 + stepx;
                fraction ← fraction − dy;
            end;
            y0 ← y0 + stepy;
            fraction ← fraction + dx;
            unsignedbackground↑[y0,x0] ← color;
        end
    end
end;
```

= 2*dy − dx

Algorithm 67. Bresenham's algorithm in Pascal.

Table 15.1. Relative performance

Target processor	Time (ms)	Relative speed (%)
Pentium	3720	100
P4	2650	140

15.7 Performance

The relative performance of vectorised and sequential versions of the program are given in Table 15.1.

The program was timed for 200 iterations of the main loop, using the model shown in Figure 15.2. This model contains 706 vertices and 1326 triangles. Timings were done on a 1.7 GHz P4. Thus all parameters other than the instruction-set used were held constant. The use of SSE instructions does appear to give some gain in performance, although, since these are not the only instructions added by the P4 processor, some of the gains may be due to other new opcodes. It should, of course, be remembered that a considerable part of the program time will be taken up by line drawing and updating the screen buffer, and will therefore not benefit from floating-point vectorisation.

Part IV
VIPER
Ken Renfrew

Introduction to VIPER 16

16.1 Rationale

When originally developed, Vector Pascal used a command line compiler operating in the classical Unix fashion. This interface is documented in Appendix C. However it has been conventional, at least since the release of UCSD Pascal in the late 1970s, for Pascal Compilers to be provided with an integrated development environment (IDE). The Vector Pascal IDE provides the usual capabilities of such environments, but with the additional feature of literate programming support.

16.1.1 The Literate Programming Tool

Today's pace of technological development seems to be rising beyond anything that could have been conceived only a few decades ago. It is a common "joke" that any piece of modern technology is 6 months out of date by the time it reaches the showroom.

Software development is one of the fastest moving areas of this technological stampede. With development happening at such a rate, documentation is often at best a few steps behind the reality of the code of any system. Hence anyone attempting to maintain a system is left to their own ingenuity and some out-of-date documentation.

The constant updating of this documentation would in fact almost certainly be a more time-consuming task than developing the program in the first place and hence time spent in this area can often be regarded as non-productive time.

Several attempts have been made at automating this process. The automation process is often termed literate programming. The two most successful of these are web (Knuth, 1984), a development of the TeX system which is the forefather of LaTeX (Lamport, 1994) developed by Leslie Lamport that is so widely used today, and JAVADOC. The JAVADOC system was developed by Sun Micro-systems to document programs written in JAVA by including the document details inside specially marked comments [Sch1].

The Vector Pascal literate programming tool will combine these two approaches by allowing the programmer to embed LaTeX commands within special comment markers. These will still be able to be parsed by a conventional Pascal compiler, allowing the system to be used for conventional Pascal programming.

The embedding of LaTeX commands in the program is not compulsory for those wishing to use the tool. There is a user-selectable scale of detail that will be included automatically in documentation even from a normal Pascal program.

In addition, in an attempt to make the programs' idiosyncrasies more readable and to present the programs' arguments more conventionally, there is the option of using a "mathematical syntax converter" which will change some of the more impenetrable code into conventional mathematical symbolism,[1] the finished document being written by the system in LaTeX to allow straight compilation into a postscript or .pdf document formats.

To aid further the documentation, the variables declared within the program will be cross-referenced to their instantiation point, allowing a reader to cross-reference a variable and thus remind themselves of its exact nature.

This brief description clearly shows the aids that a literate programming tool would bring to the programmer, allowing documentation to be both kept up to date and in fact created retrospectively from existing code.

16.1.2 The Mathematical Syntax Converter

A computer program by its very nature has a structure which allows it to be read by a machine. Modern high-level languages have abstracted themselves from this very successfully but nevertheless owing to this underlying requirement the syntax of a program language can hide the program's algorithm from a human reader.

Programmers often use pseudo-code to explain algorithmic arguments. Mathematical notation is usually the most clear and precise way of presenting this argument. The mathematical converter allows a developer to use this system to convert the Pascal syntax into something closer to mathematical notation[2] and much more presentable to the human reader.

This feature is unique[3] in a programming interface and provides a further level of documentation. The documentation of the algorithms involved in the program, which are arguably the program's most valuable assets.

16.2 A System Overview

As can be seen from the rationale above, the system breaks into three main sections: the program editor with the compiler, the literate programming tool and the mathematical syntax converter.

It is hoped that an improvement in performance of the supplied compiler can be achieved by statically loading the compiler's class files for all target processors[4] at start-up rather than the dynamic loading currently employed.

The IDE will follow the traditional approach, offering similar facilities to that of many other editors for different languages on the market.

---

[1] Refer to separate section for the rationale of the maths syntax converter.
[2] Precise mathematical notation, although perhaps desirable, is a more complex operation than the time allotted to the project would allow but none the less an interesting development for the future.
[3] Unique to the best of our knowledge at the time of writing.
[4] Processors currently supported are the Intel 486, Pentium P3 and Athlon K6.

Among these facilities are a syntax highlighting (for Vector Pascal, LaTeX and HTML), a project manager with automatic make file facility, the ability to run a program in the environment with redirected input and output, a function and procedure finder linked to the source code, an error line highlighter for compilation errors, an external process runner for LaTeX compilers, TeX to HTML converters and a mini browser to show approximate results of the Literate programming tool.

The Literate programming tool has been described in its rationale and incorporates the unique mathematical syntax conversion allowing a program to be converted to a mathematical argument literally at the touch of a button.

16.3   Which VIPER to Download?

VIPER is platform independent for the operating systems it supports. These operating systems are

- Linux
- Windows 9x
- Windows NT/2000/XP.

The only decision to make on the VIPER download is whether the source code is required. The source version, although much larger, contains the source code for the VIPER IDE and the Vector Pascal compiler and all files required for a developer to develop or adapt further any of the systems within VIPER. The class file download provides the required files to have an operational VIPER installation.

16.4   System Dependencies

VIPER depends on several pieces of software, all of which are freely available to download from various sources. The vital dependencies are

- Java 1.3 or newer.
- The NASM assembler.
- The gcc linker, included in Linux installations; for Windows use the cygwin or DJGPP versions of the gcc linker.

For full functionality the following systems are also required:

- A LaTeX installation. LaTeX usually comes with Linux installations. The total MiKTeX package is recommended for all Windows installations.
- A dvi viewer, usually included with a LaTeX installation. The YAP viewer included with MiKTeX is particularly recommended.
- A TeX to `HTML` converter. TTH was used in the development of the system.

It is recommended that all of the above programs are set up according to their own installation instructions and the appropriate class path established to suit the host machine's operating system.

16.5 Installing Files

Assuming that the VIPER files have been downloaded to a suitable place on the host machine, the actual installation can begin. The only decision that must be made is where to install VIPER. VIPER can be installed anywhere on the host machine provided that there are no spaces in the directory path of the target directory.

Once this decision has been made, the .zip file should be unzipped using a proprietary zip tool (e.g. WinZip, zip magic) to the source directory.

When the .zip file has been unzipped, there will be a directory called Vector Pascal in the target directory. Vector Pascal is the home directory of the VIPER system.

VIPER may be launched by

- All installations. Open a shell/DOS window change to the VIPER home directory and type the command `java viper.Viper`, taking care of the capital letter.
- Windows installations. The batch file viper.bat is included in the VIPER home directory; running this will start VIPER. A shortcut to this batch file should be placed on the host machine's desktop for the easiest start-up.
- Linux installations. The shell script viper.sh is included in the VIPER home directory; running this will start VIPER.

16.6 Setting Up the Compiler

VIPER detects the operating system installed at start-up and then moves a suitable run time library into the .../VectorPascal/ilcg/Pascal directory where it will be available for the compiler. This is done automatically each time that VIPER is started.

The compiler options will need to be set up along with the personal set-up preferred for the installation (see Section 16.7.2). The file type for the linker will need set-up. These options are

- for Linux or Windows using the Cygwin gcc use "elf"
- for Windows using the DJGPP linker use "coff".

It is important to read through the user guide to avoid learning the system the painful way!

16.7 Setting Up the System

VIPER automatically sets the compiler flags to suit the operating system on the host machine. For those who have used the Vector Pascal compiler with a command line interface, this means that the -U flag is set for Windows 9x and Windows NT installations, and not set for Linux/UNIX installations, the -o flag is set to produce an exe file with the same name as the Pascal source file. The

Figure 16.1. File format entries in Compiler Options.

.asm file and .o files are similarly named. If these flags mean nothing then that is not a problem: either ignore the preceding information or see the Vector Pascal reference manual in the help files of the VIPER system.

VIPER cannot, however, detect the versions of the gcc linker installed, this is left for the user. The -f flag of the compiler tells the compiler the file format to be used. To set this, go to Set-up/Compiler Options/Options, click the -f button and enter the file format into the adjacent text field. The format should be

- Linux Installations and Windows installations with Cygwin gcc linker format is elf.
- Windows with DJGPP linker format is coff.

The other options on the Compiler Options window are as follows:

- Smart serializes/de-serializes the code tree for the processor. This allows the compiler to 'learn' how to respond quickly to a given code segment.
- S suppresses the assembly and linking of the program (an assembler file is still produced).
- V causes the compiler to produce a verbose output to MyProg.lst when compiling MyProg.pas.
- CPUtag. This option is used in conjunction with the -cpu option. It prefixes the .exe file with the name of the CPU for which the compiler is set. when this option is used the .exe cannot be run in the IDE.
- -cpu. This option allow the source file to be compiled to a range of processors. To produce an .exe file for a range of processors the CPU tag should be set. This prevents the .exe file from being overwritten by the next compilation for a different processor. Subsequent compilations for the same processor, however, will be overwritten. Select the CPU from the list in the drop-down menu adjacent to the -cpu button.
- -ISO (not yet implemented on the Vector Pascal compiler). Compiles to ISO Standard Pascal.

16.7.1 Setting System Dependencies

VIPER depends on various other systems for full functionality. These are set in Set-up/Compiler Options/Dependencies. The fields are as follows:

1. Source Compiler. This option is only editable if the Default Compiler option is not set. This is the command that would run the compiler from the Vector Pascal directory.

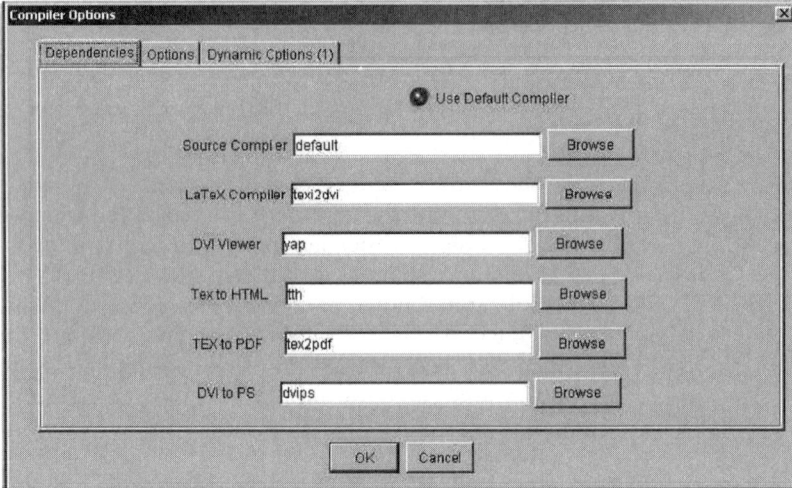

Figure 16.2. Dependencies window.

2. This is the command required to run LaTeX and is required for VPTeX to work. The recommended option for this field is `texi2dvi`.
3. DVI viewer. The dvi viewer that is to be used to view the LaTeX recommended option is YAP (Windows installations).
4. Tex to HTML. If a converter is installed on the host machine, then put the command in this field.
5. Tex to PDF. Enter the command used to convert TeX to PDF.
6. DVI to PS. Command to convert DVI files to Post Script (usually dvips).

16.7.2 Personal Set-up

Viper allows the user many options to cater for different tastes and programming styles. It is not crucial to the system to set these options but it does make for a more comfortable programming environment.

If the VIPER installation is on a network, each user may have a different personal set-up, provided that each user has a separate home directory. VIPER installs a file called `viper.properties` into this directory and updates this file whenever a change is made to the system set-up.

Note: The individual set-up should not be attempted when multiple files are open. If this is done then no harm comes to the system or any of the open files, but users may experience difficulty in closing one or more files. The solution is to use Window/Close All to close all the files. The system can then be used as normal.

Viper Options

In the Set-up menu there is the Viper Options menu option. In this are all the familiar IDE options such as font size and style, icon sizes, syntax colours, look and feel, etc.

Chapter 16 • Introduction to VIPER

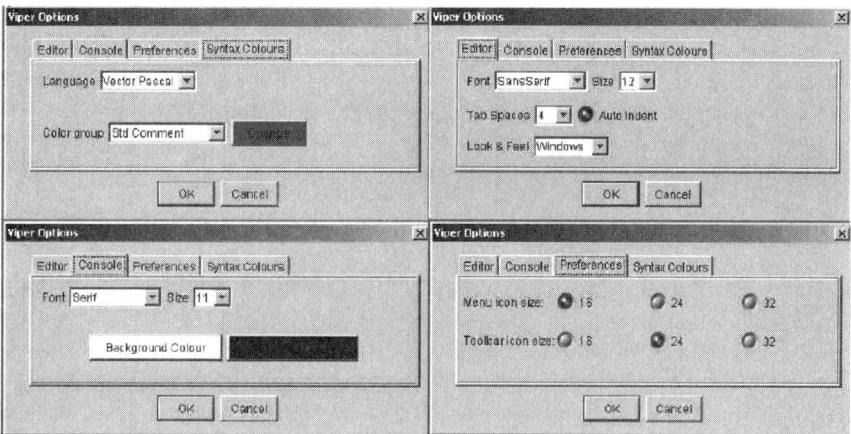

Figure 16.3. The Viper Option windows.

The different windows shown in Figure 16.3 allow the control of the VIPER IDE. The individual windows control

- **Editor.** This controls the look and feel, the font size and style, the tab size and auto indentation.
- **Console.** This controls the font style and size and the background colour of the console window.
- **Preferences.** This allows the individual set-up of the menu icon sizes and the toolbar sizes.
- **Syntax Colours.** This allows the syntax highlighting colours to be altered to personal taste. These can be adjusted for each supported language (Vector Pascal, LaTeX, HTML) independently.

16.7.3 Dynamic Compiler Options

Note: This is for advanced use only.
This feature is intended to allow VIPER to handle

- new processors as the class files become available (dynamic class loading only)
- new options for the compiler/new versions of the compiler.

The dynamically created options pages are added in the form of a new tabbed pane to the Compiler Options window (Figure 16.4). To create a new options pane the user must:

1. Open the file . . . /VectorPascal/viper/resources/dynamicOption.properties
2. Edit the file to suit the new options.
3. Save the file.

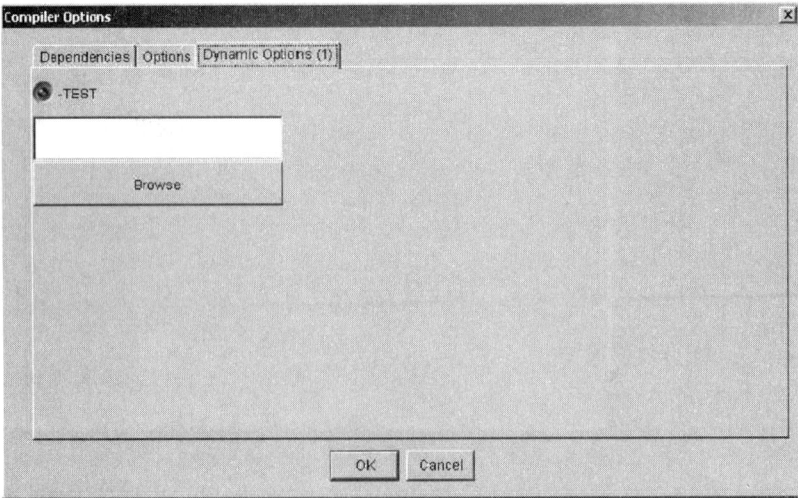

Figure 16.4. Dynamic Option window.

Editing to Add a Processor

In the file dynamicoptions.properties in the .../VectorPascal/viper/resources directory there is a list of the current processors. This list can be extended simply by adding another to the end of the list. It is best if the list ends with "others".

Note: The appropriate code generator files must be written for the Vector Pascal compiler and placed in the .../VectorPascal/ilcg/tree directory.

Editing to Add Compiler Options

The dynamicoptions.properties file can be edited to produce a new compiler option. This is done by entering a new line at the end of the file following the line above. For example:

```
CPUFLAGS:P3:K6:Pentium:IA32
#
#This is to set flags for the compiler
#NB DO NOT EDIT THIS FILE BEFORE AFTER READING THE HELP FILE
#IT IS IMPORTANT THAT THE FIELDS COME IN THE FOLLOWING ORDER
#FLAG(Type:String),DESCRIPTION(Type:String),
TEXTFIELD(Type:int),
#BROWSEBUTTON(Type: boolean)
#Any comments must be but in this area.

FLAG:DESCRIPTION:TEXTFIELD:BROWSEBUTTON
-TEST:Test description:20:true:
```

16.7.4 VIPER Option Buttons

The VIPER options are set in their respective panels with the VIPER option buttons. These have three states:

- **Grey.** The item is not selected.
- **Red.** The mouse is over the correct areas to select the item.
- **Blue.** The item is selected.

16.8 Moving VIPER

Ideally, VIPER should be installed from the downloaded zip file on any new system. If this is not possible then it is still possible to move VIPER on to a new system even if the new host machine has a different operating system.

Moving a VIPER installation from any Windows host to any other Windows host, or from one Linux installation to another is straightforward:

1. Move the entire VectorPascal directory and all sub-directories to the new system.
2. Run VIPER and in the File menu click clear recent files and then click clear recent projects.
3. Import all projects that have been moved and are to be used on the new system.

If the operating systems are different (i.e. moving from Linux to Windows or vice versa), then the system must be reset:

1. Open a shell/DOS prompt window and change directories to the VectorPascal directory.
2. Type `java ViperSystemReset` in the console window.

The system is now reset and the new installation of VIPER can be used normally.

16.9 Programming with VIPER

This section assumes that the IDE is now set up to the user's taste. To open a file, click the open file menu option and use the dialogue box to open the file in the usual way.

Familiarity with the basic editing functions of an IDE is assumed.

16.9.1 Single Files

The file will open with the syntax highlighter associated with the file suffix of the target file. The file can be edited with all the usual IDE functions (Cut, Paste, Copy, Save, Save As, Find and Replace, etc.).

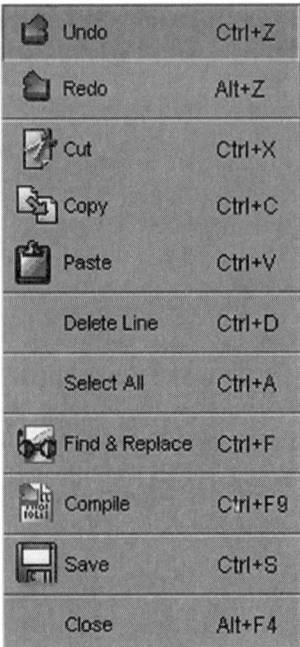

Figure 16.5. The right click menu.

VIPER features a "right click menu" to offer another method of quickly editing files (Figure 16.5).

Line numbers can be viewed either by using the statistics on the status bar at the bottom right-hand corner of the IDE or by double clicking the dark-grey panel on the left of the editor window; this line number panel can then be adjusted in size to suit the user's needs.

A new file can be opened from the file menu. Clicking on the New Document option allows the user to choose between the three types of file that VIPER supports (Pascal, LaTeX, HTML). A new file is then opened in the editor window. The file is un-named until it has been saved.

When a file has been changed since it was last saved, the name tag at the top of the editor window appears in red, otherwise it is black.

If the user attempts to close the editor before a file has been saved, the option to save the file is offered before the IDE closes.

If a file has functions and/or procedures, the function finder automatically displays these in the leftmost editor window. Clicking on the icon by a function or procedure takes the editor to the start of that section.

16.9.2 Projects

The VIPER Project Manager allows the user to construct software projects in Vector Pascal.

An existing project can be opened using the Project/Open Project menu option or icon. The project will then appear in the project window. The file

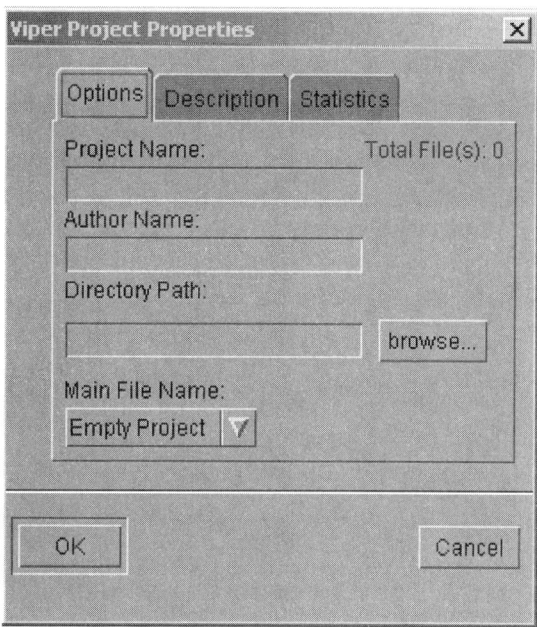

Figure 16.6. The Project Properties window.

names are in a tree structure which can be clicked to open the file in the editor window.

To create a new project, the user clicks on the new project icon and the Project Properties dialogue box will appear (Figure 16.6).

The text fields are then filled in to create the empty project. The directory path should be the parent directory for the project's home directory. This home directory will be given the project's name.

Once the project has been created, the files can be added and removed as required:

- **Adding.** Click the Add Files icon and enter or browse for the required file. This copies the file to the project directory.
- **Removing.** Highlight the file to be removed and click the Remove Files icon. **Warning.** This deletes the file from the project directory.

Other files may be placed in the project directory but if they are not added to the project they will not be a member of the project.

The makefile for the project is automatically created as ProjectName.mke. The user should not edit either this or the .prj file directly.

Importing Projects

Projects can be imported from other VIPER installations by the import project facility. This can be found in Project/Import Project. Any project coming from another VIPER must be imported via this facility.

Backing-up Projects

The import project facility can be used to move an existing project to another directory of the same machine. This Back-Up project is not just a copy of the project but is fully functional with all the facilities of the VIPER system.

16.9.3 Embedding LaTeX in Vector Pascal

The special comment (*! comment body *) is used to embed LaTeX in the Vector Pascal source file. Anything within these comments will be treated as if it were LaTeX both by the VPTEX system and the syntax highlighter.

There is no need to put LaTeX commands in the special comments unless a specific result is required (see Section 16.15).

16.10 Compiling Files in VIPER

16.10.1 Compiling Single Files

Assuming the compiler has been set up, the compilation of a file is very simple. Simply click the Compile icon (or menu option) and the compiler will compile the file in the editor window with the options selected.

The resulting files are placed in the same directory as the source file and are named the same as the source file with the corresponding suffix.

Compiling a File to Executable for Several Processors

If a file is to be compiled for several different processors, the CPUTAG and -CPU options must be set in the Set-up/Compiler Options/Options panel. The file MyProg.pas would then be compiled to ProcessorNameMyProg.exe. This process can be done for each processor on the available processor list.

Note: A file compiled in this manner cannot be run within the IDE.

16.10.2 Compiling Projects

Projects can be compiled in two ways:

- Make a project. This compiles the files that are not up-to-date but does not compile any file that is up-to-date.
- Build a project. This compiles all the files in the project regardless of whether the files are up-to-date.

The Vector Pascal compiler used in the traditional command line interface mode will check one level of dependency in a project. If there are more levels of dependency the VIPER project manager will automatically make a `makefile` and recursively check all levels of dependency in the project.

As VIPER compiles a file, the file is opened in the IDE and if an error is found compilation stops and the error is highlighted.

16.11 Running Programs in VIPER

Note: Projects requiring input from the user **must** have the input redirected.

When a program has been compiled, the resulting executable can be run in the IDE by clicking on the Run icon. A redirect input box then appears (Figure 16.7). If the program requires input from the user then an input file must be set. This file should contain all the data that the program requires to run to completion.

Similarly, the output may be redirected. This, however, is not compulsory; if the output is not redirected, the output of the program appears in the console window. If the output is redirected then the output is written to the file set-up in the run dialogue window.

16.12 Making VPTEX

Making VPTEX is as simple as clicking the Build VPTEX icon or menu option. If a project is open then the VPTEX is made for the whole project, otherwise the VPTEX is made for the file in the editor window.

16.12.1 VPTEX Options

The level of documentation is set by the user in the VPTEX Options panel (Figure 16.8). This panel can be found in the TEX/VPTEX Options menu item. There are five levels of detail that can be chosen:

- Function and Procedure headings only
- level 1 plus all special comments

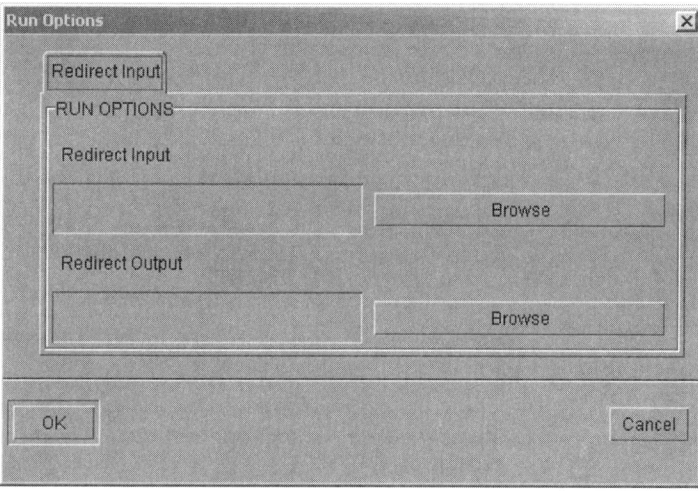

Figure 16.7. The Run Options panel.

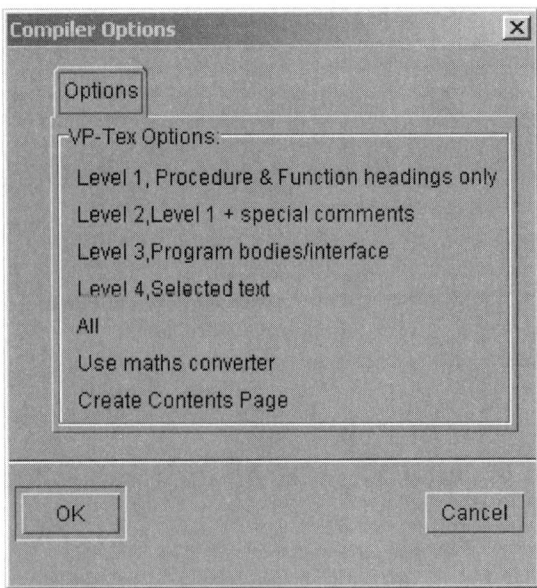

Figure 16.8. The VPTEX Options panel.

- program bodies and interfaces
- selected text
- all source code.

In addition to the above options, the user can choose whether a contents page is to be included or not. This is set by clicking the Create Contents Page button.

16.12.2 VPMath

The VPMath system converts Vector Pascal code to mathematical syntax. This makes the program more human readable and in general more concise.

The VPMath system is invoked automatically when the VPTEX is made if the Use Math Converter is set in the Tex/VPTEX Options menu item.

16.13 LATEX in VIPER

Most of the features of the VIPER editor used in the creation/editing of Vector Pascal files can also be used for creating/editing LATEX documents.

Opening a LATEX document in VIPER automatically invokes the LATEX syntax highlighter and the Function Methods finder automatically changes to a Section/Sub-section finder.

This allows the user to click on a Section icon in the left-hand window and the editor will jump to that section.

16.14 HTML in VIPER

VIPER allows the user to edit/write HTML pages. The system for HTML is very straightforward. Create a new HTML file or open an existing file to be edited. Once the file has been altered, click on the run button just as if to run a Vector Pascal executable.

When a new HTML file is created or an existing one opened, the HTML syntax highlighter is automatically loaded.

The default browser that is installed on the host machine will open with the HTML page displayed.

16.15 Writing Code to Generate Good VPTEX

VPTEX is a tool included in the VIPER IDE for Vector Pascal. It automatically produces and formats a LaTeX listing of the source file or files on which it is called. By defining three distinct types of comments, VPTEX also allows the programmer to add extensive descriptions of their code to the listing, creating full LaTeX documentation for their Vector Pascal programs or projects. Mathematical translation can also be performed on the source code listing to produce a more generic and succinct description of the program's algorithms and structures.

The three types of comments available are as follows:

Special Comments: A special comment is started in the source code with the comment command (*! and terminated with *). Special comments appear in the LaTeX as running prose and are of most use in giving extensive comments and descriptions of the program. Special comments can include LaTeX commands, with some limitations, to improve further the readability of the documentation.

Margin Comments: Normal Pascal {...} comments which appear immediately at the end of a line of code are placed in the left-hand margin adjacent to their source code line in the LaTeX documentation. These are of principal use when a small description of the content of a single line is required.

Normal Comments: Normal Pascal {...} comments which appear on a line of their own will appear in the LaTeX in typewriter font.

16.15.1 Use of Special Comments

As outlined above, special comments are the principal means of describing a program in the documentation. To maximise the effectiveness of the literate programming facility, source code should be written with large amounts of special comments and with the program's documentation in mind. The ability to include LaTeX commands within special comments allows the programmer to affect directly the look of the LaTeX documentation, but there are some limits to the use of LaTeX commands within special comments:

- Do not include any preamble within special comments. The preamble for the LaTeX documents is automatically produced by VPTEX.
- Always use full text series altering commands such as \textbf{...} rather than their shorthand equivalents such as \bf{...}.
- Bear in mind that any text entered in special comments must be compilable LaTeX for the documentation to compile. This means that the following characters are control characters and should not be entered verbatim into special comments: & $ % _ { } ^ ~ \.

Special comments can be particularly useful for controlling the structure of a LaTeX document. The following are guidelines as to how to structure the documentation.

- For an individual program or unit file, the LaTeX document produced by VPTEX will be an article, so sections are the highest level description that can be applied to a block of text.
- It is usually useful to include an introduction to the program at the start of the Pascal source file using the \section{Introduction} command at the start of an opening special comment.
- A special comment containing just a structure command (\section, \subsection, etc.) can be extremely useful in sectioning off different parts of the source code to add structure to the code listing. For example, the declarations could be prefaced with (*! \section{Declarations} *) or the main program could be prefaced with a similar command. Each procedure or function is automatically placed within its own section by VPTEX, so do not add structuring special comments to these sections of code.

To produce a well-documented program, it is important that special comments are regularly employed to add verbose descriptions of the source code. It is not uncommon for a LaTeX documentation file to contain many pages of special comments split into sections and subsections between small sections of code. VPTEX also automatically creates a contents page so the structure of the special comments will be reflected in the contents page.

Note: With the current release of the Vector Pascal compiler, special comments containing *s other than at the opening (*! and closing *) tags will not compile.

16.15.2 Use of Margin Comments

Margin comments are useful for providing short descriptions of the purpose of individual lines of code. If the meaning of a particular code line is especially cryptic, or the significance of the line needs to be emphasised, a margin comment stating the purpose of that line may be useful. It should be noted that because margin comments necessarily reside in the left-hand margin of the finished document, lengthy comments will spill on to many lines and break up the flow of the code. It is advised that margin comments should not be more than 10 or so words, with the other types of comments available if a longer description is required.

The VPTEX tool automatically breaks lines following the **var** and **const** keywords. Therefore, the declaration following these keywords will be placed on a new line, but any margin comment for this line will not. It is recommended that the programmer takes a new line after the **var** and **const** keywords.

16.15.3 Use of Ordinary Pascal Comments

The function of normal Pascal comments has been superseded in most cases by VPTEX's Special Comments. However, normal comments can still be useful in a number of circumstances. The following list details the recommended usage of normal Pascal comments, but the user is, of course, free to make use of them in any particular circumstances.

- First, because normal comments are displayed in typewriter font, any spacing within these comments set out by the programmer will be preserved in the documentation. This is not the case for special comments which are displayed in a serifed, variable-width font. This property of normal comments makes them particularly suitable for laying out tables and arrays simply, although a special comment can make use of LaTeX's ability to typeset tables for a more advanced layout.
- Second, normal comments do not break up the flow of a code listing to the same extent as special comments and so are more useful for offering a running commentary on code lines, without the space limitations of margin comments.
- If a comment is reasonably short, the programmer may find that a normal comment will have a better appearance than a special comment. Since special comments are offset from the program, listing a small special comment may constitute a waste of the space set aside for it.

16.15.4 Levels of Detail Within Documentation

Depending on the sort of documentation required, VPTEX allows the programmer to specify the detail of the program documentation. The five levels are:

1. **Procedure and Function Headings Only:** For documentation of ADTs it is often useful simply to provide a list of the functions and procedures by which a programmer may make use of the ADT. VPTEX supports this by providing the option to create documentation consisting of only function and procedure headings. It is advised that a contents page is not included with this level of detail.
2. **Special Comments with Function and Procedure Headings:** To add commentary and descriptions to the above level of detail, option 2 will add any special comments to the documentation. This allows the programmer

to provide descriptions of their procedures and functions and to add structure to the documentation. A contents page is advised for this level of detail.

3. **Program Bodies and Unit Interfaces:** This level of detail includes all comments. It is again very useful for documenting ADTs as the interfaces provided by units will be documented, but none of the implementation will be included. A contents page is recommended.

4. **Selected Text:** Special VPTEX comments commands have been defined to allow the programmer to select which sections of the program to document. The commands are (*!begin*) to mark the start of a selected region, and (*!end*) to mark the end. Any text, including special comments, not contained within these tags will be ignored by VPTEX if this level of detail is selected. The start and end of the main program file will always be included in the documentation regardless of selection. This feature is of particular use when preparing reports regarding particular sections of code within long projects as only the sections of interest will be documented. Again, a contents page is recommended.

5. **All Code and Comments:** For a completely documented code listing, of particular use for system maintenance, VPTEX can produce a complete listing of a program or project's source code, including special and normal comments. A contents page is strongly recommended, particularly for long programs or projects.

Note: All levels of detail support margin comments.

16.15.5 Mathematical Translation: Motivation and Guidelines

VPTEX has the option of automatically translating the program code into conventional mathematical notation. Complex VectorPascal expressions such as

`x:=if(iota 0 div 2 pow (dim-iota 1)) mod 2=0 then 1 else -1;`

are translated into more tidy and comprehensible mathematical representations such as

$$x \leftarrow \begin{cases} 1 & \text{if } \left(\frac{\iota_0}{2^{dim-\iota_1}}\right) \mathbf{mod}\ 2 = 0 \\ 0 & \text{otherwise} \end{cases};$$

No action is required to obtain mathematical translation, provided that it is turned on (VPTEX Options). However, the benefits of using it increase with the number of mathematical structures in the document. In particular, the following will benefit from mathematical translation:

- array indexing/slicing, e.g thisArray$_{i,j}$/thatArray$_{low...high}$
- assignments, e.g. myVariable $\leftarrow$ yourVariable
- reduction operations on arrays, e.g. myVariable $\leftarrow \sum$oneDArray
- conditional updates (as shown above)
- a number of standard mathematical function such as $\sqrt{\ }$

- mathematical operations, e.g. x^y, $\frac{a}{b}$, $i \times j$
- English names of Greek letters (lower-case only), e.g. α, β, γ, δ.

Mathematical translation is particularly useful if the documentation is for people without knowledge of Pascal or a similar language. The only time when mathematical translation is not advisable is when the reader is maintaining the code itself, in which case the need for cross-reference will usually dominate the need for clarity and conventional notation.

16.15.6 LaTeX Packages

All VPTEX documents only include packages `graphicx` and `epsfig`. These packages are included to allow the programmer to include graphics and diagrams to help document their programs. Any LaTeX commands that the programmer may wish to use which are specific to other packages cannot be included in VPTEX special comments.

Appendix A: Compiler Porting Tools

Vector Pascal is an open-source project. It aims to create a productive and efficient program development environment for SIMD programming. In order to validate the concepts it has been developed initially for the Intel family of processors running Linux and Microsoft Windows. However, it has been intended from the outset that the technology should be portable to other families of CPUs. This Appendix addresses some of the issues involved in porting the compiler to new systems.

A.1 Dependencies

The Vector Pascal compiler tool-set can be divided along two axes as shown in Figure A.1.

1. Tools can be divided into (a) those provided as part of the release and (b) those provided as part of the operating environment.
   (a) These are mainly written in Java, the exceptions being a small run-time library in C, a Pascal System unit and several machine descriptions.
   (b) These are all available as standard under Linux, and Windows versions are freely downloadable from the web.
2. Tools can further be divided into (a) those required for program preparation and documentation, (b) those for code translation tools and (c) those for code generator preparation.
   (a) The program preparation tools are the VIPER IDE described in Chapter 16, along with the standard LaTeX document preparation system, DVI viewers and the TTH tool to prepare web-enabled versions of Vector Pascal program descriptions.
   (b) The program translation tools are:
      i. The `ilcg.pascal` Java package which contains the Pascal compiler itself and classes to support Pascal-type declarations. This carries out the first stage of code translation, from Pascal to an ILCG tree (Cockshott, 2000).
      ii. A set of machine-generated code generators for CPUs such as the Pentium and the K6. These carry out the second phase of code translation – into an assembler file.
      iii. The `ilcg.tree` Java package, which supports the internal representation of ILCG trees (see Section A.3).

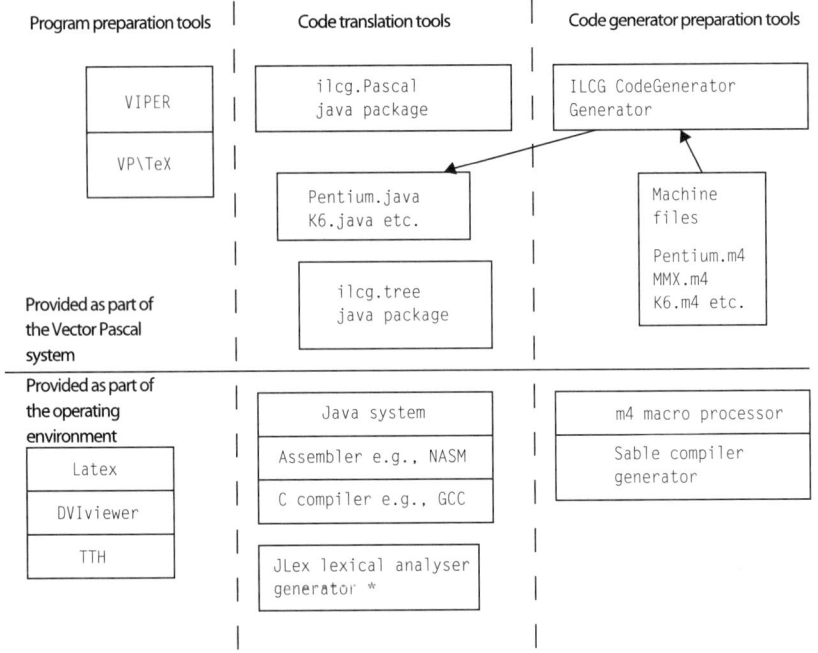

Figure A.1. Vector Pascal toolset.

iv. The Java system, which is needed to run all of the above.
v. An assembler, which is necessary to carry out the third phase of code translation, from an assembler file to a relocatable object file.
vi. A C compiler and linkage system is needed to compile the C run-time library and to link the relocatable object files into final executables.
vii. In addition, if one wants to alter the reserved words of Vector Pascal or make other lexical changes, one needs the JLex lexical analyser generator.

A.2 Compiler Structure

The structure of the Vector Pascal translation system is shown in Figure A.2. The main program class of the compiler `ilcg.Pascal.PascalCompiler.java` translates the source code of the program into an internal structure called an ILCG tree (Cockshott, 2000). A machine-generated code generator then translates this into assembler code. An example would be the class ilcg.tree.IA32. An assembler and linker specified in descendent class of the code generator then translate the assembler code into an executable file.

Consider first the path followed from a source file. The phases that it goes through are

- The source file (1) is parsed by a Java class PascalCompiler.class (2), a hand-written, recursive descent parser (Watt and Brown, 2000), and results

Appendix A • Compiler Porting Tools

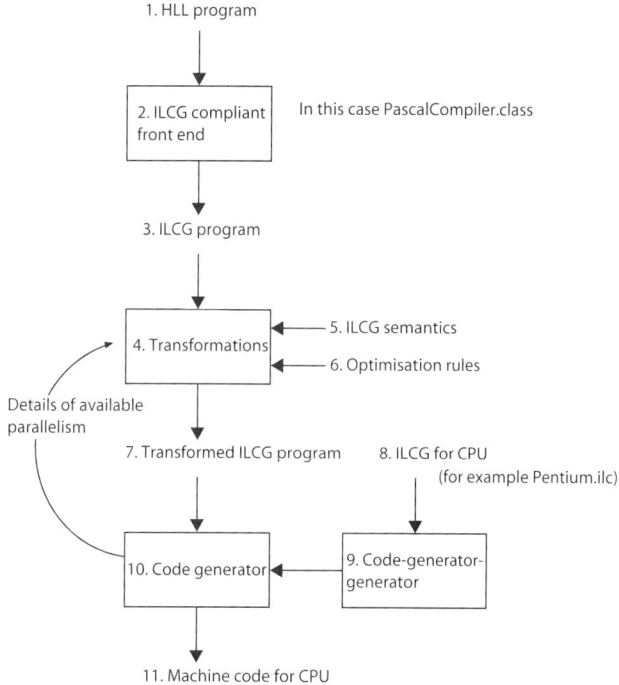

Figure A.2. The translation of Vector Pascal to assembler.

in a Java data structure (3), an ILCG tree, which is basically a semantic tree for the program.

- The resulting tree is transformed (4) from sequential to parallel form and machine-independent optimisations are performed. Since ILCG trees are Java objects, they can contain methods to self-optimise. Each class contains, for instance, a method `eval` which attempts to evaluate a tree at compile time. Another method, `simplify`, applies generic machine-independent transformations to the code. Thus the `simplify` method of the class `For` can perform loop unrolling, removal of redundant loops, etc. Other methods allow tree walkers to apply context-specific transformations.
- The resulting ilcg tree (7) is walked over by a class that encapsulates the semantics of the target machine's instruction-set (10), for example Pentium.class. During code generation the tree is further transformed, as machine-specific register optimisations are performed. The output of this process is an assembler file (11).
- This is then fed through an appropriate assembler and linker, assumed to be externally provided to generate an executable program.

A.2.1 Vectorisation

The parser initially generates serial code for all constructs. It then interrogates the current code generator class to determine the degree of parallelism possible

```
{ var i;
  for i=1 to 9 step 1 do {
    v1[^i]:=+(^(v2[^i]),^(v3[^i]));
  };
}
```

Figure A.3. Sequential form of array assignment.

```
{ var i;
  for i=1 to 8 step 2 do {
    (ref int32 vector (2))mem(+(@v1,*(-(^i,1),4))):=
      +(^((ref int32 vector (2))mem(+(@v2,*(-(^i,1),4)))),
        ^((ref int32 vector (2))mem(+(@v3,*(-(^i,1),4)))));
  };
  for i=9 to 9 step 1 do {
    v1[^i]:=+(^(v2[^i]),^(v3[^i]));
  };
}
```

Figure A.4. Parallelised loop.

for the types of operations performed in a loop, and if these are greater than one, it vectorises the code.

Given the declaration

var v1,v2,v3: array[1..9] of integer;

then the statement

v1 := v2 + v3;

would first be translated to the ILCG sequence shown in Figure A.3. In the example above, variable names such as v1 and i have been used for clarity. In reality i would be an addressing expression such as

`(ref int32)mem(+(^((ref int32)ebp), -1860))`

which encodes both the type and the address of the variable. The code generator is queried as to the parallelism available on the type int32 and, since it is a Pentium with MMX, returns 2. The loop is then split into two, a portion that can be executed in parallel and a residual sequential component, resulting in the ILCG shown in Figure A.4. In the parallel part of the code, the array subscripts have been replaced by explictly cast memory addresses. This coerces the locations from their original types to the type required by the vectorisation. Applying the simplify method of the For class, the following generic transformations are performed:

1. The second loop is replaced by a single statement.
2. The parallel loop is unrolled twofold.
3. The For class is replaced by a sequence of statements with explicit gotos.

```
{ var i;
  i:=1;
  leb4af11b47e:
  if >(2,0) thenif >(^i,8) thengoto leb4af11b47f
              else null
                    fi
       else if <(^i,8) thengoto leb4af11b47f
       else null
       fi
  fi;
  (ref int32 vector (2))mem(+(@v1,*(-(^i,1),4))):=
       +(^((ref int32 vector (2))mem(+(@v2,*(-(^i,1),4)))),
         ^((ref int32 vector (2))mem(+(@v3,*(-(^i,1),4)))));
  i:=+(^i,2);
  (ref int32 vector (2))mem(+(@v1,*(-(^i,1),4))):=
       +(^((ref int32 vector (2))mem(+(@v2,*(-(^i,1),4)))),
         ^((ref int32 vector (2))mem(+(@v3,*(-(^i,1),4)))));
  i:=+(^i,2);
  goto leb4af11b47e;
  leb4af11b47f:
  i:=9;
  v1[^i]:=+(^(v2[^i]),^(v3[^i]));
}
```

Figure A.5. After applying simplify to the tree.

```
 mov DWORD ecx,1
leb4b08729615:
 cmp DWORD ecx,8
 jg near leb4b08729616
 lea edi,[ecx-(1)]; substituting in edi with 3 occurrences
 movq MM1,[epb+edi*4+-1620]
 paddd MM1,[epb+edi*4+-1640]
 movq [epb+edi*4+-1600],MM1
 lea ecx,[ecx+2]
 lea edi,[ecx-(1)]; substituting in edi with 3 occurrences
 movq MM1,[epb+edi*4+-1620]
 padd MM1,[epb+edi*4+-1640]
 movq [epb+edi*4+-1600],MM1
 lea ecx,[ecx+2]
 jmp leb4b08729615
leb4b08729616:
```

Figure A.6. The result of matching the parallelised loop against the Pentium instruction-set.

The result is shown in Figure A.5. When the `eval` method is invoked, constant folding causes the loop test condition to be evaluated to

```
if>(^i,8) thengoto leb4af11b47f
```

A.2.2 Porting Strategy

To port the compiler to a new machine, say a G5, it is necessary to

1. Write a new machine description `G5.ilc` in ILCG source code.
2. Compile this to a code generator in java with the ilcg compiler generator using a command of the form

   ```
   java ilcg.ILCG cpus/G5.ilc ilcg/tree/G5.java G5
   ```

3. Write an interface class `ilcg/tree/G5CG` which is a subclass of G5 and which invokes the assembler and linker. The linker and assembler used will depend on the machine but one can assume that at least a `gcc` assembler and linker will be available. The class `G5CG` must take responsibility to handle the translation of procedure calls from the abstract form provided in ILCG to the concrete form required by the G5 processor.
4. The class `G5CG` should also export the method `getparallelism` which specifies to the vectoriser the degree of parallelism available for given data types. An example for a P4 is given in Figure A.7. Note that although a P4 is potentially capable of performing 16-way parallelism on 8-bit operands, the measured speed when doing this on is less than that measured for 8-way parallelism. This is due to the restriction placed on unaligned loads of 16-byte quantities in the P4 architecture. For image processing operations, aligned accesses are the exception. Thus, when specifying the degree of parallelism for a processor, one should not simply give the maximal degree supported by the architecture. The maximal level of parallelism is not necessarily the fastest.

```
public int getParallelism(String elementType)
{ if(elementType.equals(Node.int32)) return 2;
  if(elementType.equals(Node.int16)) return 4;
  if(elementType.equals(Node.int8)) return 8;
  if(elementType.equals(Node.uint32)) return 2;
  if(elementType.equals(Node.uint16)) return 4;
  if(elementType.equals(Node.uint8)) return 8;
  if(elementType.equals(Node.ieee32)) return 4;
  if(elementType.equals(Node.ieee64)) return 1;
  return 1;
}
```

Figure A.7. The method `getParallelism` for a P4 processor.

Sample machine descriptions are given on the Vector Pascal website to help those wishing to port the compiler. These are given in the ILCG machine description language, an outline of which follows.

A.3 ILCG

The purpose of ILCG (Intermediate Language for Code Generation) is to mediate between CPU instruction-sets and high-level language programs. It both provides a representation to which compilers can translate a variety of source-level programming languages and also a notation for defining the semantics of CPU instructions.

Its purpose is to act as an input to two types of programs:

1. ILCG structures produced by an HLL compiler are input to an automatically constructed code generator, working on the syntax matching principles described by Graham (1980). This then generates equivalent sequences of assembler statements.
2. Machine descriptions written as ILCG source files are input to code-generator-generators, which produce java programs that perform function (1) above.

So far, one HLL compiler producing ILCG structures as output exists: the Vector Pascal compiler. There also exists one code-generator-generator, which produces code generators that use a top-down pattern matching technique analogous to Prolog unification. ILCG is intended to be flexible enough to describe a wide variety of machine architectures. In particular, it can specify both SISD and SIMD instructions and either stack-based or register-based machines. However, it does assume certain things about the machine: that certain basic types are supported and that the machine is addressed at the byte level.

In ILCG, all type conversions, dereferences, etc., have to be made absolutely explicit. In what follows we will designate terminals of the language in bold, e.g. **octet**, and non-terminal in italics, e.g. *word8*.

A.4 Supported Types

A.4.1 Data Formats

The data in a memory can be distinguished initially in terms of the number of bits in the individually addressable chunks. The addressable chunks are assumed to be the powers of two from 3 to 7, so we thus have as allowed formats *word8*, *word16*, *word32*, *word64*, *word128*. These are treated as non-terminals in the grammar of ILCG.

When data are being explicitly operated on without regard to their type, we have terminals which stand for these formats: **octet**, **halfword**, **word**, **doubleword**, **quadword**.

A.4.2 Typed Formats

Each of these underlying formats can contain information of different types, either signed or unsigned integers, floats, etc. ILCG allows the following integer types as terminals: **int8**, **uint8**, **int16**, **uint16**, **int32**, **uint32**, **int64**, **uint64**, to stand for signed and unsigned integers of the appropriate lengths.

The integers are logically grouped into *signed* and *unsigned*. As non-terminal types they are represented as *byte, short, integer, long* and *ubyte, ushort, uinteger, ulong*.

Floating-point numbers are assumed to be either 32- or 64-bit with 32-bit numbers given the non-terminal symbols *float, double*. If we wish to specify a particular representation of floats of doubles we can use the terminals **ieee32**, **ieee64**.

A.4.3 ref Types

ILCG uses a simplified version of the Algol-68 reference typing model. A value can be a reference to another type. Thus an integer when used as an address of a 64-bit floating-point number would be a **ref ieee64**. Ref types include registers. An integer register would be a **ref int32** when holding an integer, a **ref ref int32** when holding the address of an integer, etc.

A.5 Supported Operations

A.5.1 Type Casts

The syntax for the type casts is C style so we have for example (ieee64) int32 to represent a conversion of a 32-bit integer to a 64-bit real. These type casts act as constraints on the pattern matcher during code generation. They do not perform any data transformation. They are inserted into machine descriptions to constrain the types of the arguments that will be matched for an instruction. They are also used by compilers to decorate ILCG trees in order both to enforce, and to allow limited breaking of, the type rules.

A.5.2 Arithmetic

The allowed dyadic arithmetic operations are addition, saturated addition, multiplication, saturated multiplication, subtraction, saturated subtraction, division and remainder with operator symbols +, +:, *, *:, −, −:, **div**, **mod**.

The concrete syntax is prefix with bracketing. Thus the infix operation $3 + 5 \div 7$ would be represented as +(**3, div (5, 7)**).

A.5.3 Memory

Memory is explicitly represented. All accesses to memory are represented by array operations on a predefined array **mem**. Thus location 100 in memory is represented as **mem(100)**. The type of such an expression is *address*. It can be cast to a reference type of a given format. Thus we could have (**ref int32**)**mem(100)**.

A.5.4 Assignment

We have a set of storage operators corresponding to the word lengths supported. These have the form of infix operators. The size of the store being performed depends on the size of the right-hand side. A valid storage statement might be (**ref octet**)**mem**(299) :=(**int8**) 99.

The first argument is always a reference and the second argument a value of the appropriate format.

If the left-hand side is a format, the right-hand side must be a value of the appropriate size. If the left-hand side is an explicit type rather than a format, the right-hand side must have the same type.

A.5.5 Dereferencing

Dereferencing is done explicitly when a value other than a literal is required. There is a dereference operator, which converts a reference into the value that it references. A valid load expression might be (**octet**)↑((**ref octet**)**mem**(99)).

The argument to the load operator must be a reference.

A.6 Machine Description

Ilcg can be used to describe the semantics of machine instructions. A machine description typically consists of a set of register declarations followed by a set of instruction formats and a set of operations. This approach works well only with machines that have an orthogonal instruction set, i.e. those that allow addressing modes and operators to be combined in an independent manner.

A.6.1 Registers

When entering machine descriptions in ilcg, registers can be declared along with their type, hence

> **register word EBX assembles['ebx'];**
> **reserved register word ESP assembles['esp'];**

would declare **EBX** to be of type **ref word**.

Aliasing

A register can be declared to be a sub-field of another register, hence we could write

> **alias register octet AL = EAX(0:7) assembles['al'];**
> **alias register octet BL = EBX(0:7) assembles['bl'];**

to indicate that **BL** occupies the bottom 8 bits of register **EBX**. In this notation bit zero is taken to be the least significant bit of a value. There are assumed to be two pregiven registers **FP**, **GP** that are used by compilers to point to areas of memory. These can be aliased to a particular real register:

register word EBP assembles['ebp'];
alias register word FP = EBP(0:31) assembles['ebp'];

Additional registers may be reserved, indicating that the code generator must not use them to hold temporary values:

reserved register word ESP assembles['esp'];

A.6.2 Register Sets

A set of registers that are used in the same way by the instruction-set can be defined:

pattern reg means [*EBP|EBX|ESI|EDI|ECX|EAX|EDX|ESP*];
pattern breg means [*AL|AH|BL|BH|CL|CH|DL|DH*];

All registers in an register set should be of the same length.

A.6.3 Register Arrays

Some machine designs have regular arrays of registers. Rather than have these exhaustively enumerated, it is convenient to have a means of providing an array of registers. This can be declared as

register vector(8)doubleword MM assembles['MM'i];

This declares the symbol MMX to stand for the entire MMX register set. It implicitly defines how the register names are to be printed in the assembly language by defining an indexing variable i that is used in the assembly language definition.

We also need a syntax for explicitly identifying individual registers in the set. This is done by using the dyadic subscript operator **subscript(MM,2)**, which would be of type **ref doubleword**.

A.6.4 Register Stacks

Whereas some machines have registers organised as an array, another class of machines, those oriented around postfix instruction-sets, have register stacks.

The ilcg syntax allows register stacks to be declared:

register stack (8)ieee64 FP assembles[' '];

Two access operations are supported on stacks:

- **PUSH** is a void dyadic operator taking a stack of type ref t as first argument and a value of type t as the second argument. Thus we might have **PUSH(FP,↑mem(20))**.
- **POP** is a monadic operator returning t on stacks of type t. So we might have **mem(20) := POP(FP)**. In addition, there are two predicates on stacks that can be used in pattern preconditions.

- **FULL** is a monadic Boolean operator on stacks.
- **EMPTY** is a monadic Boolean operator on stacks.

A.6.5 Instruction Formats

An instruction format is an abstraction over a class of concrete instructions. It abstracts over particular operations and types thereof whilst specifying how arguments can be combined:

**instruction pattern
RR(operator op, anyreg r1, anyreg r2, int t)
means[r1 := (t) op(↑((ref t) r1),↑((ref t) r2))]
assembles[op ' ' r1 ',' r2];**

In the above example, we specify a register to register instruction format that uses the first register as a source and a destination whereas the second register is only a destination. The result is returned in register r1.

We might, however, wish to have a more powerful abstraction, which was capable of taking more abstract specifications for its arguments. For example, many machines allow arguments to instructions to be addressing modes that can be either registers or memory references. For us to be able to specify this in an instruction format we need to be able to provide grammar non-terminals as arguments to the instruction formats.

For example, we might want to be able to say

**instruction pattern
RRM(operator op, reg r1, maddrmode rm, int t)
means [r1 := (t) op(↑((ref t) r1),↑((ref t) rm))]
assembles[op ' ' r1 ',' rm];**

This implies that addrmode and reg must be non-terminals. Since the non-terminals required by different machines will vary, there must be a means of declaring such non-terminals in ilcg.

An example would be

**pattern regindirf(reg r)
means[↑(r)] assembles[r];
pattern baseplusoffsetf(reg r, signed s)
means[+(↑(r),const s)] assembles[r'+'s];
pattern addrform means[baseplusoffsetf|regindirf];
pattern maddrmode(addrform f)
means[mem(f)] assembles['[f]'];**

This gives us a way of including non-terminals as parameters to patterns.

A.7 Grammar of ILCG

The following grammar is given in Sable (Gagnon, 1998) compatible form. The Sable parser generator is used to generate a parser for ILCG from this grammar. The ILCG parser then translates a CPU specification into a tree structure which is then walked by an ILCG-tree-walk-generator to produce an ILCG-tree-walk Java class specific to that CPU.

If the ILCG grammar is extended, for example to allow new arithmetic operators, then the ILCG-tree-walk-generator must itself be modified to generate translation rules for the new operators.

/*

A.8 ILCG Grammar

This is a definition of the grammar of ILCG using the Sable grammar specification lanaguage. It is input to Sable to generate a parser for machine descriptions in ilcg.

```
*/
  Package ilcg;
/*
```

A.8.1 Helpers

Helpers are regular expressions macros used in the definition of terminal symbols of the grammar.

```
*/
Helpers
  letter=[['A'..'Z']+['a'..'z']];
  digit=['0'..'9'];
  alphanum=[letter+['0'..'9']];
  cr=13;
  lf=10;
  tab=9;
    digit_sequence=digit+;
    fractional_constant=digit_sequence?'.'digit_sequence|
    digit_sequence '.';
  sign='+'|'-';
  exponent_part=('e'|'E') sign? digit_sequence;
  floating_suffix='f'|'F'|'l'|'L';
  // This eol definition takes care of different platforms
  eol=cr lf | cr | lf;
  not_cr_lf=[[32..127] - [cr+lf]];
  exponent=('e'|'E');
  quote=''';
  all=[0..127];
  schar=[all-'''];
  not_star=[all - '*'];
  not_star_slash=[not_star - '/'];
/*
```

A.8.2 Tokens

The tokens section defines the terminal symbols of the grammar.

```
*/
Tokens
  floating_constant =
      fractional_constant exponent_part? floating_suffix? |
      digit_sequence exponent_part floating_suffix?;
/*
```

Terminals specifying data formats:

```
*/
  void='void';
  octet='octet'; int8='int8'; uint8='uint8';
  halfword='halfword'; int16='int16'; uint16='uint16';
  word='word'; int32='int32';
  uint32='uint32'; ieee32='ieee32';
  doubleword='doubleword'; int64='int64';
  uint64='uint64'; ieee64='ieee64';
  quadword='quadword';
/*
```

Terminals describing reserved words:

```
*/
  function='function';
  flag='flag';
  location='loc';
  procedure='instruction';
  returns='returns';
  label='label';
  goto='goto';
  for='for';
  to='to';
  step='step';
  do='do';
  ref='ref';
  const='const';
  reg='register';
  operation='operation';
  alias='alias';
  instruction='instruction';
  address='address';
  vector='vector';
  stack='stack';
  sideeffect='sideeffect';
  if='if';
  reserved='reserved';
```

```
  precondition='precondition';
  instructionset='instructionset';
/*
```

Terminals for describing new patterns:

```
*/
  pattern='pattern';
  means='means';
  assembles='assembles';
/*
```

Terminals specifying operators:

```
*/
  colon=':';
  semicolon=';';
  comma=',';
  dot='.';
  bra='(';

  ket=')';
  plus='+';
  satplus='+:';
  satminus='-:';
  map='->';
  equals='=';
  le='<=';
  ge='>=';
  ne='<>';
  lt='<';
  gt='>';
  minus='-';
  times='*';
  exponentiate='**';
  divide='div';
  and='AND';
  or='OR';
  xor='XOR';
  not='NOT';
  sin='SIN';
  cos='COS';
  abs='ABS';
  tan='TAN';
  remainder='MOD';
  store=':=';
  deref='^';
  push='PUSH';
  pop='POP';
  call='APPLY';
```

```
  full='FULL';
  empty='EMPTY';
  subscript='SUBSCRIPT';
  intlit=digit+;
  vbar='|';
  sket=']';
  sbra='[';
  end='end';
  typetoken='type';
  mem='mem';
  string=quote schar+quote;
/*
```

Identifiers come after reserved words in the grammar:

```
*/
  identifier=letter alphanum*;
  blank=(' '|cr|lf|tab)+;
  comment='/*' not_star*'*'+
              (not_star_slash not_star*'*'+)*'/';
Ignored Tokens
blank,comment;
/*
```

A.8.3 Non-terminal Symbols

```
*/
Productions
  program=statementlist instructionlist;
  instructionlist=instructionset sbra alternatives sket;
/*
```

Non-terminals specifying data formats:

```
*/
  format={octet} octet|
         {halfword} halfword|
         {word} word|
         {doubleword} doubleword|
         {quadword} quadword|
         {tformat}tformat;
/*
```

Non-terminals corresponding to type descriptions:

```
*/
  reference=ref type ;
  array=vector bra number ket;
  aggregate={stack} stack bra number ket|{vector}array|{non};
  type={format} format|{typeid} typeid|{array}type array|
```

```
  {cartesian}sbra type cartesian* sket|
{map}bra [arg]:type map [result]:type ket;
  cartesian=comma type;

    tformat={signed} signed|
  {unsigned}unsigned|
  {ieee32}ieee32|
  {ieee63}ieee64;
    signed=int32|
  {int8}  int8|
  {int16} int16|
  {int64} int64;
    unsigned=uint32|
  {uint8}  uint8|
  {uint16} uint16|
  {uint64} uint64;
/*
```

Non-terminals corresponding to typed values:

```
*/
  value={refval}refval|
  {rhs}rhs|{void}void|
  {cartval}cartval|
  {dyadic}dyadic bra [left]:value comma [right]:value ket|
  {monadic}monadic bra value ket;
/*
```

Value corresponding to a cartesian product type, e.g. record initialisers:

```
*/
  cartval=sbra value carttail* sket;
  carttail=comma value;
/*
```

Conditions used in defining control structures:

```
*/
condition=
{dyadic} dyadic bra[left]:condition comma[right]:condition
ket|
{monadic}monadic bra condition ket|
{id}identifier|
{number}number;
  rhs={number}number|
      {cast}bra type ket value|
      {const}const identifier|
      {deref}deref bra refval ket;
  refval=loc| {refcast} bra reference ket loc;
```

Appendix A • Compiler Porting Tools

```
        loc={id}identifier|
            {memory}mem bra value ket;
        number={reallit} optionalsign reallit|
            {integer} optionalsign intlit;
        optionalsign=|{plus}plus|{minus}minus;
        reallit=floating_constant;
/*
```
Operators
```
*/
dyadic={plus} plus|
{minus} minus|
{identifier} identifier|
{exp} exponentiate|
{times}   times|
{divide} divide|
{lt}lt|
{gt}gt|
{call}call|
{le}le|
{ge}ge|
{eq}equals|
{ne}ne|
{push}push|
{subscript}subscript|
{satplus}satplus|
{satminus}satminus|
{remainder}remainder|
{or}or|
{and}and|
{xor}xor;
monadic={not}not|
{full}full|
{empty}empty|
{pop}pop|
{sin}sin|
{cos}cos|
{tan}tan|
{abs}abs;
/*
```
Register declaration:
```
*/
registerdecl=reservation reg aggregate format identifier
assembles sbra string sket;
reservation={reserved}reserved|{unreserved};
aliasdecl=
     alias reg aggregate format [child]:identifier equals
```

```
        [parent]:identifier bra [lowbit]:intlit colon
        [highbit]:intlit ket assembles sbra string sket;
opdecl=operation identifier means operator assembles sbra
string sket;
operator={plus}plus|
         {minus}minus|
         {times}times|
         {lt}lt|
         {gt}gt|
       {le}le|
         {ge}ge|
         {eq}equals|
         {ne}ne|
         {divide}divide|
       {remainder}remainder|
         {or}or|
         {and}and|
         {xor}xor;
/*
```

Pattern declarations:

```
*/
assign= refval store value;
meaning={value}value|
     {assign}assign|
    {goto}goto value|
    {if}if bra value ket meaning|
{for} for refval store [start]:value
     to [stop]:value step [increment]:value do meaning|
    {loc}location value;
patterndecl=pattern identifier paramlist means sbra
meaning     sket
assemblesto
sideeffects
precond
     |{alternatives}pattern identifier means sbra alternatives
     sket;

paramlist=bra param paramtail* ket|{nullparam}bra ket;
param=typeid identifier|
{typeparam}typetoken identifier|
{label}label identifier;
typeid=identifier;
paramtail=comma param;
alternatives=type alts*;
alts=vbar type;
precond=precondition sbra condition sket|
     {unconditional};
```

```
asideeffect=sideeffect returnval;
sideeffects=asideeffect*;
assemblesto=assembles sbra assemblypattern sket;
assemblypattern=assemblertoken*;
assemblertoken={string} string |
               {identifier} identifier;
returnval=returns identifier;
/*
```

Statements:

```
*/
statement={aliasdecl} aliasdecl|
          {registerdecl} registerdecl |
          {addressmode} address patterndecl|
          {instructionformat} procedure patterndecl|
          {opdecl} opdecl|
          {flag} flag identifier equals intlit|
      {typerename} typetoken format equals identifier|
          {patterndecl} patterndecl;
statementlist=statement semicolon statements*;
statements= statement semicolon;
//
```

Appendix B: Software Download

The software is available for downloading from the website associated with this book:

www.dcs.gla.ac.uk/~wpc/SIMD.html

It can be downloaded in two possible versions, both of which are distributed as .jar files:

1. Source form: this is a compressed directory tree snapshot containing the Java, C, Pascal and ILCG sources required to build the compiler.
2. Binary version, which contains the mmpc.jar and viper.jar files necessary to run the compiled version of the compiler and Viper, along with the run-time library as a C source file, and the Pascal source of the system unit.

If the binary is downloaded, it should be unpacked into a directory and one should set up a shell variable mmpcdir to point to this directory. This shell variable is used by the compiler to locate the directory containing the system unit and run-time library. One should then place the directory pointed to by mmpcdir on the path.

The binary version utilises Java, Nasm, gcc and latex, all of which are either installed or readily available for Linux systems. If one compiles with garbage collection enabled, it should be ensured that the gcc system includes the Boehm garbage collector. For Windows environments these utilities may have to be downloaded. They are available from multiple websites.

The website for this book also contains the sources for the example programs and units used in the book.

Appendix C: Using the Command Line Compiler

C.1 Invoking the Compiler

The compiler is invoked with the command

`vpc filename`

where filename is the name of a Pascal program or unit. For example,

`vpc test`

will compile the program test.pas and generate an executable file `test`, (`test.exe` under windows).

The command `vpc` is a shell script which invokes the Java run-time system to execute a `.jar` file containing the compiler classes. Instead of running vpc, the Java interpreter can be directly invoked as follows:

`java -jar mmpc.jar filename`

The `vpc` script sets various compiler options appropriate to the operating system being used.

C.1.1 Environment Variable

The environment variable `mmpcdir` must be set to the directory which contains the `mmpc.jar` file, the run-time library `rtl.o` and the `system.pas` file.

C.1.2 Compiler Options

The following flags can be supplied to the compiler:

- `-Afilename` Defines the assembler file to be created. In the absence of this option, the assembler file is `p.asm`.
- `-Ddirname` Defines the directory in which to find `rtl.o` and `system.pas`.
- `-V` Causes the code generator to produce a verbose diagnostic listing to `foo.lst` when compiling `foo.pas`.
- `-oexefile` Causes the linker to output to `exefile` instead of the default output of `p.exe`.

Table C.1. Code generators supported

CGFLAG	Description
IA32	Generates code for the Intel 486 instruction-set
Pentium	Generates code for the Intel P6 with MMX instruction-set
K6	Generates code for the AMD K6 instruction-set, use for Athlon
P3	Generates code for the Intel PIII processor family
P4	Generates code for the Intel PIV family and Athlon XP

-U   Defines whether references to external procedures in the assembler file should be preceded by an under-bar, _. This is required for the coff object format but not for elf.

-S   Suppresses assembly and linking of the program. An assembler file is still generated.

-fFORMAT   Specifies the object format to be generated by the assembler. The object formats currently used are elf when compiling under Unix or when compiling under Windows using the cygwin version of the gcc linker, or coff when using the djgpp version of the gcc linker. For other formats, consult the NASM documentation.

-cpuCGFLAG   Specifies the code generator to be used. Currently the code generators shown in Table C.1 are supported.

C.1.3 Dependencies

The Vector Pascal compiler depends upon a number of other utilities which are usually pre-installed on Linux systems, and are freely available for Windows systems.

- NASM   The net-wide assembler. This is used to convert the output of the code generator to linkable modules. It is freely available on the web for Windows.
- gcc   The GNU C Compiler, used to compile the run-time library and to link modules produced by the assembler to the run-time library.
- Java   The Java virtual machine must be available to interpret the compiler. There are a number of Java interpreters and just-in-time compilers are freely available for Windows.

C.2 Calling Conventions

Procedure parameters are passed using a modified C calling convention to facilitate calls to external C procedures. Parameters are pushed on to the stack from right to left. Value parameters are pushed entirely on to the stack and var parameters are pushed as addresses.

Example

```
unit callconv;
interface
type intarr = array[1..8] of integer;
procedure foo(var a:intarr;b:intarr;c:integer);
implementation
procedure foo(var a:intarr;b:intarr;c:integer);
begin
end;
var x,y:intarr;
begin
    foo(x,y,3);
end.
```

This would generate the following code for the procedure foo:

```
; procedure generated by code generator class ilcg.tree.
PentiumCG
1e8e68de10c5:
;       foo
 enter spaceforfoo-4*1,1
;8
 1e8e68de118a:
spaceforfoo equ 4
;.... code for foo goes here
fooexit:
leave
 ret 0
```

and the calling code is

```
push DWORD 3            ; push rightmost argument
lea esp,[esp-32]        ; create space for the array
mov DWORD[ebp-52],0     ; for loop to copy the array
1e8e68de87fd:           ; the loop is
                        ; unrolled twice and
cmp DWORD [ebp-52],7    ; parallelised to copy
                        ; 16 bytes per cycle
jg near 1e8e68de87fe
mov ebx,DWORD[ebp-52]
imul ebx,4
movq MM1,[ebx+1e8e68dddaa2-48]
movq [esp+ebx],MM1
mov eax,DWORD[ebp+-52]
lea ebx,[eax+2]
imul ebx,4
movq MM1,[ebx+1e8e68dddaa2-48]
movq [esp+ebx],MM1
lea ebx,[ebp+-52]
```

```
add DWORD[ebx],4
jmp 1e8e68de87fd
1e8e68de87fe:                         ; end of array
                                      ; copying loop
push DWORD 1e8e68dddaa2-32            ; push the address of the
                                      ; var parameter
EMMS                                  ; clear MMX state
 call 1e8e68de10c5                    ; call the local
                                      ; label for foo
add esp,40                            ; free space on the stack
```

Function Results

Function results are returned in registers for scalars following the C calling convention for the operating system on which the compiler is implemented. Records, strings and sets are returned by the caller passing an implicit parameter containing the address of a temporary buffer in the calling environment into which the result can be assigned. Given the following program:

program
type t1 = **set of** char;
var x,y:t1;
function bar:t1;**begin** bar := y;**end**;
begin
  x := bar;
end.

The call of bar would generate

```
push ebp
add dword[esp],-128        ; address of buffer on stack
call 1e8eb6156ca8          ; call bar to place
                           ; result in buffer
add esp,4                  ; discard the address
mov DWORD[ebp+-132],0      ; for loop to copy
                           ; the set 16 bytes
1e8eb615d99f:              ; at a time into x using the
                           ; MMX registers
cmp DWORD[ebp+-132],31
jg near 1e8eb615d9910
mov ebx,DWORD[ebp+-132]
movq MM1,[ebx+ebp+-128]
movq [ebx+ebp+-64],MM1
mov eax,DWORD[ebp+-132]
lea ebx,[eax+8]
movq MM1,[ebx+ebp+-128]
movq [ebx+ebp+-64],MM1
lea ebx,[ebp+-132]
```

```
add DWORD[ebx],16
jmp 1e8eb615d99f
1e8eb615d9910:
```

C.3 Array Representation

A static array is represented simply by the number of bytes required to store the array being allocated in the global segment or on the stack.

A dynamic array is always represented on the heap. Since its rank is known to the compiler, what need to be stored at run time are the bounds and the means to access it. For simplicity we make the format of dynamic and conformant arrays the same. Thus for schema

s(a,b,c,d:integer) = array[a..b,c..d] of integer

whose run-time bounds are evaluated to be $2\ldots4, 3\ldots7$, we would have the structure shown in Table C.2.

The base address for a schematic array on the heap will point at the first byte after the array header show. For a conformant array, it will point at the first data byte of the array or array range being passed as a parameter. The step field specifies the length of an element of the second dimension in bytes. It is included to allow for the case where we have a conformant array formal parameter:

x:array[a..b:integer,c..d:integer] of integer

to which we pass as actual parameter the range

p[2..4,3..7]

as actual parameter, where

p:array[1..10,1..10] of integer.

In this case the base address would point at @p[2,3] and the step would be 40, the length of 10 integers.

C.3.1 Range Checking

When arrays are indexed, the compiler plants run-time checks to see if the indices are within bounds. In many cases the optimiser is able to remove these

Table C.2. Structure of an array

Address	Field	Value
x	Base of data	Address of first integer in the array
x + 4	a	2
x + 8	b	4
x + 12	Step	40
x + 16	c	3
x + 20	d	7

checks, but in those cases where it is unable to do so, some performance degradation can occur. Range checks can be disabled or enabled by the compiler directives.

{$r−} {disable range checks}
{$r+} {enable range checks}

Performance can be further enhanced by the practice of declaring arrays to have lower bounds of zero. The optimiser is generally able to generate more efficient code for zero-based arrays.

References

3L Limited (1995). *Parallel C V2.2, Software Product Description*. 3L Limited.
Advanced Micro Devices (1999). *3DNOW! Technology Manual*. Advanced Micro Devices.
Aho, AV, Ganapathi, M and TJiang, SWK (1989). Code generation using tree matching and dynamic programming. *ACM Trans. Programming Lang. Syst.*, **11**, 491–516.
Blelloch, GE (1995). NESL: *A Nested Data-Parallel Language*. Carnegie Mellon University, CMU-CS-95-170, September 1995.
Burke, C (1995). *J User Manual*. ISI, Toronto.
Cattell, RGG (1980). Automatic derivation of code generators from machine descriptions. *ACM Trans. Programming Lang. Syst.*, **2**, 173–190.
Chaitin, G (1997). Elegant Lisp Programs, in *The Limits of Mathematics*, Springer, New York, pp. 29–56.
Cheong, G and Lam, M (1997). An optimizer for multimedia instruction sets, presented at the 2nd SUIF Workshop, Stanford University, August 1997.
Cherry, GW (1980). *Pascal Programming Structures*. Reston Publishing, Reston, VA.
Cockshott, P (2000). *Direct Compilation of High Level Languages for Multimedia Instruction-sets*. Department of Computer Science, University of Glasgow.
Cole, M (1989). *Algorithmic Skeletons: Structured Management of Parallel Computation*. Research Monographs in Parallel and Distributed Computing. Pitman, London.
Ewing, AK, Richardson, H, Simpson, AD and Kulkarni, R (1999). *Writing Data Parallel Programs with High Performance Fortran, Ver. 1.3.1*. Edinburgh Parallel Computing Centre, Edinburgh.
Gagnon, E (1998). *SABLECC, An object-oriented compiler framework*. School of Computer Science, McGill University, Montreal.
Graham, SL (1980). Table driven code generation. *IEEE Comput.*, **13**(8), 25–37.
Hennessy, JL and Patterson, DA (2003). *Computer Architecture. A Quantitative Approach*, 3rd edn. Morgan Kaufmann, San Francisco.
Intel (1999). *Intel Architecture Software Developer's Manual*, Vols 1 and 2. Intel.
Intel (2000). *Willamette Processor Software Developer's Guide*. Intel.
ISO (1991a). *Extended Pascal*. ISO 10206:1990.
ISO (1991b). *Pascal*. ISO 7185:1990.
Iverson, KE (1962). *A Programming Language*. Wiley, New York, p. 16.

Iverson, KE (1980). Notation as a tool of thought. *Commun. ACM*, **23**, 444–465.
Iverson, KE (1991). A personal view of APL. *IBM Syst. J.*, **30**(4).
Iverson, KE (2000). *J Introduction and Dictionary*. Iverson Software Inc. (ISI), Toronto, 1995. 4, pp. 347–361.
Jensen, K and Wirth, N (1978). *PASCAL User Manual and Report*. Springer, New York.
Johnston, D (1995). *C++ Parallel Systems*. ECH: Engineering Computing Newsletter, No. 55. Daresbury Laboratory/Rutherford Appleton Laboratory, Daresbury, pp. 6–7.
Knuth, D (1994). *Computers and Typesetting*. Addison Wesley, Boston.
Krall, A and Lelait, S (2000). Compilation techniques for multimedia processors. *Int. J. Parallel Programming*, **28**, 347–361.
Lamport, L (1994). *LaTeX a Document Preparation System*. Addison Wesley, Boston.
Leupers, R (1999). Compiler optimization for media processors, presented at EMMSEC 99, Sweden.
Marx, K (1976). *Das Kapital, Vol. I*. Penguin/New Left Review, Harmondsworth.
Metcalf, M and Reid, J (1996). *The F Programming Language*. Oxford University Press, Oxford.
Michaelson, G, Scaife, N, Bristow, P and King, P (2001). Nested algorithmic skeletons from higher order functions. Special Issue on High Level Models and Languages for Parallel Processing. *Parallel Algorithms Applications*, **16**, 181–206.
Peleg, A, Wilke, S and Weiser, U (1997). Intel MMX for multimedia PCs. *Commun. ACM*, **40**(1).
Schwartz, JT, Dewar, RBK, Dubinsky, E and Schonberg, E (1986). *Programming with Sets: an Introduction to SETL*. Springer, New York.
Shannon, C (1948). A mathematical theory of communication. *Bell Syst. Tech. J.*, **27**, 379–423 and 623–656.
Snyder, L (1999). *A Programmer's Guide to ZPL*. MIT Press, Cambridge, MA.
Srereman, N and Govindarajan, G (2000). A vectorizing compiler for multimedia extensions. *Int. J. Parallel Programming*, **28**, 363–400.
Strachey, C (1967). *Fundamental Concepts of Programming Languages*. Lecture Notes from the International Summer School in Programming Languages, Copenhagen.
Tannenbaum, AS (1976). A tutorial on ALGOL 68. *Comput. Surv.*, **8**, 155–190.
Texas Instruments (1998). *TMS320C62xx CPU and Instruction Set Reference Guide*. Texas Instruments.
Turner, D (1986). An overview of MIRANDA. *SIGPLAN Notices*, December.
van der Meulen, SG (1977). ALGOL 68 might have beens. *SIGPLAN Notices*, **12**(6).
Watt, DA and Brown, DF (2000). *Programming Language Processors in Java*. Prentice Hall, Englewood Cliffs, NJ.
Wirth, N (1996). Recollections about the development of Pascal, in *History of Programming Languages – II*. ACM Press, New York, pp. 97–111.

Index

3D 279
3DNow 39, 279
3DNOW 19–20
64-bit 42
8-bit 270

abstractions 109
addition 4, 130
ADDPS 27
address 13, 18, 30, 32
ah 31
al 31
Algol 68 113
algorithm(s) 6, 8, 22, 212
algorithmic 8
all 114
Alpha 119
AltiVec 22
AMD 9, 24, 30, 42, 45, 118, 279, 338
Amdahl's Law 7, 276
AND 212
and 31
any 114
APL 109, 114, 116, 148
Append 189
Apple 118, 119
applicative 148
Apply-to-Each 113
architectural 28
Architecture 13
arithmetic 5, 8, 14, 130, 183
array(s) 6, 115, 193
   arguments 110
   assignment 147
   expression 148
artifacts 245
as 28
ASCII 126, 217, 223, 266
aspect ratio 247
assembler 30, 118
assign procedure 188–189

Athlon 9, 46
atomic operation 283
average 272
ax 31
axes 39
axis 40

bandwidth 220
base 125
basic block 25
BEGIN 127
bh 31
binary 4, 187, 190
   digit 265–266
   trees 213
bit 5, 231, 265
bitmap 212, 220
bl 31
block 25
blockread 196
blockwrite 196
bmp 251
Boehm 182
Boolean 129, 183, 212
Borland 9, 34, 119, 182
bp 31
Bresenham's 289
buffer(s) 148, 283
bx 31
byte 32, 129

C 23, 28, 33, 35, 45, 113, 118, 223
C** 116
C++ 15, 28, 116–117
   compiler 34
cache line 17–18
cache(s) 6, 12, 18
   occupancy 148
calculators 5
cardinality 221
categorizer 276

345

CC++ 116
ch 31
char 129
characters 126, 191
chdir 224
checks 216
Chinese 126
Chip(s) 3, 18
circuits 3
CISC 32
cl 31
clock(s) 3, 5–6, 9
  speed 5
clockwork 3
cmplx 126
code 15, 30, 212
  generator 119
codebook 267, 270–271, 277
CODEC 265
coff 34
colon 129, 192
colour 229, 277
  plane 229
column 191, 233
compact 212, 220
compile 24
compiler(s) 6, 8, 15, 27–28, 35, 109, 110, 118, 182, 188, 212
  directive 216
  technology 118
  287 9
  486 9
  486 *See* table [convperf] 118
Complex 126, 129
complexity 8
compression 265–266, 272–273, 277
computer(s) 4–5, 181
concatenation 130, 145
conductor 4
configurations 266
CONST 127
Constant 30–31
constructor 179
contrast 230, 233
control characters 266
convolution 14, 114
corruption 266
CPU 6, 8, 12, 18, 28, 31
  386 5
  4004 5
  8080 5
  8086 5

CR 217
crash 181
Crusoe 270
crystals 3
CSP 116
cursor 187, 189–190
cx 31
cycle 4
Cygwin 34
Cyrix 13

data parallel 117, 120
database(s) 218, 219
data-flow 148
data type(s) 11, 15
db 33
DCT 266
dd 33
DEC Pascal 188
decibels 273
decimal 125, 192
declarations 127
decode 270
Delphi 9
deprecated 218
detail 276
dh 31
di 31
digit(s) 4, 192
direction 143
directory 220
disjoint 273
disk 187, 220
display 251
dispose 181–182
division 31, 130
Djgpp 34
dl 31
DMA 220
dot product 9, 142, 145
double 129
Doublewords 33
dq 33
drawline 289
DSP 11
dual buffer 283
duplicate 39
dw 33
dword 32
dynamic 31
  loading 119
  sets 213

Index

eax 31
EBCDIC 188
ebp 31, 33
ebx 31
ecx 31, 36
edges 266
edi 31, 36, 38
edx 31
efficiency 212
efficient 8, 212
element(s) 111, 193
elimination 183
emms 42
energy 273
enter 33
entryname 224
epb 35
epsreal 126
equality 180
error(s) 245, 272
esi 31
esp 31
estimate 272
estimators 272
etern 34
Euclidean 17
evaluated 147
evaluation 130
exponent 126
expressions 190
Extended Pascal 188
extern 34

F[Metcalf96] 109–110
false 125
   positive 221–222
field 181, 193
file(s) 181, 187–190, 219, 220
  binary 187
  .bmp 251
  .zip 265
filepos 195
filter 233
filtering 231
Flags 18
floating point 13, 20, 30, 33, 126, 128
format 32
Formating 191
Fortran 109, 111, 116–117
Fortran 90 109, 114–115, 148
FPU 13, 21
Free-Pascal 119

frequency 247–248
function(s) 8, 110–111
functional language 109

G4 22, 23, 119
galactic 280
garbage 182
  collection 182
  collector 182
gcc 23, 34, 119, 228
generic 213
  set 213
geometric 142
getmem 181–182
GHz 3
global 34
graphics 251
grep 219, 228

H261 266
hash 220
hashing 221
hazards 147–148
hexadecimal 125
High Performance Fortran 109–110, 116
hole 284, 289
horizontally 233
HPF 117–118
HVQ 268

IA32 13, 22, 338
ICL 11
identifiers 127
identity matrix 282
ILCG 119
image(s) 11, 229, 233, 251, 265, 267, 272
  plane 285
  processing 111, 276
imperative 182
  languages 148
implementation(s) 126, 212
indexfiles 228
index-sets 220, 222
indices 197, 199
  implicit 197, 199
induction 38
inflection 266
information 265
  theory 265
Inner Product 142
instructions 6, 9, 15

instructionset 270
int64 129
integer(s) 125, 182, 193
Intel 13, 20, 23, 45, 118, 187, 270, 279, 338
  language 148
ioresult 216
iota 199
ISO 188
iteration 6
Iverson 110, 114

J 111, 114, 116
Java 118–119
jumps 6

K6 9, 338
kernel 14, 114, 232

labels 30, 218
language 119
lea 37
leave 33
length 142–143
letters 266
lexeme 213
library 213
Linux 28, 34, 119, 188, 222–223
literal 128
literature 272
load 22
loading 13
locations 31
logarithmically 273
loop(s) 15, 17, 19, 25, 38, 197
lossless 265
lossy 265
LZW 265

mantissa 126
Map 110
mask 244
MASM 28
matrices 142
matrix 42, 111, 273
  calculation 41
  multiplication 41
  product 142
maxdims 136
maximum 114
maxint 125
maxreal 126

MAXVAL 114
mean(s) 272
memorised 4
memory 12, 18, 30, 32, 181
  leaks 182, 213
Metadata 270
meters 280
MHz 3
Microsoft 34, 119
MIMD 110
minchar 126
minimum 114
MINVAL 114
MIRANDA 111
ML 117
mm0 31
MMX 13, 15, 22, 23, 27, 31, 109, 118, 212–213, 230, 265, 270
modulus 31
Moire 248
motor 266
Motorola 118, 187
MOVNTPS 21
MOVNTQ 21
movq 43
MOVSS 21
MPEG 265–266
MS-DOS 119
multiplication 130
multiply 31

Nasm 29, 31, 34
nervous 266
Nesl 111, 113, 116–117
neurons 266
NIAL 148
n-tuple 187
NUL 217
numbers 30
numeric 183
Nyquist 248

obj 34
observations 272
Occam 116–117
occurence 219
offsets 35
opendir 224
OpenGL 279
operating system 187
operation-code 30
operation(s) 14, 39

Index

operator 31, 109, 114, 183
  & 31
  << 31
  >> 31
  + 31
  * 31
  / 31
  // 31
  := 129
optimisations 212
optimised 228
OR 212
or 31
ordered 213
ordering 219
ordinal 182–183, 213, 220–221
orthogonal 39
oscillator 3
output 192
overflows 145

P3 37, 338
P4 5, 9, 12, 20, 22, 37
packed 15
padded 193
palette 277
parallel 118, 147, 235, 248
  C 117
  code 117
  machines 109
parallelised 248
parallelism 12, 109
parameter 181
Partition 273
Pascal 9, 23, 118, 119, 182, 187–188, 190–191, 193, 212, 218–219
  Prospero 212
  Standard 182
  Turbo 188
  Vector 9, 117–118, 148, 182, 188, 212, 279
patch 267
patterns 276
  recognizer 276
PC 109, 117, 118, 119
pC++ 116
pchar 223
pdir 223
pdirentry 223
Pentium 5–6, 12, 19, 26, 279, 338
performance 11
persistent 187

perspective 288
pi 128
pipeline 5, 15
pixel(s) 111, 129, 233, 229, 245
Pointer 180
polymorphism 204
portable 119
precision 145
PREFETCH 21, 29
primary keys 219
prime 211
printed 193
procedure(s) 189–190, 191
processor(s) 6, 11–12
PRODUCT 114
program(s) 9, 181
projection 143
Prospero Pascal 212
PSNR 272
push 35
PXOR 37
Pythagoras 142

quadwords 33
quartz 3
query 219
qword 32

RAM 181, 187
randomised 247
range checking 235
rank 114
readdir 224
real 190, 192
  numbers 126
  output 192
reciprocals 17
record 175, 180, 187, 218
reduction 114, 144
redundancy 266
redundant 265
region 233
regions of interest 111
register(s) 3, 9, 11, 13, 22, 24, 25, 30–31, 33
remainder 35, 38
rendering 247
repetition 145
resb 33
reshape 115
resize 247
ret 33

retina 266
Rewrite 189
ringing 235
RISC 22
root 5
rotation(s) 40, 42, 287
Russell's paradox 182

sample 248
saturated 15
scalar(s) 6, 24, 39, 110, 144, 193, 272, 273
  code 117
  expression 148
  output 193
scaled 39
scaling 42
schema 203
school 4
screen buffer 279, 283
SDL 251, 253, 283, 285
search 219
searchindex 228
searching 8
SECTION 32
seek 195, 220
semantics 28, 148, 183
sequence(s) 111, 113
SETL 111
set(s) 182, 212, 220, 228
  type 182
shaded 279
sharpened 234
sharpening 233
shortint 129
shrinking 247
si 31
signal 273
SIMD 11–12, 17, 21–22, 23, 25, 28–29, 109–110, 113, 116–118, 129, 248, 265, 267
  instruction-set 118
singleton 219
SISD 118
sorted 213
source 148
sp 31
space 39
SPARC 23, 119
spatial frequency 235, 248
speed 6, 212
spoken word 266

SQRT 110
square 5, 272
square root 5
SSE 23, 44, 276
st0 31
stack 35
stalls 15
Standard Pascal 119
state machine 218
statically allocated 148
stimulae 266
storage efficiency 228
store 22, 187
Strachey 118
string(s) 126, 129, 130, 181, 224
strpas 224
structured programming 218
sub-atomic 280
subranges 182
subtract 31
subtraction 130, 212
SUIF 23
SUM 114
SUN 23
super-computers 109
Surfaces 39
system 189

technology 12
temporary 193
text 188, 190
  retrieval 228
TMT 9
  Pascal 23, 119
training 272–273
trans 199
transform 282
translate 39
translation 42
Texas 12
Trans-Meta Crusoe 213
Transputer 116
tree 213
triangle 39
triples 39
true 125
tuple 187
Turbo Pascal 119, 181–182, 188
type system 181

Unicode 126, 223
unicodestring2ascii 224

Index

unit vector 143
units 219–220
unrolling 25
uses 254

variable(s) 127, 129, 181, 187, 189
variant 177
vector 22, 24–25, 35, 37, 41–42, 114, 117, 144, 193, 273
  basis 40
  column 41
  quantisation 266
  quantizers 271
  row 41
  unit 40
Vector Pascal 9, 117–118, 148, 182, 188, 212, 279
VectorC 24–25
vectorised 35, 144
vertex 39
vertical 14, 248
vibrations 3
video 268
Visual C 15

visual cortex 266
voice 266
volatile 187
vqdecode 271
vqencode 271
VRML 280

weights 233
WHERE 113–114
win32 34
Windows 20, 28, 34, 223
wireframe 279
WITH 181
word 32
write 191
writeln 191

XMM 20–22
xmm0 31
xor 37

ZF 111
ZPL 110